ANABAPTISM

A Social History, 1525–1618

ANABAPTISM

A Social History, 1525-1618

SWITZERLAND, AUSTRIA, MORAVIA,
SOUTH AND CENTRAL GERMANY

CLAUS-PETER CLASEN

Cornell University Press

ITHACA AND LONDON

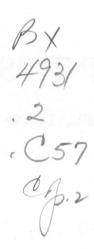

First published 1972 by Cornell University Press.
Published in the United Kingdom by Cornell University Press Ltd.,
2–4 Brook Street, London W1Y 1AA.

International Standard Book Number 0-8014-0696-X
Library of Congress Catalog Card Number 78-37751

PRINTED IN THE UNITED STATES OF AMERICA
BY VAIL-BALLOU PRESS, INC.

*Librarians: Library of Congress cataloging information
appears on the last page of the book.*

Contents

v

Tables

Maps

Preface

In studying sixteenth-century Anabaptism, one might concentrate on the religious concepts of the movement or one might take a biographical approach, singling out the founders and prominent leaders. Either of these approaches has serious drawbacks, however. The Anabaptists were not purely religious thinkers like the fourteenth-century mystics; they envisaged a new form of society. Nor were they isolated intellectuals like the humanist scholars. On the contrary, they were a movement of thousands of ordinary peasants and craftsmen. I have, therefore, chosen to approach the Anabaptist movement from the point of view of social history.

For almost a hundred years, church historians have been preoccupied with the origins of Anabaptism. Recently it has become fashionable to classify the radical groups of the Reformation period into various sociological categories. Unfortunately, the more arduous task of studying and interpreting the mass of Anabaptist documents has heretofore been neglected, with the result that little is known about the structure and nature of the Anabaptist movement itself. The present volume is therefore devoted to the evolution of the Anabaptist movement from its beginnings in 1525 until the outbreak of the Thirty Years' War in 1618, and not to such matters as the intellectual origins of Anabaptism or its relation to other radical thought of the sixteenth century.

The Anabaptist movement presents fascinating problems to

the social historian. Was Anabaptism really a major religious movement, like Lutheranism, affecting large sections of sixteenth-century German society? A study of the numerical strength and geographical expansion of Anabaptism will shed light on this question. Why did the Anabaptists split into so many small and mutually hostile groups? Could it be that the early free-church movement had more destructive tendencies than is assumed today? Did the Anabaptists develop new forms of religious life and daily behavior? Were they revolutionaries? To answer this question this book considers the relationship between the Peasants' War of 1525 and Anabaptism, the revolutionary trends within the Anabaptist movement, and the attitude of the brethren toward government, war, property, commerce, finance, and marriage. Particular emphasis is given to the communistic society of the Hutterite Brethren. How are we to explain that Anabaptism flourished in some areas for almost a century but disappeared in others within a few years? What factors, in other words, determined the advance and survival of the sect? Finally, there is the persecution. The question of how many Anabaptists were executed is investigated here for the first time, and the policies of Catholic and Protestant governments toward the Anabaptists are compared to shed new light on the evolution of religious toleration during the sixteenth century.

For practical reasons this study is limited to the Anabaptists in south and central Germany, Switzerland, Austria, and Moravia; the Anabaptist movements in the Netherlands and northwest Germany, including the Kingdom of Münster, are not discussed here. While during the past forty years an immense amount of documentary material has been published on the Anabaptists in the southern half of the Holy Roman Empire, similar materials have yet to be located and collected for the Anabaptist movement in the northern half. It would take many years to collect these documents in the Dutch and north German archives. Before new materials are accumulated, it seems appropriate to interpret the thousands of documents that have been published so far.

There are other good reasons for treating the Anabaptists in the southern part of the Empire by themselves. In spite of their considerable diversity, they had more in common with each other than with the Anabaptists in the Netherlands and north Germany. Their religious and political doctrines were shaped by the early Anabaptists in Switzerland and by Hut, Marbeck, and the Hutterites, not by Menno Simons, who exerted such an overpowering influence on the brethren in the Netherlands and north Germany. Finally, there is the question of significance. Some historians cling to the view that the Kingdom of Münster was the most characteristic and most important manifestation of Anabaptism. Undoubtedly it was a sensational episode. But whereas this kingdom collapsed after only a year, the Anabaptists in the southern half of the Empire made a serious and sustained effort for more than a century to change both the religious life and the society of their age. Contrary to popular belief, current even among historians, their efforts were much more impressive and lasting than the aberrations of the Dutch spiritualists in Münster.

Three categories of material on Anabaptism are at the historian's disposal: documentary material originating with government and church officials; material originating with the Anabaptists themselves; and material originating with third parties. A social history of Anabaptism must be based largely on sources in the first category. Since both the government officials and the pastors were hostile to the Anabaptists, it may be asked whether this type of material is not biased. In order to answer this question one must distinguish between official records dealing with individual Anabaptists and those dealing with Anabaptists in general. Those dealing with individual Anabaptists comprise transcripts of visitations; minutes of interrogations; reports to and from local officials and pastors; financial accounts dealing with Anabaptist property; minutes and decisions of town, higher government, or church councils; recantations; sentences of courts; and financial accounts concerning executions. Of these, the transcripts of visitations and minutes of interrogations are the most important, because they resulted from direct contact between local officials and individual Anabaptists and because they constitute the largest part of the material. The material dealing with individual Anabaptists occasionally lacks depth and completeness, but it is on the whole reliable. Having been intended for government use rather than for dissemination to the public, it is generally free of polemics. Officials who wanted to suppress the Anabaptist movement first had to find out what its aims were and who belonged to it; hence these documents are of a strongly factual nature. While they are not always totally objective, the documents on individual Anabaptists, especially the transcripts and minutes, are the most detailed and penetrating sources on the life and thought of the brethren. Indeed, serious work on the Anabaptist movement dates only from the time when this type of documentary material became available.

The second kind of material originating with state and church authorities deals with the movement in general. It consists of memoranda of lawyers and government commissions, drafts and final versions of laws and church ordinances, correspondence between governments, and the minutes and decisions of diets. Although this material affords some insight into how the fight against Anabaptism was organized and conducted, it is too general to shed much light on the Anabaptists themselves. Moreover, some governments clearly misrepresented the position of the Anabaptists, either because they themselves were poorly informed or because they aimed at defaming the brethren. The historian can nevertheless derive useful information from these sources. The documents discussed so far make up the bulk of the *Täuferakten,* or material on Anabaptism, that has been published during the past forty years.

Still within the first main category are materials on Anabaptism originating with theologians and pastors. The most valuable of these documents are the transcripts of disputations, though not all of them are equally valuable. Some were obviously edited by theologians or officials who were inclined to devote pages to the arguments of church representatives and only a few lines to those of the Anabaptists. Most disputations were devoted to questions of theology, and only a few dealt with political problems, which are of greater interest here. The works of theologians who discussed and refuted the Anabaptist doctrines are likewise of limited value to the social historian. Fortunately, a few pastors were also interested in the origins of Anabaptism, the various groups within it, and the life of the brethren. One has only to read a few pages of their books, however, to realize that they disliked the Anabaptists intensely. Christoph Erhard and Christoph Andreas Fischer, for example, wrote their books in order to incite the authorities to drive the Anabaptists out of Moravia. Wild rumors were indiscriminately recorded along with facts. Yet even these books sometimes contain significant information on the Anabaptist movement. The historian cannot afford to discard them altogether, but must exercise discretion and common sense in using them. Finally, letters written by theologians and pastors occasionally contain important references to the Anabaptists.

If the social historian depends largely on materials originating with government and church, he must also consider sources originating with the Anabaptists themselves. Some of this material is of a literary nature. The brethren wrote a considerable number of treatises and justifications of faith dealing mainly with theological matters. A few authors also discussed political, economic, social, and eschatological doctrines, however; their works are obviously of prime importance. In addition there is the literature produced by the Anabaptists for various practical purposes. The Hutterites composed a great body of liturgical literature, sermons, and hymns, and carefully treasured the letters written by brethren. They also produced several collections of detailed ordinances dealing with practical problems in their communities. Contracts with lords, land registers, and instructions for mission- aries are also invaluable sources for the study of Hutterite Ana- baptism. The Anabaptists in Germany and Switzerland collected some of the letters written by fellow believers, but they pro- duced only a few ordinances and hardly any liturgical literature. Still another Anabaptist source is the Hutterite chronicles, espe- cially the *Geschichtbuech*. Though these historical works are strongly biased in favor of the Hutterites, they are indispensable for studying the history and organization of the Hutterite com- munities.

The third category of material to be consulted originated with neither church or state authorities nor the Anabaptists them- selves, but with third parties—chroniclers or visitors or travelers who had occasion to observe the Anabaptists. Although these accounts were often written in a hostile spirit, they contain so much precious factual information that they are indispensable. At the same time, they must be used with great discretion.

In my view a social history of the Anabaptists must be based strictly on fact. Psychological and sociological theories in the manner of Karl Mannheim and Norman Cohn are fascinating, but when the historian investigates the evolution of actual Ana- baptist groups in specific towns, these speculations turn out to be highly simplistic and of little help. In particular, Mannheim's brilliant theories are based on insufficient knowledge and persis- tently contradict the documentary evidence. The aim of this study is to understand Anabaptism in the context of sixteenth- century German society, not to formulate a sociological model.

Since Anabaptism attracted a great number of people, a quan- titative approach is useful, not to say essential. Some basic and fascinating aspects of the movement cannot be investigated with- out resort to figures; indeed, serious mistakes could have been avoided if earlier historians had only asked how strong the movement was. One reason why quantifying methods were not applied to Anabaptism heretofore is simply that there are

no statistical tables available: the Anabaptists did not keep lists
of their membership, for example. Nonetheless, the transcripts
of visitations, minutes of interrogations, and reports of the officials contain an immense amount of information on the Anabaptists. It is, of course, very time-consuming to cull the names of
Anabaptists and related information from the thousands of documents. But who can really write social history without solid
evidence? If the historian establishes certain categories of questions and gathers all the evidence available, he soon accumulates
a large mass of data. The interpretation of these data offers some
surprising insights into Anabaptism.

Naturally, the evidence is not equally complete in all areas.
Thanks to the careful work of many sixteenth-century officials,
we know the names of practically all of the Anabaptists in some
areas, such as the city of Augsburg in 1527 and 1528 and the
Duchy of Württemberg during the second half of the sixteenth
century. In other areas, however, the exact number of Anabaptists is unknown, either because the officials never discovered all
of them or because the records have been lost. But these are
difficulties a historian always faces, whatever evidence he uses.
They certainly do not excuse him from collecting and analyzing
the material which is available. The figures presented here cannot
be expected to pinpoint the precise strength of Anabaptism in
every area, then, but they do bring the proportions of the movement into better focus.

A social history of Anabaptism presents peculiar difficulties. A
study of a highly centralized organization, such as the Society of
Jesus, can be based on the decisions of superiors and the official
correspondence. Most Anabaptist groups, however, were totally
decentralized, with a minimum of organization. In his *Chronica*
of 1531, Sebastian Franck observed with consternation that the
Anabaptists held quite divergent views on almost any given subject. It would be misleading, therefore, to single out a certain
view as the central Anabaptist doctrine just because it is held by
the Mennonites today, for in reality each of several views might

xviiiPREFACE

have had the same validity in different groups. At the risk of making the narrative a bit complex at times, I have tried to deal with all the divergent tendencies within Anabaptism.

Mennonite historians and other church historians in this country regard the Anabaptists with much warmth and sympathy. I have the impression that their sympathy is often based on religious convictions and moral sentiments. As a social historian primarily interested in sixteenth-century German society, I prefer to approach the Anabaptists from a different angle. I confess that ideologies, whether Christian or Marxist, do not interest me very much. I am not particularly concerned with the rediscovery of Christian truths or the establishment of God's kingdom. I am, however, greatly interested in the question whether during the sixteenth century, or even today, the political doctrines of the Anabaptists could be considered a workable basis for the functioning of society. Once this question has been asked, Anabaptism appears in a new light.

Grants from the Social Science Research Council and the American Council of Learned Societies enabled me to collect material at German archives and at the rich Mennonite Historical Library at Goshen, Indiana, in the fall of 1967. Two graduate students at the University of California, Los Angeles, Konrad Dinkel and James Mininger, helped me check the figures presented in this study.

Parts of Chapter 6 on ecstatic experiences are drawn from my article "Medieval Heresies in the Reformation," in the December 1963 issue of *Church History*, by permission of the editors.

CLAUS-PETER CLASEN

Los Angeles

ANABAPTISM

A Social History, 1525–1618

I

Early Developments
in Zurich

The early Reformation in Zurich was a time of great religious confusion. By 1520 Huldreich Zwingli had rejected Catholic doctrine, and in the following years his decidedly evangelical preaching was accepted in Zurich by a growing number of burghers; yet the forms of Catholic worship were maintained in the town until 1525. From 1522 onward this disparity between the new evangelical doctrines and the continued observance of Catholic ceremonies fostered in Zurich the same radical tendencies that had already begun to flourish in Wittenberg. It was then that the Anabaptist movement came into being.

The first open defiance of the Church's authority in Zurich occurred during Lent in 1522, when a number of Zwingli's more ardent supporters broke their fast by sitting down to a dish of sausage at Froschauer the printer's house. Among these radicals were four future Anabaptists: Heinrich Aberli, Bartolme Pur, Lorenz Hochrütiner, and Hans Oggenfuss. The same year several zealous burghers, among them Aberli, Pur, and Conrad Grebel, attempted to rouse the population against the monasteries. To the town council's injunction to cease agitating, Grebel angrily replied that the devil himself must be sitting on the town council, since one of the councilors had ridiculed the preaching of the gospel. If the councilors stood in the way of the progress of the gospel, they would themselves be destroyed. He left, loudly slamming the door of the council chamber.

In August 1523, Zwingli proposed certain modifications to

the worship service in his treatise "De Canone Missae." References to the sacrificial character of the mass were to be eliminated, but many of the mass's forms were to be essentially retained. Zwingli's proposals, in particular those favoring the preservation of clerical dress, Latin hymns, and certain liturgical prayers of long standing, were at once fiercely criticized for their halfheartedness. The inclusion of prayers for those of little faith was especially irritating to critics, who urged that only the Lord's Prayer be said.

In September 1523, Zurich witnessed various iconoclastic acts in which the radicals Simon Stumpf, Hochrütiner, and Oggenfuss smashed pictures, lamps, and crosses. Shortly afterward, Ludwig Hätzer advocated the removal of all pictures from churches. In October, at a public debate held by the town council on the scriptural bases for the mass and the use of images, Zwingli successfully argued that the sacrificial character of the mass had no justification in the Bible. To Conrad Grebel's demand that the priests be taught at once how to celebrate the mass, Zwingli replied that the town council must decide on the appropriate manner of celebration; at this the radical Stumpf angrily objected that such a decision, having already been made in the Spirit of God, could not be allocated to the town council. This short exchange reveals the striking differences between Zwingli and the radicals. The latter would not tolerate the mass as it was observed by the burghers, who continued to live in the religious atmosphere of their youth. Further, the radicals unequivocally denied the right of secular authorities to judge religious matters. When the discussion came to the ceremonies themselves, Grebel revealed another side of his thinking, one that has since been called a "tendency to legalism," or literal Biblicism.[1] Communion was to be celebrated exactly as the Last Supper is reported in the gospel: plain bread was to be used instead of wafers, and each believer was to put the bread in his own mouth.

As Grebel had feared, the public debate of 1523 did not result in the abolition of the mass. The more radical of Zwingli's

followers now became increasingly disillusioned. In all proba-
bility radicals like Stumpf and Grebel went in turn to Zwingli
and other pastors even as late as 1523 to propose that, as in the
times of the apostles, believers should separate from the rest of
the populace and establish a new church of true Christians. They
were confident of a multitude of believers, far outnumbering the
unbelievers. The true Christians would then elect a new town
council. According to Zwingli, Stumpf also proposed that the
new church should not be contaminated by usury. Notably,
then, the idea of a church of believers segregated from the godless, a basic concept of the future Anabaptist movement, had
already been voiced. But the radicals did not yet believe it was
unchristian to hold political office.

Deep into 1523 each radical continued to act on his own
account; there was no organized radical faction. Late in the
year, however, the radicals began to gather in conventicles or
"schools." We have already encountered some of those—Aberli,
Pur, Oggenfuss, Grebel, Hätzer—who were to frequent these
conventicles. Others were Andreas Castelberger, Felix Manz,
Wilhelm Reublin, and Johannes Brötli. What sort of men were
they? Three were simple craftsmen (two bakers and one tailor).
Six were educated to one degree or another: Grebel, who had
studied at the university, Castelberger, who was a bookseller, and
Reublin, Brötli, Manz and Hätzer, who had been trained as
priests. It is true that those of intellectual background were in a
dominant position, though their intellectuality was limited. Only
one, Ludwig Hätzer, was a man of exceptional gifts, and though
Hätzer was attracted in 1523 and 1524 to the radical cause, he
never became an Anabaptist.

Of this group Grebel and Manz emerged as leaders. Grebel,
the son of a wealthy iron merchant, dignitary, and town councilor, had attended the universities of Basel, Vienna, and Paris,
returning to Zurich in 1520 without having taken his degree. Until 1525 he lived in his father's house at Zurich. But the relations
between father and son were very strained: the son chafed under

the financial dependence on his father, and the father had been incensed by his son's loose living at Vienna and Paris and his later marriage to a girl of low descent without dowry. The young Grebel approached Zwingli in connection with a lecture-ship at a new school to be established in Zurich, but these lecture-ships were not filled until June 1525, months after Grebel's role in the Anabaptist movement had rendered his appointment to such a post impossible. The authorship of two treatises has been attributed to him,[2] but in general he wrote only letters.

Felix Manz was the son of a Zurich priest. It is not known whether he attended university, but he certainly had a very good education: he was conversant with Latin and Greek, and in 1522 studied Hebrew. Like Grebel, he seems to have angled for a lectureship, although when the radical movement came into being in Zurich he was not working for a living. Manz's mani-festo, addressed to the town council in late 1524 or early 1525, indicates that he was a pioneer of Anabaptist theology.[3]

Although Grebel was a talented man, and Manz particularly so, neither was the intellectual match of the Swiss reformers Zwingli, Johannes Oecolampadius, and Berchtold Haller. What distinguished Grebel and Manz was their uncompromising piety and courage, the products of a relentless zeal common to all the Zurich radicals, however different their backgrounds otherwise may have been. The Anabaptist doctrines were evolved not by sentimental men whose hearts had been moved by the gospel, but by strong-willed, impatient men who for two or three years had been demanding immediate action, with utter disregard for practical considerations or public opinion. Why wait? they demanded. There could be no compromise with God's word. Annul the fasting laws, drive out the monks, smash images, get rid of the mass without further delay, establish a church of true Christians, elect a new and Christian town council. Perhaps this impatience was in part the product of youth, for some of the leading radicals were still young men. Born around 1500, Manz and Hätzer were 23 or 24 in 1524, and Grebel 25 or 26.

Even so, the question of age should not be given undue importance. Other young intellectuals in Zurich never became radicals, and besides, the firebrand Wilhelm Reublin was already 44.

At their nightly meetings the radicals probably read and discussed not only the Scriptures but current theological literature. In 1524 they began to advance ideas that made any agreement with Zwingli impossible: they rejected infant baptism in favor of baptizing only conscientious believers. Since the spring of 1524 Wilhelm Reublin, the pastor of Witikon, had been advising his parishioners not to have their children baptized. Brötli, who was formerly pastor of Zollikon, may also have preached against infant baptism by the summer of 1524. Zwingli was later to write that he and his fellow pastors had wondered at first why the radicals were so excited over the question of baptism; subsequently they realized that if infant baptism was rejected, it would be necessary for the radicals to baptize conscientious believers, thus establishing a new church. In other words, Zwingli recognized the essential concern of the radicals to be the establishment of a separate church of Christian purists.

The Zurich group now set about establishing relations with other radicals in Germany who regretted Luther's reformation as being incomplete and inadequate. Grebel wrote to Andreas Karlstadt in July or August 1524; Castelberger also wrote soon after. When in October 1524, Dr. Gerhard Westerburg went to Zurich and then to Basel in order to have Karlstadt's seven treatises printed, Manz accompanied him. By October or November of 1524, several of Karlstadt's treatises were circulating among the Zurich radicals. Above all, the radicals were anxious to make contact with the great theologian Thomas Müntzer. In fact, their letter to Müntzer of September 5, 1524, contained their program for radical reform. Away, it urged, with any mixture of divine and human! An end to that anti-Christian and false deference to the weak, which the preachers had reduced to idolatry! Communion supper must be celebrated in the very way it was begun by Christ: it should put believers in mind of the Lord and teach

them that they, too, were of one body. It should not be held in
churches, and common bread and drinking vessels should be
used. Infant baptism was no more than a "senseless, blasphemous
abomination against all Scripture"; only consenting believers
should be baptized. Discipline according to Matthew 18:15–18
must be practiced before the celebration of the Supper. No force
must be used against sinners, nor indeed must they be slain, as
Müntzer had suggested, for the gospel and those who believed
in it should not be protected by the sword. The singing of hymns
was held to be contrary to the Holy Writ. The preachers were
no longer to live on benefices accruing to them through usury
and tithes.[4]

To the people of Zurich the radicals' ideas about baptism
were probably the most astonishing. Almost as unfamiliar was
the doctrine that a Christian might not bear arms. How had
Grebel and his friends come about these doctrines? Had they
discovered them in the Scriptures? This conjecture is quite possible but cannot be proved. It is equally possible that the Zurich
radicals were influenced by other individuals and movements.

In 1560 Heinrich Bullinger affirmed in his work on the origin
of Anabaptism that Müntzer, the spiritualist and revolutionary,
was the father of the Anabaptist movement. According to Bullinger, Müntzer spent eight weeks in the fall of 1524 at Griessen
in the Klettgau and in the area nearby, inciting the peasants to
rebellion and propounding his doctrines of rebaptism and the
inner heavenly Word. Müntzer, wrote Bullinger, became "only
too well known to certain people at Zurich." A few years later
Bullinger was to declare that Müntzer actually visited Balthasar
Hubmaier, a prominent preacher, at Waldshut, and that Grebel,
Manz, and "other restless heads" from Zurich visited Müntzer
at Griessen, absorbing from him the doctrine of rebaptism. Up
to the twentieth century Bullinger's thesis greatly influenced historians, but Mennonite historians have since shown that Bullinger
advanced his theory only from 1554 onward.[5] Although they do
not deny that Müntzer was in the Klettgau and Hegau in the

fall of 1524 and that he visited Oecolampadius, they insist that in the absence of documentary evidence on Müntzer's movements in that area, Bullinger's account cannot be accepted. Bullinger fabricated this thesis for political purposes, these historians say, to prove that Anabaptism had originated not in Zwinglian Zurich but in Lutheran Saxony.

The Mennonites may be going too far, however, in denying that Müntzer exercised any influence at all on the founders of Anabaptism. In their letter of September 5, 1524, Grebel and his friends expressed keen interest in Müntzer. Supposing that they had known of Müntzer's sojourn close to Zurich in October and November 1524, it was quite conceivable that they went to see him. Müntzerite ideas may also have been handed on through such intermediaries as the goldsmith Hans Hujuff, a member of the Grebel circle who indeed visited Müntzer before the letter was sent. Even if Müntzer was not visited by someone from Zurich, the Zurich group may well have been influenced by his writings.

The revolutionary spiritualists at Zwickau had already rejected infant baptism in 1521. In 1522 their arguments had greatly embarrassed Philip Melanchthon, Nikolaus von Amsdorf, and Luther. By 1524, in his treatise "On the Fictitious Faith," Müntzer too repudiated infant baptism as a useless ceremony, arguing that in the apostles' time, only adults who had received extensive instruction were accepted as catechumens. Though Müntzer never reached the point of baptizing adults as far as we know, he clearly held the conviction that only believing and well-instructed adults should be baptized. This treatise of Müntzer's, as well as his "Protestation," had been read by Grebel and his friends by September 1524.

If Müntzer had never in his writings rejected infant baptism, if Grebel and his companions had never read those writings, if, instead of writing to Müntzer on friendly terms, they had never addressed so much as a word to him, and if Müntzer had never spent those two mysterious months on the Swiss border, then the historian might with justification say that Anabaptism evolved independently of Thomas Müntzer. The evidence does not allow of a definite statement either way, but there are indeed indications that the Zurich radicals were influenced by Müntzer's ideas. This is not of course tantamount to saying that Müntzer was the father of Anabaptism, but there can be no doubt of the certain influence exercised by the Zwickau prophets and Thomas Müntzer on the Anabaptist movement in Thuringia.

The nineteenth-century historians Urban Heberle and Ludwig Keller suggested that certain medieval heresies like those of the Waldensians and the Bohemian Brethren had influenced the radicals, and there are indeed striking resemblances between these heresies and Anabaptism. The Waldensians and Bohemian Brethren also emphasized the Scriptures as the exclusive authority, demanded retreat from the world, expressed doubts about infant baptism, refused to take oaths and render military service, censured the power and privileges of the clergy, and rejected church buildings. Although no direct influence on the Zurich group has yet been discovered, heretical ideas and even books may very well have circulated in the Swiss towns.

In 1878 Albrecht Ritschl put forward the argument that the Anabaptists had revived the medieval ideals of monastic reform, with particular reference to the Franciscans. He observed a link between, on the one hand, the first rule of Saint Francis and the Franciscan order of the Tertiarians, and on the other, the rigid piety of the Anabaptists. Both practiced strict separation from the world, common ownership of possessions, and simplicity of dress, and refused to occupy secular position, shed blood, or take an oath. Also, the spiritualistic and eschatological concerns of the Anabaptists, which were foreign to the spirit of the Reformation, were said to have derived from the mysticism and eschatological speculation that characterized the late Middle Ages. This thesis has been discarded by most historians, perhaps too hastily. Further study could very well produce new evidence to support it.

Some scholars have asserted that Erasmus was one of the spiritual fathers of Anabaptism.[6] The strict Biblicism of the Anabaptists, their emphasis on Christian discipleship, their view of the church as a brotherhood united by love, and their rejection of war—all have been seen as originating in Erasmian thought. In fact, there are formulas for true Christian living in the *Enchiridion* that might have been written by an Anabaptist. Mennonite historians, however, question that Erasmus had any real influence on the first Anabaptist leaders. They argue that as a student, Grebel was influenced by humanists who did not share Erasmus' view of church reform. And after his return to Zurich, Grebel became a follower of Zwingli, not of Erasmus. One might add that Grebel's legalism, his aggressive separatism, and his views on the creation of a new church were also alien to the spirit of Erasmus. Yet the Zurich radicals may well have read the *Enchiridion* and other writings of Erasmus, and gained fresh insights from them.

According to the Swiss historian Fritz Blanke, the Zurich radical movement stemmed largely from the Zwinglian Reformation. Blanke traced the development of Anabaptist theology from the religious understanding of Luther and Zwingli. Like the Reformers, the Anabaptists held that unregenerate man was corrupt and could be saved by grace alone; repentance was thus the center of the Christian life. One did not repent to earn forgiveness, but as a response to the forgiveness already granted through Christ. Furthermore, Grebel clearly took his views on the celebration of the Lord's Supper from Zwingli, and even his views on baptism owed much to Zwingli's teaching. Grebel himself is supposed to have said that Zwingli "had brought him into this thing."

Hans J. Hillerbrand has also emphasized that the early radicals passed from Catholicism first to the Reformation and only then to Anabaptism, and not directly from the first to the last. But while Hillerbrand agreed that the radicals had accepted basic tenets of the Reformation, he also pointed to important differences between the Lutheran and the Anabaptist concept of jus-

tification.[7] Luther denied free will; the Anabaptists affirmed it.
Luther had no doubts about the reality of original sin; many
Anabaptists entertained the concept only in ambiguous terms, rejecting the notion that it stigmatized children. Luther and the
Anabaptists both taught that man was saved by faith. But for
Luther even the faithful Christian remained a sinner, whereas
for many Anabaptists the baptized believer could overcome sin
by committing himself to a new life of holiness and suffering as
Christ's disciple. Hillerbrand suggested that these peculiar views
of the radicals were due to the influence of Erasmus, Karlstadt,
and Müntzer.[8] According to Hillerbrand the radicals received
from them the strong concern for truly Christian living as opposed to Luther's emphasis on faith alone, and the tendency to
spiritualize the sacraments. Of particular interest is the reference
to Karlstadt, whose contribution to early Anabaptism had heretofore been overlooked. His influence is said to have extended to
three areas: the demand for radical commitment to Christian living, the repudiation of infant baptism, and the symbolic interpretation of the sacrament of the altar. Hillerbrand is undoubtedly right in arguing that Anabaptism derived from several
sources, and not just one. And yet we still do not know how
precisely these various intellectual influences combined to create
a new religious movement.

When in 1524 the radicals took to preaching their doctrines
publicly, tension began to mount. The pastors called the radicals
devils in the guise of angels. In turn Grebel called Zwingli and
the other preachers corrupters of the Scriptures. Even so, the
radicals endeavored to convert Zwingli and the government to
their views. On two occasions between mid-October and mid-
December 1524, they met Zwingli and two pastors in the presence of four town councilors to discuss their differences, but the
discussions led nowhere.

In a treatise on the various enemies of the Reformation "Who
Give Rise to Rebellion," published in December 1524, Zwingli
spoke of differences of opinion among the radicals. At one mo-

ment, he said, they do not want a government at all; at another they accept a government, but refuse to admit that a true Christian can hold public office. At one moment they want their own church under government protection; at another they will not have the magistrate protecting the preaching of the gospel. At one moment they say that priests should be made away with; at another that the priests should be allowed to preach freely. Zwingli went on to complain that when children were baptized, the radicals would cry out against infant baptism as the greatest abomination in Christendom. Anyone who joined their number would be acclaimed as having the true spirit; anyone who did not would no longer be greeted by them. They spread their doctrines wherever possible, in dark corners, streets, and shops. When forbidden to do this, they gathered in conventicles and denounced others so bitterly that one might "bathe in the abundance of gall." In sum, they created more mischief daily than Africa can produce strange animals.

The town council was finally forced to take action when on January 12, 1525, a peasant of Zollikon loudly interrupted a sermon on baptism. To refute the radicals and put an end to the agitation, a public debate on baptism was held on January 17, 1525. The following day the council decreed that thereafter all children were to be baptized; parents who refused to comply would be banished. On January 21 Grebel and Manz were forbidden to hold further conventicles or to discuss the problem of baptism. Several radicals who were not burghers of Zurich, such as Reublin, Hätzer, and Brötli, were ordered to leave within a week.

If the town council really hoped to end this troublesome affair by decree, it was greatly mistaken. For the radicals were also convinced that the time for talking was over. Bluntly defying authority, they repudiated the traditional practice whereby decisions on church doctrine were made by theologians and enforced by the government. The radicals themselves had already decided what the correct doctrines were and would simply establish their own church to carry them out. What matter if Zwingli and the town council disapproved? The radical movement not only could survive without assistance from the authorities but would be hard for the authorities to stop as long as its doctrines were accepted by the people. The radicals proved to be right: once the new doctrines had taken root among the people, the movement could simply not be destroyed. The great contribution of the Zurich radicals to the Reformation was not their view on baptism or Christian discipleship or political power, but their rigid determination to start their reform whether the government liked it or not. They wanted a reformation by the people, not by the government.

During a meeting on Saturday evening, January 21, 1525, the very day Grebel and Manz had been forbidden to hold conventicles or even to discuss baptism, Grebel took the extraordinary step of baptizing an adult person, the priest Georg Blaurock, who in turn baptized all the other adults present. The next day Grebel celebrated the Last Supper, and the first adult was baptized in the nearby village of Zollikon; within a week no fewer than 35 persons there had accepted baptism. Thus the first Anabaptist congregation had formed, and with it a new religious movement had arisen.

Strangely enough, the radicals never devised a name for their movement as a whole. They definitely refused to call themselves Anabaptists (Wiedertäufer or Täufer). The names they sometimes did use for themselves were more of a descriptive or rhetorical nature. All through the sixteenth century the radicals referred to themselves as brethren or brethren and sisters in the Lord or in Jesus Christ. Of course, Catholic priests also referred to one another as brethren, and so did Protestant ministers. Sometimes the radicals used flamboyant names such as Secret Disciples of Christ, Elect Saints, True Community of Saints, Children of God, Members of God's Body, or Children of Light.[9] Anabaptists in Swabia, the Tirol, and northern Thuringia referred to themselves as True Lovers of God,[10] a term already used by heretics in the Middle Ages. The radicals also spoke of themselves as a brotherhood.[11] But these names were not uniformly accepted by all Anabaptists, nor did they distinguish them from other religious groups.

Since the radicals never really gave themselves one clear name, the label given them by their contemporaries stuck for good. The name Anabaptists was not a sinister attempt to vilify the brethren but a simple necessity, for how else were people to refer to them? Grebel and Manz and their followers had amazed their contemporaries above all by their intense preoccupation with believers' baptism; it was only natural that this practice became the distinctive mark of the strange new group.

In a decree of March 8, 1525, the Zurich town council spoke for the first time of Töffer, "Baptizers." During an interrogation between March 6 and 25, 1525, the verb *widertouffen*, "to rebaptize," and the noun *Widertouff*, "rebaptism," were used.[12] Zwingli used the actual term Widertouffer in a treatise published in May 1525.[13] During the following years both the terms Toufer and Widertouffer appear in the Zurich documents. In Austria and in south and central Germany, Wiedertäufer in various spellings became the common term, Täufer being used by the authorities only occasionally.[14] Rarely do we find other terms such as Frytouffer, which appeared at Basel; Touffbrüder, again at Basel and here and there in Germany; Contrateuffer, in the bishopric of Speyer; Gartenbrüder and Gartenschwestern, at Augsburg; [15] and Schwermer, in Thuringia and Nuremberg. The Greek word Anabaptista was used only seldom in documents written in German, though more frequently in letters, books, diaries, and memoranda written in Latin from 1527 on, and probably even earlier.[16] In his principal work against the sect Zwingli used the term Catabaptista, which was also employed by theologians such as Bucer and Capito in their Latin correspondence and books.[17] Some Anabaptists protested against being called Wiedertäufer, which meant both "Anti-baptizer" and "Rebaptizer." They were not against baptism, of course, nor from their point of view did they wish to rebaptize anyone, since they regarded the first baptism in infancy as no baptism at all. The term Täufer, "Baptizer," might have been less offensive to them. This name too was given them by the authorities, however, and was not used by the brethren as a group name.

When the fight against this tenacious and elusive sect became more and more bitter, the officials and pastors vented their fury by calling the Anabaptists a large variety of insulting names: "senseless, unchristian animals," "vermin," "evil rogues," "vicious criminals," "night crows," "Enthusiasts," "pious villains," "fickle spirits," "hole-and-corner preachers." They complained of what they termed "contemptible, accursed Anabaptism," of sneaking bands of Anabaptists, and of "that foul disease." [18] In one area in Hesse feelings were so virulent that "Anabaptist" became a word of insult.[19] Of course, the Anabaptists were invariably branded sectarians, though they denied ever having formed a sect, insisting that they were God's congregation: monks and nuns formed sects, but not they; indeed, the Catholics, Lutherans, and Zwinglians were heretics and idolatrous sectarians.[20]

2

Advance and
Numerical Strength

Since the development of Anabaptism between 1525 and 1618 was uneven, it seems appropriate to divide the period into three shorter ones for purposes of study: the early years of expansion, 1525 to 1529; the period from the Diet of Augsburg to the Augsburg Interim, 1530 to 1549; and the years of Protestant Orthodoxy and the Catholic Counter Reformation, 1550 to 1618. From a political point of view, the area under examination was splintered into a bewildering variety of territories and cities. In Switzerland the Anabaptists appeared in not less than 21 territories, in the Holy Roman Empire in 23 ecclesiastical territories, in 20 large and 27 small secular territories, and in 37 free imperial cities. It would thus be impossible to base our investigation on political units, and in any case the Anabaptists disregarded political frontiers. We shall therefore divide this area into nine larger geographical regions: Switzerland, the Rhine valley, Swabia, the Tirol, Austria, a southeastern area with Bavaria as the center, Franconia, Thuringia, and Hesse.

Three criteria are useful to measure the strength of the Anabaptist movement in a specific area: the number of individual Anabaptists; the number of towns and villages affected; and the number of leaders, among whom we shall include apostles, properly appointed ministers, and inspired brethren who made their rounds preaching and baptizing. Even if the data for one of these criteria are incomplete, the other two should indicate the intensity of the Anabaptist expansion. We shall add as a fourth cate-

gory the number of Hutterite missions sent to an area, though
this factor is not in itself a reliable indicator of the strength of
the movement, since Anabaptism sometimes flourished in areas
where the Hutterites did not missionize.

After the first adult was baptized at Zurich, the new doctrines rapidly spread to other parts of German-speaking Switzerland: in January 1525 to Schaffhausen, in March to St. Gallen,
in April to the Hapsburg town of Waldshut near the Swiss border, in May to Graubünden, in August to Basel, and in November to Bern. Although a great number of people seem to have
been involved in the Anabaptist disturbances at Waldshut and
St. Gallen, the Zurich area remained the most strongly affected
by the new religious movement. Some unreliable evidence indicates that in 1525 adult baptism was already taking place also in
the Strasbourg area and in central Germany.[1] Even should this
evidence be correct, a few instances of adult baptism did not
give rise to a movement. The Anabaptist movement in Germany
and Austria began only in 1526, when the Anabaptist leaders
from Switzerland carried their doctrines into the Empire. Three
lines of expansion can be distinguished: to Strasbourg, to Augsburg, and finally to the Tirol and Austria. In March 1526,
Reublin advanced the Anabaptist doctrines at Strasbourg. Soon
Anabaptists also appeared in nearby Landau, and at Horb and
Rottenburg in Swabia. At Augsburg, in May 1526, Hubmaier
baptized Hans Denck, who in turn baptized Hans Hut, who
within a few months began his phenomenal mission in Franconia. From eastern Switzerland the Anabaptists crossed the
mountains into the Tirol and Austria. By 1526 they were already baptizing adults in the Inn valley. Before the year was
over radical doctrines were being preached by a cowherd in the
Puster valley, and Anabaptist circles were reportedly formed at
Freistadt and Steyr.

In 1527 the Anabaptist leaders, often following important
waterways such as the Rhine, Danube, and Main rivers, spread
their message with growing speed, penetrating more and more

towns and villages. One line of expansion—the route taken, for example, by Denck—ran from Strasbourg along the Rhine valley to Bergzabern, Landau, and Worms, whence the sect spread to the Palatinate and the Kraichgau. Another direction, taken by Reublin and Michael Sattler, was from Strasbourg to Swabia, especially to Horb, Rottenburg, Esslingen, and Ulm. A third line of expansion, followed by the group around Hans Hut, was from northern Franconia to Königsberg, Staffelstein, and Nuremberg, or to Schweinfurt, Iphofen, and Windsheim. Other leaders carried the message from northern Franconia to Thuringia and Hesse. Hut was also the principal apostle in Austria, traveling from Vienna to Melk, Freistadt, Vöcklabruck, and Steyr, where he commissioned four new apostles, who in turn fanned out to various Austrian towns and to Salzburg, Passau, and Munich. From Augsburg leaders such as Lienhart Schiemer, Eukarius Kellermann, and Joachim Mertz went to the duchy of Bavaria and then to Salzburg or the Tirol. Others such as Martin Zehentmaier were sent from Augsburg to the imperial cities in Swabia. In addition to these major lines of expansion, the sect spread in many other directions: Anabaptists from Salzburg and Austria appeared in Franconia, for example, and in 1527 leaders were sent off from Augsburg to Switzerland, Worms, and Thuringia.

The rapid advance of Anabaptism was the work of an increasing number of indefatigable leaders, whether they were actually ministers or simply brethren eager to spread the new doctrines. During the period from 1525 to 1529, as Table 1 shows, no fewer than 257 such leaders appeared, and there were probably more. Indeed, the claim made in 1527 by the Thuringian leader Hans Römer that five hundred leaders were propagating the Anabaptist doctrines was not entirely unfounded.[2] It was in this way that the outlawed sect spread over vast areas of Switzerland, Austria, and south and central Germany within only a few years. Frequently towns were the centers of early Anabaptism: the imperial cities of Strasbourg and Worms in the Rhine valley, and Augsburg, Esslingen, Kaufbeuren, and Schwäbisch Gmünd in

Table 1. New Anabaptist leaders, 1525–1529

Area	1525	1526	1527	1528	1529	Total
Switzerland	34	6	12	9	10	71
Rhine valley	1	2	9	3	3	18
Swabia	0	2	17	15	7	41
Tirol	0	1	7	8	17	33
Austria	0	1	17	13	0	31
Southeast	0	0	19	3	0	22
Franconia	0	15	11	4	0	30
Thuringia	0	1	4	1	2	8
Hesse	0	0	1	2	0	3
Total	35	28	97	58	39	257

Swabia; the capital cities of Munich, Passau, Salzburg, and Vienna; the upper Austrian towns of Steyr, Freistadt, and Linz and the Tirolese towns of Rattenberg, Kitzbühel, and Bozen. Whereas in 1525 Anabaptists appeared in only 43 communities, in 1526 they appeared in 57; in 1527, in 181; in 1528, in 199; and in 1529, in 188. From 1525 through 1529, then, the sect had found followers in more than five hundred cities, country towns, and villages. There were Anabaptist groups in most major towns in Switzerland, in almost all larger imperial towns in south Germany, and in many towns in upper and lower Austria (Map 1). The sect's swift expansion is all the more remarkable because it was not centrally planned (as the expansion of the Society of Jesus, established twenty years later, would be) but depended on the zeal of the individual leaders. Only at the meeting at Augsburg in August 1527 do the leaders seem to have carefully selected areas where missionaries would be sent.[3]

Between 1525 and 1529, Anabaptism flourished most in the territory of Zurich, in the imperial cities of the southwest, in the prince-bishoprics of Würzburg, Bamberg, Passau, and Salzburg, the duchies of Bavaria and Ansbach, and the Hapsburg territories of Austria, the Tirol, and Hohenberg. Anabaptists

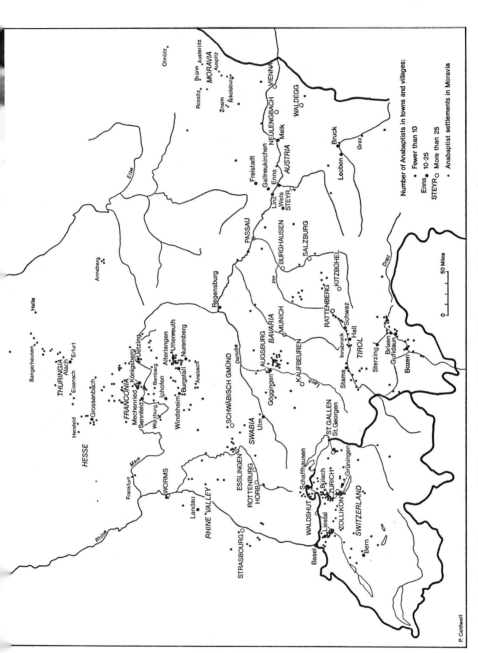

1. Anabaptism in Towns and Villages, South and Central Germany, Switzerland and Austria, 1525–1529

Number of Anabaptists in towns and villages:
- Fewer than 10
- 10–25 Enns
- More than 25 STEYR○
- Anabaptist settlements in Moravia

0   50 Miles

P. Caldwell

also began to appear, though not in large numbers, in Thuringia and the Palatinate in 1527, and in the duchy of Württemberg, Baden, and the bishopric of Speyer in 1528. In some areas a surprisingly large number of communities were affected by Anabaptism: 116 in Switzerland, 107 in Franconia, and 74 in the Tirol, as Table 2 shows. By contrast, in Swabia, the Rhine valley, Bavaria, and Austria, the movement was centered in a smaller number of communities. The congregations in the individual communities, however, were sometimes very large: this is why Swabia and the Rhine valley had a very large number of Anabaptists even though relatively few communities were affected in those areas during the early period.

In the entire area of Switzerland, Austria, and south and central Germany, 3,617 Anabaptists were discovered between 1525 and 1529. Switzerland was strongly affected by Anabaptism compared to other areas individually. Compared to the Empire in general, however, it ceased to be the center of the Anabaptist sect within a few years. Already in 1526 there were Anabaptists in almost as many communities in the Empire as in Switzerland.[4] Of the 507 towns and villages that had Anabaptists between 1525 and 1529, 391, or 77 percent, were in the Empire. The number of believers demonstrates even more positively that the Swiss were soon to be in a minority among the Anabaptists. From 1525 to 1529 only 588 Anabaptists, or 16 percent, lived in Switzerland.

The number of believers also indicates that few large congregations were formed on Swiss soil. Although Zurich was the birthplace of Anabaptism, there was never a large congregation there. Between 1525 and the end of 1529, only 29 people joined the movement in Zurich, and in later years hardly any joined. At Basel only nineteen people accepted baptism between 1525 and 1529, and at Schaffhausen, ten. Anabaptism gave rise to a truly strong movement only in three areas in Switzerland: Zollikon, the district of Grüningen, and the area of St. Gallen–Appenzell. In the Empire, however, congregations with more than thirty believers existed in no less than seventeen communities

Table 2. The expansion of Anabaptism, 1525–1618

Area	Anabaptist converts				Communities affected *				Leaders †				Hutterite missions		
	1525–1529	1530–1549	1550–1618	Total	1525–1529	1530–1549	1550–1618	1525–1618	1525–1529	1530–1549	1550–1618	Total	1530–1549	1550–1618	Total
Switzerland	588	478	481	1,547	116	182	128	363	72(71)	40(27)	22(21)	123(119)	1	18	19
Rhine valley	549	336	1,054	1,939	29	72	246	294	26(18)	36(33)	43(42)	103(93)	1	17	18
Swabia	654	703	1,575	2,932	39	178	252	379	55(41)	45(41)	26(26)	123(108)	7	20	27
Tirol	455	1,178	379	2,012	74	150	97	212	35(33)	39(35)	3(3)	73(71)	16	25	41
Austria	422	99	16	537	35	24	7	55	33(31)	1(1)	3(0)	34(32)	8	2	10
Southeast	323	83	98	504	57	20	29	96	32(22)	4(3)	1(1)	37(26)	4	16	20
Franconia	466	157	31	654	107	46	14	151	32(30)	7(6)	0(0)	39(36)	1	1	2
Thuringia	112	202	21	335	35	65	8	94	8(8)	14(14)	1(1)	23(23)	0	2	2
Hesse	48	451	216	715	15	96	95	177	4(3)	21(14)	3(3)	24(20)	8	13	21
Total	3,617	3,687	3,871	11,175	507	833	876	1,281	(257)	(174)	(97)	(528)	46	114	161

* We are counting all communities affected by Anabaptism within a given period of time. The same community might have had Anabaptists in two or all three periods. Therefore the total number of communities affected is smaller than the sum of communities added up horizontally.

† Leaders active in an area in a given period regardless of whether they also preached in other areas or in other periods. The figures in parentheses result when leaders are counted only once, at the time and in the area of their first appearance.

between 1525 and 1529. None of the sectarian circles in Switzerland could compare with the large congregations at Augsburg,
Esslingen, Strasbourg, and Linz. To be sure, certain basic doctrines and practices of the new sect appeared first in Switzerland,
but the statistical evidence should caution us against overrating
the Swiss character of Anabaptism.

Alarmed by this burgeoning new movement, governments responded with a campaign of fierce and bloody persecution. Between 1527 and 1529 almost all congregations in the imperial
cities with the exception of those in Strasbourg and Augsburg
were exterminated or reduced to insignificance. By 1528 Anabaptism had also been eliminated in the towns and villages of
Bavaria and Salzburg, and by 1529 in Franconia, the Palatinate,
and Austria. It was this persecution that in 1528 and 1529 sealed
the fate of Anabaptism as a mass movement in our area, and this
several years before the Anabaptist Kingdom of 1535 was destroyed at Münster.[5]

From 1530 to 1549 the Tirol, Swabia, and Switzerland predominated in number of Anabaptist converts, of communities
affected by Anabaptism, and of new Anabaptist leaders, as Table
2 and Map 2 show. In the Tirol not fewer than 1,178 persons
in 150 towns and villages joined the sect during these years. In
Switzerland the districts of Bern and Zurich were strongly affected. In southwest Germany, Anabaptism was strong in the
city of Strasbourg, in the Bruhrain and the Kraichgau, the duchy
of Württemberg, and the areas of Lauingen and Kempten. The
sect even expanded in several imperial cities, such as Esslingen,
Heilbronn, Kaufbeuren, and Ulm, and particularly Augsburg.
However, these cities were no longer the predominating centers
of the movement that they had been before 1530. In central Germany the sect appeared in the areas of Mühlhausen and Frankenhausen, the border districts of Electoral Saxony, Hesse, Fulda,
and Hersfeld, and in the areas of Marburg-Alsfeld and Grünberg in Hesse. In Franconia the movement was already subsiding,
though Anabaptists were still discovered in 46 towns and villages.

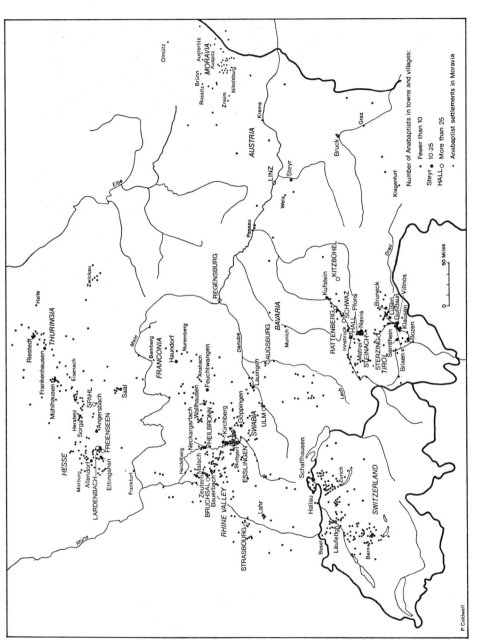

Number of Anabaptists in towns and villages:

- Fewer than 10
- Steyr ● 10–25
- HALL ○ More than 25
- ● Anabaptist settlements in Moravia

50 Miles

P. Caldwell

2. Anabaptism in Towns and Villages, South and Central Germany, Switzerland and Austria, 1530–1549

In Austria and Bavaria the sect had largely disappeared by 1530. Though Anabaptists were relentlessly persecuted in the Tirol, the movement continued to attract great numbers of converts there until about 1550. In most areas of south and central Germany, however, Anabaptism was successfully suppressed during the 1530s; only in the duchy of Württemberg did it prove impossible to quash the sect.

After 1550 the largest number of Anabaptist converts were to be found in Swabia, the Rhine valley, and Switzerland. In Swabia, Anabaptism flourished more than ever in the duchy of Württemberg. In the Rhine valley it was mostly to be found in the Palatinate west of the Rhine, and to a smaller extent in Alsace. In Switzerland it centered in the Aargau and in the districts of Zurich and Solothurn. The sect still had many adherents also in Hesse and the Tirol. There were few traces of it in Bavaria and Thuringia during this period, however, and in Austria and Franconia it was practically nonexistent.

In most areas where Anabaptists appeared in the second half of the sixteenth century (Map 3), the movement was short-lived. In the Tirol, Anabaptism remained relatively strong until the 1580s, then fell off sharply; few Anabaptists were left in the Tirol in the early seventeenth century. The movement also petered out in the 1580s in Alsace, and in the 1590s in Solothurn. But in the Palatinate, in the territory of Zurich and the Aargau, and to a smaller extent in Württemberg and Hesse the sectarians were still quite active at the outbreak of the Thirty Years' War.

During the entire period from 1525 to 1618, as Table 2 again shows, Swabia, Switzerland, the Rhine valley, and the Tirol clearly emerge as the areas of the most intensive Anabaptist activity. Here we find the largest total number of leaders, of towns and villages affected, and of Anabaptists. Among the remaining areas Hesse was on the whole the most strongly affected. In Franconia, the Southeast, Austria and Thuringia the movement aroused a lot of turmoil for a few years, but was short-lived.

From 1525 to 1618, 528 Anabaptist leaders were active in

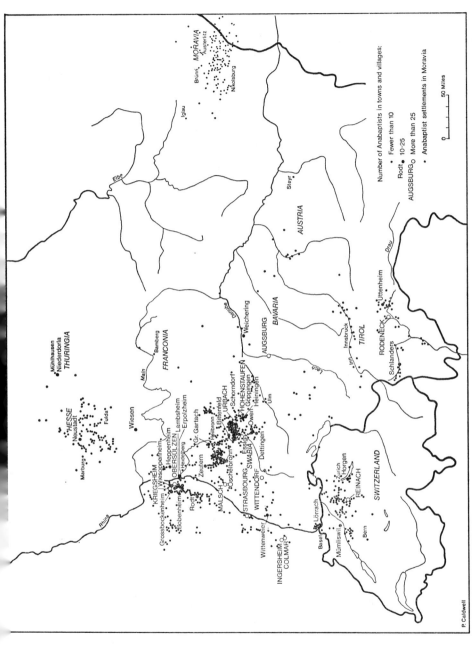

Number of Anabaptists in towns and villages:
- • Fewer than 10
- Rodt• 10-25
- AUGSBURG○ More than 25
- • Anabaptist settlements in Moravia

0   50 Miles

THURINGIA
Mühlhausen
Niederdorla

HESSE
Neustadt
Marburg
Fulda

Wiesen

Elbe

FRANCONIA
Bamberg

MORAVIA
Brünn•
Austerlitz
Nikolsburg

Iglau

AUSTRIA
Steyr

BAVARIA
Weichering
AUGSBURG
Lech
Inn
Innsbruck
TIROL
RODENECK Uttenheim
Schlanders
Drau

Main
Danube

KRIEGSHEIM
Grossbockenheim
Bobenheim
Wiesoppenheim
Heppenheim
OBERSÜLZEN
Lambsheim
Erpolzheim
Rodt
Heidelberg
Gr. Gartach
Zeutern
MALSCH
Hellbronn
Bittenfeld
URBACH
HOHENSTAUFEN
Schorndorf•
Göppingen
Eislingen
Owen Heiningen
Ulm
Oschelbronn
STRASBOURG
SWABIA
WITTENDORF
Dettingen
Wittenweier
INGERSHEIM
COLMAR

Rhine

Basel
Lörrach
Mümliswil
Bern
SWITZERLAND
Zürich
Horgen
REINACH

P. Caldwell

3. Anabaptism in Towns and Villages, South and Central Germany, Switzerland and Austria, 1550–1618

Switzerland, Austria, and south and central Germany. In addition 161 Hutterite missions appeared in this area. Altogether, 11,175 persons are known to have joined the sect. Anabaptism achieved its most rapid growth during the earliest period, or to be precise in 1527 and 1528. Although in the 1530s it continued to attract many followers, from the 1540s on the number of converts dropped steadily, except for a temporary upturn in the 1570s. With every decade that passed up to the Thirty Years' War, fewer and fewer people joined the sect. The decline in the rate of growth of Anabaptism becomes apparent when we look at the average number of converts per year for the three periods: between 1525 and 1529 there were an average of about 723 converts in 101 communities per year; between 1530 and 1549, about 184 converts in 42 communities per year; and finally, between 1550 and 1618, only about 56 converts in 13 communities per year.

In reality, there were undoubtedly many more than 11,175 Anabaptists between 1525 and 1618. The Hutterites who emigrated from south and central Germany, Switzerland, and Austria may well have numbered in themselves more than ten thousand. If the average Hutterite community had at least a hundred inhabitants, and if a new generation of Hutterites appeared about every thirty years, we would have to reckon with 17,400 Hutterites. In addition, there were still other Anabaptist groups in Moravia, and of course many Anabaptists, especially Swiss Brethren, did not emigrate.

Let us assume that in the course of almost a hundred years, from 1525 to 1618, Anabaptism did indeed attract about thirty thousand persons in our area—an average of three thousand persons every ten years, or three hundred every year. Considering that we are now dealing with an enormous area, comprising south and central Germany, Switzerland, and Austria, an area that in the sixteenth century was inhabited by millions of people, three thousand new Anabaptists every ten years is really a modest figure. The sixteen hundred Anabaptists known to us in the

Tirol from 1526 to 1550 constituted only 0.4 percent of the total population of 375,000.[6] In the duchy of Württemberg, which had 400,000 to 450,000 inhabitants, the Church Council of 1570 listed 129 Anabaptists, or a mere 0.03 percent of the population.

To be sure, at certain times the sect was concentrated in certain areas. But even at Augsburg only about 1.2 percent of the population became Anabaptists between 1526 and 1528, and Augsburg had the largest Anabaptist congregation in the Empire! [7] From 1527 to 1530 the Anabaptists at Esslingen constituted between 1 and 2 percent of the population. Only in a few villages did a larger proportion of the people accept Anabaptism: at Urbach in Württemberg as many as 9 percent of the villagers seem to have been involved with the sect between 1590 and 1609.

The number of towns and villages affected by Anabaptism might give a better indication of the strength of the movement. From 1525 to 1618 Anabaptists appeared in at least 1,821 towns and villages—an enormous number indeed. In the duchy of Württemberg, for example, Anabaptists were to be found in one-fourth to one-fifth of all communities. In most of these 1,821 communities, however, the sect appeared for only a very short time. In 78 communities Anabaptists appeared for a span of ten years; in only fourteen communities, for twenty years; and in exceedingly few communities for thirty or more years. At Augsburg, Anabaptism existed almost without interruption from 1526 to 1573, but Augsburg was an exception. In not a single community did Anabaptists appear for more than fifty years.

The number of believers in an individual community was also very modest. In only five towns and villages in Switzerland, Germany, and Austria did more than a hundred persons become Anabaptists between 1525 and 1618; in another 36, 31 to 100 persons became Anabaptists. These 41 towns and villages were in fact nuclei of the movement, which radiated out into the surrounding area. However, the communities with more than thirty

Anabaptists constituted only 2.2 percent of all towns and villages
affected, and in the course of the sixteenth century, the number
of communities with large Anabaptist congregations declined. In
5.8 percent of all communities affected, ten to thirty persons
joined the sect; in 9.2 percent, five to nine persons; and in 67
percent, fewer than five persons. In other words, in 76 percent
of all towns and villages affected by Anabaptism, fewer than ten
persons accepted the new doctrines in the course of almost a
century! Anabaptism may have spread to a very large number
of communities, but for the most part it appealed to an extremely
small number of persons in a given community.

Why should Anabaptism have taken this particular form of
expansion? Some leaders, such as Hans Hut, deliberately set out
to spread their doctrines in as many villages as possible. Frequently government persecution prevented the leaders from staying in a place for a longer period of time and establishing larger
congregations. Above all, the peculiar nature of the Anabaptist
message—its strange political doctrines and excessive religious
and moral demands—seem to have appealed to only a few. A
leader was more likely to find one follower in a great number
of communities than many followers in only one. Government
persecution and the limited appeal of Anabaptism also explain
why Anabaptism was able to maintain itself in most towns and
villages for a short time only.

This evidence raises the question whether Anabaptism may
realistically be described as a Radical Reformation—"a tremendous movement at the core of Christendom," which according
to George H. Williams had the same impact on modern European society as the Magisterial Reformation, the Counter Reformation, Renaissance Humanism, and Nationalism.[8] The term
Reformation would certainly imply that large numbers of people
were involved, as happened in numerous towns that adopted the
Lutheran or Zwinglian Reformation. For example, at Schwäbisch
Hall and Reutlingen, the massed burghers literally drove the
town council into adopting the Lutheran reform, and at Ulm

and Esslingen an overwhelming number of burghers voted in referendums for the new belief. But nowhere, with the possible exception of the Tirol, did large numbers of people flock to the Anabaptists. In all other areas where Anabaptist leaders preached, most towns and villages were never affected by the sect at all. And of the towns and villages that were affected, 76 percent had no more than ten Anabaptists in the course of three or four generations. The Spiritualists and Evangelical Rationalists, who are said to have formed the other two major divisions of the Radical Reformation, had even fewer followers. From a quantitative point of view, then, the Anabaptist movement was so insignificant that it is misleading to use the term Reformation at all. Anabaptism was no more than a small separatist movement.

3

Divisions within the
Anabaptist Movement

Classifications by Sixteenth-Century Authors

Their sixteenth-century contemporaries soon noted that the Anabaptists were divided into a bewildering mass of groups that seemed to disagree with one another entirely. Already in 1531 Sebastian Franck was writing in his "Chronicon" of the perplexing diversity in the Anabaptist doctrines. But he made no real attempt to classify the Anabaptists, mentioning only a few groups by name: the Apostolic Brethren, the Silent Brethren, and brethren who experienced ecstasies, visions, and dreams.[1] In 1538 Kaspar Hedio presented a list of thirteen groups; in 1544 Johannes Gast listed seven; and in 1566 Wendel Arzt also listed seven.[2] Hedio, Gast, and Arzt did not divide the Anabaptists into the three groups—Swiss Brethren, Mennonites, and Hutterites—that according to nineteenth-century historians made up the movement. But are these sixteenth-century lists complete? Some of the groups, particularly those mentioned by Arzt, did indeed exist. Yet we have no information as to the whereabouts of such groups as the Silent Anabaptists, the Praying Anabaptists, and others.

We face the same problem in Bullinger's discussion of the "marvelous and manifold divisions and bands" of the Anabaptists.[3] Bullinger introduced the important distinction between the large body of "General Anabaptists" and the variety of special groups. The General Anabaptists whom Bullinger considered to be the original group upheld those doctrines we ascribe to the

Swiss Brethren. Soon, however, some Anabaptists had revelations and introduced all sorts of innovations that were rejected by other Anabaptists, who in turn established their own peculiarities. It was not long before the various groups began to ban and curse each other.

Bullinger distinguished the following special groups: the Apostolic Anabaptists; the Secluded, Spiritual Anabaptists; the Holy, Pure, and Sinless Anabaptists; the Taciturn Anabaptists; the Praying and Quiescent Anabaptists; two groups of Free Anabaptists; the Followers of Hans Hut; the Augustinian Brethren; the Münsterite Anabaptists; and the Abominable Anabaptists, consisting of Servetus, Melchior Hofmann, David Georgians and Libertines, those who taught that at the Last Day God would pardon everyone, and those who discarded the Old Testament as having been abolished by Christ. He admitted that he had received much of his information from books written against the Anabaptists, particularly Zwingli's *Elenchus*, and to some extent the books of Franck, Hedio, and Gast, yet he also said that he used books and statements by the Anabaptists themselves, mentioning two particular Anabaptist writings. Recently a German historian concluded that Bullinger's classification is valueless because it is based on anti-Anabaptist literature.[4] Obviously, Bullinger's work has to be used with much caution; yet one hesitates to think that men of high intellectual caliber like Franck, Zwingli, and Bullinger only repeated scabrous rumors circulating about the Anabaptists. Early Anabaptism in particular evidenced a variety of trends, and some Anabaptists may indeed have deserved the names Apostolic, Holy, Silent, or Ecstatic Brethren.

In his book *Evangelische Inquisition* (1573), Georg Eder distinguished 38 different Anabaptist groups. Christoph Erhard used this list in his own book, *Gründliche Kurtz verfaste Historia* (1588), adding five more groups. Neither Eder nor Erhard indicated where the groups were located within the Empire or whether they still existed.[5] The Anabaptists themselves rarely enumerated their various groups. One leader, Sebold Feuchter, claimed at Augsburg in 1533 that there were three sects among the brethren: first, the Swiss, who were ready and willing to use force; second, those who refused to render taxes or payments of any kind to the government; and third, those who paid whatever was due. Feuchter, then, was aware of disagreements among the brethren, but even so he was mistaken in saying that the Swiss advocated the use of force.

While these classifications reveal the bewildered curiosity of sixteenth-century authors over the diversity of Anabaptist groups, they tend to be incomplete, fanciful, and vague. It might be more rewarding to base our study of the various Anabaptist groups on documentary evidence.

The Major Groups

In all, twenty Anabaptist groups can be distinguished in our area. Only six of them, however, played roles of major importance: the Swiss Brethren, the followers of Hans Hut, the group that formed around Pilgram Marbeck, the Thuringian Anabaptists, the group that formed around Georg Schnabel, and the Hutterites. These six major groups held certain basic beliefs in common. They emphasized separation from the world and a life of discipleship. They believed that through the baptism of believers and the strict practice of excommunication it was possible to establish a congregation of pure Christians. They introduced a lay ministry. And they demanded the limitation of secular government to secular matters. But there were equally fundamental differences between these groups as well.

The Swiss Brethren distinguished themselves by their uncompromising stand in political matters: they scrupulously denied that a Christian might hold government office, swear an oath, sue in court, or fight in war. Unlike the Hutterites, who also took this position, they allowed themselves to own personal property. Emanating from Zurich, the Swiss Brethren dominated the Anabaptist movement in Switzerland and the valley of the

upper Rhine, and spread to Swabia and Hesse. In Swabia, however, they encountered Anabaptist groups influenced by Hut,
and did not get farther east than Augsburg. There were no Swiss
congregations in Franconia, Thuringia, or Bavaria, but Swiss settlements existed in Moravia right up to the Thirty Years' War.

The second influential group originated with the Franconian
bookseller Hans Hut, who had been deeply impressed by Müntzer's theology.[6] Müntzer's view that the path to salvation led
through bitter spiritual suffering lived on in Hut's Gospel of All
Creatures. Possibly Hans Denck may also have influenced Hut's
baptismal theology. Both regarded questions of government,
oaths, and the use of weapons as externals of secondary importance. What distinguished Hut from other Anabaptist leaders
was his fiery preaching on eschatological matters; he proclaimed
that the Last Day would come in 1528. In spite of his special
views, Hut looked on the Anabaptists in Switzerland as his fellow believers.[7] Originating in northern Franconia near the Thuringian border, Hut's type of Anabaptism spread through Franconia during 1526–27, and through Bavaria, lower and upper
Austria, Salzburg, and the Tirol in 1527. It reached into Swabia,
but did not advance farther west than Esslingen. There were no
Huttian congregations in the Rhine valley or Switzerland.

Pilgram Marbeck, the central figure in the third major group,
rejected the rigid legalism of the Swiss Brethren. Love and faith,
and not the letter of the Scripture, should guide the believer.
Marbeck's friend Leupold Scharnschlager criticized the Swiss
Brethren for constantly ordering the believers: "Wear not this";
"Wear not that." Nor could Marbeck's followers accept the
Hutterite preaching that only those who shared their property
would find the Savior. Though Marbeck and his followers agreed
with Hut in placing love above laws and rules, they did not
preach Hut's Gospel of All Creatures or Hut's explosive eschatology. They were distinguished from the Schnabel group in
Hesse by their Christology: though Marbeck taught that one
could not separate the humanity and deity of Christ, he clearly

emphasized the humanity. Marbeck and his followers referred
to themselves as the "Christ-believing allies and participants in
the sadness which is Christ." Others simply called them Pilgramites. Owing to Marbeck's wanderings his followers can be discovered at Strasbourg and the Kinzig and Leber valleys in the
1530s and 1540s, possibly at Esslingen in 1544, at Graubünden
and Augsburg from the 1540s to the 1560s, and again in the
Leber valley in the 1560s and 1590s. In Moravia, Marbeck
groups may already have existed in the 1530s and 1540s, and
definitely existed in the second half of the sixteenth century.
One group is mentioned at Austerlitz as late as 1617.

The fourth group, the Thuringian Anabaptists, were decisively set apart from other Anabaptist groups by the lingering
influence of Thomas Müntzer. Hans Römer, the first Anabaptist leader in Thuringia, even made preparations for a new uprising, and some of Römer's followers still used Müntzer's liturgical
writings. Müntzer's ideas also persisted among nonrevolutionary
Anabaptists in Thuringia. Two believers in the area of Mühlhausen actually maintained that Müntzer had brought them to
their faith; another embraced Müntzer's views on infant baptism,
Christ's atonement, and inspiration. The leader Jakob Storger
publicly declared that Müntzer had been one of the prophets
predicted in the Revelation. Thuringian Anabaptism was also
influenced by leaders from Franconia and Salzburg, by a disciple
of Wolfgang Brandhuber in upper Austria, by Andreas Karlstadt, and possibly by the Zwickau prophets as well. The Anabaptists in the areas of Mühlhausen, Frankenhausen, and the
Harz Mountains were extremely bitter, condemning infant baptism as a bath for dogs and pigs. Some used Karlstadt's interpretation of the Lord's Supper; others spoke of the hands of the
priest as the flesh and blood under the elements. Some brethren
cut bread into wine for the Lord's Supper. Others held a special
view of the Trinity.[8] In the area of Eisenach some brethren had
a strong spiritualistic tendency, repudiated the resurrection of
the body,[9] spoke of marriage as an eternal spiritual estate, and

held that drinking from the cup meant the shedding of one's blood. Outside of their theological views, the Thuringian Anabaptists were distinguished by social and political radicalism, which was more common in their group than in any other. In western Thuringia we find communistic tendencies in the environs of Zella St. Blasii in 1527 and Eisenach in 1537. The Anabaptists in Thuringia, then, cannot be classified as Swiss Brethren or followers of Hut or Marbeck, but must be considered a group in themselves. Thuringian Anabaptism appeared only in the areas of Erfurt, Mühlhausen, Eisenach, Sangerhausen, and the Harz Mountains.

The fifth group, which formed around Georg Schnabel in Hesse, differed from the Swiss Brethren in that it recognized as Christian government, military service, and the swearing of oaths. It did not share the political radicalism of the Thuringian Anabaptists. The group held to Melchior Hofmann's doctrine of incarnation and believed that there was no forgiveness of sins against the Holy Ghost. In 1538 they also thought that the end of the world was near, though they did not preach Hut's eschatology, nor for that matter his Gospel of All Creatures. Two leaders of this group, Lienhart Fälber and Peter Tesch, had come from the duchy of Jülich, where Hofmann's doctrines had been preached. Tesch was strongly influenced by Hofmann, and may have introduced Schnabel to Hofmann's views on incarnation and perhaps also to his eschatological orientation. In any case Schnabel employed expressions that are characteristic of Hofmann. It is not clear, however, where Schnabel acquired his political views. The Schnabel group appeared only in Hesse, and only during the 1530s; we find Swiss Brethren in the same area during the second half of the sixteenth century.

The Hutterites, the sixth group, effected a profound social revolution by establishing communities in which all property was held in common and the family practically abolished, in spite of marriage. They were far less democratic than the other Anabaptist groups, establishing an authoritarian hierarchy.

Though their communities were situated in Moravia, the Hutterites were active in a larger area than any other group. They roused powerful movements in the Tirol, Swabia, and Hesse, and also sent missionaries into the Rhine valley, Bavaria, and Switzerland. Only Franconia and Thuringia remained largely untouched by their influence.

During the second half of the sixteenth century, the Hutterites, the Swiss Brethren, and to a smaller extent Marbeck's followers were the only important groups in Germany, Switzerland, and Austria. Hut's followers, the Thuringian Anabaptists, and Schnabel's followers had disappeared. In Hesse the Schnabel group collapsed owing to the defection of its leaders; in Thuringia, Franconia, and Bavaria, Anabaptism was simply suppressed by the governments.

Schisms and Their Causes

In 1529 the governor of Styria had the impression that each Anabaptist group invented its own doctrines and kept multiplying them. If the Anabaptists were not quite so individualistic as that, one nevertheless wonders why this already small sect split further into not less than twenty different groups. Several reasons are evident. First, Anabaptism was spread over an enormous area at a time of primitive means of communication. How were the brethren in Switzerland to know what the Anabaptists in the Harz Mountains were doing? Second, there was never an Anabaptist hierarchy to supervise the congregations as a whole: each congregation was practically independent. Third, the Anabaptists themselves encouraged an almost unbridled individualism by rejecting all human authority and the use of force in religious matters. If a person received odd inspirations or discovered exotic doctrines and practices in the New Testament, the congregation could not prevent him from voicing his opinions; they could only exclude him, a tactic that hardly bothered a new prophet. He was still free to establish his own sect. The principle that religious activities should be free from secular interference—employed so skillfully by the Anabaptists against the governments—backfired against the Anabaptists themselves, leading to their irreconcilable divisions. The immediate causes of the internal quarrels and divisions varied from disagreements over doctrine to clashes of personality to power conflicts among the leaders themselves.

In May 1527 at Nikolsburg, Hubmaier and Hut, the two most gifted leaders in south Germany, came into conflict over 52 points of heresy that Hut was alleged to have taught. In later years, too, differences over doctrine divided even close congregations. In 1557 the leaders of two Swiss congregations around Worms and Kreuznach, Farwendel and Theobald, clashed violently over the doctrines of original sin and sins of soul and flesh. Finally leaders from fifty congregations met at Strasbourg in an attempt to restore peace. The Hutterite Chronicle reports that the discussions gave rise to violent outbursts in which Farwendel called Theobald a false prophet and a liar. In the end the leaders calmed the antagonists by calling their dispute the product of mere human reasoning. Farwendel and Theobald shook hands in front of the assembly. But in spite of this touching scene, they soon clashed again, and their followers went different ways.

Sometimes differences of opinion over doctrine were intensified owing to the ambition of dissatisfied leaders. In 1529, for example, feelings were high among the believers of the Jakob Widemann community at Austerlitz over the privileged position of their leaders and other matters. These differences might have been ironed out in discussion. But the Anabaptist apostle Reublin smarted under a community injunction against individual preaching, and simply preached anyway. When called to account by Widemann, Reublin accused him and his friends of false doctrines and practices. Neither Widemann nor Reublin could yield without losing his authority. As a result Reublin and Georg Zaunring and their adherents separated from Widemann's congregation and went to Auspitz.

Some schisms resulted purely from power struggles between
ambitious and gifted leaders. When for example Jakob Hutter,
the Tirolese leader, tried to assume leadership functions after his
arrival at Auspitz in August 1533, he was firmly opposed by
Sigmund Schützinger, the head of the Auspitz congregation, and
by Philipp Plener and Gabriel Ascherham, the leaders of two
affiliated Anabaptist groups. After angry exchanges, Hutter demanded that the matter be brought before the entire congregation. The congregation recommended that both Schützinger and
Hutter be leaders although Schützinger should have precedence.
Hutter accepted the compromise with bad grace. When a few
weeks later it was discovered that Schützinger had hidden
money, Hutter decided to crush his rivals once and for all.
Schützinger was expelled and Plener and Ascherham were excommunicated. The followers of Plener and Ascherham in turn
ceased to regard the Hutterites as fellow believers.[10] We look in
vain for basic differences of doctrine that could have unleashed
this most venomous of all Anabaptist quarrels in Moravia. Its
cause was nothing more or less than Hutter's determined drive
for leadership, on the one hand, and on the other, the incensed
opposition of Schützinger, Plener, and Ascherham, who resented
Hutter's ambition and envied his talent.

Group Relations

The various Anabaptist groups viewed one another not with
forbearance and understanding but with bitter hatred. Any
deviation advocated by one group from the basic Anabaptist
beliefs was branded treasonous by the others. Brotherly love
turned into abiding ill will. In Strasbourg ugly disputes over
doctrinal matters broke out at meetings.[11] Marbeck seems to have
been a particularly contentious leader. In 1531 he quarreled
with Hans Bünderlin; in 1533, with Hofmann. In the 1540s he
and his flock at Graubünden had an angry exchange with the
Swiss Brethren at Appenzell in which the two groups even refused to recognize each other as congregations of God. Marbeck

denounced the Swiss Brethren and the Hutterites as "two harmful and destructive sects." [12]

Where, as in parts of Moravia, two or three Anabaptist groups occupied the same town or area, doctrinal disputes often embittered their relations. Following their altercation of 1533, the Philippites would have no more to do with the Hutterites, refusing to work, sit, or eat with them even when they were employed by the same lord. The Hutterite Chronicle rather smugly observes that the Hutterites, too, would have preferred to keep to themselves, but were bound to take jobs wherever they could find them. Soon enough, however, the Hutterites also refused to mingle with false brethren—not because they were conceited, they hastened to point out, but because the Holy Ghost had ordered believers to avoid those who pretended to be brethren but in reality led disorderly lives.

Among these so-called false brethren, as far as the Hutterites were concerned, the Swiss Brethren held first place. It is with some consternation that we observe the deep enmity prevailing between the two leading Anabaptist groups during the sixteenth century. The Hutterites accused the Swiss Brethren of a wide array of offenses: abandoning the true community, retaining private property, leading dissolute lives like worldly people and paying taxes for purposes of war and "idol's money" (*Götzenopfer*), making a mockery of the office of minister, teaching erroneous doctrines of original sin, and failing to stay away from other false Anabaptist groups.[13]

The Swiss Brethren retaliated by accusing the Hutterites of a long list of pernicious tenets and practices, which included requiring the believer to emigrate to Moravia; emigrating without paying debts; advocating the common ownership of property, and thus refusing to return property to brethren who left the communities; admitting into their number ostensibly penitent robbers and murderers; condemning peddling and trading; practicing doubtful marital customs and permitting divorce on the ground of different beliefs; using harsh methods in rearing their children, including separating the children from their parents; conferring special privileges on their leaders; avoiding other Anabaptist groups; refusing to pay for food and clothes in prison and refusing to pay taxes on the ground that they might be used for military purposes; and finally, maintaining that infant baptism was harmful.[14] The Swiss Brethren thus condemned not only the common ownership of goods but all the Hutterite customs of communal living.

The Hutterites querulously protested that they were disliked by all other Anabaptist groups, and they were quite right. The Pilgramites in Moravia even excommunicated them. Farwendel, the leader of the Swiss Brethren near Kreuznach, called the Hutterites a cursed people; he was so violently opposed to them that when in 1557 a large number of Swiss Brethren defected and went to Moravia, he excommunicated himself for not having guarded his flock sufficiently against the Hutterite leaders.

When in 1573 Paul Glock, a Hutterite missionary, and Lienhard Sommer and Jakob Gantz, two leaders of the Swiss Brethren, lay in the same prison at Hohenwittlingen in Württemberg, Glock and Sommer soon began to quarrel angrily. Glock, who could hardly sleep for two nights because of the dispute, finally asked Sommer to read Peter Riedemann's *Account of Our Religion*. Two days later Sommer replied that this book contained unbiblical, human ideas. Glock retorted that an opinion was not wrong just because one could not support it with a biblical passage. This argument only kindled the flame: Sommer rejected the Hutterites more vigorously than ever, while to Glock's way of thinking "he had a bitter heart full of gall with many lies." Glock offered Sommer pen and paper to write down his arguments, but Sommer refused any further communication.[15] The situation is tragic and grotesque: even while they suffered together in prison, the two Anabaptists could not overcome their disagreement and mutual aversion. This acrimony and petulance contrasts sharply with the pious discipleship some historians have attributed to the Anabaptists. The Hutterites even doubted

whether people of other Anabaptist groups who had died for
their faith should be called martyrs: one leader suggested eva-
sively that these people should be left to the judgment of the
Lord.[16] But there were also magnanimous Hutterites. Hieronymus Käls wrote from his prison in Vienna in 1536 that though
the Austerlitzers did not live according to the rule of Christ, they
had witnessed to the truth until their death and would also enter
the kingdom of God.[17] Indeed, some of the martyrs listed in the
Hutterite Chronicle were not Hutterites at all. And if the Hutterites were only too well acquainted with the divisions among
the Anabaptists in Moravia and southern Germany, they nonetheless expressed loud indignation at the divisions among the
Mennonites in Prussia.

Whatever the relations of the various other Anabaptist groups,
all agreed in condemning the Anabaptist Kingdom of Münster.
Christoph Erhard observed that the Hutterites were agonized
whenever they were compared to the Münsterites. Angrily they
spoke of the Münsterites as the devil's brethren, with whom they
wished no communion whatever.[18]

One of the curious effects of the hostility among the various
Anabaptist groups was that brethren who had been excluded by
one congregation quickly joined the enemy. After his expulsion
by the Hutterites at Auspitz, Adam Schlegel immediately joined
the Plener group and soon held a high position. For that matter,
there was considerable rivalry among Anabaptist groups in attracting members. Thus leaders of both the Swiss Brethren and
the Hutterites sometimes preached in the same area at about the
same time. Around Kirrweiler in the Rhine valley, for example,
we find Swiss Brethren in the 1550s and 1560s and between 1590
and 1610; yet "many" Anabaptists, presumably Hutterites, are
said to have emigrated from eleven towns and villages near
Kirrweiler in 1566. Occasionally we even find Swiss Brethren
and Hutterites in the same villages, as for example at Urbach,
Schlechtbach, Schnait, Lorch, and Beutelsbach in the Rems valley in Württemberg.

The presence of both Swiss Brethren and Hutterites in the same place was not a coincidence but a deliberate consequence of Hutterite policy. The Hutterites thought it would be easier to convert those who had already accepted adult baptism than to convert heathens, that is Lutherans and Zwinglians. Sometimes they were successful. In 1557 they persuaded the leader Lorenz Hueff and many of his followers near Kreuznach to come to Moravia. In more than one village Hutterite Anabaptism replaced Swiss Anabaptism. In 1553, 1561, and 1574 we find Swiss Brethren at Frankweiler in the duchy of Pfalz-Zweibrücken, whence several were finally expelled before 1584; that same year, however, the pastor of Frankweiler reported the infiltration of Hutterites into the village. Newly converted Hutterite believers would suddenly leave for Moravia. But the Hutterites also experienced failures: around 1540 Riedemann preached without success in the Neckar basin because the Swiss leaders had "devastated" everything. It goes without saying that this rivalry was not limited to Hutterites and Swiss Brethren. In 1530 attempts were already being made by Hofmannites at Strasbourg to entice Swiss Brethren into their ranks.[19]

When the member of one Anabaptist group joined another, was his first baptism recognized? The problem presented itself so often that the Swiss leaders decided at Strasbourg in 1568 to accept the original baptism if it had been performed in the right spirit. The Hutterites did not rebaptize converts from other groups either, but admitted them simply by laying a hand on their heads.

Some Anabaptists felt no qualms at the manifold divisions within their movement. Even if there were more sects, a brother at Austerlitz wrote in 1539, he would not worry, for the brethren were divided only over externals, not over doctrine. And even if there were divisions over doctrine, he continued, he still would not be disturbed, for there had been false prophets and false doctors before and after the coming of Christ.[20] There were

Anabaptists who went even further, simply denying that there were any divisions among the believers at all.

Attempts to Settle Differences

Other Anabaptists, however, were undoubtedly embarrassed by the rifts within their small movement. Even so, only occasionally do we find evidence of meetings held or letters exchanged on this subject, though many unrecorded efforts may have been made to overcome differences between Anabaptist groups. The earliest known attempt to unite disagreeing factions was a meeting held at Schleitheim in February 1527 where Michael Sattler and other leaders discussed various doctrines on which they had previously "failed to agree in true understanding." The accord was laid down in the Brotherly Agreement: "In this we have perceived the oneness of the spirit of our father and common Christ with us. For the Lord is the Lord of peace and not of dispute."

Yet the Anabaptist movement continued to split into groups. Worried by this development, Pilgram Marbeck made great efforts in the 1540s to reach an understanding with other groups. While he was on good terms with the Swiss Brethren in Swabia, his correspondence with those at Appenzell and St. Gallen from 1542 to 1551 is full of rancor. Nor was he successful with the Hutterites. The Hutterite Chronicle reports that he came to them in 1541 pretending to unite the believers in all countries. But he soon clashed with the Hutterite leaders when he went so far as to assume the functions of leadership: he said his prayers too loudly during worship, and was promptly told to keep his mouth shut. Outraged, he shouted that he would rather unite with the Turks or the Pope than with the Hutterites, and stormed away. We may assume that he and the Hutterites had many more such differences. For all Marbeck's efforts to bring the Anabaptists together, they were as much divided as ever when he died in 1556.[21]

In the second half of the sixteenth century, the south German Anabaptists made several attempts to discuss disputed doctrines especially with the brethren in the Netherlands and north Germany. On August 24, 1555, brethren and elders of "many places"—we may assume that these were Swiss Brethren and followers of Marbeck [22]—met at Strasbourg to talk over the wretched controversy on Christ's incarnation that divided the Mennonites. Refusing to take sides, they declared that either position might be justified according to the Scriptures; it was best simply to obey God's commandments and live pure in heart. In 1557 leaders from Moravia, Swabia, Switzerland, Württemberg, Breisgau, and other areas held another unusual meeting in an inn at Strasbourg. They referred to themselves as "Upperland Brethren," and claimed to represent fifty congregations within a range of 150 miles (which would amount to some seven or eight hundred statute miles) stretching from the Eifel Mountains to Moravia.[23] We would call them Swiss Brethren. They tried to settle the quarrel of Farwendel and Theobald and rejected the extreme position on discipline and marital avoidance adopted by the Mennonites of northern Germany and the Netherlands at Wismar in 1554. The leaders besought Menno and the Dutch brethren to strive after unity: let us, they said, "be one people at peace with ourselves." Menno harshly rejected their letter, and in 1559 the Dutch elders even pronounced the ban on the upper German brethren.

Yet the ideal of unity was not forgotten. In 1567 the Swiss Brethren in and outside Moravia asked the Hutterites by letter for clarification on seven controversial points of doctrine. The Hutterites sent such a cutting reply that the Swiss leaders did not even care to read it to the congregation.[24] This exchange of letters might have had something to do with the conference held by "ministers and bishops of many places" at Strasbourg in 1568. At any rate, there the Swiss leaders again refused to espouse the Mennonite position on avoidance and incarnation. At the disputation at Frankenthal in 1571, too, the Swiss Brethren reiterated their differences with the Mennonite views. Even so, they began talks in 1575 with the "Flemish" Mennonites, who in 1566 had separated form the "Friesians." But when the Flemish emissaries who had come to the Neckar valley insisted on a new baptism of the south German brethren, on the strict use of the ban, and on shunning, the talks collapsed. Finally, fifteen years later, in 1591, the leaders of the Swiss Brethren in the upper Rhine valley and certain northwest German and Dutch Anabaptists drew up a compromise on incarnation and avoidance. They also agreed on numerous questions of congregational life.[25]

The Hutterites, too, aimed at reaching an understanding with other groups, though it is doubtful that they ever envisaged a compromise: to them, unity implied the acceptance of their doctrines and way of life by other groups. When in 1536 Onofrius Griesinger was sent to the Tirol, he also visited Switzerland, conveying written and oral messages. But his mission failed, for the barrier between Swiss Brethren and Hutterites was already well established. The Hutterites also made considerable efforts to win over the Philippites, who after their expulsion from Auspitz in 1535 had returned to Württemberg, Baden, Strasbourg, and the Palatinate. In 1538 Riedemann asked them not to make agreements with other Anabaptist groups before they had heard the Hutterite explanation of the quarrel of 1533, and in 1539 he himself attended a meeting of Philippite leaders at Heilbronn. All hopes for a union were dashed, however, when the Philippites adamantly rejected the Hutterite belief in communal property. The Philippites in the area of Worms refused even to hear Riedemann. In 1537 the Philippites in upper Austria got in touch with the Hutterites, who sent them leaders to organize their congregations. But in spite of the pleas of Bishop Hans Amon in 1540, most of these Austrian Philippites also refused to emigrate to Moravia. Under Riedemann's inspiration the Hutterites wrote to the Hessian leader Mathes Hasenhan in 1538, explaining why Hans Both and his followers had been thrown out of the Hutterite community in 1533 and denying that the Hut-

terites had ever attacked Melchior Rinck, who was greatly respected in Hesse. But though Riedemann himself went to Hesse
in 1539, he could not overcome Hasenhan's distaste for the
Hutterite doctrines and practices. In and around 1540, however,
a considerable number of Hessians did emigrate to Moravia.

Many years later, during 1603–4, the Hutterites tried to merge
with the Mennonites in Prussia. While the Hutterites established
a community at Elbing, two Mennonite leaders came to Moravia
with some of their followers to observe the Hutterite life. After
their return to Prussia, the Mennonites at first made a favorable
report, and the understanding seems to have been that the Mennonites would join the Hutterites. But suddenly one of the Mennonite leaders changed his mind and refused to go to Moravia,
calling the communities murder caves where young and old
failed to get their proper food and died. The entire project collapsed, the Hutterites complaining that they had spent a good
deal of money for nothing. But while the Hutterites were never
able to convert a whole group to their way of life, they were
occasionally able to attract individual leaders, sometimes with a
large following, of the Swiss Brethren, the Austerlitzers, and the
Gabrielites. Lorenz Hueff and his followers around Kreuznach
joined the Hutterites only after carefully scrutinizing the Hutterites' doctrines and practices. In spite of their desire to win
converts, the Hutterite leaders who negotiated with Hueff were
not hasty either: they admonished the Swiss Brethren to be
aware of the doctrinal differences between the two groups;
they talked to the individual converts about their repentance
and faith; and they prayed to God to pardon the converts' errors
after the converts had recited a confession of faith.[26] The Hutterites made even more fuss when it came to admitting leaders
who had formerly criticized them.[27] In none of these cases, of
course, did the Hutterites merge with other groups; they simply
converted members of other groups to the Hutterite faith.

The sixteenth-century Anabaptists, then, never succeeded in
uniting their divided movement. While the Anabaptist move-

ment was still fluid in the 1520s, it soon crystallized into factions with sharp differences. A loose understanding, such as the Concept of Cologne of 1591, was the most that could be achieved. There was never an Anabaptist movement with common doctrines and practices, and to this day the descendants of the Anabaptists remain divided.

The extreme divisions within the Anabaptist movement raise the question whether in an age of religious turmoil a certain amount of governmental control over religious affairs was not preferable to unlimited religious freedom. The example of the Anabaptists indicates that during the Reformation any pious person could find followers if he had leadership qualities. Arbitrary doctrines or even eccentric speculations were advanced as divine intuitions. Admittedly, whenever governments, church councils, and universities decided on the truth of a doctrine, they were likely to be oppressive and intolerant. The authorities were not guided by religious inspiration, however, but by common sense and certain secular realities. They knew they were responsible for keeping order among hundreds of thousands of people. Thus they would never have authorized a Hut or a Hofmann to proclaim their fantastic notions on the Lord's Day or tolerated the ecstatic aberrations that characterized some Anabaptist groups.

Of course, eccentrics among the Anabaptists were rare. The Anabaptist leaders were on the whole decent, pious men, if a little too self-assured. Nobody will deny that their theological speculations, their piety, and their high moral standards form a fine chapter in the history of religion in the sixteenth century. Yet the origin and development of these small Anabaptist groups were invariably accompanied by violent rows and outbursts of hatred that were surely contrary to the spirit of Christianity. To maintain their identity these small groups practiced a strict legalism and fastidious observance of all regulations that was as narrow-minded as the ceremonialism of the late medieval church.

Preoccupied with the idea of religious freedom, modern admirers of Anabaptism tend to disregard the negative aspects of the early free church movement. The divisions within Anabaptism suggest, to the contrary, that in the sixteenth century the regulation of religious matters by educated theologians and governments was to some extent a matter of common sense.

4

Organization

In spite of their subjectivism the Anabaptists did not reject organized religion, as did some of the sixteenth-century spiritualists. Actually, the Anabaptists attempted to restore the type of church that had existed at the time of the apostles. Thus they introduced to Switzerland, Germany, and Austria a congregational type of church organization in which converts voluntarily joined independent congregations that were neither subordinate to a church hierarchy nor subject to governmental interference. Some of the earliest leaders, such as Reublin and Schiemer, referred to themselves as bishops and might have enjoyed special prestige in congregations they had founded. There is, however, no evidence showing that the brethren in our area had conceived of a system where the bishop, like a Catholic bishop or a Protestant church council, would have disciplinary powers over several congregations.

Conferences and Ordinances

While there was no hierarchy above the level of the individual congregation, the congregation leaders gathered occasionally to discuss doctrine and practical questions. The meeting of Sattler with other leaders at Schleitheim near Schaffhausen in February 1527 has already been mentioned. Before May 13, 1527, leaders from Augsburg, Lindau, and Memmingen gathered at Basel; we do not know whether they had attended the meeting at Schleitheim.[1] In August 1527 two or three important meetings were held at Augsburg. Outstanding south German and Austrian leaders were present, such as Hans Hut, Lienhart Dorfbrunner,

Jakob Kautz, Jakob Widemann, and Hans Schlaffer, and surely also the Augsburg leaders Jakob Gross, Sigmund Salminger, and Jakob Dachser.[2] Most of the sixty participants were probably simple believers at Augsburg. The purposes of the meeting were to organize apostolic missions, to discuss Hut's controversial eschatology, and perhaps to discuss also the conflicting views of different groups on government and on bearing arms and swearing oaths.

In 1528 another meeting of "many leaders and up to 100 Anabaptists" was held at Christmas in the village of Teufen near Appenzell. We do not know the reasons for this meeting. Some evidence suggests that leaders from the Strasbourg area met in 1535. In 1539 the Philippite leaders from the areas of Strasbourg, Worms, and Heilbronn gathered at Heilbronn. There is no record of other meetings of Anabaptist leaders in the 1530s and 1540s, though of course others may have been held. As we have already seen, in 1555, 1557, and 1568 the Anabaptist leaders of south Germany held conferences at Strasbourg, and in 1591 several south German leaders met with Dutch and north German brethren at Cologne.

In some of these meetings agreements or ordinances were drawn up to define correct doctrine, to decide on important practices, or to unite various branches. The oldest known ordinance is the seven articles drafted by Sattler and his fellow leaders at Schleitheim in February 1527. The Schleitheim Articles rejected libertinistic tendencies and defined the views of the Swiss Brethren on baptism, ban, breaking of the bread, separation from nonbelievers, leaders, government, and swearing oaths.[3] The articles deal with the theological foundations of these doctrines rather than their practical application.

The seven theses Kautz published at Worms on June 9, 1527, for a proposed disputation with the evangelical ministers might be regarded as a summary of the beliefs of the Anabaptists in this city. They deal with the outer and inner Word, baptism, the Lord's Supper, Christ's work and man's sanctification.[4] In 1527 at Erfurt, Römer referred to an ordinance in Bavaria that would also be introduced in Thuringia.[5] It is possible that during 1527–28 the brethren in Franconia also had an ordinance.[6] An ordinance adopted in 1527 or 1529 by a congregation, probably in the Tirol, dealt with meetings, excommunication, economic matters, and the Lord's Supper.[7]

Around 1540 Scharnschlager wrote an important "Church Order for Members of Christ's Body" dealing with the practical problems of meetings, leadership, excommunication, and the common fund.[8] The ministers and elders of "many congregations" who in 1568 met at Strasbourg issued a "discipline" of 23 points that was renewed at another Strasbourg meeting in 1607. It laid down rules concerning the appointment of leaders, the communion service, the avoidance of excommunicated sinners, marriage, caring for the bereaved, and everyday problems such as dress, commerce, and debts.[9] The Concept of Cologne of 1591 discussed both doctrine and congregational life.[10]

Unfortunately, these written agreements and ordinances offer only a limited insight into the organization of the Anabaptist movement. For one thing, it is uncertain to what extent the congregations really complied with them, since there were no means of enforcement such as the regular visitations by superintendents, archdeacons, and bishops in the established church. For another, many customs and practices that were followed were never formally enacted. We must therefore supplement the ordinances with the statements made by Anabaptists in the course of interrogations.

The Leaders

Although some Anabaptists asserted that they did not have priests, apostles, or leaders, God or Christ being their only superior, the ordinary Anabaptist congregation in fact had a leader. But unlike the Catholic priest or the Protestant pastor, the Anabaptist leader was not part of the ruling hierarchy of a city or territory. The brethren referred to their leaders as ministers or

servants, shepherds, elders, teachers, or *vorsteher*. Melchior Hofmann distinguished between apostles and leaders of local congregations. The apostles wandered from place to place, without
attaching themselves to a specific congregation, to spread the
new belief all over Switzerland, Austria, and Germany. The
work of the local leaders was confined to one congregation.

What were the qualifications of a minister? Referring to
I Timothy 3:7, Sattler insisted that those chosen must have a
good reputation among nonbelievers. Moral purity was an absolute prerequisite, for the life and the function of a minister
could not be separated. The minister also had to be conversant
with the Scriptures, a hard condition for most Anabaptists, who
were craftsmen and peasants with little or no education, to meet;
even so, many knew the Scriptures astonishingly well. But the
most decisive factor was the call from God. The brethren agreed
with the Lutheran theologians that only those who had been
summoned should preach, teach, and baptize, but they added,
that those summoned had to be called by Christ, not by the government, and confirmed by the congregation.

When asked who had chosen the first Anabaptist leaders, Hut
and Riedemann replied, God. Just as God had sent prophets to
Israel, so now He had conferred the power of His spirit on a
chosen few. Soon, however, the divine appointment was replaced
by a more tangible procedure. Some of the first apostles were
commissioned by other apostles, "as Timothy and Titus had
been commissioned by Paul." At Steyr, Hut commissioned Hieronymus from Mannsee, Schiemer, Dorfbrunner, and Jakob
Portner to preach and baptize.[11] Others were sent out by an
assembly of leaders, such as the concilium at Augsburg in August 1527. Then congregations began to commission apostles,
sometimes by drawing lots.

We observe a similar development from appointment to election among the local leaders. Usually leaders were elected as
soon as the congregations were formed, although we do not
know precisely what form the elections took. When on or about

Shrove Tuesday 1527, the believers at Augsburg decided to elect a minister, they first prayed to God and then drew lots. It is possible that in some Anabaptist groups the leaders were elected not by the congregation but by an assembly of brethren from various congregations. In 1539, for example, the Philippites from the areas of Worms, Strasbourg, and Heilbronn gathered at Heilbronn to elect ministers. It is not entirely clear what procedures were used for electing leaders in later years. There may have been elections by vote in Württemberg in 1562.[12] The Thuringian Anabaptists declared in the 1560s that the minister must be chosen by lot.[13] Obviously they assumed that this method left the decision to God.

Whatever the procedure, the minister was chosen by the congregation and not appointed by ecclesiastical superiors or even the government. The demand for popular election of parish priests, made by the peasants in the uprising of 1525, was fully carried out by the Anabaptists. (Only the Hutterites had an authoritarian tendency, as we shall later see.) Immediately after the election the new minister was installed through the laying-on of hands by the elders.[14] In order to prevent the spread of wrong doctrines, newly elected ministers sometimes received instruction by older ones.[15] Furthermore, a minister was appointed on probation, and his election was confirmed only later.[16] As an acting minister, he could not perform all the functions of a confirmed minister: thus in 1630 the Swiss Brethren ruled that in exceptional cases, when a confirmed minister was not available, an acting servant who had a good testimony could also break the bread, baptize, marry couples, punish, and exclude.[17] The Mennonite congregations in north Germany prepared themselves with fasting and prayers for the election of a minister, but it is not known whether the Anabaptists in our area also followed this custom.

Many early congregations, such as those at Worms, Esslingen, and Schwäbisch Gmünd, had only one minister at a time. Since a minister's arrest could thus easily lead to the dissolution of his congregation, the Schleitheim Articles emphasized that if a minister was expelled or killed, another should immediately be ordered to take his place. Some early congregations had two or more ministers. Jörg Nespitzer considered the task of preaching and baptizing at Augsburg to be too heavy for one person alone. Sometimes a minister who had been expelled or was escaping from the authorities would find refuge in another congregation, assisting the local minister. Then there were the apostles, who sometimes made a brief appearance in a congregation. In 1527 and 1528 there were about fifteen apostles and leaders of other congregations preaching and baptizing in Augsburg; here, however, the circumstances were exceptional.

In some instances, by contrast, there were hardly enough ministers to go around. Scharnschlager was already complaining in his "Church Order" of 1540 that there was a "shortage of faithful workers" to lead the congregations. Indeed, in 1562 the Anabaptists in the Rems valley in Württemberg were without a minister, for the old minister was dead and a new one not yet elected. Occasionally a minister from the Palatinate visited this congregation. Also, the same man might be elected minister by more than one congregation: Christof Rudolph served believers in the areas of both Fulda and Mühlhausen.

What were the duties of an Anabaptist minister? According to the Schleitheim Confession he was to "read, admonish and teach, to warn, to discipline, to ban in the church, to lead out in prayer . . . , to lift up the bread when it was to be broken." [18] In other words, the Anabaptist minister had the same tasks as the priest in a Catholic or the pastor in a Protestant church.

The minister was not the only leader in the congregation. At Augsburg in 1527 and Strasbourg in 1545 we hear of a "helper," who assisted the minister. Then there were the elders. At meetings near Strasbourg in 1545 and 1557, the "most prominent" members of the congregations—by which, we may assume, is meant the elders—discussed certain matters with the minister at a distance from the assembled believers. The Strasbourg Discipline ruled in 1568 that on their trips to neighboring congregations, ministers should be accompanied by elders, who would instruct the new elders in their task. The number of elders is unknown, and little is known of their function except that they sometimes had pastoral duties.[19] In any case, the Strasbourg Discipline indicates that the minister was superior to the elder.

As for their apostles, the Anabaptists prayed that they would have strength to spread the Word of God fearlessly. How exactly did the Anabaptist apostles preach the new belief? Hans Hut, the most effective of them, was accompanied by some of his new converts on his missionary travels. When he left the area of Koburg, Eukarius Kellermann, Jörg Volk, Joachim Mertz, and Sebastian joined him; at Königsberg, Wolf Schominger and Hans Beutel; at Ostheim, Thomas Spiegel; at Uetzing, Hans Weischenfelder. All these men also took to preaching and baptizing, presumably inspired by the example of Christ's disciples. Similarly, in Thuringia Hans Römer wandered around accompanied by three disciples.

The early Anabaptists commonly believed that the true apostle wandered from place to place, preaching and suffering persecution as the apostle Paul had done. Often nobody knew where the apostle had come from. He preached and baptized, and then left during the night or early morning at two or three o'clock without telling anyone where he was going. Sometimes believers did not even know the name of the man who had taught them the way to salvation. Thus inquiring officials were unable to elicit more than fanciful descriptions of the apostle's red or blackish-brown beard, his yellow hair, or his long black coat. Under these conditions a deep relationship between apostles and newly converted believers could hardly develop. Many converts, having received only the most elementary instruction in the new faith, readily abandoned it when persecution set in.

Hans Hut in particular never remained in one place for any length of time. Within twelve to fifteen months he rushed three times to Augsburg, all over Franconia, to Nikolsburg, and finally

through lower and upper Austria. His itinerary was not in fact
as haphazard as it might appear. He went to Augsburg because
it was the center of the movement, to Nikolsburg in order to
reach an understanding with Hubmaier. He then traveled from
Nikolsburg to Augsburg via Vienna, following the Danube.

Hut and his followers split into small groups in order to reach
the largest possible number of people. In Franconia he did not
preach in the major towns, such as Bamberg, Würzburg, and
Nuremberg, but only in country towns and villages. In Austria
he went directly to the more sizable towns, realizing that he
would have a larger audience there than in villages and hamlets.
Hut may have been seeking to save as many people as he could
before the imminent Day of Judgment, and he probably sought
also to bring about the triumph of Anabaptism by winning over
the masses. But these goals were never reached. The number of
people who accepted rebaptism remained relatively small; moreover, the governments soon got wind of Hut's activities and took
severe reprisals.

Some apostles addressed themselves first to relatives, friends,
and other acquaintances. One of Hut's first converts was the
cooper in his native village, Haina. It is also possible that he already knew Kellermann at Koburg, and Kilian Volkammer and
Sebastian at nearby Gross-Walbur, who were among his first
followers. Hut and his disciples then went to Königsberg, where
Kellermann's brother-in-law Wolf Schominger lived, and afterward to Ostheim, where Schominger's two married sisters lived.
Thus the appearance of Hut and his friends in specific villages
in northern Franconia was not a simple matter of chance. Obviously traveling in some haste, they talked to only a few persons
in most villages. When Hut and Kellermann came to Passau, they
went straight to Kellermann's sister, the wife of Jörg Nespitzer.
At Augsburg, Nespitzer and Kellermann stayed with their
brother-in-law, Thoma Paur, who also accepted the faith. Impressed by the new apostles, some people recommended them
to their own friends and relatives.

When an apostle had no prearranged contacts of this kind, he would simply walk into a house, as Hut entered a woman's house at Uttenreuth, saying: "Sister, is it your wish to know the Word of God?" News would spread among the peasants that someone was preaching in a nearby mill, barn, or stable, and wondering what was afoot, they would come to take a look. A few might sense that the proceedings were not altogether orthodox. A man at Bussbach remembered very well the fate of his father in the peasant uprising, yet his curiosity proved too strong for him. Another peasant at Bussbach, about to tell his neighbor that the strange preachers had arrived, asked his neighbor to send his children out of the room. The neighbor replied that his children knew how to keep quiet.

The Anabaptist leaders spread their faith wherever they went. Sometimes they explained their beliefs to passengers while they were traveling on the Danube. In 1528 two men asked a peasant at Burgstall for lodging; though they were sent away, they returned four weeks later, were let in, and soon began reading from the Scriptures. In Thuringia, Römer told people to invite their neighbors over, and then preached to them while they were drinking beer. Some fellows even claimed they had been baptized while drunk.

If the Anabaptist leaders were resourceful enough in finding ways of approaching the people, we yet wonder how they induced them to take the unusual and unheard-of step of undergoing a second baptism. Ambrosius Spittelmaier said that whenever he came to an inn, he would ask other guests such questions as whether the pastor in the town or village preached the gospel; what the true gospel was; whether they were Christians; what sort of Christian lives they were leading; and whether they had everything in common with their fellow believers.[20] Hut seems to have impressed on people the imminence of the end of the world and the necessity for suffering. Römer in Thuringia also stressed the end of the world, demanded an austere Christian life, and alluded to some secret knowledge. In December 1527 he told two men at Eisleben that he knew they were among the believers elected by God to be saved through baptism. Those who accepted baptism, he promised, would have no more cares over food, drink, or dress. One of the two men later admitted that he had been greatly taken aback at this claim, and had in fact wondered whether it were not a fraud; but then it had occurred to him that if there really was so little time left, he should not spurn the offer of grace.[21]

Some leaders impressed their listeners by claiming that they had never been refuted by Catholics or Lutherans; they were willing to defend their doctrines with their blood and a thousand books. Others asked the people why they hesitated to embrace the true belief when the rich, whose wits were sharper than theirs, had already accepted it. Burkhart Braun sought to impress one Bernhart Zurkendorffer in Augsburg by pointing in the direction of Austria, where Anabaptism was spreading rapidly: three noblemen with long red beards and a prior had already been baptized. When Zurkendorffer replied that he would prefer to wait until Anabaptism was officially sanctioned, Braun reproved him: "You do not know whether you will be alive tomorrow." Still Zurkendorffer was not convinced. A few days later he told Braun he would not accept baptism because the town council did not allow it. Braun now tried a different approach: he himself had been imprisoned for three days at Augsburg and had yet been released. If baptism had been a crime, they would have put him on trial. When Zurkendorffer still hesitated, Braun said flatly: "Then take my body as a pledge that it is right." "Why do you make so much fuss?" another brother quickly chimed in. "You know that you are a sinner; follow Christ, do penance, and accept baptism." Zurkendorffer agreed that he wanted to be saved, but he still had doubts: "If this should be contrary to God and the authorities, I shall be in a sad plight." Braun now urged him: "You know that you have sinned; kneel down and do penance." The unhappy Zurkendorffer finally had to yield.[22]

Things did not always go so smoothly, however. When one Anabaptist tried to convert the wife of a fellow believer, she angrily told him to stop talking to her like that in her house. Two men in Thuringia curtly told an Anabaptist leader they would first like to discuss the matter with other people. Of course, the Anabaptists themselves realized that few people, hardly one in a thousand, accepted the Word of God. Why? Because it was the Word of the Cross.

Some Anabaptists insisted that the apostles should not have property or a fixed residence. Like Christ and His disciples they should wander about the earth in poverty, serving others for nothing, content with whatever food was given them. And it is true that the early Anabaptist apostles came close to this ideal. When Hans Krüsi preached at St. Gallen, the believers would give him either food or money. Other leaders too were given lodging, hot meals or bread and cheese, money, or warm clothing. Hut, for example, was sometimes offered two or three florins, and on one occasion even a hundred.[23] The Austrian government claimed that the leaders had the addresses of fellow believers who would help them. Indeed, when in 1527 Spittelmaier traveled from Linz to Erlangen, he had a list of people who would offer him lodging.

Some leaders who had sold their possessions were able to pay their own way. Since most were craftsmen, they were almost always certain of finding a job for a few weeks, a fact that increased their mobility. We hear of leaders who supported themselves by working on building sites, in vineyards, as tailors or barrel makers. Yet some, like Dorfbrunner, who had formerly been a priest and later a craftsman, did not ply their craft after they became Anabaptist leaders.

Being determined to follow the example of Christ and His disciples, many of the early apostles did not concern themselves too greatly over the fate of their families. Hut's family was reduced to utter chaos. The wives of Krüsi, Kellermann, Gross, Salminger, and Nespitzer wandered from place to place for weeks and even months, earning meager livings as seamstresses and maidservants. Repeatedly they were arrested, imprisoned, driven out. Sattler's wife was even executed.

Apart from the Hutterites it was only in the 1520s that the Anabaptists sent out apostles. In vain do we look in the second half of the sixteenth century for Swiss Brethren apostles who went from place to place, proclaiming their doctrines. How was it that the Anabaptists in Germany, Switzerland, and Austria lost their missionary zeal? For one thing, after the first enthusiasm had passed, the Anabaptist leaders themselves became wary of wandering apostles whom nobody really knew. Jakob Hutter, possibly fearing lest unauthorized apostles spread erroneous doctrine, warned in the 1530s against those who preached baptism on their own, without the permission of either leaders or brethren.[24] For another, most leaders of later years did not share the intensity of Hut's eschatological speculations, and hence they did not share his sense of urgency about converting unregenerate mankind.

We may assume, too, that the leaders were disappointed, for the first apostles had made immense efforts to spread the true gospel through Switzerland, Germany, and Austria, and yet their enthusiasm, sacrifices, and suffering had succeeded in creating not a mass movement but only a small sect. The Anabaptists might have thought that if the people in Franconia and Austria rejected the gospel, nobody could force it on them. Instead of thinking of grandiose missions, then, the new generation of leaders considered it their primary duty to take care of the few believers who remained and perhaps to spread their doctrines within the confines of their own region, but not beyond. There was also the practical problem posed by the shortage of leaders. The few men who accepted the dangerous task of preaching were needed by their own congregations, not out traveling around the countryside.

By the second half of the sixteenth century, then, at the latest, the Anabaptist leader was head of a specific congregation. This raised the important question whether he should be a full-time minister, supported by the congregation, or a lay minister who would continue to earn his living as a craftsman or peasant. Sattler might have envisaged a professional ministry,[25] and around 1539 the brethren in Hesse do seem to have supported their minister.[26] But most Anabaptist leaders kept their former jobs. Two leaders at Augsburg, a glassmaker and a mason, declared in 1533 that nobody had given them a penny: they were not belly preachers or money preachers.

Anabaptist congregations did recognize, however, that the leaders who devoted so much time and effort to them must receive at least some support. Scharnschlager suggested in 1540 that the leaders be given material support in addition to the work they were able to do. The Strasbourg Discipline also ordered that the minister and elders be provided with all necessities when they were sent out to comfort prisoners and bereaved believers. The Anabaptists of Switzerland and south Germany thus arrived at a compromise between the completely honorary lay leader and the salaried professional pastor. In a sense, the entire matter was a source of embarrassment, for the early Anabaptists had furiously assailed the pastors for accepting a salary.

In an effort to protect the minister from possible intrigue, the Schleitheim Articles stipulated that he should "not be dealt with except on the testimony of two or three persons," and that he was to be disciplined before the entire congregation. Scharnschlager emphasized that the minister be "given due respect and be obeyed, for he is worthy of double honor." Even so there seems to have been unrest. When in 1539 Riedemann visited several congregations in Germany, he found nothing but quarrels between leaders and congregations. At Lauingen spiritualistic tendencies had undermined the authority of the leaders: pressured by an inspired brother, four leaders confessed that they had not received their positions from the Lord and resigned. The Philippites in Württemberg accused one of their former leaders of lying, another of having maladministered their money. When

Riedemann came to Hesse the brethren there were on the point of deposing their minister, Mathes Hasenhan.[27] In point of fact, there was a case in later years where one Lerch, a leader of the Strasbourg congregation, was expelled for embezzlement.[28] Most Anabaptist leaders, however, seem to have been conscientious in the performance of their tasks.

The Size of the Congregations

Since the congregations varied greatly in size, it might be useful to distinguish three categories: large congregations, of one hundred to five hundred; medium-sized congregations, of twenty to ninety-nine; and small congregations, of fewer than twenty. Really large congregations formed only during the first years of the Anabaptist movement: for example, there was a congregation of 360 in Waldshut in 1525; of about three hundred in Augsburg during 1526–28; of about a hundred in Strasbourg [29] during 1526–30 and in Rattenberg during 1527–31. Medium-sized congregations began to predominate as early as the 1520s and 1530s: about eighty believers in Zollikon; seventy in Passau, Salzburg, Kitzbühel, and Esslingen; sixty in Linz and Ulm; fifty in Vienna; forty in Worms, Kaufbeuren, Schwäbisch Gmünd, Hall in the Tirol, and the area of Mühlhausen; thirty to forty in Rottenburg, Horb, Colmar, and the area of Hersfeld; thirty in Munich and Nuremberg; and twenty to thirty in Burghausen, Regensburg, Wels, Enns, Steyr, Bozen, Brixen, Gufidaun, Heilbronn, and the areas of Iphofen and Königsberg. Finally, a very large number of groups, such as those of the Staffelstein, Windsheim, Rothenburg, and Ansbach areas in Franconia, had fewer than twenty members.

Whereas some congregations existed only for a few years, months, or even weeks, others survived the persecution and persisted for twenty or thirty years. From references occasionally made by Anabaptists to specific congregations, we can be certain that in 1591 there were congregations at Weissenburg in Alsace, Landau, Neustadt, Lambsheim, Worms, and Kreuznach. But how large were these congregations in the second half of the sixteenth century? The leaders assembled at Strasbourg in 1557 made the unlikely claim that some of their congregations had five hundred to six hundred believers. The Anabaptist group that in the 1550s and early 1560s existed in the area of Mühlhausen in Thuringia had only fifteen members; the group of Swiss Brethren in Hesse in 1578, only fourteen believers in eleven towns and villages. Of course, the small size of these groups might be due to the decline of Anabaptism in Thuringia and Hesse. But even in Württemberg, where relatively speaking, Anabaptism flourished in the 1560s, the congregations were not very large. In 1562, 22 men and women from fourteen towns and villages gathered in a forest near Esslingen. We can be certain that this Anabaptist congregation in the area of the Rems valley did not number more than thirty or forty. The congregations of Landau, Neustadt, Lambsheim, Worms, and Kreuznach in the Rhine valley were larger. About 315 Anabaptists in 74 towns and villages are known to us in the area from Landau to Kreuznach between 1580 and 1609, or about sixty believers in each of the five congregations. It is only fair to add that the situation in the Rhine valley was not typical: by 1600 Anabaptism was much stronger there than elsewhere in the Empire. To judge by the size of meetings, most Anabaptist groups in the second half of the sixteenth century did not exceed thirty or forty believers.

The modest size of most congregations might be one of the reasons why the Anabaptists were content with lay ministers who devoted most of their time to farming and craftsmanship and only some of their time to pastoral duties. There was no need for a full-time ministry, nor could a group of thirty or forty believers provide full financial support for a minister and his family. The size of the congregations also helps explain why sometimes one leader headed two congregations.

Meetings

Meeting for worship occupied an important place in the life of the isolated and harassed Anabaptists. Two types of meetings can be distinguished, though the difference is not always clear: the small conventicle of three to ten persons, and the general assembly, the "Gemein Versammlung," which was attended by a larger number of believers. Anabaptist meetings, whether small or large, were most frequent in the early years of the movement. When the first Anabaptist congregation formed at Zollikon during the week of January 22 to 29, 1525, meetings were held daily. There was hardly a house in the village where the brethren did not meet. At Augsburg fifty meetings are known to have been held in 1527, and sixty from January to mid-April, 1528. The total number of meetings in 1527 and 1528 may well have reached 150. On Easter morning, 1528, there were even two meetings held at the same time—one in the city, the other in nearby Pfersee.

After the first ardor had passed, the Anabaptists gathered for worship at regular intervals, whether once a week, once every two weeks, once a month, or once every two or three months. The Anabaptists in the Mühlhausen area, for example, were visited twice a month by a minister in 1537. Most meetings were held on Saturday or Sunday, though sometimes meetings were also held on weekdays. The Anabaptists in the area of Romrod in Hesse met on Wednesday and Saturday in 1530, those at Strasbourg on Sundays in the 1530s, those in the area of Schorndorf once a month on Sunday morning. Obviously the Anabaptists preferred to gather on Saturday evening or Sunday because they had to work during the week. They also liked to meet on Christmas, Easter, and Whitsunday. Fairs, attracting crowds of peasants from the villages, also offered a good opportunity for holding assemblies. During the fair on July 25, 1540, at Grünberg in Hesse, both the Swiss Brethren and the Hutterites held meetings.

Occasionally the leaders chided individual Anabaptists for not attending meetings often enough. A man at Esslingen replied that he had too much work to do. Scharnschlager complained of brethren whose enthusiasm was only lukewarm and who had an excuse ready whenever a meeting was announced to them: "I must go on a journey—today I must do this, tomorrow that." Some Anabaptists also came to doubt the value of meetings. As a Strasbourg Anabaptist said in 1557, when asked why he did not attend meetings, the Lord had warned against those who claimed that Christ was in the woods or fields.

We may distinguish between meetings held in houses and those held in the open country, such as in a forest or a deserted chapel. Each type had its advantages and disadvantages. Brethren who gathered in a townhouse were independent of the weather and did not waste much time walking long distances. But there were many difficulties. First, it was difficult to find a house where the believers could meet. In 1527 and 1528, when Anabaptism was still in its beginnings in Germany, believers sometimes met in inns where the guest rooms were large and the innkeeper was glad of a chance to make money. Soon, however, Anabaptist meetings were strictly prohibited, and public meetings such as those at Sorga in Hesse in the early 1530s became rare.

To make matters worse, many Anabaptists were unable to receive their fellow believers in their own homes. Some husbands forbade their wives even to mention the Anabaptists; one woman said that if her husband found an Anabaptist minister in the house, he would throw him downstairs. Other Anabaptists made various excuses to keep the leaders from using their houses for meetings. A craftsman at Augsburg excused himself on the ground that his trade involved the property of others. When Jörg Nespitzer asked permission to hold a gathering of only eight or nine believers in an upstairs room, the lady of the house said she had to think of her children. She and her brother Gall turned Nespitzer away. But another brother of hers, Jerg, was willing to let the Anabaptists in; at this a loud quarrel broke out between the two brothers, and Jerg finally arranged for the meeting to be held in the cellar. On another occasion the same woman slammed the door in Nespitzer's face.[30] Nespitzer admitted in 1528 that he was at a loss to know where to hold meetings.

Even if a house was available, was it suitable for a meeting? To escape the unwanted attention of the authorities, it should preferably be situated in a side street or at the end of a village; yet believers must be able to find it easily. More important was the question whether the rooms were large enough, a consideration that explains why more than half the meetings at Augsburg were held not in the houses of the poor but on fair-sized premises. Very large meetings had to be held in cellars. Sometimes elaborate preparations were made to avoid arousing suspicion. A good three days before Easter, Susanna Doucher at Augsburg began to close the shutters and cover the windows with carpets and blankets—a wise precaution, for when people heard strange mumbling in a house, they immediately suspected that a clandestine meeting was being held.

In 1527 and 1528 the Anabaptists at Augsburg gathered in the houses of 33 fellow believers and in fourteen places outside the city walls. They continually changed their meeting place for fear of arrest. At Esslingen 26 of the 33 meetings in 1527 and 1528 were held in houses of burghers, and a few outside the city. The brethren at Esslingen also changed their meeting place, gathering in 27 different locations.

If they did not meet in houses, city people gathered within the city walls in gardens, or water towers, in quiet spots near the town gates or the moat. Outside the city walls they might meet on meadows near rivers, such as the Lech and Wertach rivers near Augsburg; in gravel pits or stone quarries; on fowling floors; or in inns and private houses in neighboring villages. In the small towns and villages of the Tirol, Franconia, Württemberg, the Palatinate, and Hesse, the Anabaptists occasionally gathered in one another's houses but preferred to meet outdoors, "on God's holy earth," in forests and on mountains, in fields and meadows, near rivers, creeks, and reservoirs, in mills, sheepfolds, barns, stables, sheds on vineyards, in deserted monasteries or field chapels, in abandoned brothels, or in the ruins of former villages. Sometimes officials talked of razing these old buildings to prevent the sectarians from meeting here.

Meeting in mountain forests obviously had many advantages: there was no problem of space, and above all the believers were safe. Few outdoor meetings were ever rounded up by the authorities. But there was the question of weather: most open-air meetings were held in late spring and summer when the nights were not too cool. In winter, when deep snow covered the narrow paths, the huts high up on the mountains were not accessible. Where did Anabaptists meet then? "Wherever God tells us to," one brother replied.

Frequently Anabaptists met in frontier regions where the rights of jurisdiction were shared by two or more governments, such as the border area of Hesse, Hersfeld, Fulda, and Saxony. Since the governments disagreed on how to proceed against the sectarians, no effective measures were taken at all for several years.

The size of the Anabaptist meetings is difficult to establish. Most figures are estimates by participants or officials and are undoubtedly too high. Seldom is a complete list of participants available. At any rate, some meetings in Switzerland in 1525 were quite small. Only a few people took part in the memorable meeting on January 21, 1525, when the first believers were baptized. But there were also larger gatherings that same year: two hundred persons thronged the house of Hans Murer, and forty gathered in the village church of Zollikon.

Most meetings at Augsburg were no more than conventicles. Three large meetings of about sixty believers were held in August 1527, however, in the houses of Fischer the weaver, Finder the butcher, and Huber the lacemaker. On April 2, 1528, there was yet another assembly of about sixty believers in Barbara Schleifer's cellar, which could not even hold all the people who wished to enter. Whenever someone left, others came in. According to the chronicler Clemens Sender, two hundred people attended the famous Easter morning assembly at Susanna Doucher's house. This figure may have been exaggerated, but the meeting was indeed large: though "many honorable people" had already left, the officials were yet able to arrest 95 Anabaptists there.

In Franconia we hear of meetings with thirty believers, though one woman declared they never met except in the evening around the distaff. In Württemberg and Hesse we know of meetings with four, five, ten, twenty, thirty to fifty, one hundred, and even 180 participants. In the Tirol, the Palatinate, and Baden, the authorities reported large gatherings of two hundred, three hundred to four hundred and even a thousand Anabaptists. The meetings in the Eckbolsheim Forest near Strasbourg may have been quite large, since they were attended by believers from many areas. In 1545 we hear of three hundred participants, in 1557 of one hundred, and in 1576 of two hundred. But meetings of such a size were exceptional. Most gatherings, especially in the second half of the century, consisted of only twenty or thirty persons; a meeting of thirty to fifty was considered large. Even so, the Anabaptists of Horgen, near Zurich, declared in 1613 that more people came to their meetings than they cared to receive. The government, they said, should give them a chapel. Then it would be seen who attracted more people—the Anabaptists or the official pastor.[31]

A special problem was how to inform believers of meetings. Anabaptists at Augsburg in 1528 and at Schorndorf in 1539 said that at the end of one meeting they arranged the time and place of the next. The early leaders, however, often did not know where they would meet again. There was also the danger of betrayal: thus the Anabaptists of Augsburg and of the Zurich area sent word to one another by a brother or sister of their own number or by their children, and around Basel the leader Mathis Gysin himself notified the believers. The authorities often suspected that passing on the word was the task of one particular brother. Indeed, at Strasbourg a particular brother had the duty of carrying messages and letters. In Württemberg the Anabaptists sometimes exchanged information in the inns.

Or a written message was sent: "The Grace and Peace of the Lord through our Lord and Savior. Amen. Beloved Jacob and dear Elspeth, I send you word that next Tuesday a meeting will be held at the house at Schilken where last we met. Do not be late this time and do you also let the old man at Westhofen know of this. Trust in God, peace be with all you who love God in your hearts." [32]

Even when the believers had been told where and when a meeting would be held, it was not certain that they would find the place. Strangers could easily get lost in big cities such as Augsburg and Strasbourg. The leaders would therefore tell a few brethren to stroll around in the streets and casually guide the believers to the house where the meeting was held. To ensure that believers would find her house without attracting the neighbors' attention, Susanna Doucher chalked a sign on the door. Sometimes a brother or sister would be sitting behind the door to let the faithful in. Naturally the Anabaptists could not enter the house in a large group without arousing curiosity, so they walked in singly.

Since it was even more difficult to indicate meeting places in forests or on mountain slopes, the Anabaptists would sometimes station believers on the way. Strasbourgers who on a June evening in 1576 followed several Anabaptists out of the city came across some women who took them for brethren from out of town. After the women had told them the way and the watchword, they passed a guard who had been placed at the Eckbolsheim Forest. They had walked for quite a while in the forest when they came upon the Anabaptists, who were standing around in small groups. After all the believers had gathered, they walked still farther into the forest, to a point somewhere between the villages of Lingolsheim and Wolfisheim, where they lit candles. When the Strasbourgers, after a heated discussion with the Anabaptists, made ready to leave at two o'clock in the morning, they found that they did not know the way out of the huge forest. The Anabaptists finally sent a guide with them to the nearest road.[33] In short, the meetings were perforce held in very secluded places.

There were Anabaptists at Augsburg and Württemberg who simply could not find the arranged meeting place. Therefore the leaders often established landmarks, such as the well-known "Esslingen oak-tree" in the forest near Esslingen, the well of Friedrichsborn in a forest near Alsfeld in Hesse, the conspicuous pulpit-like rock in a forest near Urbach.

Since the officials could easily find Anabaptist meetings by following the Anabaptists, the brethren attempted to delude spies by carrying tools as if they were only workmen going out on a job. Following two suspicious persons to a forest near Strasbourg, two boys saw bricklayers, bricklayers' men, reed makers, and weavers carrying various tools such as pointed hammers, and villagers with saws and pitchforks. One man later said that on arriving at the forest, he had noticed only about sixty people, but that at about ten in the evening, someone gave a signal and another three hundred came suddenly out of the brush.[34]

Though some brethren did not hesitate to gather in daytime, for example during regular church services, most preferred to meet at night, when they would not miss any work and would also be much safer. The large meetings near Strasbourg in 1545, 1557, and 1576 were all held at night. The leader would stand beside an open fire, or two men with burning candles or lanterns would be at his side. Occasionally it was so dark that the believers did not even know who else was present. The early morning was also a favorite meeting time of the Anabaptists: the great Augsburg meeting of Easter 1528 began several hours before dawn.

The duration of the meetings varied. Small conventicles probably did not last longer than one or two hours. There were also longer meetings like the gathering at Augsburg on April 2, 1528, which lasted from six in the evening until five in the morning. On July 24, 1545, the believers at Strasbourg gathered from ten in the evening until sunrise. Since the meetings lasted so long, food was sometimes distributed. The Bernese Anabaptists decided in 1527 that "the food for meals during meetings should be provided by the brethren in whose houses the meetings were held." [35] Of course, some believers brought their own bread. At Augsburg soup, cabbage, wine, and bread were distributed; at Strasbourg, wine and pears; at Colmar, wine and bread. While couples ate together, single persons ate separately. If food had to be bought, the richer brethren would pay for the poorer.

Meetings in the Tirol sometimes lasted two or three days, for in this sparsely populated country believers were obliged to travel long distances to the meeting place and could not return home the same day. They slept in huts built for them in the forests. Searching for Anabaptists, the officials repeatedly came across these huts and burned them down. Sometimes the believers would stay in the houses of fellow believers. On one occasion a farmhouse was so packed with Anabaptists that the farmer, who was not a believer, had to sleep in the oxhouse. Another problem was food. Preparing for a meeting in the Puster valley in 1533, the brethren bought two oxen, ground six "sters" of rye, baked three "sters" of flour into bread and bought cheese.[36] We hear of Anabaptists threshing grain and butchering an ox. One man was told to collect a lot of eggs. Strong brethren were appointed to carry the large quantities of food up to the mountains, and also to guide the believers along perilous and lonely mountain paths to the meeting places. The Tirolese Anabaptists kept lists of how many people had been allowed to stay in this or that farm, and how much food they had received. At times the brethren protected their meetings with guards or watchdogs. It was easy to discern a stranger's approach on moonlit nights or to hear his footsteps crunching on the frozen snow.

Whatever pains were taken to arrange a meeting, some breth-

ren seemed less than delighted with the results. When a sermon
was particularly long, many hurried home immediately afterward. Some leaders were chagrined to see that people even left
before the meeting had ended. This happened so often that the
Strasbourg Discipline finally forbade leaving a meeting without
cause. Sometimes, too, simple communication was a problem.
A Tirolese journeyman said at Augsburg that he had had difficulty understanding Plener, a "Rhinelander," and people in Lucerne said they had not understood a leader from Bohemia. It is
in fact surprising that differences in dialect did not cause difficulty more often. Anabaptists meeting at Strasbourg recognized
their preacher by his accent as being from the Breisgau, and Hessian Anabaptists realized that they had been addressed by a Swabian. Neither group in these cases had trouble understanding the
sermon, however.

Occasionally Anabaptist meetings were attended by some who
were not members of the congregation proper. A man in Hesse
said that he had taken his children along. At Augsburg, however, Anabaptists denied that children were present during their
gatherings. Obviously, then, there was no rule, but we can assume that generally children were not taken to meetings, especially at night.

The records are more revealing on the question of adult visitors. The Anabaptists knew that some came to their meetings
only "out of curiosity and to provide themselves with gossip." [37]
In a village unusual behavior easily attracted attention. When
late one evening in July 1596 a man was seen outside the village
of Ötisheim with food and a bottle of wine, but declined to say
where he was going, the peasants immediately followed him and
ended up in a Hutterite meeting.[38] There was so little excitement in village life that the peasants were intrigued by the many
wild rumors they heard about the Anabaptists. No fewer than
150 curious peasants stood looking on at a nocturnal meeting
of fifteen Swiss Brethren in the forest near Alsfeld. Called to
account by the officials, the peasants cleverly argued that they

had only followed the Anabaptists to find out who they were and report them to the authorities. Curiously enough, even the pastor of a nearby village appeared at this meeting—to acquaint himself, as he later claimed, with the life and doctrines of the sectarians. Surprised at his appearance, the Anabaptists' first thought was to leave at once. Then they sent two men to him to apologize for their nocturnal meeting and to ask whether the authorities planned to descend on them. The pastor calmed their fears. As the meeting proceeded, he strolled among the people, recognizing to his anger quite a number of his own parishioners. Finally he lay down under a beech tree and listened to the lengthy sermons.[39]

People would sometimes attend a meeting by chance, as happened on the evening of May 27, 1584, in a small forest near Ulrichstein in Hesse. A man from nearby Köddingen had been in the forest picking herbs, as he subsequently explained. On his way home he learned that an Anabaptist leader would preach in the forest that evening, so he went to see what was happening. Similarly, a father and son were tending their cows on a nearby meadow when they became aware of the Anabaptist meeting.[40] Many peasants swore they would never have gone to the meetings if they had known that it was forbidden to do so. Nor were they always respectful toward the Anabaptists. There were peasants who ridiculed the preacher or who relieved their boredom during a five-hour sermon by throwing fir cones at the believers.[41]

The governments of the sixteenth century could not tolerate these clandestine gatherings. The pastors asked the Anabaptists why they always preached secretly in lonely places and solitary houses, in forest churches and in darkness. If their beliefs were right the Anabaptists would not fear to preach in public. The brethren easily countered this dubious argument: they would gladly hold meetings in the cathedral itself so long as they were safe from violence. They also pointed to the example of Christ and the apostles, who had preached day and night in solitary places. Martin Luther himself had recommended that "one should meet behind closed doors." Nonetheless, the authorities particularly objected to the Anabaptist practice of gathering at night in badly lit cellars and dark forests: noctu congregari was a repulsive practice. In 1556 the Heidelberg Church Council ruled that these clandestine meetings would not in any circumstances be tolerated. They caused not only "speciem schismatis" in the church, but also "speciem seditionis" in civil society, and they gave rise to disobedience and unchastity.[42]

Connections between Congregations

Though Anabaptist congregations were sometimes separated by long distances, they were not really isolated. For one thing, the brethren would visit each other. In 1529 a leader in the area of Basel visited "the other Anabaptist brethren" at the Kaiserstuhl, and in 1533 Hessian Anabaptists came to a meeting near Kreuznach in the Palatinate. Strasbourg in particular was a meeting place for Anabaptists of the upper Rhine area. In 1576 five leaders and many believers from Switzerland, Breisgau, Westerich, Westerburg, and upper and lower Alsace assembled near Strasbourg on the pretext of attending the fair. For that matter, Swiss Brethren from south Germany and Switzerland might have gathered at Strasbourg every summer. In 1605 it was reported that some three hundred brethren from an area stretching from Switzerland to Frankfurt gathered annually at Modenbach in the Palatinate to celebrate the Lord's Supper. Clearly their attendance was facilitated by the Rhine waterway.

In addition there was a lively exchange of letters in the late 1520s between congregations. In 1528 the brethren of Esslingen dispatched Hans Leupold to Worms with a letter for the Anabaptist congregation there. This letter was read in the course of a meeting, and three weeks later Leupold returned with a letter from Worms to Esslingen. On his arrest in 1529 an Esslingen leader said that his congregation had received letters from congregations at Basel, Worms, Augsburg, and Strasbourg.[43]

Many of these letters contained comforting words and exhortations to remain steadfast. Others consisted of long theological discussions on disputed doctrines or practices. Still others were more practical in nature. In 1528 Brandhuber informed the brethren at Freistadt that he was still at Passau; that his brother baptized at Linz; that God would come to the aid of the imprisoned brethren; and that they should not trust the messenger who was delivering the letter.[44]

Although the ordinary Anabaptists met only a small number of fellow believers in their gatherings, they knew that they were part of a larger movement in many countries. Thus the believers at Strasbourg prayed for the "brotherhoods" in upper Alsace, Baden, and Breisgau. The knowledge that they were not forsaken in a hostile environment undoubtedly gave the brethren strength and confidence to persevere in their faith. We shall later see that refugees in particular kept alive the contacts between congregations.

A visitor to sixteenth-century Switzerland, Württemberg, or the Palatinate would have found two church systems—one official, the other clandestine. The official Protestant church, whether it was Lutheran or Calvinist, had its authoritarian hierarchy of pastors, its church buildings, and its public services. Theoretically, it accounted for the religious life of the entire population. Then there was the secret, proscribed church of the Anabaptists. If Anabaptism was elusive and hard to lay hands on, it was by no means an amorphous or chaotic movement. Anabaptism was organized around independent congregations that elected their own ministers and held regular meetings.

It appears that Anabaptism fed on an undercurrent of resentment against the domination of church life by the professional clergy. Luther's doctrine of the priesthood of all believers had already freed the layman from domination by the priest, with his supposedly supernatural attributes. Still the Lutheran and Reformed churches retained the procedure whereby the pastor,

having of course studied theology at the university, was assigned
to his flock by the higher church authorities. By approving the
Ordinance of the Common Chest at Leisnig in 1523, Luther recognized the need for greater participation by laymen in running
the church; but after the peasant uprising he apparently changed
his mind. It remained for the Anabaptists to carry out this democratic principle to the fullest extent.

5

The Rejection of
the Official Church

The Pastors

Numerous brethren withdrew from the churches quietly, intent only on following the teachings of Jesus in their own way. But there were also many who angrily expressed their dislike and contempt for official pastors, whether they were Zwinglians, Lutherans, or Catholics. The Anabaptists fully shared the vituperative language of their age. Already in 1524 we find Grebel referring arrogantly to the "negligent scribes and doctors at Wittenberg." According to Blaurock, the Pope, Luther, Zwingli, Leo Judd, and the like were thieves and murderers of Christ. Grebel and Blaurock had set the tone for the future: the pastors were later called false prophets and Pharisees; seducers and blasphemers; hypocrites; frauds; liars; false vipers; cursed rogues; belly preachers; barking and chasing dogs; godless, filthy, perfidious villains; husbandmen of lies, foul bastards; poisonous snakes; monstrous dragons; angels of Satan; blind guides who strained at a gnat but swallowed a camel. One pastor was called a fat sow; another, whose name was Basileus, a basilisk. Their sermons were stinking lies. "May God's passion rape them; they cheated us in the past and now they seduce us more shamefully than ever," one brother in Switzerland yelled. How are we to explain this hatred of the "bloodthirsty gang of prophets"? [1]

First of all, the Anabaptists were embittered by persecution. "You have driven me from the village and my young children. May the penance of God be denied to you," an angry Swiss

Anabaptist told his pastor. The brethren complained that all those who did not accept the pastors' teachings were condemned as villains, devils, false prophets, and enthusiasts. In order to protect themselves from criticism, the pastors had assumed a position of superiority, claiming that only they had the right to interpret the Scriptures and that laymen should keep to their crafts. Many Anabaptists were convinced that it was the pastors who incited the government to drive them out of the country and confiscate their property. Like the Pharisees the pastors shouted, "Crucify!" Why is it, Rinck asked bitterly, that the Pharisees and scribes are protected by the government even though they do not pay taxes, whereas the believers, who pay all dues, are driven out of the country?

Strictly separating religion and politics, the Anabaptists also criticized the pastors for seeking support from the governments. The pastors should not complain that the emperor and princes used force in matters of belief, they said, for the pastors themselves were doing the same thing. Some Anabaptists accused even Lutheran pastors of distorting Luther's message of freedom of belief. Others called Luther a neo-Pope, liar, and goat: indeed, they considered him to be even worse than the Pope, for in Catholic times there had at least been a crumb of compassion. Catholics had not thrown people into prison or driven them from their homes.

The opposition of the Anabaptists to the professional pastors went still deeper. As the authorities often accused the Anabaptist leaders of usurping the pastoral office, so the Anabaptists asked who had given the pastors authority to preach. The pastors had never been called by God or elected by the congregation. Those appointed by the government were no more than servants of princes. The prerequisite for a call to the ministry so far as the Anabaptists were concerned was inner conversion, which none of the pastors had ever experienced. They substituted the memorizing of scriptural passages for inner rebirth, much as rich men talked of hunger and thirst without ever having experienced them. The Anabaptists also criticized the Reformers for failing to missionize like the apostles. The Swiss leader Jakob Gross, for example, said that if Zwingli and Judd were true evangelists, they would travel like the messengers of God and proclaim His word.

Nor could the Anabaptists understand why a pastor must attend university. Christ's words were clear and could be preached by simple men. Indeed, Christ had preferred to have in His service shepherds, fishermen, and other common people. The pastors, by contrast, learned nothing at the universities but heathen fables, and practiced the deceptions of the courts of chancery rather than the teaching of Christ. They were so full of conceit that they themselves did not understand what they said or wrote. But damned was he who criticized them, for then they would rise in anger and strike out with their sharp pens. One man said bluntly: "The old priests shat on us, and the new ones do the same." [2] Some Anabaptists admitted they did not even care for doctors in their own sect. They had not learned their belief from any human being, be he Luther, Müntzer, or Nikolaus Storch. The Anabaptist movement is an indubitable revelation of how deeply some laymen distrusted the learned priest.

The Anabaptists also criticized the differences between various pastors. Whenever two or three preached on the same scriptural passage, they said, each one had a different interpretation; worse still, they changed with every wind. Whereas Zwingli had once taught that one should not baptize children, he reversed his stand a few years later. As a further example the brethren pointed to the frequent religious changes in the area of Mühlhausen and the Palatinate. Such an inconstant faith could not be the true one; whatever the pastors preached must then be nonsense. Zwingli, the false prophet, had wrought more violence on the Scriptures than the old Pope. Melanchthon's preaching had killed more people than all the hangmen together. Why did people listen to their lies?

The Anabaptists accused not only the Catholic priests but also the Lutheran pastors of paying too much attention to external matters. By closing monasteries, abolishing masses, tearing down altars, destroying ornaments, and preaching vehemently the pastors had turned the hearts of their congregations to violence and destruction, and not to love and God.

If the pastors were wrong in their preaching, they were just as wrong in their way of life, both material and moral. Grebel and Brötli were already insisting in 1525 that those who lived on benefices and wages could never preach the truth.[3] During the public debates at Bern in 1531 and at Zofingen in 1532, the brethren attacked the very basis, economically speaking, of the professional ministry. First, pastors' salaries were based on interest payments and usury ("Zinss und Wuchergut"), and consequently the pastors were not in a position to censure and punish usury. Second, the pastors lived on property the church had wrongfully acquired by luring the poor into giving it away. Third, a fixed salary was contrary to Christ's command to give freely what one had received freely. On principle, the pastor should earn his living by working with his hands. The apostles, who traveled too much to support themselves, should be given food and shelter, but again, not a fixed salary.[4] Such stipulations went even beyond the Twelve Articles presented by the peasants in 1525, which had proposed that the tithes be used to pay the pastors. Soon the German Anabaptists too were angrily denouncing the pastors for living on salaries. "Take up your hoe and work, you godless bastard!" one Hutterite shouted.[5] The pastors, the Anabaptists maintained, looked on their task as a business, not a calling. No preacher offered the Lord's Supper unless he got a *zwölfer*; no pastor officiated at a burial unless he got a *fünfer*. Some brethren claimed that this materialistic attitude had even worsened since the Reformation.

The Anabaptists fiercely castigated the pastors as well for their comfortable way of life—their robes and caps, their collations, their heartening drafts, their leisure, their warm and well-appointed chambers, padded chairs, and feather beds. The pastors cut themselves off from the people, lived behind walls, wore smart shoes, and demanded to be called "Doctor," "Master," or "Rabbi." "I suppose you expect me to call you my lord," one Anabaptist said to his pastor. Another shouted in the faces of Lutheran theologians that the apostles had never worn gowns furred with fox skins.[6]

The Anabaptists never tired of railing against what they regarded as the immorality of both Catholic priests and Protestant pastors. Throughout the sixteenth century they clamoured angrily that the pastors did not practice what they preached: they preached in the morning and proved gluttons at noon; their wives even joined in the dance. How could such people be qualified to forgive sins? Since the pastors led such a "vicious, vainglorious, and evil life," the Anabaptists insisted their preaching had to be wrong. For one's life and one's preaching could not be separated. The ministry of the established churches, in short, was worthless.

Protestant theologians were outraged, of course, over this crude but effective attempt to discredit the pastoral work of the church. Article Eight of the Augsburg Confession explicitly condemned the belief held by both the Donatists and the Anabaptists that the efficacy of the pastoral functions depended on the holiness and piety of the pastor. But did the pastors on the whole really have such low moral and religious standards? During the early years of the Reformation, many ministers indeed lacked the proper moral and theological qualifications. In 1533, Justus Menius himself deplored the fact that both the pastor and the vicar at Herda—a center of Anabaptism—led disorderly lives. At Strasbourg a few years later Eckart zum Drübel, a severe critic of the Anabaptists, castigated the pastors for lingering in their wives' chambers, coveting rich parishes, and surpassing each other in arrogance. Several books and pamphlets of the sixteenth century also criticized the Protestant pastors, but they tended to exaggerate because they either aimed at reforming the clergy or were written in a hostile spirit. More objective were the reports of the commissions that periodically—in some areas twice a year—inspected every parish, questioning village officials and parishioners on how the pastors performed their duties and what kind of life they were leading.

One of the areas strongly affected by Anabaptism from the 1530s to the Thirty Years' War was the Rems valley in Württemberg, and particularly the district of Schorndorf. The semi-annual reports of the visitations from 1581 to 1590 reveal that 42 pastors were active in 26 parishes during these years.[7] One of the pastors was dismissed because he had been in a violent quarrel, and cursed and sworn. Nine others were censured for shortcomings of a minor order: for example, one preached too vehemently; two were in debt; two more drank too much wine; one quarreled with his neighbors; another had family problems. Clearly none of these were grave transgressions, but the censured pastors had to mend their ways or run the risk of dismissal. Out of the 42 pastors, then, 32 were found to be irreproachable and were characterized as industrious, diligent, and learned. Village officials and parishioners repeatedly commended and praised their pastor for his devotion to his parish work and his exemplary Christian life. There is no question that three-fourths of the pastors in the Schorndorf district went conscientiously about the performance of their duties. As we have seen, the remaining fourth were obliged by their superiors to mend their minor weaknesses.

The massive charges of immorality and incompetence made by the Anabaptists against the pastors thus appear to be exaggerated. If the pastors' moral and professional standards were not really deserving of hatred and contempt, why were the Anabaptists so vituperative? It may be that the relentless persecution they suffered at the hand of the authorities had vitiated their outlook, making them unable to see conditions as they really were. More important, the Anabaptists had a totally different view of the ministry, having rejected the traditional role of the pastor as an appointed and salaried functionary of the higher church authorities, separated from the people by special knowledge or powers. And since the Anabaptists condemned the professional ministry as an institution, they were prone to exaggerate the failings of individual pastors out of all proportion.

Church Services

Given their deep-rooted aversion to the pastors, it is not surprising that the Anabaptists refused to attend church services. Some said they would rather leave the country. One woman attended once a month but declared that she would be much more pious if she did not go at all. To the chagrin of the pastors, some Anabaptists also kept their families and servants from attending church or refused to send their children to be instructed in the catechism. A brother at Strasbourg even maltreated his wife when she went to church. Sometimes the Anabaptists expressed their defiance of churches in more curious ways. A brother might refuse to be present at the solemnization in church of a relative's marriage. A woman accompanied the funeral procession of her two brothers to the gates of the cemetery, but then quickly walked away. There were also brethren who ridiculed people attending church or taking part in processions.[8] The Anabaptists were obviously aware that by refusing to attend church services they violated the law, for all burghers were required to attend church. Why then did they risk fines and jail sentences rather than go to church at least once in a while? In their interrogations the Anabaptists gave a variety of reasons.

Many Anabaptist leaders impressed on their followers that they could not serve both Christ and the devil: therefore they must never go to mass, sermons, baptism, or confession.[9] There were, however, some early Anabaptist leaders who allowed the believers to attend Catholic mass or Protestant services in order to avoid persecution. Apparently these leaders felt that one should distinguish between physical presence and spiritual consent. But this view, which might have appealed to many brethren, was strongly opposed in two anonymous pamphlets. What

man, the author asked, would knowingly imbibe poison, imag-
ining that his skill would keep him from being harmed? [10]

Some Anabaptists argued that they had books of their own,
which they could read as well as the pastor, and Christ Himself
to preach to them every day. Why, then, should they go to
church? Furthermore, the New Testament did not say that the
faithful should gather in churches built of wood and stone; on
the contrary, they should worship God alone in their rooms, for
the true temple was the heart. It was on this authority that Hubmaier's cohorts at Waldshut razed a local chapel to the ground.
Some Anabaptists maintained that at the time of Christ there had
been no church apart from the temple at Jerusalem. The temple
mentioned in Revelation 2 was not a cathedral or church but
the wide earth: that is where the Anabaptists worshiped. Riedemann claimed that the churches were merely old heathen temples that the Germans had converted into churches when they
were forced to accept Christianity. As a result people had never
really abandoned their heathen practices; under Christianity the
old gods were simply called saints.[11]

The Anabaptists also condemned churches because they were
filled with idols—that is, wood carvings, statues, and pictures
that had been carried over from heathen times. The Holy Cross,
after all, was nothing but wood, like a stick one threw at a dog
or crammed into a stove. In Pfalz-Zweibrücken offensive pictures were actually removed from churches because of the Anabaptists.[12] The Anabaptists also objected to organ music.[13]

The rejection of church buildings seems to have been strongest in Thuringia and Hesse, and among the Hutterites. Some
Anabaptists, however, were willing to use them for their own
purposes. Jörg Schad even baptized in the village church at
Zollikon in 1525, and brethren at Basel and Zurich asked the
town council to assign a church building to them.[14]

But if a few Anabaptists felt that church buildings were not
so objectionable, almost all refused to attend the official church
services, as we have seen. Their main reason was a moral one:

the Lutheran pastors, not to mention the Catholic priests, had failed to change their parishioners' lives. One reason for this failure was that the Lutheran teaching was basically wrong: the Lutherans taught nothing but faith—a false and fictitious faith. The scribes told no one how faith was acquired, and by emphasizing the premise that Christ had done enough to save mankind, they made it possible for people to continue their evil ways. Fornicators, adulterers, drunkards, and usurers were absolved and offered peace though they never thought of abandoning their sins and doing penance. Another reason for the failure of the Lutheran church was that anyone could belong to it, no matter what sin he had committed. The Anabaptists agreed, of course, that all men should be taught the Word of God in meetings; but only those who lived by it were to be received as members of the church.

To the Anabaptist way of thinking, then, conditions in the Protestant churches were nothing less than catastrophic. Leupold said in 1528 that the Lutheran belief had been preached at Augsburg for seven years, but that he had yet to see it bear fruit. There was no difference between the Catholic town of Schwäbisch Gmünd and the Lutheran town of Schwäbisch Hall. "Show me but one in the village who lives according to the gospel," one woman told the pastor. "Not one has been turned to piety through your sermons."

The Anabaptists were not ones to mince words: the church was not a church at all, but a "horde and assembly of fornicators, adulterers, liars, blasphemers, drinkers, braggarts, misers, and all sort of unclean spirits." However, when an Anabaptist woman at Strasbourg was asked by the pastors whether she knew a public sinner who was admitted to the Lord's Supper, and whether she had on her own account reported or reprimanded a sinner, she could not name a single instance. She added that if ever she had helped to punish anyone, she would have had her skull beaten in.[15]

One wonders whether the Anabaptists were unaware that a

great effort was being made in the Protestant churches to raise moral standards, and that some territorial churches had ecclesiastical discipline and held regular church visitations. Conditions may have been bad in some congregations, but there is no evidence that they were generally as deplorable as the Anabaptists claimed they were. Not the actual conditions, but the peculiar cast of mind of the brethren explains their charges of immorality. Possibly their ethical standards were abnormally high—so high that no large group could have been selective enough to meet them. Possibly, too, plain sectarian hatred prevented the Anabaptists from seeing anything but damnation in the world.

Under pressure from the authorities, some Anabaptists at last attended services, but their hearts were certainly not in it. There were Anabaptists who remained standing at the door of the church and walked away immediately after the gospel had been read or before the pastor had finished his sermon. One man chose a seat behind a large column to prevent the pastor from seeing whether he was present or not. He listened to the sermon but hurried out of the church whenever the Lord's Supper was celebrated or children were being baptized. Some brethren would leave the church whenever the pastor spoke against their doctrines. Occasionally even the parishioners left the church when the pastor preached too violently against the Anabaptists. Finally, there were Anabaptists who felt uneasy about their flagrant disobedience and offered all manner of excuses: they had too much work to do; they had a dispute to settle; their clothes were unworthy; their hearing was faulty or the church too cold.

Needless to say, the pastors were affronted and enraged by the deliberate contempt that was shown their services. They foresaw that if the Anabaptists were permitted to set church services at nought and call the sermon lies, people would no longer come to church. Indeed, in 1529 the pastors in the territory of Zurich reported that in villages that had Anabaptists, few or hardly any people came to church, and those who did come were usually very late. Even then they remained outside the doors in the

churchyard, engaging in all sorts of horseplay, and laughing and
ridiculing the divine Word and its preachers. Sometimes, without provocation, they even dared to interrupt the sermon with
indecent words.[16] In short, the willfulness of the Anabaptists was
having its effect on the entire parish.

Acts of Violence

Especially in the early years of the movement, some Anabaptists were more aggressive than is generally assumed. The tendency to violent intolerance was not limited to revolutionary
Anabaptism in the Netherlands and northwest Germany, but
also appeared in the south. In 1525 Blaurock sent a letter to
Friedrich Myconius that, according to Zwingli, was more insulting than any waffle vendor he had ever heard. One entire line
read: "Blind, blind, blind, blind, blind, blind."[17] There were
leaders who could not contain their rage when people did not
accept their doctrines: "Shame on you, with your God. Give us
a game at the tables; that is your God." Or, "You Martinians
won't last long; God will strike you down and throw you into
hell."[18] There were Anabaptists in south Germany who expressed their indignation at the obstinacy of the heathens by
shaking off the dust from their shoes.[19] Though it is apparent
that they were simply following the example of the apostles, the
governments looked on this gesture as an unpardonable act of
defiance.

People were even more surprised by violent scenes some Anabaptists staged in churches. One of the first brethren at Zollikon,
Hans Hottinger, suddenly shouted during a sermon: "Leave the
church, leave the church, and beware of false prophets." In 1526,
while Mathias Zell was delivering a sermon at Strasbourg, an
Anabaptist called out: "You are disobeying the Holy Spirit; you
are lying. On authority of the spirit, I order you to leave the pulpit and let the spirit speak through me." In several towns and villages, such as Zurich, Hinwil, "Rigaschwyl," Lucerne, Oberntief,
Schmalkalden, Tüngeda, Homberg, Esslingen, and Urbach, Ana-

baptists also interrupted the sermon or the religious instruction by storming into the church or making loud remarks. For example, when the pastor at Urbach in Württemberg was explaining the Pauline doctrine of justification to some children and servants, one father suddenly challenged him. Why did he not also read the first three chapters of James? Were these not God's Word as much as the epistles of Paul? An angry scene developed, and finally the pastor sent for the village bailiff. At times pastors and Anabaptists carried on loud arguments in front of the congregation.[20]

Some zealous brethren actually tried to preach in the churches. During the service at Zollikon on Sunday, January 29, 1525, the famous Blaurock himself stopped the vicar from going to the pulpit and asked what he was up to. Surprised, the vicar explained that he was going to preach the Word of God, but Blaurock angrily riposted: "You have not been sent by God, but I have." When the vicar at last began to deliver his sermon, Blaurock interrupted him by making loud remarks or striking on the pew with a stick. In the village of Hinwil, Blaurock actually took possession of the pulpit before the pastor arrived. Similar scenes are reported from Strasbourg, Colmar, and the Tirol.[21]

Some Anabaptists were clearly animated by an urge toward violent action. At Rodeneck in the Tirol, during the celebration of the mass, one Anabaptist grabbed the chalice and paten from the altar and threw them at the church door. Then he also snatched the Host, threw it on the floor, and trampled on it. We hear of Anabaptists at St. Georgen, in Basel and Speyer breaking open altars, throwing out the "accursed bones" (*Schelmenbeine*), burning or smashing crucifixes, and overthrowing statues of the Virgin.[22]

Of course, the vast majority of Anabaptists never committed violent acts of this nature. Nevertheless, these acts were the result of a hatred of pastors and established churches that had been stirred up by the Anabaptist leaders. They were well within the tradition of Conrad Grebel.

It is not hard to see why the quarrel between the Anabaptists and the pastors remained so bitter all through the sixteenth century. Though the Protestants had abolished Catholic dogma, they had kept the traditional type of community church, an ecclesiastical hierarchy, and the notion that pastors should get their theological education at the university. The Anabaptists not only rejected fundamental doctrines but introduced a completely new type of church organization, replacing the monopoly of the authoritarian and compulsory state church with independent, voluntary congregations, and the special class of supernaturally endowed or learned pastors with an elected lay ministry. The charges of immorality hurled by the Anabaptists so furiously against pastors and churches must be seen against this background: to justify their new concept of church organization, the brethren greatly exaggerated the depravity of the traditional church.

Judgments on whether the Anabaptists' congregational church was more Christian than the existing state churches must be left to those interested in theology. For the purposes of the social historian, the Anabaptists were trying to destroy the traditional church which embraced all members of a town or village. No doubt, most people preferred the church to sectarianism. And as guardians of the church, the governments could hardly be expected to sustain the assault upon the traditional church without striking back at the sectarians who tried to destroy it.

6

Spiritual Life

The Anabaptists organized their congregations for a spiritual purpose: to establish a congregation of saints. In this process they looked to the Bible as their standard, and particularly to the New Testament, the Old Testament being considered valid only insofar as it did not contradict the spirit of the New Testament. The New Testament not only was the source and criterion of all Christian doctrine but contained God's word on all political, economic, and social institutions. Not surprisingly, the brethren read the Bible more often than any other book, and it influenced their way of speaking and writing. The Bible told them that the disciples of Christ had at all times been persecuted, that their belief was right, and that they would not be forsaken by the Lord. Indeed, we fail to understand the views and actions of the brethren unless we keep in mind that they were following the New Testament more strictly and literally than Luther or Calvin.

What, then, was the spiritual life of the Anabaptists like? How did they worship, baptize, deal with sinners, and celebrate the Lord's Supper? Were eschatological predictions and ecstatic experiences common among them? Finally, was their daily life truly different from that of their Catholic and Protestant neighbors? The answers to these questions will bring us to the heart of Anabaptist piety.

Worship

The small conventicle played an important role in the life of the Anabaptists, especially in areas where the number of Anabaptists was small. The faithful would gather to read and discuss the Scriptures, and to pray for understanding and for strength to bear the cross. At times the conventicles were quite informal. A burgher at Strasbourg often saw the Anabaptists lying on their backs in a garden with their legs pulled up, each holding a book on his knees and reciting prayers toward heaven. Whenever someone approached, they would jump to their feet. At Augsburg three or four brethren would take a walk around the city walls, talking of the Word of God. The secrecy, intimacy, and earnestness of these small meetings probably left a strong impression on the participants.

The larger meetings were more formal. The Church Order of 1527 or 1529 ruled that only one speaker should be heard at a time, and that the audience must pay careful attention. All through the sixteenth century, in fact, Anabaptists in various places such as Appenzell in Switzerland, Esslingen in Swabia, Lambsheim in the Palatinate, and Mühlhausen in Thuringia emphasized that not only the preacher but anyone present at their meetings was allowed to speak; only the authoritarian Hutterites do not seem to have adopted this custom. As for the order in which speakers would be heard, Scharnschlager left it to inspiration: the believers should speak "one after the other, according to the manner in which they received" the Word. As the Anabaptists well knew, this innovation was a revolutionary one, though in the last analysis it probably derived from Luther's notion of the priesthood of all believers. Brethren in the Palatinate even sent word to the Calvinist pastor at Lambsheim that he should not always refute their doctrines in the church, where only he was allowed to talk. He should come to their meetings, where everyone was allowed to speak, but had also to accept the decision of the congregation.[1]

In practice the Anabaptists themselves did restrict this liberty. Already in 1527 the Anabaptists at Uttenreuth in Franconia agreed that those who had not been sufficiently instructed in the Word of God should not speak. And a man at Esslingen who "produced nothing but talk and no grounding in the Scriptures" was told to be quiet.[2] Actually, in none of the larger meetings of which we have detailed accounts did a simple believer get up and deliver a sermon. Even among the brethren only the leaders seem to have had both the authority and the ability to preach.

Repeatedly we hear that the Anabaptists knelt while pray-ing—in Zurich, at Mühlhausen, at Esslingen, and in Hesse. A peasant who walked through a forest in Württemberg saw a hundred men and women kneeling for quite a time while a man standing among them preached and prayed in a loud voice. Other people observed the Anabaptists look toward heaven, as if they saw God Himself.[3] Even when they gathered outdoors, the brethren customarily took off their hats during the service.

The Lord's Prayer seems to have been used frequently, but not exclusively. Manz often read a fiery prayer from a piece of paper at the beginning of the service, and one man in Thu-ringia even said he could not remember all the prayers his minister had recited. The Anabaptists prayed with much emotion. Breth-ren in the Rems valley "fell on their faces," clasped their hands, and cried, "The Lord be praised." In 1545 believers near Stras-bourg were seen crying and weeping as they prayed. In another meeting near Strasbourg the Anabaptists, grouped around oak trees, prayed for fifteen to thirty minutes. One admittedly hos-tile observer reported that the Anabaptists spread their arms and beat their breasts, and mumbled during their prayers. Not a word they uttered could be understood as they continuously raised their eyes to heaven and sighed, "groaning and grunting like a tired old nag pulling a cart."[4]

Referring to the word of James, "Confess your sins one to the other," Anthonius Kürschner introduced at St. Gallen the prac-tice of confessing before the congregation. But the result was unexpectedly disappointing: the brethren and sisters were an-noyed or dejected when they heard that this or that man had stolen or had committed adultery. Public confessions thus did not become part of Anabaptist worship.

How, then, was a typical Anabaptist meeting conducted? The

three hundred believers who on Saturday, July 24, 1545, gathered in a forest near Strasbourg from 10:00 P.M. until 1:00 A.M. listened to sermons and readings from the Bible. First the preacher spoke of the flight of the children of Israel from Egypt, identifying the Anabaptists with the Israelites. Like the Egyptians, he said, all those who were not believers—that is, Papists, Lutherans, and Zwinglians—would be slain by God. He also read Chapter 11 of the Revelation, emphasizing that one had to find God in the desert and darkness. Then another preacher rose to his feet, had a candle lit, and read from Hebrews 11, and of Christ's abiding at the house of Zachaeus, the publican. A third preacher criticized the Lutheran doctrine of justification, emphasizing the importance of good works. The Anabaptists then dealt with practical matters such as deposing a helper and appointing a new one, and readmitting into their community a banned brother. Afterward they prayed with great earnestness, or at least most of them did: one man with a lantern went around waking up those who had fallen asleep.[5]

Thirty years later the form of meetings in the Strasbourg area was basically similar. A vicar who clandestinely attended a large meeting in the same forest on July 4, 1576, reported that after all the believers had arrived, five vorstehers or elders stepped forward. The oldest among them, one brother Peter, took a shabby copy of the New Testament and read a lesson. His example was followed by the other four. Although they had put on their spectacles, their reading was somewhat "cool" because of the poor light. Then each of the five delivered a sermon that lasted about a quarter of an hour. The tenor of these sermons was that the believers should thank God that they had been elected and no longer belonged to the world or were affected by gross sins. During the sermons some believers stood or leaned against trees, while others sat or lay on their sides on the ground; some lay face down, and others drowsed or even slept. A brother continuously walked around, shaking those who were dozing or sleeping: "Get up, brother," or "Wake up, brother; listen to the

Word of God." After the sermons and prayers, greetings from others were conveyed to the assembly. For example, a believer said, "Petronella in the Breisgau has asked me to present her excuses for her absence. She is ill. She sends you her greetings, in the Name of the Lord." [6]

A night meeting held by Swiss Brethren on Whitmonday of 1578 in a forest in Hesse differed only slightly from the meeting at Strasbourg. First the congregation said a psalm; then the vorsteher, Hans Pauli, preached for about two hours, repeatedly bringing in passages from the Bible. Referring to Cain and Abel, he declared that the pious had been persecuted from the beginning of the world, and he charged the believers to live in penitence and humility. Then they prayed for emperor, king, dukes, and lords. At last the vorsteher asked: "Brethren, have you aught to say?" Someone stepped forward and said that a brother had asked for their prayers to strengthen his faith. "He who desires this, say Amen." Another man stepped forward, saying that a sister had sent them peace and asked for their prayers; others made similar statements for about an hour. The congregation then fell on their knees and said the Lord's Prayer aloud. They parted without having appointed a further meeting. [7]

Like the service in the official church, then, the Anabaptist service consisted of singing, reading from the Scriptures, one or more sermons, and prayer. The differences were striking, nonetheless. Dressed in his best clothes, the Lutheran or Catholic attended church on Sunday morning together with the other villagers because it was both customary and ordered by the government. The Anabaptist slid away furtively into the forest, disobeying the orders of the government, because he needed spiritual help. Whereas the well-ordered service in the church allowed hymns as the only emotional expression, the Anabaptist meetings were punctuated by outbursts of anguish and hope. Whereas in the church only the pastor preached, in the forest anyone could speak. Then, too, the Anabaptist meetings were held in much simpler surroundings than a church. There was no splendid church building with stone columns, carved pulpit, or stained glass windows, but only the forest lit by a few candles; no organ music and elaborate liturgy, but only a simple hymn and greetings from absent believers; no priest in a surplice or parson in a black gown, but only a lay preacher in his work clothes. By rejecting the culture of the church, the Anabaptists may have achieved part of their aim: their simple meetings were probably quite similar to the gatherings of Jesus and the early Christians. Indeed, they seem to have filled a need for an intimate, emotional expression of piety that the official churches of the sixteenth century failed to recognize.

Baptism

Criticism of Infant Baptism

Following Luther and Zwingli the Anabaptists rejected the Catholic doctrine of seven sacraments. In point of fact, they did not recognize any sacraments at all, but "signs," of which, according to Dorfbrunner, there were only two: baptism and the breaking of the bread. When a Hessian brother was reminded of Ephesians 5:32—"This is a sacrament"—he replied that his Bible, the Froschau edition, read: "This mystery is great." [8]

The Anabaptists took baptism very seriously, for it was through baptism that the believer entered the community of saints. Infant baptism, however, was regarded with nothing but revulsion and contempt: a man whose boy had been baptized by the order of the authorities washed off the "dirt" immediately afterward. For infant baptism originated with the devil. It was a simple water bath, a dog's bath, a pig's bath, a foul bath, a filthy ablution, a malpractice and an act of idolatry, an abomination, a curse, the greatest blasphemy that had ever existed.[9] In January 1525 the brethren at Zollikon removed or possibly even smashed their baptismal font. The pious followers of Hubmaier at Waldshut threw theirs into the Rhine.

The Anabaptists formulated a whole series of thoughtful and persuasive arguments against infant baptism, deeply impressing laymen and causing pastors no little embarrassment. In the first place, infant baptism had no basis in either the Old or the New Testament. The argument that baptism had taken the place of circumcision was unfounded, the Anabaptists said, for though Christ and the apostles had been circumcised on the eighth day, they were still baptized at the age of thirty. Christ, too, should be called an Anabaptist. Above all, Christ had explicitly ordered in Matthew 28:19 and Mark 16:15 that only believing people be baptized. Again and again the brethren quoted Christ's command: "Go ye into all the world, and preach the gospel to every creature. He that believeth and is baptized shall be saved; but he that believeth not shall be damned." Nor was it possible to unearth one instance when the apostles baptized children or called in godparents. Baptizing nonbelievers, as the Catholics and Lutherans did, was as absurd as telling snowflakes to fly to heaven.

The Anabaptists further pointed out that infant baptism had been unknown to the Christian churches for several hundred years. At the time of Pope Nicholas, believers had been baptized at the age of twelve. Only later did the popes decide to have first ailing children and then all children baptized, for as long as a man had a choice whether or not to be baptized, the number of heathens had increased. Through infant baptism the popes had hoped to keep everyone in the Christian fold. According to Rinck infant baptism had been introduced at the same time as the principle that priests should remain celibate. According to the Hutterite Klaus Felbinger, it was just a means to enrich the priests. Whatever the reason, infant baptism was just an invention of the popes. Thus at the enforced baptism of her child, a woman pointedly instructed the deacon to sing the hymn "And beware of human rules" before the baptism took place.

Still further, the Anabaptists emphatically argued that a child was not sensible of faith, for faith came from the hearing of the Word of God. Children could not understand the covenant of a true conscience with God, and therefore should not be baptized. Why not take a newborn child, one Hutterite suggested, and preach to it for a week? If the child believes your false doctrines, it may be baptized.[10] In reality a baptized child six weeks old was no more pious than one who had not yet been baptized. And if children needed the sacrament of baptism, why not also that of the Lord's Supper? The Anabaptists always insisted that a child should be baptized only when he had attained the age of understanding, for the sacraments should be held in awe, not because they passed man's comprehension but because they were instituted by Christ Himself. Otherwise there was the risk of giving free rein to such superstitious practices as preserving the water with which a child had been baptized.

When it came to the question of baptizing children because they had been tainted with original sin, some Anabaptists in central Germany seem to have cast out the notion of original sin altogether. Man, like all other creatures, was created good and pure; therefore all children were in a state of innocence and blessedness.[11] Many Anabaptists, however, admitted that there was a leaning toward evil in man. The Hutterites held that through his sin, Adam had imparted this evil tendency to all mankind. But if children were potential sinners, this weakness was not held against them. Children who died entered the kingdom of heaven even without baptism.

One Anabaptist reasoned that although the child of a thief might have the inclination of his father, the evil in the child's nature had not yet made its appearance. Therefore the child could not justifiably be punished by the most pitiless judge, and certainly not by God, whose mercy was greater than that of all men.[12] A number of Anabaptists argued against the supposed sinfulness of children by a syllogism: God will not receive sinners into His kingdom; since the kingdom belongs to children, how could they be sinners? [13] Others cited a more convincing argument. Until children had reason with which to distinguish between good and evil, they were neither right nor wrong and remained free of sin; not having committed any sins, they did not need penance, confession, or baptism. But sin grew daily in

the child: evil lusts entered and he began to feel ashamed. Now
baptism was needed to free him from sin.

Some Anabaptists tried to prove the necessity of adult baptism
by maintaining that they were not sure whether they had ever
been baptized. One man's parents, admittedly, had said he had
been baptized, but how could he know for sure, having at that
time been a child without understanding? His godparent had
spoken the words "I believe," but that had been forty years ago.
He did not know whether his godparent had really believed or
not.[14] Other Anabaptists argued that having been baptized as
children had not made any difference in their lives. It had never
reminded them of sins or made them desist from sinning or given
them a good conscience. Infant baptism, then, was useless, unnecessary, and ineffective; it was a blind and foolish affair, a
ceremony without content. Moreover, it was harmful: all the
sins and vices in Christendom had resulted from it, for it offered
evil and infamous people an opportunity to call themselves Christians.[15]

With all their references to the Bible, these arguments against
infant baptism seem to have been based primarily on common
sense and a strong feeling for justice. To the Anabaptists their
own experience was apparently a more valuable teacher than
traditional dogma.

There were also a few Anabaptists who did not condemn infant baptism outright. Infant baptism, they declared, should not
be a burning question: children might be baptized without detri-
ment to the truth. Fritz Erbe, the well-known Anabaptist captive
in Hesse, thought that each individual should be allowed to decide whether to abide by his first baptism or to be rebaptized. He
added, however, that in his view it was better to baptize only
those children who had understanding.[16]

Most people who heard these arguments in the sixteenth century must have been shocked and horrified by what sounded like
wild blasphemies. Baptism was of far more consequence to the
ordinary Christian than such questions as the mass, pilgrimages,

and saints. First of all, it concerned their infant offspring. No doubt those who were sincere in their Christian faith wished to see their children received into the communion of saints. Second, baptism was not just a matter of theology, but a custom observed, indeed greatly loved, in every town and village of Christendom for many centuries. Baptism followed birth as the seasons one another: even Luther or Zwingli probably would not have commanded the authority to abolish it. And now these illiterate tailors and peasants were claiming that the whole of Christendom had erred for more than a thousand years. They not only rejected the baptism of children, but vilified and ridiculed it. Even more amazing, these people took to baptizing fellows fifty or sixty years old who had already been baptized as children. It was not hard to conclude that the Anabaptists were out of their minds.

The Meaning of Baptism

The theologians recorded the Anabaptists' objections to infant baptism in considerable detail because they had to refute them. Lacking a similar motive for recording the Anabaptists' views on baptism, they did not always do so with the same care. Yet many individual Anabaptists in Franconia, Thuringia, and Hesse explained their views on baptism in detail. These various pronouncements, considered in the light of writings by Anabaptist leaders, will tell us what baptism meant to the brethren.

Riedemann, for example, insisted that man must be reborn to inherit Christ. Man first heard the Word; then he believed it; and then his faith was sealed by the power of the Holy Spirit: God created him anew. Those who were thus reborn should be baptized.[17] While all Anabaptists would have agreed with this general statement, not all shared completely identical views of the meaning of baptism. Let us look in particular at Hubmaier and Hut, whose writings and preaching greatly influenced the Anabaptists in our area.[18]

Hubmaier spoke of baptism by the spirit, by water, and by

blood. Baptism by the spirit is the inner act of regeneration, the renewal of soul and spirit, that Hubmaier seems to have conceived of as being complete before the outward ceremony. This inner act must be testified to by the outward ceremony, baptism by water. But the outward ceremony is more than just a testimony; it is a pledge: first, a pledge to Christ to lead a pure life, and second, a pledge to the congregation to be a member of the church and accept its disciplinary authority. Finally, Hubmaier spoke of a baptism by blood. By this he meant first the anguish man experiences when he encounters the law, and after baptism, the continued suffering of temptation and persecution by the world; and second, man's agony on the deathbed.

Like Hubmaier, Hut also distinguished a threefold baptism by the spirit, by water, and by blood. But he gave the first term in particular a different meaning. The inner, spiritual baptism, which Hut also called a covenant with God, was the essential one. It consisted of three stages. The first was fully to realize the awful omnipotence and power of God in all creatures. The second was to be cleansed in the "bath of rebirth." Following Thomas Müntzer, Hut interpreted the term "water" as used in the Gospel according to Saint John to mean spirit, not physical water. Man has to rid himself of all creaturely love, of absolutely everything that binds him to the world, and surrender to God. In fighting his own flesh and blood, he will be thrown into the water of tribulation, into such suffering that he thinks he is even forsaken by God himself. This is why the entry to heaven is also called the door of death. Christ trod this path, and His disciples must also tread it, for the notion that Christ's suffering would release all mankind from suffering is wrong. The example of all creatures—the Gospel of All Creatures, as Hut called it— also teaches man that he must suffer to realize the purpose of his existence. A fish or chicken cannot kill, clean, and roast itself, but must suffer at the hand of man to reach its ends. When it has undergone the debasement of being chewed and swallowed by man, its purpose of existence has been realized. Similarly, man can fulfill the purpose of his life only through suffering, or in Hut's formulation, nobody can find the sweet Son of God unless he has first tasted the bitter Christ in justification. Having abandoned the world and being purged of sin and lust, the soul finally reaches the third stage of inner baptism: redemption. Even though the redeemed man may still sin and fall, he will do so only by frailty, and will not be condemned.

The outer baptism by water, in Hut's view, is first a covenant with the Lord to continue the struggle against the self throughout life, and second a pledge to accept the disciplinary power of the church. Baptism by blood, finally, is the persecution that never fails to come when the name of Christ is confessed. Often it leads to martyrdom.

Hut also attached eschatological significance to baptism. Only those who had received the sign of baptism on their foreheads would be saved during the persecution that was to precede the coming of Christ and the Last Day in 1528. Such references to the sign on the foreheads of believers seem to have confused some of Hut's followers, many of whom had heard him only for an hour or two. Many Anabaptists in the areas of Staffelstein and Erlangen in Franconia and Freistadt in upper Austria maintained that Hut and his disciples had not baptized them but had given them the sign. Hut had said: "I give you the sign in the name of the Father, the Son, and the Holy Ghost." [19] Some even considered their baptism to be the definitive ceremony, the second being only a sign or promise to desist from sin, to be pious, and to suffer persecution. In reality, however, Hut considered the sign an intrinsic part of baptism. Some believers of the Staffelstein and Erlangen areas were explicit in their testimony that Hut had used the words "I baptize you" when he had baptized them.[20]

Hut's view of baptism as the covenant of a good conscience with God and a seal was widespread in Franconia. Here we also find Hut's doctrine that one had to be baptized through grief, agony, and tribulation. Suffering imprisonment was being baptized. In Thuringia baptism also signified the acceptance of future suffering.[21]

By contrast, some Anabaptist statements notably did not emphasize suffering: those made by Gross at Strasbourg in 1526, for example; by Plener's followers in the Palatinate in 1529; by Rinck's disciples in the environs of Vacha in 1531; by Tesch's and Schnabel's followers in Hesse in 1538; and by the Hutterite leaders Riedemann and Felbinger. These Anabaptists stressed the view that baptism was the covenant of a good conscience with God.

Some Anabaptists drew a careful distinction between outer and inner baptism. Whereas the flesh receives the outer baptism, the spirit must be baptized in the spirit of God.[22] The Anabaptists in the area of Mühlhausen around 1560 seem to have attributed little significance to the outer ceremony, emphasizing that the believer had to be baptized with fire and spirit. The river Jordan, in which Christ had been baptized, had not been water but the Word of God. A woman at Eisenach even argued that the outward ceremony of baptism was useless; water was no more than water, and people could be saved just as well without it.[23] There is no evidence, however, that the Thuringian Anabaptists discarded the ceremony of baptism. Sometimes a believer did not have an opportunity to be baptized before he was executed. Such a person, Plener said, was baptized in his own blood.[24]

The Ceremony of Baptism

In general only elected leaders were allowed to baptize. Occasionally believers had to wait for baptism because there was no minister in the area. During the first years of the movement, however, a few ordinary brethren performed baptismal rites at Augsburg and Esslingen. One brother from Linz even went so far as to say that any Christian might perform the rites if the spirit urged him.[25] At St. Gallen in the 1540s the congregation would designate an ordinary brother to baptize whenever a "church servant" was not available.[26]

In the 1520s many people, especially in Franconia, Thuringia, and Augsburg, accepted baptism at the end of the first meeting they attended. Possibly they were influenced by anxiety over the impending end of the world. Even those who thought the problem over for a while sometimes made their final decision suddenly. But some leaders were wary of baptizing such ready converts. Hans Kendtner explained at Augsburg that he had not baptized everyone who had requested it, but had first examined the believer's life and faith. We hear of believers pursuing a leader for five or six weeks together, entreating him to baptize them. The leaders at Colmar used to wait six months before they baptized a believer. Juveniles, too, were baptized only when it was clear that they believed, and not when they reached any particular age.

On a few occasions the early Swiss leaders baptized large groups of 35 or 40 people, but these were exceptional incidents.[27] Hut baptized ten persons at Hans Strigel's house at Uttenreuth in 1527. In general only one or two persons, or sometimes as many as five, were baptized at a time in Germany and Switzerland. Mass conversion was rare among the Anabaptists in our area.

The brethren baptized in rooms, barns, water towers, and inns, in fields, meadows, forests, gardens, and clay pits, at wells and near creeks, even in churches—that is, wherever it was likely that they would not be disturbed. People at Uttenreuth said that Hut and his friends liked to go to a creek to baptize. Indeed, when the brethren held meetings near water, the authorities suspected that baptism was taking place. The ceremony might take place whenever a meeting was held, either during daytime or at night.

In 1526 Hubmaier described how the ceremony of baptism was performed at Nikolsburg and "elsewhere." Whoever desired to be baptized presented himself to the minister, who questioned him on the law, the gospel, the articles of faith, his moral views, and his ability to recite prayers. If the believer passed this test, the minister would present him to the church, asking the

brethren and sisters to kneel down and pray to God to grant this
man the grace and power of the Holy Spirit. Then the believer
would answer several questions, affirming his belief in the articles of the Christian faith, his willingness to resist the devil, and
his desire to be baptized. The minister would baptize the believer by pouring water on his head.[28]

Hans Schlaffer contradicted this account in 1528, saying that
the rites at Nikolsburg were in fact quite different: first a general sermon was delivered, and then whoever wanted to be baptized, was baptized. The individual believer thus did not have
to render evidence of his faith, and as a result not all those who
were baptized really changed their way of life. According to
Schlaffer, Hut reprimanded Hubmaier for this practice, which
in turn led to the division between Hut and the brethren at
Nikolsburg. Hut's manner of baptizing was first to read several
chapters of the Bible and give an interpretation of them. Sometimes he then told the believers to kneel down in front of a
table. The believers would confess their sinfulness and their desire to desist from sinning. Hut then poured water into a bowl,
and having moistened one or two fingers in it, made a cross on
the forehead of the believers while uttering the words, "I be-
stow on you the sign"—or "I baptize you"—"in the Name of
the Father, the Son, and the Holy Spirit." On other occasions,
it appears, he actually poured water on the believers. He then
exhorted the newly baptized believers to abide by the will of
the Father, to endure suffering with patience, and never to lie,
swear, or do wrong.[29]

Other early leaders in Germany, Switzerland, and Austria baptized in a very similar manner. The believer had to answer certain questions concerning his faith and his willingness to lead a
new life and submit to the discipline of the congregation. All
those present would kneel down.[30] (In one case, however, one
of the peasants pulled at his neighbor's sleeves because everybody
was standing up.) A prayer would be recited for the believer.
Sometimes he was absolved from sin before the actual ceremony.

Water was poured from a pitcher into a bowl, a cup, or any other vessel: at Waldshut in 1525, a bucket of water was placed in the church, and in two instances, in Switzerland in 1525 and Bavaria in 1527, the leader took a little water from the tracks made by wagon wheels in the road. The minister would then perform the baptism by making either one or three crosses on the believer's forehead, by laying his wet hand on the believer's head, by sprinkling a few drops of water into his face or under his eyes, or else by actually pouring water over the believer. In one case, this last procedure was done three times.[31] There were often exhortations after baptism. At Rothenburg the minister gave his hand to a woman, calling her sister. Nespitzer at Iphofen told the believers that he had erased their names from the book of the dead and inscribed them in the book of the living. In Thuringia the newly baptized were embraced and congratulated by Römer, and then drank beer. Other Thuringian Anabaptists sang hymns and psalms.

On two occasions baptism apparently took place without water.[32] In contrast there is the account of how in 1525 Wolfgang Uolimann, formerly a monk and now an enthusiastic leader of the radicals at St. Gallen, waded naked into the Rhine river at Schaffhausen and was submerged by Grebel.[33] We do not know whether this was Grebel's or Uolimann's idea. No other baptism by immersion was reported.[34]

The Anabaptists retained their simple form of baptism throughout the century. When, for example, at the meeting near Strasbourg on June 5, 1557, two men asked to be baptized, the two leaders first preached on the meaning of baptism, refuting the Lutheran and Catholic positions. Then they presented the two to the congregation, inquiring whether they had lived in a Christian way and were worthy of baptism. They unanimously were considered worthy. The leaders now plied the two men with a number of questions: "Is this the congregation of God, is this the true baptism, and are you willing to revoke the first baptism, which you received in ignorance? Are you willing, if the need

arise, to sell your property for this congregation?" The two
knelt down and were baptized. The leaders then praised God
that the congregation had received two new members.[35]

Newly baptized believers kept their old names, with only a
few exceptions.[36] Of course, the brethren gave names to their
newly born children, even though they were not baptized.
Grebel called his little daughter Rachel.

The Tirolese government claimed in 1528 that the Anabaptists had a book in which the names of eight hundred believers
in the town of Schwaz were listed. Other governments were
also trying to get hold of such lists, perhaps spurred on by the
thought of Thomas Müntzer's famous register. While Hut's disciple Thomas Spiegel stated in 1527 that Hut had written down
the names of all people he had baptized, Anabaptists at Passau,
Esslingen, and Treffurt denied that such lists or registers ever
existed. Who, they argued, could write down the names of all
believers? In the event, they seem to have won their point, for
no lists of believers were ever discovered in our area.

Banning, or Exclusion

As we have seen, the baptized believer promised to submit to
the disciplinary power of the congregation. If he led a sinful life,
the congregation could punish him by banning, a procedure discussed in detail particularly by Hubmaier. He distinguished public sins, which should be punished publicly and right away, from
secret sins, which should first be punished secretly. A person
who had committed a secret sin should be reminded in private
of his baptismal vow. If he remained obstinate, he should again
be admonished, this time in the presence of two or three witnesses. The sinner might object to having his secret sins revealed:
what sinner would like to publicly denounced? Hubmaier
answered that the believers must be more interested in Christ's
command and in the sinner's salvation than in any false and
hypocritical regard for honor. Finally, if a sinner persisted in his
error despite these measures, he could be banned, or excluded,
according to a formula drawn up by Hubmaier.[37]

The Anabaptist articles of faith and ordinances of 1527, 1529, 1540, 1591, and 1630 also dealt with the ban.[38] Scharnschlager reminded the leaders that the ban was not intended to destroy the sinner. Before it was applied, the leaders should carefully consider whether the sinner's transgression was secret or public, whether it was great or small, and how often the sinner had been warned. As Hubmaier had said, for one believer to admonish another was a delicate matter; some would retort, "Who are you, brother, to admonish me? Are you not also guilty of this or that?"

Which concrete offenses were punished by exclusion? Scharnschlager spoke of vices of the flesh, false teaching, and licentious living; others spoke of defection, lack of charity, blasphemy, and vice. We know instances where people were excluded because they defected, advanced wrong doctrines, rebelled against the leaders, rendered an oath of allegiance to the ruler, engaged in prohibited business deals, married unbelievers, quarreled with their spouses, drunk too heavily, fornicated, or embezzled the congregation's money. Poaching was also punished by exclusion.[39]

How was the actual banning done? In a meeting near Strasbourg on June 5, 1557, the vorsteher first explained the true apostolic practice of banning, accusing Lutherans, Catholics, and other "sectarians" of ignoring it for the sake of material profit. Hans of Kolbsheim and his wife Margarethe, a couple who had been quarreling for a considerable time, were then questioned by the elders in front of the congregation. The interrogation revealed that the man had accused his wife of adultery, without cause, and had beaten her. After every member of the congregation had rendered his verdict, the husband was excluded. Strangely enough, he himself voted for his own exclusion. But after his punishment had been announced, he immediately asked to be readmitted. His request was denied. At this moment a burgher of Strasbourg, who was present only out of curiosity about the Anabaptists, had the impertinence to interrupt the proceedings by asking whether it was really Christian not to readmit a sinner who had done penance and accepted his punishment. His

question immensely angered the brethren, who began to shout at
him, giving him no opportunity of defending his view. The leaders quickly stopped the violent altercation, and the husband was
not readmitted. After this disturbance the minister presented another sinner, called Barbara, a seamstress and burgher of Strasbourg, who for a certain time had broken with the congregation.
After she had confessed the sinful life she had been leading, she
was again received into the congregation.[40]

Apparently a person who was to be banned had to be present
during the proceedings. In 1533, for example, Ascherham refused to recognize his exclusion by the followers of Jakob Hutter
because it had been pronounced in his absence.

The practical effect of the ban was strict separation from the
congregation. According to Hubmaier, a believer should not
have anything to do with a banned person, neither greeting him
nor eating and drinking with him. If a banned person was to be
avoided, however, he was not to be beaten or killed. The necessities of life, such as food, drink, and lodging, should be offered
to him, for they were also offered to Jews and heathens. Friendship, however, which might also be extended to Jews and heathens, could never be extended to a banned person. As for marital
relations between a banned person and his spouse, in 1557 the so-
called Upperland Brethren in south Germany rejected the strict
avoidance demanded by Menno Simons. Husband and wife
should not be separated on account of the ban, they said, for
the order of marriage was higher than that of avoidance.[41]

The brethren in the area of Basel and probably also in other
areas applied various degrees of punishment. A sinner might first
be refused material help from the congregation. If he persisted in
sinning, he would then be excluded from the Lord's Supper,
sometimes for as long as a year. Some congregations, too, generally punished more severely than others. The congregation at
the Blauen, near Basel, was known to be particularly strict.[42]
During 1542–43, while he was at Graubünden, Marbeck accused the Swiss Brethren of Appenzell of banning wrongdoers

too rashly. They responded by accusing him of extending Christ's mercy too far.[43] Some Swiss leaders had a high opinion of their own authority: Martin Lincki declared that those he had banned would also be banned in the next world.[44] No wonder that some banned people had bitter feelings. Christ, they said, had come to the sinners and the weak; the Anabaptists, however, excluded them.[45]

Sinners who truly repented were to be readmitted into the congregation. Hubmaier emphasized that a sinner should be pardoned as often as he showed true penitence and remorse. In practice, however, the Anabaptists were very cautious about readmitting excluded sinners. The brethren at Strasbourg withheld their pardon for a considerable time from a man who had defected to the Lutherans.[46] A repentant sinner at Augsburg who returned to his congregation in 1530 or 1531 was required to kneel down while the vorsteher laid his hands on his head in the name of the Father, the Son, and the Holy Spirit. Afterward, several brethren shook hands with him. This ceremony was not considered a fresh baptism, however. In later years some Anabaptists must have criticized the practice of making a penitent believer kneel down and humble himself, for in 1568 the Swiss leaders at Strasbourg passed a special ruling to affirm that this custom should be followed. They acknowledged, however, that the true humiliation must take place in the heart.

The Anabaptists attached much importance to the exercise of the ban, just as they did to the establishment of a congregation of true believers. Many people seem to have joined the sect not because the Anabaptists held this or that doctrine but because they exercised strict discipline. For example, one of the reasons why the Lutheran deacon Johannes Walch joined the brethren in 1582 was the absence of church discipline in the Lutheran church in Württemberg. Repeatedly Anabaptists told the pastors that they would gladly return to the official church if only the ban was introduced. The Anabaptist and Lutheran churches would then unite, one man said. Pastors who had to deal with many Anabaptists sometimes directly asked their superiors to introduce the ban.

We wonder whether the Anabaptists realized that rigorous banning was not simply a religious matter. Since the believers were forbidden to have anything to do with the banned sinner, the ban obviously affected the sinner's economic and social position as well as his spiritual life. If the Anabaptists had ever succeeded in winning over the majority of the population in one area, the ban would inevitably have led to a social distinction between the saints and the sinners: quite conceivably, indeed, to the dictatorship of the saints over the mass of unregenerate sinners.

The Lord's Supper
Criticism of the Real Presence Doctrine

The ban's aim, of course, was to maintain the purity of the congregation that celebrated the Lord's Supper. We have seen that the brethren discarded the term "Sacrament." The early Anabaptists in Switzerland used the Zwinglian term "Table of God," or "Table of the Lord," or simply "Table." Some brethren in Switzerland, however, rejected the term "Table" as nonscriptural, instead favoring "Supper," a term already used by Grebel in his letter of 1524 to Müntzer. The Anabaptists in Germany, Austria, and Moravia generally spoke of the "Breaking of the Bread," [47] the "Supper," or "Lord's Supper." Some Anabaptists, particularly in Thuringia, spoke of the "Testament."

The Anabaptists in our area largely shared Zwingli's views on the Supper, but they profoundly objected to the Catholic and Lutheran doctrines of transsubstantiation and consubstantiation— that is, the doctrines that the flesh and blood of Christ were present in the bread and wine used for the ceremony. This doctrine, they said, was just a human invention, humbug and hocus pocus, an abomination, blasphemy, idolatry, and filthy lucre. What Christ had offered for salvation the Catholics and Lutherans turned into a poison causing eternal death. The Sacrament was a dumb idol of wheat, a filthy god, a dead god, dog's food, a devil pure and simple, and devil's magic. Contemptuously the Anabaptists spoke of the chalice of abomination, the chalice of the Babylonian whore, and a cursed chalice. A woman dying of the plague said she would prefer a piece of fresh bread; it would help her more than "that morsel of turnip." [48]

Not being equipped to discuss the intricate questions of the Real Presence and the effects of the Lord's Supper, many Anabaptists simply said they could not believe that Christ's flesh and blood were in the bread and wine. Quite a number of them elaborated on their criticisms, however. Some dwelt on the events of Holy Week: Christ Himself was present in body during the Last Supper, but there is no evidence that the disciples ate Him. Christ broke the bread and not His body. Anabaptists in the area of Mühlhausen asked how the disciples could have eaten and drunk Jesus on Thursday when he was arrested and crucified on Friday. After all, the Jews had tortured not the bread but the body of Christ. When Christ said: "This is My body, which is given for you," He was referring to future time. In other words Christ gave His disciples only bread and wine.

In Franconia in 1526, Volk and Kellermann, both disciples of Hut, taught an interpretation obviously adopted from Karlstadt. When the Lord said: "This is My body, which is given for you," He was pointing to Himself, referring not to the bread but to His own body. The same interpretation was also offered by several Anabaptist leaders in Thuringia from the 1530s to the 1560s.[49] It appeared in Württemberg in 1563 and 1602.[50]

Citing the Easter Day message "He has risen; He is not here" (Mark 16:6), many Anabaptists pointed out that Christ was seated on the right hand of His Father and would not come again until the Last Day. It was impossible for Christ to be both in heaven and on earth at the same time; God had only one body, not two or three. Moreover, He would hardly come down every time mass was celebrated and have himself killed all over again. Other brethren held the notion of eating Christ's body up to ridicule. May God in His mercy ever guard her from doing so, one woman prayed ironically. Also, bread and wine were too small to contain Christ: how could He be in the Lord's Supper in his entire length, thickness, and width, as the Lutheran pastors claimed? Still others argued that the body of Christ could not possibly have been eaten so many hundred thousand times: it would have been consumed long ago.

Some Anabaptists in northern Thuringia surprised the theologians by saying that flesh and blood were indeed under the bread and wine, but only in the form of the hands of the priest who lifted the elements.[51] Other brethren in Thuringia and Hesse argued as follows: whatever was of the body and blood could be seen; the flesh and blood in the bread and wine could not be seen, touched, or tasted; ergo, the flesh and blood were not there.

There were also Anabaptists who said that it was a violation of the Ten Commandments to make a god of bread. How could people seriously believe that God would let himself be baked in an oven? It was written in the Gospel of John, "I am the bread of life which has descended from heaven," not "which has been baked in the oven." "If bread were the true body of Christ," said an Anabaptist at Erlangen, "I could make myself many gods by stuffing my belly." [52]

Some found it downright revolting to assume that God was in the bread and wine. It would be a poor god who let himself be broken by priests, bitten off, sipped at, chewed, and swallowed. Christ Himself had said that whatever entered by the mouth descended into the belly and left through the natural orifice—surely a desecration of the beloved Son by anyone's standards. No doubt this thought was in the mind of an Anabaptist leader who said in 1529: the communicant shits into Christ's body.[53] Of course, arguments of this kind only served to confirm the authorities' view that the Anabaptists were horrendous blasphemers.

Other Anabaptists objected to the picture of the Cross on the Host, pointing out that God had forbidden man to make images of Him in heaven, on earth, or in the water. The theologians replied: "Then, since you object to the picture, we shall give you a host without one; yet you do not cavil at the image on coins, do you?" When the Anabaptist replied that he did not eat coins, the theologians riposted: "And neither do you eat cookies with pictures on them." [54]

When the brethren referred to Christ's having said that He did not dwell in temples built by human hands, the theologians argued that this statement referred only to God, and not to Christ. Riedemann replied that if Christ appeared in the temples after he had become man, this could only show that He really was a man and as such could not be in more than one place at a given moment. But could it not be argued that now, after his glorification, Christ was everywhere? The fact is, Riedemann said, that Christ held the Supper with His disciples before He was glorified. It is true that God or the deity extends into all created things: as wood into wood, as bread into bread, as man into man whom He has made an especial dwelling for Himself. Why, then, should one seek Him in bread, or in one bread more than in any other? [55]

Like the Waldensians, some Anabaptists insisted that the efficacy of the Sacrament depended on the worthiness of the priest and the believer. A brother in Lutheran Württemberg strongly opposed the doctrine that even a godless pastor could offer the Supper, and laymen very well receive it. In general the Anabaptists refused to partake of the Lord's Supper in the churches. From time to time Anabaptists were discovered who had not attended the Lord's Supper for years, sometimes even ten or twenty years. Those who under pressure finally agreed to attend church services still vehemently refused to take the Sacrament; the few who did simply regarded it as bread and wine only.

In criticizing the Catholic and Lutheran doctrines of the Sacrament, the Anabaptists appealed not only to the Scriptures but also to reason, common sense, and experience. Although the ordinary brethren had not devised these arguments themselves but had received them from their leaders, they took them very seriously. It would be misleading to call the Anabaptists rationalists, for they had in fact rejected the rationalism of the Anti-Trinitarians. Nevertheless, the Anabaptist craftsmen and peasants turned to a sort of coarse, simple rationalism that undermined old and venerable doctrines. The Anabaptists lived in a spiritual world that was different from that of their Catholic and Protestant neighbors.

The Meaning of the Lord's Supper

As an Anabaptist at Erlangen intimated in 1529, the brethren did not always agree on the Lord's Supper even among themselves. In the 1530s, some Anabaptists in Hesse and Thuringia seem to have discarded the traditional Lord's Supper entirely. They thought nothing of the Sacrament because they had bread and wine every day; one might as well recite the words of the institution whenever one had food and drink. Similar views were expressed in Württemberg in later years: "He had the Lord's Supper at home every time he said grace before and after a meal." Why should this believer partake of the Supper elsewhere? [56]

Rinck's followers in Hesse professed simple ignorance of what the Lord's Supper meant. They regarded it as a deep and difficult matter, and with much sighing diligently warned all who partook of it to exercise great caution.[57] Most Anabaptists had more definite views, however. Some brethren in Thuringia, Franconia, and Swabia explained that the words "Whoso eateth my flesh and drinketh my blood, hath eternal life" must be understood not literally but spiritually, in the light of John 6.[58] Christ, they said, had often used figures of speech to explain spiritual matters to common people, who saw but did not perceive. The bread signified the spiritual bread, the gospel. When the believers accepted the Word of God, then they ate the body of

Christ in the spirit. A man at Marbach bluntly told the pastor he would abide by the Lord's Supper as described in John 6; the pastor could have the other two versions of the gospel and Saint Paul.[59]

Anabaptists in Franconia who seem to have been influenced by Hut emphasized the aspects of unity and suffering in the Supper. As the grains first had to be ground into flour, mixed with water, and baked in the oven, so the believers through suffering should also become one loaf. Similarly, many grapes were turned into one wine in the vine press.[60] Christ had broken the bread also as a sign that His disciples should be broken for His sake. Numerous brethren in Franconia, and here and there in Thuringia and Austria, saw an even greater symbol of suffering in the wine. The blood of Christ was not, they said, in the chalice. The chalice was in the blood of Christ, as the Lord's words clearly showed: "This chalice is the new testament in my blood." The Lord drank of the chalice and ordered His disciples to drink too—that is to suffer. This is why the Scriptures say that one does not enter the kingdom of God unless he drinks of the chalice. The brethren admitted, however, that it was hard to go with the Lord to the Mount of Olives.[61]

Some of Hut's disciples spoke of Christ's dwelling in the believer. An Anabaptist at Uttenreuth said, for example, that when a man was a Christian, he had the blood of Christ; and when suffering entered the body, the chalice was in the blood.[62] Though they did not mention the chalice, the Anabaptists in northern Thuringia also emphasized the significance of suffering: when a man shed his blood in the name of God, he celebrated the true memory of Christ.[63] The ideas of unity and suffering also appear in the confessions of faith of the Hutterite leaders Riedemann and Felbinger.[64]

The Anabaptists all over south and central Germany, Austria, and Moravia, whether Swiss Brethren, followers of Hut, or Hutterites, also celebrated the Supper as an act of remembrance: or as the Hutterite Chronicle described it, as a beautiful and gracious remembrance of the bitter suffering and death of the Lord, and a fervent expression of gratitude for salvation from our sins.

The Ceremony of the Lord's Supper

In his letter to Müntzer of September 1524, Grebel said that in celebrating the Supper the words of Matthew 26, Luke 22, and Corinthians 11 should be recited. These were the words of a covenant, he said, not of consecration. Common bread should be used. No priest should officiate, but if a priest had to be there, he should at least not wear the stole. The Supper should not be celebrated in temples, but presumably in houses or outdoors; and it should be celebrated often. Though Grebel mentioned that Christ and the Corinthians had celebrated it in the evening, he did not establish a preferred time.[65]

The first Anabaptist celebration of the Supper of which we have a detailed account took place at Rudi Thoman's house in Zollikon on January 25, 1525.[66] Among those present were Reublin, Brötli, Manz, and Blaurock. Blaurock broke a loaf of bread into pieces. He also had nearby a container of wine. He then said: "Whosoever believes that God has saved him through His death and rose-colored blood, may come and eat the bread with me and drink the wine." All present pressed forward to take a piece of bread and a drink of wine.[67]

The Anabaptists in Switzerland celebrated the Supper in houses, in barns, in orchards, and allegedly even in prison, though no evidence of its being celebrated there has been found.[68] They celebrated it on weekdays as well as important feast days. To Anabaptists the Supper was a very serious matter indeed: only baptized believers were allowed to participate, for those who broke the bread had to be free of sin.[69] In the Lutheran church, the brethren complained, everyone could go to the Lord's Supper like sows to the trough.[70] The Anabaptists also insisted that the Lord's Supper had to change the believer's life. One woman said she was not worthy of the Supper, for though she had taken it, she had again fallen into grievous sin.[71] Most Anabaptists, however, pointed not to their own sins but to the sins of others.[72] The sins of Lutherans and Catholics, indeed, were another reason why the Anabaptists refused to attend the Supper in the official churches.

Hubmaier suggested that common bread and wine be put on the table. The minister and the believers would kneel down and confess their sins before God. Then the minister would explain the meaning of Christ's death. He would ask several formal questions, recite the words of institution, break the bread and give a piece to each participant, and give each participant also a sip of wine. After this all the believers would sit to hear a final exhortation.[73] Hut and his followers had a simpler ceremony. After baptizing, the minister would explain the meaning of the Supper. Reciting the words "Take this in remembrance of me," he would give each person a bite of bread and a sip of wine. In the large meeting of sixty believers at Augsburg on April 2, 1528, two jugs of wine and nine to ten rolls were distributed.

Some Anabaptists in Thuringia and neighboring Hessian villages celebrated the Supper in an unusual manner. The leader broke off several pieces of bread, dipped them into the wine, blessed them, and gave a piece to everyone. In 1535 the refugees at Halberstadt also cut off pieces of bread and put them into the wine. Then each took a sop and divided it. One man later said that he had taken the Supper only once, but that once in this manner was sufficient for a lifetime. The custom of dipping pieces of bread into wine was carried from Halberstadt to Schneeberg near Zwickau.[74] Apparently it was not practiced outside Thuringia, or at least not by the Swiss Brethren.

In the procedure followed by the Swiss Brethren in the Palatinate, the minister laid a slice of white or dark bread on a cloth spread on the ground. While reciting the words of institution, he broke off pieces for each person present, setting the first aside for himself. Then he took up a bottle, a bowl, or other drinking vessel and gave each person a drink of wine.[75]

The question whether the minister should break the bread and distribute it or whether the individual believers themselves should break it led to disputes in some congregations. In the Rems valley in Württemberg, contrary to the practice of the Palatinate, each believer himself took a piece of bread and drank from the vessel.[76] The Strasbourg Discipline of 1568 concluded that no strict rule could be laid down, and that nobody should be forced to accept a new practice. The believers were told, however, to take the Supper in their own congregation, not in a neighboring one.[77]

When in 1525 Hubmaier celebrated the Lord's Supper at Waldshut, he washed the feet of the believers. Later, at Nikolsburg, he discontinued the practice. Other leaders, however, like Schiemer, were strict in demanding it. We find the custom in the lower Inn valley in the Tirol and at Halberstadt.[78] Some hymns of the Swiss Brethren and Hutterites emphasized the obligation of foot-washing as an expression of humility and love.[79] The Hutterites even had an established sermon on the subject, based on John 13:1–20.[80] The Anabaptists of Germany, Switzerland, Austria, and Moravia mentioned foot-washing so rarely, however, that it is doubtful whether they practiced it at all. Nor is the practice mentioned by those who described the Lord's Supper as celebrated by the Swiss Brethren in the Palatinate in 1553 and in Hesse in 1578. The south German and Dutch leaders discussed the question at Cologne in 1591 and decided that if he was asked to, a believer should let his feet be washed and also wash the feet of others.[81] Such a decision indicates that the custom was not generally practiced.

Eschatology

The religious life of most Anabaptist congregations was a sober one, especially during the movement's later years, centering on worship, the ban, and the Lord's Supper. But during the movement's first years some Anabaptists were intensely preoccupied with Christ's imminent return. Hut's eschatological predictions for 1528 influenced many Anabaptists in Franconia, Austria, Swabia, and possibly also Thuringia and Hesse. But since the eschatology of Hut and his followers might have had a political orientation, we shall discuss it in connection with the revolutionary trends in Anabaptism. Here we are concerned with those Anabaptists who thought of the return of Christ only in spiritual terms.

Contrary to what is usually believed, even the early congregation at Zollikon was affected by the eschatological mania.[82] In June 1525 groups of the brethren of Zollikon came to Zurich, shouting in the streets: "Woe, woe, dreadful woe to Zurich!" They wore willow twigs and ropes instead of belts, fulfilling Isaiah's prophecy that at the day of judgment, the believers would wear "instead of a girdle, a rope." Loudly condemning Zwingli as the red dragon of the Revelation and his fellow pastors as the dragon's seven heads, they warned the burghers, "If you do not repent, a dreadful calamity will befall you." Like Jonah, they gave Zurich forty days of grace.[83]

At St. Gallen too, prophets claimed that the Lord would come at Christmas 1525. When He did not show up, they changed the date to Easter 1526. In May 1527, Michael Sattler, supposedly the spiritual head of Swiss Anabaptism, declared that all portents had been fulfilled and that the Lord would soon appear. Sattler's long quotations show that he was influenced by the prophecy of the Fourth Book of Esdras. Similar predictions were made at Strasbourg in 1527, at Augsburg and Reutlingen in 1528, at Basel and Lucerne in 1529, and at Heilbronn and Wiesloch in 1530.[84] Melchior Hofmann taught that after the siege of Strasbourg and the massacre of the godless in 1533, he and his 144,000 followers would go to meet the returning Christ. While Hofmann's speculations contributed to the rise of the Kingdom of Münster, they had no influence in south Germany, Switzerland, or Moravia. In general it may be said that even in the 1520s eschatological expectations were limited to some Anabaptist groups only. By no means did eschatology dominate the thought of all Anabaptists.[85]

In the 1530s only scattered believers here and there in Thuringia, Hesse, and Franconia were still inspired by the hope that the Lord would soon return.[86] In 1536 an Anabaptist at Rothenburg accused Luther of disregarding the Revelation of Saint John, which like the Third and Fourth Book of Esdras, he said, pointed to that very time for the Lord's return. The Hessian leaders Tesch and Schnabel were also fascinated by the Revelation of Saint John and the Book of Esdras. In 1538 they said that God would send two prophets to destroy the realm of the Antichrist and build the temple, the foundations of which had already been laid. They did not know who these prophets were, however, or when they would appear. In 1538, too, Joachimite ideas were current among the brethren of Schneeberg in Saxony.[87] Ten years later, during the Smalcaldic War, the followers of Marbeck in Alsace were convinced that the Last Day was at hand.[88]

By the second half of the sixteenth century, eschatological predictions were rare. Some Hutterites still thought that the end was near.[89] In 1578 the Swiss Brethren in Hesse also believed that they were living in the Last Day, although they strictly condemned rebellion. Their leader said he knew what the common rabble had in mind. It could be read in the chronicles and had been seen in the peasant uprising: "May God protect us all from it!"

Eschatological predictions were not limited to the Anabaptists. It is well known that Luther and Calvin, too, were convinced that the Day of the Lord was near. Yet the predictions of the Anabaptists were really different. Unlike the Reformers, some Anabaptists announced a precise date for the return of Christ. And while Luther and Calvin waited for the coming of Christ in hope and confidence, the Anabaptists proclaimed it as a day of retribution when the unbelievers would be mercilessly exterminated. These frenzied dreams might have been a reaction to the brutal imprisonment, torture, and executions the brethren had to endure, but they were also related to ecstatic trends that had appeared from the early days of Anabaptism.

Ecstatic Experiences

Having divested baptism and the Lord's Supper of the awe-some supernatural power they held for Catholics and Lutherans, the Anabaptists encountered the divine in a different form: the working of the Holy Spirit. Many Anabaptists placed a stronger emphasis on the working of the spirit than either the Lutherans or the Zwinglians did. The Swiss Brethren declared that God's word was not limited to the written word of the Scripture, which they called the Outer Word, but manifested itself also through the Holy Spirit, the Inner Word. Indeed, to understand the meaning of the Scripture, the believer must have inner enlightenment. Although the Bible was the source of all truths, it remained a dead letter without the Inner Word. The Inner Word did not go beyond the Scripture, however: a revelation was recognized by the congregation only if it agreed with the New Testament. For that matter, Hut and his followers went even further. Since it was God Himself who spoke in the Holy Spirit, the inner voice was more reliable and more complete than the Scripture. Ultimately the believer heeded the inner voice more than the Scripture, for the inner voice taught him everything he had to know. Even in prison, when he might be deprived of the Scripture, the inner voice could guide him.

In general the spiritualistic trend of Anabaptism remained moderate enough; most Anabaptists never underwent ecstatic experiences. Under special circumstances, however, the strong emphasis on the spirit as opposed to the letter of the Scripture could produce intense emotional and ecstatic states in believers. This is in fact what happened in certain areas, especially during the first years of the movement.

Felix Manz himself admitted that once or twice during his imprisonment the epistles of Saint Paul had visually appeared to him.[90] In the first congregation at Zollikon, baptisms were often accompanied by much emotion. Men and women would cry loudly and complain of their sins and ask with tears in their eyes

for the sign of baptism. In 1527, for example, in a meeting held
by Anthoni Roggenacher at Zollikon, a man fell on his knees,
and crying to God with his eyes full of tears, besought the congregation's prayers. All then fell on their knees and prayed. During the prayer the man beat his face with his fist so hard that
blood began flowing from his nose and mouth. Falling backward,
he lay prostrate for a while on the ground, and then was baptized. At that moment a girl entered and asked to be baptized
also. Once again the congregation knelt and prayed. When suddenly the girl screamed loudly, Roggenacher explained that the
devil was leaving her. She, too, was baptized.[91] Experiences of
this sort seem mild, however, compared to the excesses that arose
in some Anabaptist congregations.

In 1525 or 1526 a girl named Margret Hottinger, an Anabaptist of Zollikon whose family and relatives had also joined the
new sect, declared that she was God. Although some were rather
taken aback, her followers defended her by referring to Christ's
word: "Have you not read in the law that you are God's? Whoever keeps my commands stays in me and I in him." She talked
of matters that nobody could comprehend. She might say, for
example: "Has it not been written, cursed be he who has hung
on the cross? Or that whoever prayed, committed a sin?" At the
same time she led a strict and pure life.[92]

Margret Hottinger was by no means unique. Ulrich Bolt, a
former priest at Schwyz, remarked in 1528 that shortly after his
rebaptism he had come across Anabaptists who said: "I am God;
I am Christ; I am deified; I am sure I cannot sin any more."
They justified these views by quoting Christ: "He that eateth
my flesh, and drinketh my blood, dwelleth in me and I in
him." [93] We do not know where Bolt met these people or
whether he had been at St. Gallen; in any case it was there, in
1525 and 1526, that the most extreme doctrines were advanced.
From the start the Anabaptists at St. Gallen had a spiritualistic
tendency. They began by declaring that the Heavenly Father
spoke through them, but soon went further. In describing their

doctrines the chronicler Kessler admits that they were hardly the teaching of the fathers of Anabaptism. At the same time he leaves no doubt that the Anabaptist teachings provided the starting point for the startling events at St. Gallen.

For some months, according to Kessler, hardly a week passed without the appearance of some new teacher of special doctrines; one of these teachers was Hans Denck.[94] Indeed, a hectic atmosphere prevailed, possibly due in part to the severe persecution the brethren suffered from June 1525 on. Some made public confessions; some began to behave like children; some women cut off their curls; some exhorted people to do penance before the Day of the Lord. Carrying their emphasis on the spirit to the extreme, some threw their copies of the New Testament into the fire or tore them to pieces, exclaiming that the letter killed and the spirit quickened. Challenged to prove their views with the Scripture, they would laugh and shout, "'Woe, woe, you scribes," and pointing with their finger to their breasts, exclaim, "Here, here." Others gave a fatalistic interpretation to Zwingli's doctrine of predestination. They would simply sit and refrain from any activity, claiming that if God was to effect anything through them, He would do so in any case. When a thought entered their minds, they would say, "This is the Father's will." They even stopped praying, on the theory that if God was going to do something for them, He would do it whether they asked Him to or not.

Some people at St. Gallen had strange ecstatic experiences: they would "die," as they said, referring to Saint Paul's words: "I die daily." [95] Johannes Kessler, who himself witnessed these scenes, reports that when the believers were assembled, some would suddenly fall backward on the ground or against a wall and lie there writhing. They would twist their hands and fingers, while their faces were torn by endless sighs and a "breaking heart." Kessler says they looked as if they were about to cry out from the heart but feared to do so, trying to overcome their anguish. All this was done with great straining and outpouring of sweat. When they recovered consciousness, they would talk of divine and high matters, "witnessing," as they called it. Whatever they said was regarded as God's word and esteemed higher than the Scriptures. If anyone should try to question their mode of "witnessing," as Kessler did, they cried in a loud voice as if he had committed murder, beating themselves all the while: "Woe, you scribes, woe, you Pharisees and hypocrites." These acts of "dying" and "witnessing" became so frequent that the town council of St. Gallen formally prohibited them.

Kessler reports that most people thought such scenes were all a fake. But a friend of his, Niklaus Guldi, who also had formerly "died," assured him that no fraud was involved. The person who "died" was forced to do so against his will. Guldi himself had felt as if he had epilepsy. Such sweat and such contortions would be impossible to produce, he said, without inner agony. Guldi reminded Kessler of the *spiritus phytonis* in *The Aeneid* that had possessed the Sibyl. Kessler was convinced that a spiritual power was involved, though he considered it an evil spirit, as described in Acts 16.[96]

Whatever the psychological causes of these phenomena, they have occurred again and again in times of religious excitement, and not only among Anabaptists. Scenes of religious ecstasy are reported in both the Old and the New Testament. The bodily convulsions of the pilgrims in the chapel of Mary the Beautiful at Regensburg in 1523 were signs of religious ecstasy. The Wesleyan Revival in England, the first Great Awakening from 1834 onward in Northeastern America, the Great Awakening of the Middle West at the beginning of the nineteenth century, and the numerous Pentecostal movements of the early twentieth century produced phenomena that were similar or even identical with the events at St. Gallen in 1525 and 1526. People would scream, fall on the ground, suffer convulsions, and lie there for hours. At an outdoor revival meeting held at Cane Ridge, Kentucky, in 1801, people shouted, sobbed, leaped in the air, writhed on the ground, and suffered bodily contortions. "At no time was

the floor less than half covered. Some lay quiet, unable to move
or speak. Some talked but could not move. Some beat the floor
with their heels. Some, shrieking in agony, bounded like live
fish out of water. Many lay down and rolled over tree stumps
and benches and then plunged, shouting 'Lost Lost!' into the
forest." [97] The "gift of tongues," the "holy laugh," the "barks,"
and the "jerks" are various expressions of ecstatic piety that even
today are cultivated by some sects in America. In general these
sects also have deep faith in the coming of the millennium.

The strong spiritualistic trend at St. Gallen was connected,
too, with unbridled sexuality. Kessler reports that these Anabaptists, who had hitherto made a great show of their humility,
suddenly began to wear extravagant dress. Inspired by the example of the Prodigal Son, they would give each other rings—
first of wood, then of bone and of silver, and finally of gold—
as a sign of their new life and marriage to God. According to
Kessler, however, these rings served only to incite fleshly love.
These people would engage in wild promiscuity, copulating like
animals in the fields and forests. Both married and unmarried
women were involved. The records of the town council indicate
that several persons were present during these sexual acts. For
example, on February 15, 1526, the town council noted that five
couples had "taken to one another" in the choir of a church. On
March 11, 1526, the town council questioned seven persons who
had run around in shirts or undershirts only, and who had kissed,
caressed, and lain with one another. Called to account, these
people would say defiantly: "Why do you judge, you hypocrites? We have died to the flesh and passed through death.
Whatever we do is done by the Father, in spite of us." Some
referred to Christ's words: "If He renders you free, you are
truly free." There is little doubt that these acts were religiously
motivated. According to the chronicler Hermann Miles, during
a meeting held sometime before Christmas of 1526 or 1527 by
three hundred Anabaptists at Haslen near Teufen in Appenzell,
some brethren changed their best clothes for their worst and

then lay on the ground as if they were dead. When they awoke they took off the old clothes and again put on the good clothes, for Paul says in Hebrews 4, "Do away with the old man and put on the new one." Afterward they undressed completely and lay naked on one another.[98]

One St. Gallen family, the Guldis, were particularly affected by the new piety. By 1525, Niklaus Guldi was well known in Anabaptist circles at St. Gallen, Zurich, Zollikon, and Aarau. He was arrested at St. Gallen in November or December 1525 and released on January 22, 1526, after he had promised on oath to stay away from the Anabaptists and their like. Instead he kept in touch with the sectarians and also engaged in the experience of "dying." On March 11, 1526, at the house of one Walter of Oberndorf, he conducted a ceremony that reveals his unorthodox thinking. He sliced part of a loaf of bread into 28 pieces, saying that they belonged to the dogs. Then he threw the pieces to the floor and trampled on them to show that the bread was material bread grown in the earth, as opposed to the living bread with which the soul is fed. Afterward he burned some of the bread. This act signified that like the bread, man would turn to ashes. He then cut the remaining bread into pieces and told a little girl to throw them into a forest. In the morning he ordered the girl to gather these pieces again and burn them. Guldi was arrested by the authorities at St. Gallen on March 25, 1526. Since he had already twice broken his oath, his situation was serious; but he recanted once more, and his sentence was only a term of imprisonment. Three months later, on June 18, 1526, he was released on the conditions that in the future he abstain from baptizing, "dying," reading, breaking the bread, and the like, and that he leave St. Gallen for one year. Far from keeping his promise, he appeared at Esslingen in April 1529 as an Anabaptist. By 1530, however, he is said to have forsworn Anabaptism for good. Verena Guldi, his sister, also played her part: In February 1526 she was imprisoned at St. Gallen on account of her "Anabaptist behavior," but she was released on February 15, 1526, with a warning. On March 20, however, little more than a month later, three persons were surprised in the house of the Guldis in the act of embracing.

The St. Gallen movement reached its climax with the incidents involving Verena Baumann and Thomas Schugger. Verena Baumann, a maidservant at St. Gallen who belonged to the spiritualistic circles, told two other girls, friends of hers, that she was Christ. One of these girls, Wybrat Vonwilerin, had been imprisoned at Zurich as an Anabaptist from sometime in March, at least, until April 2, 1526. Verena and Wybrat now took the biblical names Mary Magdalen and Martha. Verena left the city, establishing herself in a house at Buch near Tablat. Numerous people from St. Gallen and the surrounding villages flocked to see her; believers confessed to her the most secret and heinous of the sins they had committed in their lives. Verena herself told the people that she was to bear the Anti-christ, but shortly afterward said she was to bear the child mentioned in Revelation 12. She called herself at one moment the great whore of Babylon, but immediately afterward the living Son of God. She also appeared naked in front of the crowd, and reproved them for having lewd ideas. At the request of her relatives she was finally arrested by the abbot of St. Gallen and handed over to the town council. When she and her two girl friends were led through the streets to the town hall, they shouted, "Do penance, do penance, the Day of the Lord, the ax has already been laid to the roots of the tree." Verena's hair was flying, her face was distorted, her mouth was covered with saliva, and her fingers and body were writhing as if she were suffering from a serious illness. Taken before the town council, she tore her clothing. The authorities at St. Gallen regarded her as mentally ill and thought of entrusting her to the care of a burgher. She refused and was placed in the beadhouse, and six weeks later, when she had calmed herself, expelled from the town.[99]

The Thomas Schugger incident was even more extraordinary. During a family gathering at the elder Schugger's house near

St. Gallen on the night of February 7–8, 1526, Thomas Schugger cut off the head of his brother Lienhart in front of their parents and relatives. Schugger was sentenced to death and executed on February 16, 1526. What was the motive for this fantastic crime, which was soon known all over Germany? The chronicler Joachim Vadian, burgomaster of St. Gallen and one of the prosecutor's aides at the trial, says that both Thomas and Lienhart were Anabaptists. But Vadian does not attribute the crime to Anabaptism, suggesting that Thomas might have been drunk or had lost control of himself in some other way. The chronicler Fridli Bluntschli, however, attributes the decapitation to religious motives. Both the Schuggers and their guests were Anabaptists. Before he killed his brother, Thomas had imposed on him several trials of a religious nature that symbolized suffering and submission.

The chronicler Kessler provides a more elaborate explanation. Thomas belonged to the libertinistic group at St. Gallen, claiming that he was a prophet and lived in a higher state of perfection. Those who had passed through death to freedom, he believed, could no longer be tainted by sin whatever they did. A flutist and fiddler at dances, he encouraged people to light-heartedness and then defended himself with his views of freedom and perfection. Kessler sees the roots of the crime in these beliefs. Even in front of the judges, Thomas declared that God had acted through him when he had killed his brother. Kessler goes on to explain that like his brother Thomas, Lienhart was also obsessed with strange religious ideas. On February 6, two days before his death, he ran into the town of St. Gallen and exchanged his surcoat and sword for the staff held by the guards on duty at the marketplace, shouting wildly: "This is a staff of authority; but it is not the right one. There will be another." The following morning he and some others broke the staff into three pieces and burned them. All these acts had a religious meaning: the political authorities at St. Gallen who protected the gospel by force and persecuted the true Christians would be forced by an evil power to abandon their position and belief. The breaking and burning of the staff meant that this evil power would in turn be punished.

During the evening of February 7, according to Kessler, Thomas inflicted several brutal acts on his brother in order to test his faith. He beat him with a cudgel, tied his feet together and pulled them over a staff, and then suddenly let him fall again. He made him lie down and turned the point of a sword three times directly above his eye, and finally gave him vinegar and gall, causing him to vomit. Lienhart himself asked his brother to cut off his head. They prayed, and then Lienhart jumped up, mumbling, "Father, if thou be willing, remove this cup from me; nevertheless not my will, but thine be done." After he had knelt down, Thomas, standing behind him, said, "Father, thy will be done," to which Lienhart replied "Amen." Thomas then beheaded his brother.[100]

Naturally enough, after all these strange events the town council of St. Gallen forbade further Anabaptist meetings in the city. Kessler reports that the sectarians then assembled in the countryside, particularly in the territory of Appenzell. What actually happened is not clear. According to Kessler people left their families, threw away their possessions, and stopped working, declaring that God would feed them. Three groups, totaling at least twelve hundred believers, ran over mountains and through valleys, and worked themselves into a state of religious ecstasy. Since the believers shouted that the Last Day would dawn in eight days, many people who were concerned about their salvation also accepted baptism. Although the authorities in Appenzell finally interfered and prohibited these meetings, the sectarians came to their senses and returned home only when they began to suffer from hunger and cold.

We do not know who was really responsible for the aberrations in St. Gallen and Appenzell. It is not accurate to call those who indulged in spiritualistic excesses Anabaptists, for the Anabaptist leaders themselves, such as Grebel and Manz, preached in the area of Appenzell against unbridled spiritualism, obviously to no avail: they were called false prophets and scribes, and told to go away. Still these forms of ecstatic piety were quite certainly connected with the Anabaptist movement at St. Gallen. There is evidence that some, if not all, of the major figures involved had formerly been Anabaptists. At the least, then, the Anabaptists had prepared the ground for the ecstatic manifestations that appeared.

Spiritualistic tendencies also appeared among the Anabaptists in southwest Germany. Sattler, for example, warned believers there against brethren who claimed to have had revelations and against "vain curiosity and knowledge of matters which God had reserved to Himself only." Sattler did not condemn revelations as such, however, but only "their boastful use." [101] At Strasbourg there were several visionaries, quite apart from Melchior Hofmann. Clemens Ziegler, one of the first sectarians at Strasbourg, experienced fantastic and ugly visions between 1528 and 1533.[102] In 1530 Lienhart Jost and his wife Ursula had ecstatic experiences, and in 1533, Barbara Rebstock. It appears that Hofmann had received from Jost and his wife the idea that Strasbourg was the New Jerusalem from which 144,000 apostles would spread all over the world. Hofmann published accounts of the two Jost prophets, whose fame spread as far as the Netherlands.[103] Ecstatic experiences were also had by some Anabaptists at Reutlingen, Lauingen, and Esslingen. During a meeting at Esslingen in 1529 two strangers "knelt with their hands raised toward the sun and acted as if they were mad." One Anabaptist became alarmed: "God, where will this end?" Afterward the two strangers ran through the town, loudly calling for penance.[104]

Hut, the greatest Anabaptist leader in south Germany, had definite spiritualistic tendencies. On his travels as a bookseller through Thuringia and Saxony, he may have encountered the spiritualistic doctrines of the Zwickau prophets. God, Hut explained, had revealed many things to His elect through visions and dreams. Three kinds of dreams had to be distinguished. First were those of the flesh, reflecting what one had done during the day, and second, those inspired by the devil, such as the dreams of fornicators and usurers; none of these had any value. Finally there were the dreams revealed by the Holy Spirit. God had spoken to the prophets through such dreams, and whoever had understanding would accept them.[105]

There is no evidence that Hut's followers generally experienced dreams and visions. In Austria only one case is known. In the Erlangen region in Franconia, however, Hut's spiritualistic tendencies seem to have made a deep impression on some believers. When Hut and his disciples preached at Erlangen and in nearby villages such as Uttenreuth in early 1527, about a hundred persons in some twenty towns and villages in the area of Erlangen joined the Anabaptist sect. Although most of them abjured Anabaptism in 1528, some reappeared a few years later in a new sect led by one Hans Schmid of Uttenreuth. Schmid insisted that he had been taught by God alone: he was a prophet sent by God and the Spirit. The sect existed in the Erlangen region, with Schmid's house at Uttenreuth as its center, from Whitsunday of 1530, though Schmid seems to have had his revelations as early as 1528. New members were received into the group by Schmid after God had approved of them through Schmid's visions. By 1531 as many as 65 persons in thirteen towns and villages, 57 of whom are known to us by name, are said to have been members.

Schmid's sect distinguished itself first by its highly ecstatic character, probably the most extreme in the Reformation period. Not only Schmid himself but his followers too were blessed with a flood of visions and inspirations. Soon the theologians referred to these men and women as Träumer, or "dreamers." The Spirit spoke to the Dreamers partly through visions, and partly through voices. Most of the visions occurred at night during sleep. In this way the crucified Lord had appeared, naked and displaying the stigmata, to Schmid; at other times God came to him in the form of an ordinary man, such as the district official of Baiersdorf, a peasant, a miller, or another acquaintance. Some Dreamers, however, were poorly named, for they did not believe in dreams and visions but claimed to follow the voice of the Spirit of God.

While admitting that Schmid had launched the whole movement, his followers nevertheless contended that God alone had opened their eyes. The voice they heard was the same that had spoken to Abraham and Jacob, and later to the apostles. One Dreamer made a more sober statement to the effect that as long as the theologians differed among themselves, the Dreamers had to rely on the voice of God as their only guide. God gave the Dreamers absolute certainty. If the voice had told you to rise against the authorities, the theologians asked, would you have followed it? Schmid himself said yes, but his followers said no. One argued that caution was necessary, for the meaning of the voice was not always clear.

All Dreamers, however, heeded the urging of the Spirit on one point: sex. Indeed, it was not their extreme spiritualism but their new conception of marriage that distinguished the Dreamers from the Anabaptists. The Spirit had revealed to these men and women that their present marriages were sinful because in choosing their spouses they had followed not God's voice but only lust. Now the Spirit revealed to both the married and the unmarried whom they should wed. Some Dreamers confessed that they were disturbed by this urging of the Spirit. Hans Schmid himself claimed that at first he would rather have had his head cut off than let his wife sleep with another man. A woman confessed how angry she had been when her husband had had intercourse with another woman—in her very presence, it appears. One and all, however, submitted to what they believed was the will of God. Altogether, sixteen men and women were wed by the Spirit and several times engaged in sexual relations. Couples who were already married did not simply separate, but continued to live together without sexual intercourse.

A point remains unsolved: how are we to explain that a married man and a married woman living in separate villages both claimed that God's voice had told them to marry one another? If they had merely been following their own inclinations, several of the couples already married would certainly have remained together. In some cases, at least, Schmid himself suggested the new arrangements to his followers. For example, only after he had revealed to his maidservant that she was to be his true wife was this girl urged at night by the Spirit to yield to him.

In Franconia we also find a trait that had appeared among the spiritualists in Switzerland: some Dreamers referred to themselves as God and the root of David. The Dreamers were convinced, too, that the end of the world was drawing near. But if Schmid proclaimed that God would renew the world, this conviction never implied to him the use of physical force. Revolutionary ideas would have required a degree of rational thinking of which Schmid and his followers were hardly capable. Schmid lived in a world of spiritual fantasy. God, he believed, would call those who obeyed the Spirit: they would run toward Him like the sunshine and be glorified in Him eternally. Similarly, the Dreamers were not the sort to concern themselves over such questions as community of goods.

Hans Schmid was arrested at Uttenreuth in April 1531, after protesting against a mandate concerning Anabaptists. The government realized in making this arrest that they had discovered a sect "never before heard of." On June 10, 1531, Schmid and two other prominent members were put on trial and sentenced to death. Other Dreamers were expelled, some after receiving sentences of flogging.

Though the doctrines and practices of the Dreamers were different from those of the Anabaptists, they must be placed against a background of Anabaptism. At least nineteen Dreamers had formerly been Anabaptists, including Hans Schmid himself. Hut had preached in Uttenreuth at the house of a prominent

Dreamer, Hans Strigel. Marx Maier of Alterlangen and the Kerns of Crainthal were arrested as Anabaptists as late as the summer of 1530, Meir being a well-known Anabaptist leader. But within a few months or even weeks, Meir became a Dreamer and engaged in sexual relations with his new wife. Evidently the change was not abrupt but gradual.

The extravagant spiritualism of the Dreamers was probably prompted by Hut's talk of dreams and revelations. The demand for truly spiritual wedlock may be related to the peculiar views on marriage held by the Anabaptists in Thuringia. Elements of Hut's eschatology also lingered on in the thinking of the Dreamers. Of course, there was also a pathological element in the behavior of this sect. Some Dreamers were given to hallucinations. Walking home from a neighboring village at night, one Dreamer suddenly had visions of light and heard a voice admonishing him to stay on the right path. A woman saw in the sun a great eagle that then changed into a human face encircled in blood. As at St. Gallen, the aberrations in the area of Erlangen arose shortly after the suppression of Anabaptism. Maybe imprisonment and torture had made these people susceptible to an ecstatic type of piety.[106]

Occasionally spiritualistic tendencies also appeared among the genuine Anabaptists in Thuringia. The leader Jakob Storger thought highly of dreams that had a bearing on the gospel and believed in Müntzer's doctrine of the Inner Word; possibly Müntzer's disciples injected the spiritualistic tendency into Thuringian Anabaptism. Many Thuringian brethren said they had been taught by God Himself, not by man.[107] One woman who was wondering whether to accept baptism suddenly heard a voice from heaven when she was all alone in the forest. "Do not be afraid: I will guard you as a hen her chick."

In Thuringia the Anabaptist emphasis on the working of the Spirit also seems to have contributed to the rise of two ecstatic groups, the so-called Anabaptists in the area of Spahl and the Bloodfriends in the area of Mühlhausen. We do not know the origin of the group at Spahl, but they had had contact with the Anabaptist leaders Niklaus Schreiber and Melchior Rinck.[108] When in the early morning of March 25, 1532, the Monday before Easter, forty believers were apprehended by the abbot of Fulda's officers at a house in Spahl, they put up a formidable defense, resorting to cheeses when they ran out of ammunition and stones to throw. Among these Anabaptists were thirteen women, who it was said fought even more "devilish" than the men. During the battle three Anabaptists were killed by the officials, and three others mortally wounded, among them the preacher and "captain." The others, all of whom were also wounded, were imprisoned at Fulda. The abbot reported on March 25, 1532, that they were quite happy, singing and looking forward to Whitsun, when they believed some extraordinary event was bound to happen.

Four weeks later, on April 28, 1532, the abbot expressed his amazement at the wild and ecstatic piety of these people. To be sure, the bad air in the dungeon, the circumstances of deprivation, and emotional excitement partly explain their strange behavior, but these Anabaptists had been given to ecstatic experiences even before their arrest. On the very day of their arrest, for that matter, one of them had performed miracles to prove that he was a prophet. He claimed that he would turn water into wine as God had done, and indeed, all his followers swore he had succeeded. He had cured a beggar woman who was afflicted with leprosy by opening her mouth, blowing into it, and saying, "Be pure within and without"; and his followers had shouted, "She is pure." Some believers had fallen down as if dead and then were resuscitated by the prophet—a phenomenon reminiscent of the "dying" at St. Gallen.

In prison, when one of the believers was moved by the Spirit in the middle of the night, he would wake up all the others: "Brothers, arise, the Comforter is nigh." If one of them did not at once rise to his feet, the others would rush at him. Then they would cry out: "He who is to come for us is nigh"; "I see him, I

see him"; "How splendid is his light." Some believers would see
several stars, others a half-moon and lights as bright as fire. Then
they would suddenly be thrown to the ground by the Spirit, lie
there without moving a limb, and shout whatever the Spirit told
them to. One would howl like a dog; another would roar like
an ox; a third low like a cow or neigh like a horse. Some also
sang. "Whoever has not heard it would not believe this. I have
heard it so much that it is still in my head day and night," the
abbot wrote. Asked what the howling meant, some of the prisoners later said that the prophet had started and the others had
joined in. Sometimes men and women who were imprisoned together would kiss, declaring that God had ordered them to do
so. Or an old woman would shake a leper's rattle and they
would all dance and cry out, and after a while grow calm again.

We hear little of the actual doctrines of these Anabaptists because they apparently would divulge nothing, even under torture. According to the abbot they declared that their belief was
divine and Christian, and asked God only that their enemies be
enlightened. They recognized no lord or government but God,
and intended to hold all their property in common. To the abbot
their views seemed the same as those of the rebellious peasants
of 1525. He noted with surprise that the Anabaptists were asking
for death and accepted it happily, singing and laughing as if
they were going to a dance.

A spiritualistic sect of a different nature was discovered in the
area of Mühlhausen and Langensalza in 1551.[109] During the
1530s and 1540s this area was one of the centers of Thuringian
Anabaptism: about sixty persons in fifteen towns and villages
joined the sect. Among them was one Claus Ludwig, a peasant
in the village of Tüngeda. Ludwig refused to have his children
baptized and professed Anabaptist doctrines, though he himself
had not been rebaptized. Twice he fled to avoid having to recant. Arrested for the third time in 1546, he once more regained
his freedom when the Smalcaldic War broke out. Ludwig had
wandered about as a bagpiper. Later he claimed that while he

was in the house of an Anabaptist at Gierstädt, God had revealed to him that the Anabaptist teachings were wrong. Indeed, in January 1551 a commission of ministers reported that he was utterly opposed to Anabaptism. The honest pastors had not noticed, however, that he carefully kept his real views to himself.

We do not know when Ludwig conceived his ideas. He may have gathered a following as early as 1541. At any rate, in the 1540s rumors of secret orgies began circulating in the villages around Mühlhausen. At first the theologians dismissed them as mere gossip. In or about 1550, however, there fell into their hands a letter written by an apostate member of the sect, the pastor Sebastian Thiele, to his former fellow brethren. A pamphlet written by a second defector, Adam Weiss of Langula, must have increased suspicion. In the late summer of 1551 the first arrests were made. Altogether, 54 Bloodfriends, as these sectarians called themselves, were discovered in the following weeks. The villages of Langula and Kraula proved to be the centers of the movement. Other heretics were discovered in the city of Mühlhausen itself and in several nearby villages. At least three members of the sect were executed in 1551, and the rest apparently recanted before being released. There was one man, however, whom the authorities never succeeded in arresting—Claus Ludwig.

Like Hans Schmid, Ludwig lived in a world of ecstatic experiences. He thought of himself as Christ, the Son of God, who would bring justice to the world. The two and one-half years had passed after which, according to the Book of Daniel, the divine kingdom would be established (Daniel 7:12 and 25).[110] Everything would change. It had been revealed to Ludwig that he was to exterminate the godless with Gideon's sword and liberate the faithful. Following the Lord's word he had already chosen twelve judges among his disciples and elected the woman who, dressed in the Sun, would bear the future judge of all peoples, the Son of God. Ludwig also thought his adherents had reached a state that distinguished them from the rest of mankind.

He taught them that neither the sword nor the plague could do them any further harm. Their women would bring forth children without pain. Above all, the reborn could no longer be tainted by sin. "You claim," one of his former followers said, accusing Ludwig, "that you are without sin and cannot sin, as God cannot and does not sin." Several of Ludwig's followers, when brought before the theologians, said that they were sinless. Indeed, they regarded all inclinations and desires that are commonly called sinful as promptings of the Holy Ghost.

Through Ludwig, his followers believed, the law of the Old Testament had been abolished. The saved had attained true freedom, particularly sexual freedom: marriage had no foundation in either the Old or the New Testament. Since one who was reborn could not be touched by sin, he was free to engage in sexual relations with any saved woman. Indeed, the sexual act played an important role in the life of the reborn, for it was considered an outward sign of being received into the community of the saved. Ludwig therefore called the sexual act "Christierung." But sexual intercourse was even more than a rite of initiation; it was an act of sanctification. A woman who willingly mated with a saved man was thereby made completely free. She even became purer than she had been before. Ludwig and his followers rejected the sacraments of baptism and communion, too, as having no basis in the Bible. There was only one true sacrament: the sexual act. Man was the bread; woman, the wine. Children born of the mating of the saved would be holy.

In spite of this breakdown of ordinary morality, there were definite rules in force within the group. The brethren were obliged to render strict obedience to Ludwig. He even imposed penalties on them, such as living on bread and wine, until he had forgiven their sins. It was he who initiated a new member into the meaning of true Christianity. Thus he seems to have been the first to have sexual intercourse with each new female member.

At the meetings, which were usually attended by six to fifteen couples, Ludwig would first read from the Bible. After he had concluded his lecture, always with the words "Be fruitful and multiply," the brethren took to sexual intercourse. The holy mating did not occur only at these meetings, however. Prompted by the Spirit, an individual brother sometimes visited the wife of a fellow believer to celebrate the rite of sanctification with her. Of course, the husband of this woman knew what the two were doing. One of the Bloodfriends later confessed that he had had sexual intercourse with sixteen sisters. Since sexual relations were considered a rite of initiation and sanctification, however, the reborn had intercourse with each brother or sister only once. Married couples went on living together and brought up the children born of the "Christierung."

Ludwig told his followers to attend church services and even to take part in the communion service in order to avoid suspicion. He also advised them to deny all rumors about their sexual practices vigorously. Lying and fraud were not sins for the reborn. According to Ludwig, too, the saved must own all property in common: thus his followers should sell their homes and fields, and hand the money over to him.

Though we do not know where Ludwig had received the inspiration for his strange doctrines, they are basically identical with the doctrines of the medieval heresy of the Free Spirit. But Anabaptism also played a part: Ludwig and three of his followers had been Anabaptists or close to Anabaptism, and some of the Bloodfriends later became Anabaptists. While the Anabaptists cannot be held responsible for the aberrations of the Bloodfriends and the group at Spahl, it seems doubtful that these ecstatic sects would ever have sprouted up if the Anabaptists had not first prepared the soil.

After the 1530s Anabaptism in south and central Germany and Switzerland was largely free of ecstatic tendencies, possibly because the disaster of the Kingdom of Münster had a dampening effect. For whatever reason, only a few believers still had spiritualistic experiences. In 1541, for instance, a woman of

Augsburg had two visions of Christ in which she received orders
to run through the streets shouting, "Change your ways, for
God will punish the world." Quite properly fearing that she
might be taken for a lunatic, she instead conveyed the message to
the pastors.[111] Sometimes believers who had lain in prison for a
long time or suffered personal tragedies were susceptible to
similar experiences.

In summary, a spiritualistic tendency can be detected in Anabaptism from its very beginnings at Zurich. Though the overwhelming majority of Anabaptists never had ecstatic experiences,
the evidence shows that some individuals and groups in Switzerland, Swabia, Franconia, and Thuringia were affected by religious frenzy during the 1520s and 1530s. In four areas—St. Gallen, Erlangen, Spahl, and Mühlhausen—Anabaptist spiritualism
engendered highly ecstatic groups that ended, however, by devi-
ating from Anabaptist doctrine. These groups came into existence only after the genuine Anabaptist movement had been
suppressed by force.

Daily Life

Anabaptism was not just a set of doctrines and practices to be
followed; it deeply changed the life of the believer. In this sense
Anabaptism was not only a religious but also a social phenomenon. The change demanded of the believer implied first separation from the world, and second, a new way of life.

The world was utterly corrupt. The believer therefore had to
withdraw from it—from all popish and antipopish (Lutheran or
Zwinglian) works and services, from assemblies, church attendance, inns, sureties, and obligations of unbelief. And separate
the Anabaptists did, from Catholics because of their idols, from
Lutherans because of their ungodly life. Thus a gulf suddenly
opened between the Anabaptists and their former friends, relatives, and neighbors. Those who refused to accept baptism were
heathens, infidels, worldlings, vain devils, Satan's parishioners,
godless people, sows and dogs, goats on the left hand of Christ,

Turks and Tartars.[112] They were the stinking flesh, while the brethren were "God's spirit."

In various places such as St. Gallen, Strasbourg, Heilbronn, Dinkelsbühl, Schwäbisch Hall, and Thuringia, people observed with stupefaction that suddenly the Anabaptists no longer greeted unbaptized people, but "shuffled on with their mouths shut" like dumb oxen.[113] Some Anabaptists apparently thought it a mortal sin to touch their felt hats when passing an official. Whether or not people greeted their neighbors was held to indicate whether or not they were Anabaptists.

Why did the Anabaptists pursue this eccentricity? According to Kessler, the chronicler of St. Gallen, some brethren who strictly followed Grebel took the first epistle of Saint John as their text: if they greeted heathens, they would make themselves guilty of the heathens' sins. Other brethren, who rejected the doctrine of free will, argued that they might not wish another a good day lest God intended it to be otherwise. But the Anabaptists were unlikely to continue this odd behavior all through the sixteenth century, and even the Hutterites eventually modified it. The clergy, of course, were still entirely ignored: one impetuous Hutterite even refused to shake hands with his own stepbrother, who was a Lutheran pastor, or to the Anabaptist way of thinking, a "false prophet." However, the brethren were allowed to greet ignorant heathens, that is common people, by wishing them God's aid or by a similar salutation.

The Anabaptists divorced themselves strictly from the social life of their neighbors. They did not go to weddings, christenings, convivial gatherings, banquets, or archery matches. If they sometimes frequented bathhouses, they were unhappy with their company: one brother at Basel angrily protested that the other bathers were alternating filthy language with psalm singing. Hutterites who were employed as maids and servants in the houses of the Moravian nobility even refused to prepare hens, geese, and other food for weddings, marriage negotiations, or feasts, for these celebrations were invariably the occasion for overeating, heavy drinking, dancing, and all manner of mischief.

In 1526 the Anabaptists at Zurich criticized the town council for permitting such worldly frivolity as dancing. In later years other people sometimes made fun of the Anabaptists' adamant refusal to dance. The Anabaptists were not against the use of alcohol, but drank wine and beer in moderation. Of course, some drank too much.[114] Like many of his contemporaries, Riedemann condemned the custom of standing drinks. Ordinarily the Anabaptists did not play with dice or cards, but an Anabaptist at Augsburg mentioned in 1528 that he had gambled.[115] The brethren refrained from making obscene, malicious, or mocking remarks. Fornication occurred among them only rarely.[116] One man in Franconia who at first had been incensed by the rebaptism of his sons was not long in perceiving that they no longer cursed, fought, or went out dancing, but stayed soberly at home. As a result he and his wife also accepted baptism. But there were also Anabaptists who were simply unable to lead such a strict life as their leaders demanded, and consequently ceased to attend the meetings.[117]

Naturally the Anabaptists had some contact with their neighbors, as for example when they worked in fields or workshops, or went to the market. Otherwise they seem to have returned to the world only for purposes of charity, such as visiting the sick. Some Anabaptists worried about the social or economic effects of their radical separation from the rest of the community. When a man at Grossenbach was told to stop going to church and social gatherings, and instead to stay at home and praise God, he replied: "I am a poor fellow. If I separate from the world like this, how am I going to live? Nobody will bring me any work." The leader told him not to worry: he had more than he needed, and the End would come soon.[118]

The Anabaptists did not just reject the old forms of behavior, but developed new ones. Kessler reports that one Anabaptist leader in the areas of St. Gallen and Appenzell in 1525 had a rather unusual view of the Christian life. Since Christ had said,

"Whosoever shall not receive the kingdom of God as a little child shall not enter therein," [119] this leader urged his followers to behave like children. That is exactly what they did, especially the women. They would jump and clap their hands, sit about naked and let themselves be washed like children, throw apples at each other, and trail fir cones on the ground with a string. This strange behavior was limited to St. Gallen, however, if indeed Kessler's report is true at all.[120]

The Church Order of 1529 enjoined the believers not to behave frivolously in word or deed: they were daily to expect the suffering of the cross. Not surprisingly, there was a tone of seriousness in the behavior of the Anabaptists. One Anabaptist leader said that most believers could be recognized by their plain behavior, though he admitted that a criminal could also feign humility. When Anabaptists traveled on roads or rivers, they frequently engaged in pious conversations. Sometimes people were surprised when someone who did not talk or dress like an Anabaptist turned out to be one.

Many people admired the fine life of the Anabaptists. A Lutheran woman described them as a saintly and pious people. When one Anabaptist fugitive returned to his village, the people greeted him joyously: some said it was as if they saw the Lord Himself. Their pastor reported indignantly that the villagers would not allow him to be punished.[121] The strict bearing of the brethren became almost proverbial. Some people were suspected of being sectarians because they led calm and quiet lives or prayed ostentatiously before meals. A girl who for psychopathic reasons habitually avoided people became a suspect.[122] Conversely, the officials in one village assured the superintendent that a certain man could not be an Anabaptist, since he was as envious as anybody on two feet. To clear someone of being an Anabaptist, one only had to prove that he cursed, danced, drank heavily, started quarrels, or beat his wife.[123]

The Anabaptists did not fail to point to the paradox in their persecution. For as long as they were dissolute, quarrelsome, and

gluttonous, they were left in peace; but when they obeyed
Christ's commandments, they were punished. If a reprobate were
to desert the Hutterite community for a tavern, where he could
drink, sing bawdy songs, gamble, and dance; if he stuck a feather
in his hat and wore big frills around his neck; if he cursed and
wished syphilis on others, he was at once welcome in the world.
People would tell him he had done well to leave the brethren and
become a true Christian, and must not let himself be seduced
again.[124]

Some pastors and theologians admitted that the Anabaptists
led quiet, impeccable, and honorable lives, at least in the eyes of
the world. But they inveighed against the piety of the Anabaptists as Pharasaic hypocrisy, and feared lest simple-minded people
should be seduced by it. "Do not be deceived," Jacob Andreä
preached, "if an old Anabaptist leader appears, wearing a shabby
old coat and a felt hat with his hair sticking out of the crown
and bowing as if he were almost collapsing with holinesss. Un-
derneath these fellows are proud and arrogant, condemning all
people, even those whom they have not even seen." Martin
Bucer, too, looked sadly on the moral rigor of the Anabaptists.
Heresy, he said with fine understanding, is not this or that fantasy or doctrine, but the ambition to be better and more pious
than the people in the church. This ambition led these people to
form their own special sect. Their untimely severity and contempt for the goods of the world, which does not really help
anyone, is an old bait of Satan.[125] Amused by the Anabaptists'
manifestations of saintliness, some pastors apostrophized them—
"O new Christians"—or offered congratulations on their second
baptism.[126] To be sure, any endeavor toward saintliness leads
easily to hypocrisy, and some Anabaptists had a high regard indeed for their own virtue, maintaining that since they had left
the world and accepted baptism, they had not consciously committed any sin.[127]

The Anabaptists strongly repudiated all forms of fashion and
luxury. In 1525 some women at St. Gallen cut off their hair

around their ears, as men did, because they had suddenly realized that curling it was a form of arrogance. Similar zeal animated the German and Austrian brethren. In 1529, for example, the Austrian leader Wolfgang Brandhuber fulminated against anklets, fancy dress caps, collars, bracelets, ribbons, fine clothes with wide lace trimmings, pomanders, curling tongs, rings and front brooches, festive dress, hats, veils, ornamental hairpins, mirrors, fine shirts, and light summer skirts. Anabaptists repeatedly burst into angry words when they came across modish apparel. One leader ordered a girl to take off her jewelry and hair ribbons and start a new life. Anabaptists at Basel were indignant when Oecolampadius told them that people who wore gold and velvet could be saved as well as those who had just a coarse linen blouse.[128] As the sixteenth century wore on, however, some brethren seem to have abandoned this excessive zeal and accepted the fashions of their age. The Swiss leaders assembled at Strasbourg in 1568 thus made it a point to order that "tailors and seamstresses should abide by the plain and simple style." Still, many Anabaptists were not modest enough. In 1591 the leaders considered it necessary to remind the brethren that luxury was a sign of the world.

What, then, did Anabaptists wear? In 1529 it was reported that refugees from Strasbourg, Memmingen, and Augsburg who gathered not far from Augsburg had beards and wore long black robes.[129] As a rule, however, the brethren wore a simple version of the ordinary clothes of their age. This practice was in no way intended as a social statement—to demonstrate solidarity with the poorer classes, for example—but simply another aspect of the Anabaptists' rejection of the sinful world. A believer could expect to enter the Kingdom of God clad only in humility, not in caps and voluminous robes.

While the Swiss Brethren, the Anabaptists in Thuringia, and the Hutterites had strong views on dress, a few Anabaptists thought that this question was really unimportant. No less a leader than Hut maintained that God had never ordered believers to dress simply. Marbeck's friend Georg Probst of Augsburg was unable to understand why the Swiss Brethren of Appenzell forbade weavers to produce colored or unusual cloth.[130]

Another characteristic that separated some Anabaptists from the rest of the community was their unusual way of praying. The small group of Anabaptists that lived in a house behind Halberstadt cathedral in 1534 and 1535 would pray and sing four times a day, before and after meals, and rise twice during the night to praise God. When reciting the Lord's Prayer they prayed not for "daily bread," but for "true bread" (*wahrhafftig Brot*); and in reciting the Apostles' Creed they said that Christ suffered not "under Pontius Pilate," but "under the covenant of Pilate." Villagers at Kleineutersdorf near Orlamünde also observed in 1535 that an Anabaptist miller held strange ceremonies with his children before and after meals.

Like other revolutionaries, the Anabaptists developed a new jargon. As we have seen, many called their ministers *vorsteher*, a term that was not commonly used. Jörg Nespitzer went even still further, calling himself an *einschliesser*, or "one who includes," and baptism "an agreement to and inclusion under the chastisement of the father." A brother at Augsburg used a new term for baptism: a man was not baptized but testified (*bezeugt*).[131]

The Anabaptists referred to their fellow believers as brothers and sisters and addressed them in the second person singular, the familiar "thee" or "thou." While these customs hardly seem surprising, the Anabaptists' contemporaries were amazed by their strange new talk. Asked where she was from, one woman at Augsburg said that according to the flesh she was from Lauingen, but according to the spirit, from God. Some Anabaptists in northern Thuringia, the Tirol, Moravia, and Switzerland also modified the traditional terms of family relationship. The wife was called the "sister after the spirit," "sister after the flesh," or "conjugal sister." The husband was the "conjugal brother." The real father was in heaven: here on earth one had only a fleshly or a worldly father. We hear, too, of a "brother after the external birth" and a "brother-in-law after the flesh." One man near Orlamünde even called his daughter "sister," and she called him "brother." [132] The Anabaptists near Orlamünde also insisted that they did not have any more friends or relatives in the world. When a prison guard reminded one of them that he had been his godfather, the Anabaptist replied morosely that the guard might be the devil's godfather, but not his.

According to some Catholic authors the Anabaptists gave harmless-sounding names to the grosser vices. To get drunk was termed "to be overwhelmed with surprise" (*überzucken*). Or the Anabaptists would say of a drunkard, "He is tired; he is weak." To steal was called "to encounter something" (*begegnen*). Adultery, unchastity, and fornication were referred to as "being fresh and overconfident." [133] Possibly these euphemisms were simply derivations from the various dialects.

Mindful of the peasant uprising, the officials often inquired whether the Anabaptists had watchwords, signs, or special formulas by which they recognized each other. In fact, the brethren did have special ways of greeting each other. At Augsburg, Esslingen, Heilbronn, and Strasbourg, and in eastern Hesse, a believer would say, "The peace of the Lord be with you," to which the other believer would reply, "Amen," or "And with your spirit," or "May God thank you for it." There were still other formulations.[134] In remembrance of Saint Paul certain Austrian brethren used the sacred kiss. In 1568 the Strasbourg leaders also decided that the brothers and sisters should receive one another with the kiss of the Lord. The Anabaptists of Thuringia also had formulas of blessing when they parted from one another.[135] The Hutterite leader Riedemann took the business of greeting very seriously indeed. Both the person who greeted and the one who was being greeted had to be "children of peace." This custom possibly explains why so many Anabaptists refused to greet nonbelievers. The Hutterites shook hands and embraced each other, if they were of the same sex;

otherwise they only wished each other peace and shook hands, without embracing.

Some Anabaptists in Thuringia, the Tirol, and perhaps also the Neckar basin and the Black Forest used to carry staffs when they traveled. According to a Thuringian brother, this custom signified that all weapons should be melted down.[136] Yet carrying staffs probably did not become a general custom, for the believers obviously would have betrayed themselves in this way. Indeed, the Hutterite Chronicle says that when someone walked with only a staff in his hand, he was suspected of being an Anabaptist.

The Anabaptists not only rejected the traditional feast days as Catholic inventions but also advanced strange views concerning Sunday. Anabaptists in Franconia, Thuringia, the Tirol, and southwest Germany and the Hutterites in Moravia maintained that there was no difference between Sunday and the other days of the week. God had never forbidden working on Sunday, and as a matter of fact, Christ had done most of His work on the Sabbath. One should celebrate Sunday by desisting from sin. The refugees at Halberstadt explained that whatever sins one had committed during the week, one should repent on Sunday: indeed, the word for Sunday, Sonntag, derived from "sonen," or "to repent." The Christian was free to worship on Sunday or not.[137] There is no evidence, however, that it was the general rule for Anabaptists in Germany, Switzerland, and Austria to work on Sunday.

Following Luther and Zwingli the Anabaptists also repudiated the Catholic fasting rules. The believer could eat any food at any time, whether it was bread, meat, fish, eggs, milk, or wine; but of course he must always eat with moderation. He should not bless the food, for it had already been blessed by God.[138] As might be expected, those Anabaptists who were especially pious rejected certain dishes as too worldly. In 1540 a brother even criticized the Hutterites for raising and consuming pigeons.

A special problem for Anabaptist women was finding some-

one to attend them in childbirth, for midwives were the first to
know if parents refused to have their children baptized, especially when the children were weak and would ordinarily be
baptized hastily. A woman of Augsburg admitted that she had
never been attended by a "sworn midwife," yet refused to name
the woman who had assisted her. Since unlicensed midwives ran
the danger of severe punishment, they were hardly likely to
inform the authorities if an Anabaptist woman left her child
unbaptized. There were also Anabaptists who employed the
official midwife but bribed her to say that the child had been
weak and baptized privately, though in reality it had not been
baptized at all. Some Anabaptist women adopted the simple
expedient of giving birth in another village—we may assume in
the house of a fellow believer—returning to their own village in
due course. In 1530 a burgher informed the Strasbourg town
council that eleven children had been born during the preceding
year in a neighboring house that was greatly frequented by
Anabaptists.[139]

Naturally the authorities were alarmed when a midwife herself held Anabaptist views, for she might dissuade parents from
having their newly born children baptized. Such an incident indeed occurred at Thurnen near Bern. On occasion Anabaptist
midwives were forbidden to practice their craft, but often a
shortage of skilled women took precedence over objections to a
midwife's views.[140]

Blaurock said in 1525 or 1526 that he had nursed the sick and
buried the dead. Where did he bury them? A brother in the
village of Neerach held the earth to be free and buried his
deceased wife in a meadow behind his barn. Around 1529 the
Anabaptists at Esslingen also buried fellow believers "under a
tree without having a special burial service." Repeatedly Anabaptists in southwest Germany were interred without ceremonies, and even in vineyards.[141] Why? The reasons are simple
enough. Since they repudiated church ceremonies, the Anabaptists could hardly ask the clergy to officiate at burials. Perhaps

more tellingly, the governments prohibited pastors from burying
Anabaptists in the cemetery. In 1530, for example, the priest at
Bauerbach in Speyer refused to bury a girl who had died of the
plague. Her father therefore buried her in his garden. In the same
village the body of a maidservant who had rejected the Sacrament on her deathbed was carted to the cemetery and dumped
at the wall. Someone then dragged the body to the grave. The
authorities at Speyer ordered that in both cases a penalty should
be imposed unless the corpses were disinterred and buried elsewhere.[142] In Kempten, Anabaptists had to be buried under the
gallows. To avoid this humiliation the Anabaptists buried their
dead in their houses, in sheds, in fields, and in "culinae," special
burial places for the poor.[143] Annoyed by these strange burials,
their Catholic neighbors frequently asked the authorities to give
the Anabaptists a special burial ground. Only rarely were
Catholic governments lenient: in 1572 at Solothurn the officials
permitted the burial of an Anabaptist on his own property,
"though they had good reason to bury him under the gallows." [144]

At least some Protestant governments were tolerant. The officials at Bern allowed Anabaptists to be buried in cemeteries in
1541, for they did not want to interfere with God's judgment.
In Protestant Württemberg the Anabaptists were also buried in
the cemetery, but without either funeral orations or the passing
bell. These omissions were of no very great consequence to the
brethren: they knew the lack of burial ceremonies would hardly
affect their salvation.[145]

The Anabaptist congregations consisted not of sinless saints
but of men and women with frailties and weaknesses. Still, the
Anabaptists formed a religious elite. They took a much more
serious view of worship, baptism, exclusion, and the Lord's Supper than the average Protestant or Catholic. They displayed admirable qualities in their personal lives: an independent mind,
genuine piety, a vigorous moral sense, immense courage, and a

willingness to suffer for their faith. People of these superb qualities were surely a great loss to the Catholic and Protestant
churches.

If the Anabaptists were so admirable, why did the governments wage a ceaseless fight against them? Two basic considerations point toward the answer. First, a movement cannot be
judged solely by the piety of its members, by their high moral
standards, or by their willingness to suffer hardship or even
death for their ideals; one must also ask what these ideals were.
Second, the Anabaptists did not live by themselves on a remote
island like Thomas More's Utopians, but in the midst of a highly
developed civilization, and one that they opposed on a very deep
level. To the Anabaptists this civilization, however Christian it
claimed to be, was basically unchristian: it had to be changed or
even destroyed to allow the believer to lead a Christian life. In
other words, Anabaptism was not just a religious movement but
in many senses a social one.

7

The Anabaptists
and Society

Were the Anabaptists revolutionaries or even anarchists? We shall first consider those revolutionary tendencies in Anabaptism that appear clear-cut and then ask whether the social teachings of those who may be termed true Anabaptists posed a threat to sixteenth-century society.

Revolution

The Peasant Uprising

Did the Anabaptists incite the peasant uprising of 1524–25 or at least play a leading role in it? Such an influence could have been possible only in Switzerland and the nearby area of Waldshut, for Anabaptism had not yet spread as far as south and central Germany by 1525. There is no evidence whatsoever for the claim by Bullinger and Emil Egli that Anabaptists caused the uprising in the district of Grüningen near Zurich. Much more problematic was the role of Hubmaier at Waldshut. Already in 1525 Hubmaier was accused of having incited the peasants in the Hegau, Klettgau, and Black Forest. But since Hubmaier was not a genuine Swiss Anabaptist, rejecting as he did the political doctrines of Grebel, he cannot be considered a characteristic representative of the Anabaptists in general.

It has recently been said that while Hubmaier sympathized with the peasants, he was by no means a leader in the uprising.[1] He did not compose the Twelve Articles but only approved of them and interpreted them for the peasants. Although copies of two other important documents of the uprising, the Letter of Articles and the Constitutional Draft, were found among his papers at Waldshut, Hubmaier seems very unlikely to have written them, for they reflected not his political views but Müntzer's quite different ones. Even so, Hubmaier's influence cannot definitely be discounted, especially if Müntzer indeed visited Hubmaier at Waldshut in 1524, as Bullinger maintained he did. Hubmaier certainly was much friendlier toward the peasants than Luther, Zwingli, Melanchthon, Brenz, or any other reformer. In any case, it is clear that the Letter of Articles and the Constitutional Draft did not contain specifically Anabaptist demands, and that after the peasant uprising Hubmaier did not favor a general revolution.

If the Anabaptists did not cause the uprising, it is possible that the ideas and the spirit of the rebellious peasants lived on in the Anabaptist movement. Anabaptism is often regarded as a continuation of the Peasants' War. Indeed, in many areas where the peasants had risen in 1525, Anabaptism found numerous adherents in the next ten years: Zurich; Bern; Basel; St. Gallen; the Tirol; upper Austria; the bishoprics of Salzburg, Würzburg, Bamberg, and Speyer; Württemberg; Alsace; the Palatinate; the border areas of Hesse, Saxony, Hersfeld, and Fulda; and in Thuringia the areas of Erfurt, Mühlhausen, and Frankenhausen. The geographical evidence is not entirely satisfying, however. Upper Swabia and parts of Franconia, such as the areas of Rothenburg and Mergentheim, had been centers of the uprising in 1525, but during the following years very few Anabaptists appeared there. Conversely, there had been no uprising in 1525 in Bavaria, lower Austria, and the central districts of Hesse, yet within a few years Anabaptism had gained a wide following in these areas. Could it not have been mere coincidence, then, that the peasant uprising and the spread of Anabaptism occurred in some of the same places? Since both the uprising and the Anabaptist movement affected large areas of Switzerland, the Tirol and south and central Germany, it was inevitable that there

would be some overlapping of the regions involved. Perhaps
more to the point, during the first ten years Anabaptism was
largely centered in cities, that had not been involved in the
uprising. The geographical evidence, then, at best suggests a
certain connection between the peasant uprising and Anabaptism; in no way can it be considered proof.

Thirty-two Anabaptists are known to have taken part in the
peasant uprising, some evidence indicates five more.[2] We may be
certain, however, that there were more than 37 Anabaptists who
had been involved in the uprising. In Franconia, eastern Hesse,
and Thuringia alone, 24 ex-rebels were converted to Anabaptism, three of them, Hans Hut, Melchior Rinck, and Hans
Römer, were to play an important role in the movement. Even
so, there is no evidence that rebels became Anabaptists in great
numbers.

Why should peasants who had participated in the uprising
have been attracted by Anabaptism? The demands of the peasants and the doctrines of the Anabaptists had almost nothing in
common. The peasants were motivated not by an abstract religious principle, such as putting into practice the Sermon on
the Mount, but by a desire for social and economic change.
Although the Twelve Articles contained references to the Scriptures, they did not derive from the Scriptures; the social doctrines of the Anabaptists, on the other hand, derived directly
from the literal interpretation of the New Testament. To be
sure, both the peasants and the Anabaptists stipulated that pastors be elected by the congregation. But whereas the peasants
demanded rights and power, the Anabaptists rejected the notion
of rights and power altogether. If the peasants hated individual
princes and officials, they never for a moment thought of rejecting, as the Anabaptists did, all governments, courts of law,
capital punishment, weapons, and oaths. Political power in itself
was not unchristian to the peasants' way of thinking; it had only
fallen into the wrong hands. For their part, the Anabaptists did
not care who held power or whether that power was justly or

unjustly wielded. Government was unchristian not because the burdens it imposed on the peasants were too heavy but because it was an expression of force—in short, because it was government. If the peasants had seized power in 1525 and put into effect each of the Twelve Articles, the Anabaptists would still have cursed their government as unchristian.

The peasants and the Anabaptists worked on quite different principles, then, and pursued quite different social aims. It must be said, too, that the peasants' program seems far more practical than that of the Anabaptists. The Twelve Articles would have changed the social order, to be sure, but they made no claim to create a paradise. Even the programs developed by the more radical revolutionaries of the Bundschuh Uprisings—Joss Fritz, for example—can be considered capable of realization, though they would have required profound social and political change. But the Anabaptist doctrine that in a truly Christian society government would be replaced by love seems utopian, the wishful thinking of pious intellectuals. At least sixteenth-century officials must have thought so, for if they were not perplexed by the Anabaptist ideas they simply laughed when they heard them.

Recent Marxist historians have maintained that the peasants joined the Anabaptists because they were disillusioned after their terrible defeat in 1525. Indeed, it is possible that the peasants' disillusionment gave a boost to the Anabaptists in some areas. In the summer and fall of 1525 the Anabaptist leaders attracted large crowds in the district of Grüningen, near Zurich, which had been shaken by an uprising the previous spring. Grebel may have tried to ingratiate himself with the peasants there by accusing Zwingli of harboring all manner of cruel schemes against them.[3] By November 1525 no fewer than 103 persons had joined the sect. Though the Anabaptists constituted only a small fraction of the population,[4] many people sympathized with them. On October 8, 1525, a large crowd at Hinwil flatly refused to obey the *landvogt's* order to arrest Blaurock as he stood among them.[5] That the peasants in the district of Grüningen opposed the centralizing policy of the Zurich town council obviously added to the sympathy felt in the district for the Anabaptists, who were persecuted by the same town council. Even the local officials, the twelve *amtleute*, yielded to popular pressure, recommending in October 1525 an impartial disputation between the Anabaptists and the pastors at which, they added, Zwingli should let the Anabaptists speak and not "choke a poor fellow's words in his throat." After the disputation, held from November 6 to November 8, 1525, the Zurich town council even felt it necessary to ask the amtleute formally whether they intended to assist the government in punishing the Anabaptists or to support the disobedient sectarians. As might be expected, the *amtleute* sided with the town council, though differences between the two bodies over local jurisdictional rights sometimes impeded swift measures. In other words, sympathy for the Anabaptists had its limits. The mass of people of Grüningen agreed with the Anabaptists only in their dislike of the town council. When it came to taking sides, the people would not disobey their government for the Anabaptists' sake.[6]

While in some areas the peasants' anger against the government may have contributed to the advance of Anabaptism, there is no evidence to support the Marxist theory that after their defeat the peasants were plunged into hopeless despair and therefore found the Anabaptist doctrine of withdrawal from the world attractive. On the contrary, most peasants stayed squarely in the world. For example, the peasants in the territory of Speyer, who had fiercely fought their rulers in 1525, continued to quarrel bitterly with the Chapter during the following ten years. In the village of Bauerbach the peasants unilaterally rejected the Chapter's rights, refused to pay taxes, held back dues in kind, cut down a forest in order to finance the suits they brought against the government, pestered the government official until he entered a monastery, and violated the mandates by engaging in archery. During these same years, and in spite of government persecution, Lutheranism advanced rapidly in the villages of

Speyer. This fact invalidates further the Marxist theory that after Luther's betrayal in 1525 the peasants were no longer interested in Lutheranism. From the late 1520s onward, Anabaptism also began to appear in the area, and particularly at Bauerbach. The mentality of the Anabaptists contrasted strongly with the restless mood of most peasants. Instead of insisting on their rights, they gathered in small groups to read the New Testament and pray. When threatened by persecution some set out under the cover of night for Moravia; arrested, they let themselves be executed without resistance. Of course, the terrible defeat and slaughter of the peasants in 1525 might have shaken some so badly that they sought comfort in excessive piety. These people may indeed have been receptive to the Anabaptist message of withdrawal. They were exceptions, however, for most peasants were by no means so sensitive.

Thus the evidence—geographic, numerical, ideological, and psychological—does not show a link between the peasant uprising and the Anabaptist movement.

Revolutionary Anabaptists

Although most Anabaptists had nothing to do with the peasant uprising or with a revolutionary movement, there were a number of Anabaptist groups that displayed revolutionary tendencies. These trends centered on Hans Römer in Thuringia, Hans Hut in Franconia, and a group at Esslingen. The revolutionary demands of the peasants in the Tirol probably also influenced the early Hutterite leaders in Moravia, but the Hutterites merit a separate discussion.

Hans Römer, a furrier of Eisenach, had been a companion of Müntzer. He accompanied Müntzer and Heinrich Pfeiffer to Nuremberg in October 1524, preached in the Mühlhausen area after Müntzer's return, and was present at the battle of Frankenhausen. He escaped the massacre and may have joined the peasants of the Bildhausen group. Since he could not return to Eisenach, he then went to Etzleben and Bautzen. His activities in 1526 are not known: he may have fled to Switzerland or to Nikolsburg, or he may have met Hans Hut. He reappeared in 1527 in Thuringia, preaching Anabaptist doctrines and gathering a small circle of followers.[7] Several of these followers had also participated in the peasant uprising in 1525, such as Georg Fuchs, Meister Andreas, Dionysius Mansfeld, and Volkmar Fischer, and it is possible that the common experience of the Peasants' War brought Römer and them together. The disaster of 1525 had certainly not cooled Römer's revolutionary fervor. In 1527 he was still proclaiming that Müntzer and Pfeiffer had been the right teachers and that their execution was an injustice. More important, he and his disciples planned a new uprising.[8]

Römer's revolutionary plans were apparently connected with eschatological speculations. He preached in 1527 that according to Daniel 9 and 12, the end of the world would come in eleven months.[9] Possibly Römer acquired this idea and the idea that baptism had eschatological significance from Hut, but there is no definite evidence. In any case, unlike Hut, Römer was more interested in concrete plans than in eschatology. As a prelude to the general uprising, he planned to seize the city of Erfurt. He may have chosen Erfurt because it was torn by social, political, and religious tensions that had already culminated in a bloody revolution in 1509 and in wild riots in 1521. Römer and his friends won a considerable following in many towns and villages of Thuringia, and Römer even claimed that he had forty adherents in Erfurt. It seems unlikely that these people were aware of what Römer was planning, though he later claimed that all those he had baptized had promised to join him in his attack on Erfurt.

Römer's plan combined shrewd calculation with extravagant expectations. A week before January 1, 1528, he would pin up public letters in ten places in Erfurt announcing his intention to preach at "Our Dear Lady's Mountain" on January 1.[10] Struck with his audacity, the people would assemble to hear him. While Römer was delivering his sermon, four of his disciples, Volkmar

Fischer, Christof Peisker, Niklaus Hofmann, and the pastor of Alpersdorf, would put to the torch four houses inhabited by priests that stood on the Petersberg.[11] While the fire raged, Römer would shout to the crowd that the priests had started it to stifle the Word of God. Niklaus Hofmann would blow on a trumpet and shout, "All ye who stand by the Word of God, step over to this side." Römer was careful to appoint the particular gate by which his followers would burst into the city. They were to assemble at the fish market and then take the town hall by storm, killing the town councilors and seizing control of the city.

What was the aim of this coup? Georg Fuchs and Volkmar Fischer later said that they had intended to exterminate rulers and lords in retribution for the slaughter of the poor and summon the peasants to rise in rebellion. The city of Erfurt would have become the property of the Anabaptists and the rich would have been forced to share with the poor. The Anabaptists would have preached their belief in the whole world and killed those who refused to accept baptism. Römer himself also later declared that he had intended to establish a Christian league. As soon as it had amassed sufficient money, the league was to have purchased arms and stirred the peasants to revolt.

Römer had advised his followers to provide themselves with a stout pair of shoes, a sword, a leather coat, and half a florin for their escape in case the plot should fail. In fact, Römer's plan was discovered by the authorities that same December of 1527, possibly through betrayal. Niklaus Hofmann was arrested no later than December 27, 1527, and executed on January 10, 1528. About fifty Anabaptists and Lutherans in Erfurt and nearby towns and villages were rounded up. Twelve were executed; others were expelled from the city, mutilated, or otherwise punished. But the chief conspirators managed to escape. Römer, Peisker, and Fischer traveled to Basel, where Fischer separated from his companions. He abandoned Anabaptism altogether and went to live in Bohemia. The Erfurt town council did not forget

the revolutionaries, however. Fischer was captured on November 1, 1534, while visiting a village near Erfurt, and probably
executed. Römer was arrested at Göttingen in August 1534.
Peisker may have been arrested at Strasbourg in March 1529.
The depositions of Hofmann, Fuchs, Römer, and Fischer differed on minor points but agreed in all essentials. Although
torture was used in some of the interrogations, Römer and Hofmann are said to have made their statements without being
tortured.[12]

Without having Müntzer's intellectual caliber, Römer had
accepted some of Müntzer's revolutionary ideas. Like the Gideon
of Allstedt, he planned to establish a Christian league and exterminate princes, lords, and priests. Like Müntzer, he seems to
have thought that the godless had no right to live, and planned
to exterminate all those who refused to accept baptism. The idea
of requiring the rich to share with the poor may also have been
suggested by Müntzer. Would Römer really have had a chance
to seize Erfurt? Would the authorities have allowed him to
preach in the city? The conspirators might have started their
fires successfully, but it is hard to imagine that a large mass of
Anabaptists could have marched on Erfurt without being noticed and stopped by the local authorities. Even if the conspirators had seized Erfurt, it is not likely that the peasants would
have responded to a new call for an uprising only two and a half
years after their terrible defeat of 1525. Even so, Römer remains
the outstanding exponent of revolutionary Anabaptism in central
Germany.

While Römer's intentions are clear, those of Hans Hut are
more difficult to understand. Three questions present themselves
in particular. First, what role did Hut play in the peasant uprising? Second, did Hut's eschatology contain the idea of revolution? And third, did Hut's eschatology arouse revolutionary
tendencies in Franconia, Hesse, and southwest Germany?

Like Römer, Hans Hut was well acquainted with Thomas
Müntzer. It was to Hut, a sexton and book peddler of Bibra,
that in 1525 Müntzer entrusted the manuscript of his inflam-

matory treatise "Witness of the First Chapter of the Gospel of Luke," which Hut then had printed at Nuremberg. According to Hut, Müntzer gave him the manuscript because he was a book trader, not because he belonged to Müntzer's sect. Yet it could hardly have been by chance that Müntzer went to Hut and not to any other of the numerous book peddlers. Hut may already have been impressed with Müntzer's theology by 1525. At any rate, his later thinking unmistakably bears Müntzer's imprint.

In 1525 Hut came as a book trader to the peasant army at Frankenhausen. He was quickly arrested by the peasants and released only after Müntzer had intervened. Hut was present when Müntzer preached on the three consecutive days preceding the battle, and like Müntzer he fled into the town of Frankenhausen. There he was seized by Hessian soldiers, who freed him only after he had proved that he was a book trader carrying Luther's writings.

If Hut did not share the views of the peasants before the battle of Frankenhausen, he certainly did afterward. At the end of May 1525 he appeared at Bibra, where the castle of his former lord had been burned down by the Bildhausen peasant army. At the request of Jörg Haug of Juchsen, elected pastor by the peasants, he delivered a sermon on May 30, 1525, dealing with baptism, the Sacrament, idolatry, and the mass. But Hut's sermon was not only religious in nature. He also incited the peasants to rise up against the rulers and kill them: now was the time to revolt, he said, while the sword was in their hands.[13] Later, after his arrest at Augsburg, Hut explained that he had been impressed by Müntzer's view that the Lord had inspired the peasant uprising and that He would appear and exterminate all those who opposed the truth. Hut had been convinced that this moment had indeed arrived. When on June 5, 1525, the armies of the princes occupied Meiningen and approached Bibra, Hut left. There is a report that he then stirred up the peasants in the Würzburg area.[14]

In May 1526, Hut was baptized by Denck at Augsburg, and

within a few months he became the foremost Anabaptist leader in south Germany. Now the peasant uprising appeared to him in a very different light: the peasants had been wrong to rise up in arms.[15] At the same time he continued to proclaim dangerous eschatological ideas that resemble the revolutionary predictions of the Zwickau prophets of 1521.[16] Hut was arrested at Augsburg in September 1527.

During his first interrogations at Augsburg, on September 16 and October 5 of 1527, Hut said the Messianic disasters that according to the Scriptures would precede the Last Day could be observed on every side. Then there would be one fold and one shepherd, as written in John 10:16. He emphasized, however, that the kingdom of God would be spiritual, not material.[17] During the interrogation on November 26, 1527, conducted without torture, Hut went beyond his first statements. God had allowed man forty months in which to repent, and according to Daniel 12 these forty months would be filled with pestilence, famine, war, and the persecution of the faithful. At the end of that time God would gather His people in all countries, and the faithful would punish the authorities and sinners. God would send His angels to the four corners of the earth to gather the elect, for whom there would be a new heaven and earth. In another, undated interrogation, conducted both with and without torture, Hut recalled a sermon he had delivered at Königsberg in 1526. He had told the believers that a Christian could wield the sword, but only at God's command. Although Christians at first would be dispersed and tried, in the end the Lord would appear and gather them in; the saints would punish the sinners. Only those who now did penance would inherit the earth and life everlasting.

Of course, the authorities were deeply disturbed by the idea that at the Day of Judgment, the faithful would punish the authorities and sinners, and take possession of the earth. Was it true that Hut had taught this? Since the statements made at the interrogations might have been induced by long imprisonment or torture, they cannot be accepted as sufficient evidence in themselves. Hut had discussed the end of the world in two treatises, but the little we know of these writings does not conclusively prove that he envisaged revolutionary action by the saints on earth.[18]

During their stormy meetings at Nikolsburg in mid-May of 1527, Hubmaier accused Hut of no fewer than 52 heresies, which he claimed to have culled from Hut's writings. Hubmaier later said that he had charged Hut with inciting rebellion under the pretext of baptism and the Lord's Supper. Hut admitted at Augsburg that Hubmaier had accused him of teaching that the Last Day would occur at a specific date, that the Christians would judge the world, and that power would be taken from the rulers and given to the Christians. But Hut denied having taught the first of these three doctrines and disclaimed the latter two as they were stated. Hubmaier, he said, being envious of Hut's popularity, had distorted the meaning of passages taken from Hut's writings. In short, Hubmaier's charges have nothing further to tell us about Hut's real teachings.[19]

Hubmaier was not the only Anabaptist leader to object to Hut's doctrines. Several believers, among them the leader Hans Leupold, strongly opposed Hut's eschatological doctrines during one of the famous meetings at Augsburg in August 1527; they even left the meeting.[20] Hut himself later admitted that the brethren had not allowed him to speak of eschatology. Finally a compromise was reached: Hut promised to discuss these questions only with those who heartily desired it.[21]

What, then, did Hut teach? Certainly he taught that the end of the world would come in 1528, forty months after the Peasants' War. But did he think of the Day of Judgment in terms of social revolution, as he was accused of doing? Hut's own statements, the remnants of his writings, the accusations of Hubmaier, and the clash at Augsburg do not offer conclusive evidence. It is not clear, for example, exactly what the Anabaptists at Augsburg opposed: Hut's doctrine that the end of the

world was imminent, or his having fixed the time for the end
of the world, or his alleged revolutionary tendencies.

A disciple of Hut, Ambrosius Spittelmaier of Linz, may give
us more insight into his master's eschatology. After his arrest
on September 5, 1527, at Erlangen, Spittelmaier declared that
though God alone knew the year and hour when He would
punish the world, there were signs by which men could recognize whether the end of the world and the Day of Judgment
were near. Such signs were the present wars between empires
and nations and the collapse of popery. The fig tree was in
bloom; therefore summer and the liberation of the godly was at
hand. God would send Turks and the true cross, and the people
would flee in terror. The wealthy would throw their riches into
the streets, put on sackcloth, and feign repentance, but God
would not be satisfied with their pretense. When the end of the
world arrived, the just would gather and slay the godless in the
space of moments. One godly man would slay thousands, and
two would slay ten thousand—a statement the authorities were
particularly worried over. Finally, God would purge the world
through fire, earthquakes, and thunder and lightning. All mortals
would be struck to the ground and destroyed, and Christ would
appear in His glory to judge the quick and the dead. Then all
men would rise with their bodies and souls, the godly to life,
the godless to death.

Clearly Spittelmaier thought of the Last Day in spiritual
terms. The idea that in the end the godly would gather at a
moment's notice and miraculously slay the multitude of sinners
had nothing to do with such a worldly matter as social revolution. In all likelihood Hut's views were in the same vein.[22]

Whatever Hut himself believed, his ambiguous doctrines may
have kindled revolutionary hopes among the peasants and craftsmen in Franconia who less than two years earlier had risen in the
greatest rebellion in memory. A copy of one of Hut's books was
found at Hildburghausen in 1527. In some villages such as
Meeder, Neida, and Walbur in the "Langen Berge," where

either Hut or his disciples preached in 1526 and 1527, the peasants still talked of revolution.[23] Indeed, in February and March 1527, captured Anabaptists of the Königsberg and Staffelstein areas sounded a good deal like revolutionaries when they spoke as if they were planning the extermination of princes, lords, priests, and monks.[24] But these bloodthirsty ideas may well have been suggested to them under torture. It is striking that one Anabaptist in this area denied all such plans even when he faced torture; two, though subjected to torture, made no mention of any ideas of bloody revolution; and a further two expressly repudiated their confessions later. Four of the five Anabaptists in northern Franconia who in February and March 1527 admitted revolutionary plans had assuredly been subjected to torture, and probably the fifth as well. Another five brethren who at Bamberg confessed to the wildest revolutionary schemes, such as strangling the emperor, had just as surely been tortured. In other towns and villages in Franconia where Hut or his disciples had preached we also find mention of invasion by the Turks, the punishment of the wicked, the salvation of the baptized, and the founding of a new kingdom. Yet only one leader went so far as to assign a role in these events to the brethren themselves: according to him the prophet and his small band would pursue the godless to the sea and slay those who had not drowned.[25]

Hut also preached his eschatology in upper Austria in 1527.[26] His two most prominent disciples in Austria and the Tirol, Lienhart Schiemer and Hans Schlaffer, were indeed persuaded in 1527 or 1528 that the Day of Judgment was at hand. Nevertheless, the notion of social revolution was completely foreign to them.[27]

There is no doubt, then, that Hut's doctrines about the end of the world produced a strong echo wherever he preached. By introducing these eschatological ideas into south Germany, Hut in effect damaged the entire Anabaptist movement there irreparably, for the Hapsburg government, shocked by such teachings, responded with savage persecution. Hubmaier well knew what he was doing when he so passionately condemned Hut's doctrines. There is no concrete evidence, however, that the Anabaptists in Franconia and Austria thought of the end of the world as a social revolution. The revolutionary ideas some of them confessed to having could easily have been extracted by torture; we must remember that later in the sixteenth and seventeenth centuries the most grotesque confessions were made during witch trials. Of course, it is equally possible, and equally incapable of certain proof, that revolutionary sentiments still existed among some Anabaptists.

Some of those in eastern Hesse who had taken part in the peasant uprising of 1525 also found their way a few years later to Anabaptism. One of them was Melchior Rinck. Rinck's bitter enemies, Menius and Eberhard von der Tann, maintained that he had even played a leading role in the uprising. He had been a follower of Müntzer, they said, and had fought in the battle of Frankenhausen. Furthermore, they charged, he had never expressed regret over past mistakes and had no intention of abandoning his views: on the contrary, he had often declared that God had helped him escape from Frankenhausen and that he would execute Müntzer's plans. Whether or not his enemies portrayed him accurately, Rinck was at Worms in 1527, meeting Denck and Hätzer, and he was preaching Anabaptist doctrines in the Hersfeld area in 1528 and 1529.

The Hersfeld area had experienced serious disturbances in April 1525. The peasants had banded together at the Petersberg near Hersfeld under the leadership of Hans Plat and Heintz Hutter,[28] both of whom later joined the Anabaptists. Six others from the village of Sorga who had taken part in the 1525 rebellion also accepted Anabaptism. One of them, Gilg Schneider, even became one of the leaders of the large congregation at Sorga. This background explains why some Anabaptists in the area of Hersfeld did not at all condemn the peasant uprising. One woman declared in 1533 that Müntzer's rebellion had been God's work: the poor who had been strangled were innocent martyrs of God, and those who had killed them would soon receive their punishment. Most Anabaptists were more guarded. Ten believers at Sorga, six of whom were former rebels, told the officials that they did not know whether the uprising had been godly or not. Heintz Hutter evaded the issue by saying that he would leave this question to God. The Anabaptist minister Gilg Schneider did not call the uprising either right or wrong, and recommended the rebels to God's mercy. If these Anabaptists refused to denounce the rebels of 1525, they obviously considered the uprising at least partially justified.[29] The Hessian chancellor who conducted the interrogations was painfully surprised by these views. Only six believers at Sorga unambiguously condemned the peasant uprising.

In about the same area not only Melchior Rinck but Jörg of Staffelstein and Niklaus Schreiber preached the imminence of the Last Day in 1528 and 1529.[30] Their ideas were quite similar to those Hut had preached in 1526 and 1527. There is the prediction that a great invading army would come as a scourge though the Turks are not mentioned.[31] There is the warning that the baptized alone would be saved, and the unbaptized thrown into darkness. There is no evidence, however, that the brethren in eastern Hesse expected social revolution. They might better be described as frightened and awed by the impending judgment.[32]

We have observed the ecstatic tendencies in the Anabaptist congregation at Esslingen. This town also seems to have been a center for eschatological brooding. In the early sixteenth century Conrad Stiefel of Esslingen was already predicting a particularly bloody reformation. In the 1520s there was bitter discord at Esslingen between the small vine growers and the wealthy vineyard proprietors. But there is no evidence that these social and political tensions had any influence on the forming of eschatological doctrines. When in 1527 Christof Freisleben, one of Hut's disciples, proclaimed that the Day of the Lord had come, he made a strong impression on the Anabaptists at Esslingen. The leader of the congregation, Lienhart Lutz, who with several of his fellow believers had been expelled from Esslingen and fled to Reutlingen, was greatly excited. In early 1528 Lutz wrote to the believers at Esslingen that God's punishment would appear within half a year. It had been revealed to a sister, who may have been influenced by Hut,[33] that after Candlemas the persecution would sharply increase and last ten weeks. After these ten weeks the believers would be so violently persecuted that they would have to take refuge in rocky places and woods for an additional ten weeks and thirteen days. Then on Sunday, April 26, 1528, two weeks after Easter, the Son of Man would appear to smite His enemies—those who had not abided by His word and law but had said, "It is not necessary that we have ourselves baptized. I have believed; I have been baptized before." [34]

At about the same time a burgher at Esslingen, Mathias Dritschler, also told his friends that the world would end in the summer of 1528. All prophecies had been fulfilled except the one that the rich would throw their silver out of their houses just in order to be left alive. Dritschler said he would not give half a batzen to have a fortune of a thousand florins. He quoted Ezekiel 7, in which terrible punishment is foretold for idolatrous Judah: Judah is threatened by the Babylonians; hunger and plague strike Jerusalem; and the people in despair throw their gold and silver into the streets, for money cannot help them. In Dritschler's interpretation of this passage, the destruction of Jerusalem was equated with the Last Day. Although no particular curse is attached to the rich in Ezekiel, Dritschler predicted that they would be singled out for special punishment.[35] Obviously he hated the wealthy. The Esslingen town council looked on Dritschler as an Anabaptist, but there is in fact no proof that he was one. Nevertheless, the house in Esslingen where he uttered these predictions was that of the Dill family, who were definitely Anabaptists. Dritschler left the city before he could be apprehended. Even so much as a year later, in June 1529, he was refused permission to return.

The town council of Esslingen was sensitive to remarks of a revolutionary nature. Already in 1527 ambiguous and dangerous utterances were being reported; in March 1528 the council at last received information that the Anabaptists were indeed planning revolution and bloodshed.[36] An Anabaptist baker, Hans Pfau, who had left Esslingen before March 8, 1528, confessed during his interrogation at Heilbronn on March 24 that the brethren at Esslingen planned to make their move at Easter and baptize believers in towns, markets, and villages. Private property would be abolished, and all people would be equal. Another Anabaptist, Hans Zuber, who was arrested at Hegensberg, a village near Esslingen, confessed on March 27 that this plan had been made on February 29 at a meeting in Hegensberg of 25 believers. The brethren from the Esslingen area had decided to go to Reutlingen at Easter 1528 and there unite with some seven hundred Anabaptists from Augsburg and Zurich. In the towns they would arm themselves. Then, marching through the country, they would exterminate any civil authorities who resisted and destroy churches and monasteries. All property would be under common ownership, and the rich would share with the poor. Zuber said that on Sunday, March 15, he had separated from the Anabaptists.

The statements of Pfau and Zuber agreed on several points. Both mentioned the same Anabaptists as ringleaders of the conspiracy. Pfau said he had heard of the planned uprising prior to March 8, Zuber said the plan had been made on February 29, and both said the uprising would start at Easter 1528. Both declared that private property would be abolished. Zuber's statements appeared all the more convincing because he outlined more or less correctly the Anabaptist views on infant baptism, the Lord's Supper, auricular confession, and the veneration of the saints and of Mary.

Some of the people mentioned by Pfau and Zuber were immediately arrested at Esslingen. But though all of them were Anabaptists, they all denied knowledge of the alleged plot, even under torture. Were the statements of Pfau and Zuber simply fantasies then? Perhaps they were so badly tortured that they simply invented their stories. But this explanation would depend on the unlikely coincidence that both Pfau and Zuber made similar statements about the participants, the timing, and the methods and aims of the conspiracy even though they were interrogated at different places within three days. Of course, Pfau's statements of March 24 might have been forwarded to the government at Stuttgart, which then would have used them during Zuber's interrogation on March 26 and 27. In this case, however, the Stuttgart government would probably have pointed to the similarity between the statements made by Pfau and Zuber in its correspondence; yet it did not even mention Pfau. Even three weeks later, when faced with possible execution, Zuber took the Sacrament on the truth of his statements. As far as we know, Pfau did not retract his statements either.

Though Pfau and Zuber did not speak of the coming of Christ, they said the uprising was due to begin at Easter, more or less simultaneously, that is, with the return of Christ and the punishment of the godless as foretold by Lutz and his friends at Reutlingen. Pfau and Zuber spoke, too, of the extermination of the authorities and the church, and the abolition of private property—recurring themes in the chiliastic predictions of the time. It seems possible, then, that some Anabaptists at Esslingen did have chiliastic expectations.

During these years, probably before 1530, the authorities at Esslingen also received the prognostication of one Rubius Philippus Cataneus von Thurn.[37] Written in black and red ink, it predicted political events and harvest prospects for the years 1530 to 1550. Showing the influence of the Revelation, it also spoke of the coming of the new kingdom. In 1542 the Jews would rise, only to be suppressed in 1544. The years that followed would be characterized by messianic tribulations. A false prophet would appear, and Christendom would suffer from vice, diseases, and plagues. At last a "very holy man" would arise, and

in 1550 the infidels would be converted to Christianity. "Then
there will be one fold and one Shepherd and Lord, who will
maintain the whole world under His rule, and a golden age will
dawn." The authorities at Esslingen seem to have attributed this
prognostication to Anabaptists, although there is no evidence
that it in fact originated with them. Traces of revolutionary
tendencies also appeared among the Anabaptists in the Rhine
valley, although here again there is no firm evidence.[38]

Ultimately, the revolutionary strains in the Anabaptist movement in Thuringia, and possibly also in Franconia and at Esslingen, lead back to the great radical spiritualists of Thuringia, Thomas Müntzer and the Zwickau prophets. In this sense,
Bullinger's assertion that Müntzer was the father of Anabaptism
contained at least an element of truth. In Thuringia some of
Müntzer's disciples, such as Hans Römer, infected the Anabaptist movement with the hatred and the aspiration that had
characterized the peasant uprising. It was Müntzer's legacy,
indeed, that inspired Römer to plot another rebellion. In
Franconia the same legacy may also have contributed to the
revolutionary elements in the eschatological doctrines of Hans
Hut and his followers. There is no firm evidence, however,
that these Anabaptists really envisaged revolution in any terms
other than spiritual. At Esslingen, if a revolutionary group
indeed existed there, it was again connected to Hut's disciples.
What relation Müntzer's two disciples, Hut and Römer, bore
to each other cannot be stated with certainty, though it is
attractive, of course, to suppose that Hut influenced Römer.

In any event, the groups led by these revolutionaries or
prophets were suppressed by the authorities in 1527 and 1528,
before they could realize their plans for revolution and establish a Kingdom of Münster in south or central Germany. It
must be emphasized that the revolutionary tendencies in south
and central German Anabaptism were limited to the 1520s; in
later years revolutionary plots were totally foreign to the
spirit of Anabaptism. Nevertheless, the authorities remained

apprehensive and alert to the slightest rumor. When, in 1535, a shepherd in Ansbach spread the news of the Kingdom of Münster among the peasants, the margrave ordered his arrest: one does not put straw to fire. Two years later the Hessian chancellor inquired whether the Anabaptists in fact taught that in a short while there would no longer be knights or priests. Even as late as 1555 an Anabaptist from the Kraichgau was asked whether the brethren did not plan the suppression of all authorities once they were strong enough. He replied that no believer would ever entertain such an idea, let alone plot against the government.[39] This being the case, why did the theologians insist all through the sixteenth century that the Anabaptists undermined "church, state, and economy"? [40]

Government, War, Law Courts, and Oaths
The General Doctrine

Manz is reputed to have said in 1525 that there was more behind the rejection of infant baptism than could be revealed: in the end it would eliminate the political authorities.[41] This view was certainly shared by the governments, which accordingly questioned the Anabaptists in hundreds of interrogations on their views of governmental authority. These political questions, except for that of oaths, hardly affected the personal life of the individual believer. Yet most Anabaptists had firm views and did not hesitate to state them before the officials.[42]

The Anabaptists cannot be likened to the nineteenth-century anarchists. Most Anabaptists recognized the state as a divine creation. God had established the magistracy as a punishment for man's sins, and therefore it would exist as long as man was sinful. Government was also seen as an expression of divine love that tried to keep men from destroying each other. Indeed, without government nobody could live safely on earth. The Anabaptists left no doubt that every government, good or bad, had divine sanction. Even the pagan Nero had received his office from God.[43] The task of government was to maintain society by punishing the criminal and protecting the pious. Since governments had been created by God, every Christian was obliged to obey them, even to the extent of obeying a tyrant, for he too maintained a minimum of order. Similarly, princes were to obey their superior, the emperor, rather than rising against him as they had in the Smalcaldic War. The authority of government was limited by the higher authority of God, however. When the government demanded anything contrary to the Lord's command, the Christian was required to refuse. But even in this case the Christian was not to resort to force or rebellion.

Up to this point the Anabaptists and Luther were in perfect agreement. It was on the commandments of the Lord that they differed. First of all, the Anabaptists taught that government authority was strictly limited to secular matters. A ruler who forced his subjects to adopt a certain religion exceeded his authority and became a tyrant. The Anabaptists were horrified at instances such as the Smalcaldic War, where there was the ultimate use of force over questions of belief.

Secondly, the Anabaptists held that God created government and its coercive functions only for fallen and sinful mankind. In the kingdom of God—among Christians—the state had no place. Already in the fall of 1525 the Anabaptists at Zurich insisted that those who were sitting in law courts and town councils could not be Christians. They pointed to the example of Christ, who had refused to be made king or judge. They also explained that government, with its use of force and power, contradicted the spirit of love and pardon that Christ had enjoined upon His disciples. Sinful mankind had to be constrained by force, but the Christian should withdraw and leave the world to itself. When the government officials asked how it was possible that government was unchristian when it had been created by God, the Anabaptists replied that government was like a rod that a father used to chastise his children: finally the rod became useless, and he threw it into the fire. At God's behest, governments punished criminals, but in the end even governments would be damned. When the officials questioned this strange logic further, the Anabaptists thundered, "Man, who are you to dispute with God?"

Holding to the example and commandment of Christ, most Anabaptists refused to carry or use weapons. If the Turks invaded the country, they would defend themselves only with their prayers. If the whole world were of their faith, they pointed out, then all war and injustice would be at an end. The Hutterites and some Anabaptists in Hesse and in the area of Zurich also refused to pay war taxes. War taxes were blood taxes, they said. Other brethren in Hesse, Württemberg, and Bern personally refused to fight and kill but were willing to pay taxes, since they reasoned that the sword had been given to the government.[44]

Many Anabaptists seem to have considered it a sin to go to court, for example to secure the payment of debts. But there was no unanimity on this question either. Two Anabaptists declared at Eisenach in 1537 that a Christian could use intermediaries for lawsuits, though he himself should not make claims in court. In 1564 a Thuringian leader even conceded, though with hesitation, that a Christian might appeal to the law himself. Two of his disciples denied, however, that a Christian might have recourse to the courts; a Christian should entrust his problems to God.[45]

Some Anabaptists in Hesse, Württemberg, the Tirol, and Moravia claimed that it was unchristian to execute a criminal for murder, robbery, or any other crime if he repented and asked for pardon, for a criminal who was executed lost his eternal life also. Of course, unrepentant criminals should be executed.[46] When Hutterites explained this legal philosophy to the theologians, they would simply laugh or look at one another in silence.

The Anabaptists also refused to swear oaths of allegiance or testimony because the Lord had clearly forbidden his disciples to swear. In testifying a Christian would tell the truth anyway. An oath sworn to ensure future action was presumptuous, for no man could keep his promise without God's help. The brethren did admit, however, that the oath was necessary in the world, if not in the Christian world.

The Anabaptist position, then, was that Christ had abolished the power of government, the use of weapons, and the oath only among His disciples. Among non-Christians, that is the non-Anabaptist mass of mankind, these institutions still had their validity. Since even the believers could not entirely separate themselves from society, they too were obliged to assist the government in maintaining order, at least as long as the commands of the government did not violate the commands of God. But there could be no doubt that whoever occupied governmental office, used weapons, took an oath, or sued in court was not a Christian. Swiss Brethren and Hutterites were generally in agreement on these points. A number of believers took a more radical view, however; and a number of others took a more conservative one.

The Radical Minority

There were Anabaptists, especially in Thuringia, who held extreme views reminiscent of the revolutionary movements of the fifteenth and sixteenth centuries. In 1523, only a few years before Anabaptism appeared in western Thuringia, Nikolaus Storch, one of the spiritualists of Zwickau, had hurled violent and inflammatory charges against the ruling classes; he may well have influenced Anabaptist thought. Heinz Kraut, a prominent Thuringian leader, declared in 1535 that Christians had no need of secular authority, even if they lived in a commune, for they were all brothers. Christ had made them free. He did not condemn a government that punished evil. Yet people were making idols of everything, themselves included: they must be addressed as lords, and the cap must be taken off to them, an honor due only to God. Before his execution Kraut looked the official at Weimar, Ewalt von Brandenstein, straight in the eye and recited the old peasant rhyme: "When Adam delved and Eve span, who was then the gentleman?" The rejection of the ruling class in this instance had become part of the Anabaptist ideology.[47]

In the 1540s and again in the 1560s, Anabaptists in the area of Mühlhausen held that government was a purely human institution; it had received its authority from men only, not from God. One woman, a disciple of Müntzer, said that princes and lords had simply usurped their power, and therefore had no right to banish.[48] A few Thuringian Anabaptists even questioned the right of the authorities to levy taxes. If the government rendered her services, a woman said, she would gladly pay taxes and dues. When reminded of Christ's saying "Render to Caesar the things which are Caesar's," she replied that the coin to which Christ had referred had formerly been the property of Caesar.[49] In other words, taxes were just a form of exploitation.

There were also radicals among the first brethren in Switzerland. The leader Krüsi preached at St. Georgen in June 1525 that according to the Word of God, nobody was obliged to pay tithes or the like. When Melchior Degen, a St. Gallen official, attempted to arrest him and others, they told him openly that they had no lord or government other than God: Degen had better take to his heels, or they would teach him how. A stone was thrown, and Degen left. Though Krüsi's account of the confrontation was different, it seems clear that violence was in the air.[50] Another prominent leader, Hans Pfistermeyer, bluntly denied that a Christian could own serfs.[51] Indeed, in the Rhine valley and in Thuringia, some brethren insisted that all men were equal according to Christian law. An Anabaptist craftsman even refused to let himself be called "Master," for there was only one master—God.[52]

Some Anabaptists, such as the Thuringian leader Kraut, the Hutterites, and the brethren of the Kraichgau made a point of treating everyone as an equal, addressing each other with the familiar "thou" instead of the customary "Ihr." Even God, they pointed out, was addressed as "thou" in prayer. A Saxon even argued that only God should be called "Ihr." Some Anabaptists had the impudence to address the government of Zurich as "ye my brethren," or the judges of Zwickau as "dear men and brethren."[53] Anabaptists in upper Austria and the Tirol and the Hutterites denied that a Christian must kneel before the magistrates, call them "gracious, serene, august or wise lords," take off his hat, or even rise to his feet. After all, the Lord had said that whoever wanted to be the highest among His followers should be the servant of all. The Hutterites omitted all titles in letters. One Catholic writer complained that if Catholic subjects ever did such a thing they would be thrown into prison, but when the Hutterites did it, the lords just laughed. Actually, Cardinal Franz von Dietrichstein did not laugh but flew into a rage when he received a letter that omitted his titles.[54]

Some Anabaptists were very critical of the legal system. In 1530 an Anabaptist at Strasbourg called the syndic, Dr. Caspar Baldung, a villain who made money first by winning a case for one side and then by winning it for the other. A Hutterite in Württemberg maintained that petty thieves who had stolen a cow or ox were sentenced by men who themselves had stolen a hundred florins from the duke. "If you judge others for crimes you yourself commit," the brethren demanded, "do you think that you will escape the judgment of God?"[55]

It is hard to decide which of these Anabaptists were guided by revolutionary motives and which by a literal interpretation of the New Testament. If a large number of brethren had held these radical views, then Anabaptism would indeed have been a revolutionary movement, as the authorities suspected for a long time. But apart from Thuringia, the radicals were exceptions: the mass of Anabaptists never held these views, not even in the 1520s and 1530s. The radicals were even fewer in number than the conservative, or "common-sense" minority.

The Common-Sense Minority

The outstanding Anabaptist spokesman of a sober political philosophy was Balthasar Hubmaier, who in his treatise "On the Sword" angrily accused the brethren of misinterpreting and twisting the words of Christ and the apostles. Even if there were no other scriptural passage, Romans 13 would confirm the divine origin of government. To govern and to pronounce sentence in court as burgomaster, bailiff, or judge was by no means unchristian. If it was right to sentence a criminal in court, how could it be wrong to execute him? If the magistrates were unable to subdue evil by themselves, a citizen was obliged for the sake of his soul to answer their call for assistance, though he should first examine whether the government was moved by ambition or by the common good. If we desire to live in peace under a heathen government, Hubmaier argued, why not all the more under a Christian?

Hubmaier's views were influential first in the congregation of Waldshut and then at Nikolsburg, spreading in 1528 or 1529 to Linz; about 1540 they may have helped to persuade the Philippites of Steyr to pay war taxes and render military service.[56] Obviously Hubmaier did not depart much from Luther's political philosophy. If the Anabaptists had adopted Hubmaier's position, they would have abandoned one of their most distinctive doctrines. But their movement might not have incurred such violent suppression by the government; indeed, it might have survived, as the Baptists would a century and a half later.

Other Anabaptist leaders also rejected the Swiss doctrines, though their reasoning differed from Hubmaier's. Hans Hut and his disciples considered political doctrines of secondary importance only. Their great concern was the salvation of man's soul, not such trifling questions as whether he could carry weapons or swear an oath. When in 1527 Jakob Gross proclaimed the Swiss view at Augsburg, Hut opposed him, insisting that the Scriptures did not forbid swearing oaths, carrying weapons, or fighting in wars. These conflicting views may have been discussed at the famous council of August 1527. The followers of the Swiss and Hut also collided in the congregation at Esslingen, with the result that no binding doctrine was laid down there. In 1528 some brethren at Esslingen were even willing to use arms or at least serve as guards on the walls.[57] During the following years, too, deviationist views appeared at Esslingen and Bretten. In 1544, for example, five brethren at Esslingen clearly stated that a Christian might be a magistrate or sit in law courts and councils. They denied that a Christian might carry or use weapons, however.[58] These Anabaptists may have been influenced by the leader Pilgram Marbeck.

Marbeck and his friends maintained that love and faith, not the letter of the Scriptures, should determine the Christian attitude toward government and oaths. A Christian could hold political office and a magistrate could be a Christian, though of course he must not use his political power in religious matters. Marbeck cautioned, indeed, that it would be difficult for a Christian to be a secular magistrate. Nonetheless, Pilgramites participated in municipal government at Austerlitz.

In Hesse the leader Georg Schnabel and some of his followers also admitted in the 1530s that a Christian could be a magistrate; but they never arrived at a common view on the question of war.[59] In the second half of the sixteenth century, a few brethren at Strasbourg swore the annual oath of allegiance in front of the cathedral.[60] Despite such incidents, however, there is no doubt that Anabaptists who affirmed political institutions remained a minority.

Effects of Anabaptist Political Doctrines on Society

Whether or not the political doctrines of the Anabaptists were closer to Christ's teaching than those of Luther and Zwingli is not at issue here, but only the actual effects of the Anabaptist doctrines on sixteenth-century society. The governments quite naturally regarded the Anabaptist's condemnation of the magistracy, weapons, oaths, and law courts as not just a question of faith but an attack on all secular authority. That the Anabaptists refused to serve in any kind of government office was not so troubling: the vast majority of them would not have qualified for

such positions in any case. But the authorities were deeply disturbed by the Anabaptist doctrine that anyone who did hold office could not be a Christian. Asked by the theologians and councilors whether rulers might not be good Christians just as their
subjects were, one impetuous Hutterite replied, "How can this
be as, from the beginning of the world, there have not been people so godless as you damned Lutherans or Papists who live in all
unchastity, knavery, and depravity . . . ; how may you, with
all your depravity, be saved?" Not surprisingly, the theologians
were enraged by such insults.[61]

It should be remembered, too, that in the sixteenth century
government was still closely linked to Christianity. The right of
the prince to rule and the duty of his subjects to obey were
deduced from the Scriptures. The ruler was charged not only
with maintaining order in society, but with leading his subjects
to salvation by establishing and protecting the church. It was the
Christian faith that the government defended against the Turkish
menace. What would happen if people preached that their rulers
and officials were not Christians but in reality the enemies of
Christianity? The governments and theologians were genuinely
alarmed: "Yes, if the peasants were told that their lords, servants,
and priests were not Christians and would not be saved, they
would soon seize us, tear our hair, and strike us to the ground." [62]

Nor was the refusal of the Anabaptists to use weapons quite so
harmless as is generally assumed. All burghers in the cities and
subjects in the territories were legally obligated to render military service, although only a few might be called on to do so.
There was the danger that the religious wars in France and the
Netherlands might also engulf the Empire, and an invasion by
the Turks seemed so imminent that in 1531 Brenz wrote a treatise on "How Preachers and Laymen Should Act When the
Turks Conquer Germany." The Anabaptists, however, declared
that they would not raise so much as a finger against the Turks.
Indeed, we do know of Anabaptists in Catholic and Protestant
territories who refused to serve as soldiers or pay war taxes dur-

ing the Swiss War of 1531–32, the invasion of Württemberg in
1534, and the Smalcaldic War of 1547.[63]

Obviously the number of Anabaptists was far too small to
impair the defense capacity of any territory or town. But the
sixteenth-century governments could not accept the deliberate
disobedience of the Anabaptists in a purely political matter. The
Anabaptists, it seemed, challenged and undermined all authority.
"Their obedience is of such a nature," one theologian wrote,
"that I would rather be a subject than a ruler. For I would not
have to obey the government but the government me. . . . The
prince has to leave me unmolested, whether friend or foe is
coming, whether he is winning or losing his territory. I will have
nothing to do with it, I love my enemies." [64] The authorities
were horrified by the alleged statements of some Anabaptists
that if it were right to go to war, they would rather side with
the Turks than with the supposed Christians. In 1535 refugees
from Moravia were even asked whether some of their brethren
had not joined the Turks.

There was still another problem. The peasants often took
turns guarding villages in times of war and keeping animals out
of their fields and vineyards during the harvest. What should the
brethren do when it was their turn? The Strasbourg Discipline
of 1568 advised them to hire replacements or appear without
weapons. Yet the Anabaptists allowed themselves to go out
hunting; one man in Hesse even distinguished himself by killing
large numbers of wolves.

The question of oaths, like that of bearing arms, was also a
serious one in the sixteenth century. In many territories every
adult man and new resident had to swear an oath of allegiance.
In many imperial cities all burghers had to swear annually that
they would uphold the constitutional order. These oaths were
more than just a formality. In refusing to swear them the Anabaptists seemed to be rejecting the legitimacy of the government
—a point the governments were very sensitive about. The Heilbronn town council might tolerate the Anabaptist inclinations of

some of the burghers, but not even the richest could forgo the oath of allegiance. Anyone refusing to swear was inevitably expelled from the city. Another difficulty involving oaths arose in the case of some brethren who apparently were willing to accept offices on the village level that did not entail the use of force, such as administering the village or church property. Since they refused to swear the customary oath, the community had no legal guarantee that they would perform their duties honestly, though of course they were most likely to do so. Thus these Anabaptists violated another legal tradition of long standing.

The Anabaptists also undermined one of the bases of sixteenth-century society by insisting that civil authorities had no right to issue orders concerning matters of religion. Again we must remember that in Europe at that time governments felt responsible for the establishment of the true religion. If individual subjects refused to take orders from their government in matters of belief, were they not again challenging the authority of government itself? The officials thought so. In their view the Anabaptist philosophy ran like this: "To prevent disturbance, I am supposed to attend church, at least once on Sunday; if I like the pastor, I will obey, if not, I shall please myself entirely"; and further, "if I am ordered not to form bands or congregate in secret at questionable places, I will obey if it pleases me to do so, but if it does not, I don't give a damn for the order." It should be remembered that individual Anabaptists, not constitutional bodies such as magistrates or estates, assumed the right to decide whether obedience was due or not. The officials were all the more intolerant of this form of disobedience because they were in the process of extending their control over the administration, jurisdiction, and economy of territories that previously had been divided by innumerable privileges and exemptions.

The Anabaptists realized, of course, that they were violating laws when they refused to bear arms, swear oaths, or attend church. But to them God's commandment took precedence over men's laws. Grebel had already told his followers that in questions of faith one should seek guidance not from the government but from God. Like all revolutionaries the Anabaptists appealed to a law that ranked above positive law: in their case, to divine law.

Property
Communistic Tendencies in the Early Sixteenth Century

Since the Anabaptists regarded secular power as incompatible with Christianity, it is not surprising that they also raised the question whether Christians could own property. They were not the first to do so. A communistic tendency was inherent in Christianity from its beginnings. A form of community of goods was practiced in the first Christian congregation at Jerusalem. Later, community of goods became one of the bases of Christian monasticism. In the thirteenth century the Franciscans rejected property even when held by the monastic community, and in the fifteenth century the Brethren of the Common Life and the Beguines led a communal life. Communistic ideas also appeared in heretical movements. Among the Waldensians, the Perfect renounced all property and lived in apostolic poverty. In accordance with their chiliastic expectations, the Taborites demanded and practiced community of goods in early 1420. Doubts about private property lingered on among the Bohemian Brethren and may even have appeared in Germany.

By the early sixteenth century communistic ideas were being discussed more often than ever before. Popular interest in this subject may have been due to the prevailing poverty among the masses. In some larger cities population growth led to an increasing proletarization: at Augsburg, for example, the number of burghers without any property grew much more rapidly than the population as a whole, while a very small group of wealthy merchants and bankers amassed immense riches. In small country towns and villages, too, the overwhelming mass of the population were poor people rather than property owners. Although

most villages in Germany still retained a small amount of common land, the landless laborers were frequently prohibited from
using it. Perhaps the existence of the "common" village property
suggested to many that total community of goods was the only
way to eliminate the appalling misery in which the mass of
people lived.

In 1516 Thomas More portrayed in his *Utopia* a society based
on community of property. More suggested that the common
good demanded equality in all respects, and further that equality
could never be achieved as long as private property existed. The
German humanists seem to have been fascinated by this picture
of a new society. The second part of *Utopia* had already been
published in German by 1524, years before it was translated into
any other modern language.[65] Of course, it is hard to say how
much influence More really had in Germany. Some revolutionaries and intellectuals may already have been questioning the
existing social institutions even before More's book appeared.
Nikolaus Storch, who was close to the heretical traditions in
Bohemia, is said to have preached in Saxony and Thuringia in
1523 that God created all things to be held in common.[66]

Though in 1525 the Twelve Articles of the peasants did not
demand community of goods, some individual leaders in the
Peasants' War may have advanced communistic ideas.[67] Müntzer
supposedly admitted after his capture in 1525 that he had planned
to introduce community of goods. There is no evidence to cor-
roborate this allegation, but it at least reveals the authorities' concern about the issue.

In 1526 Johann Sichard of Basel published four letters allegedly written by Clement, supposedly the first successor to
Peter at Rome; the fourth letter stated categorically that all
goods and chattels, even wives, should be held in common.
Reference was made to Plato and to the communism of the first
congregations at Jerusalem and Rome. Sebastian Franck made this
letter known to a wide public by publishing it in his "Chronica"
schichtbibel" in 1531. Franck himself thought that private

property was a purely human invention based on avarice and force.[68]

In 1527 a Nuremberg printer, Johann Hergott, who had had contact with Thomas Müntzer,[69] was arrested either at Leipzig or at Zwickau for having distributed an extremely revolutionary pamphlet entitled "On the New Transformation of the Christian Life" and subtitled "Beware, Devil, Hell Will Be Destroyed." [70] Hergott was interrogated by Duke Georg himself and beheaded at Leipzig on May 20, 1527. Following the Joachimite tradition, Hergott had declared that the ages of God the Father and God the Son had passed, and that a new realm of the Holy Ghost was imminent. In the future society nobility by birth was to vanish, all men would be equal and none would say anymore: "This is mine." The basic social and economic unit would be the "Flur," a certain area of arable land, with God's House at its center. The people would live together in a sort of monastic community, like the Carthusians, eating from one bowl and drinking from one barrel. Children would not be educated by their parents but by the community. Everything—woods, water, pastures, and products—would be owned in common by God's House. Everyone would have to work according to his abilities, and no one would live better than his neighbor. Thus the words "our . . . our . . . our," so often recited in the Lord's Prayer, would be fulfilled. Every community would have the necessary crafts, but Hergott envisaged a largely agricultural economy; even the burghers would leave their houses in the cities to live in these communities. Hergott advocated a hierarchy of elected leaders who would not live on payments or rents but would receive their maintenance in the various Fluren they visited. Every Flur would be governed by a "purveyor of God's House." The various purveyors would elect a "lord of the country." Twelve lords of the country would in turn elect a "quarter lord." There would be four quarter lords for countries of the Latin tongue, four for countries of the Greek, and four for countries of the Hebrew. All twelve quarter lords would then elect one head: at last there would be one fold and one shepherd. Hergott's vision seems to have encompassed not only Western and Eastern Christianity but the Hebrew (and perhaps even Moslem) world. Finally, he predicted an even more profound change: all religions would merge into one.

Hergott was convinced that the new order would be established soon. God had incited the Peasants' War as a warning to princes and scribes—that is, learned judges—whom Hergott hated with wild fury. Since they had not heeded God's warning, He had aroused the Turks and infidels against them. But there was still another reason why the change was imminent. There were three tables in the world, Hergott said: the first was laden with an abundance, the second had a moderate sufficiency, and the third was downright bare, for those at the abundant table had taken the bread from it. This inequality would lead to war. God would overturn the tables of abundance and scarcity and retain the table of moderate sufficiency. This transformation would be brought about through the rise of the "nobility by virtue". The great towns, Hergott proclaimed, would be the instrument, God and the common man the craftsman. In other words, the common man would rise. Though Hergott's demand for an agrarian economy could be called backward, his vision of a new society based on communistic households, consisting of a single social class, and governed by a rational system of elected leaders was more revolutionary than the program of the peasants in 1525.

It is against this background that the Anabaptists' concern over the problem of private property must be seen.

Noncommunistic Anabaptists

The early Anabaptist leaders, such as Grebel, Manz, and Blaurock, were already being accused of advocating community of goods. Manz and Blaurock simply denied these charges.[71] Indeed, the mass of Anabaptists in south and central Germany, Switzerland, and Austria did not advocate community of goods.

Even so, their views on property differed from those of many of their sixteenth-century contemporaries. First, they insisted that since the Christian did not really live the life of this world, he must not get too involved in business affairs. As an Austrian Anabaptist put it, Christians could have property but they should not be rich.[72] Thus the Anabaptists clearly rejected the acquisitive mentality of the wealthy bourgeoisie.

Second, property signified to the Anabaptists not a legal right but a moral obligation to help their fellow men. It was this conception of property that disturbed the officials. Hubmaier said the Christian was not the lord but only the steward of his goods: he would use them to take care of his neighbor, feeding the hungry, giving drink to the thirsty, and dressing the naked. Other Anabaptists used more ambiguous terms to express fundamentally the same idea. For example, Ambrosius Spittelmaier explained in 1527 that a true Christian would not own anything on earth. This did not mean that a Christian should not work, have fields or meadows, or engage in a craft, or that he should sleep in the forest, but that he should not use these things only for himself, or say, "This house, this field, this penny is mine." He should always say "ours," just as he also prayed, "Our Father." A Christian should work not in order to stuff his house with goods or fill his stewpot with meat, but to keep his brother from suffering want. All Christians should work equally and earn their living by the sweat of their brow.

Spittelmaier, then, did not advocate the common ownership of goods; even so, his statements reveal a certain uneasiness. This internal questioning led to such ambiguities as the statement that Christians should hold all goods in common, whether spiritual or secular, because they also had the name Christian in common. The fact is, however, that Spittelmaier never advocated community of goods but simply demanded a state of mind that would lead the Christian to share his goods with the poor. The authorities, blind to this fine distinction, concluded that Spittelmaier was actually advocating community of goods. Immediately they asked who would work in the fields if all property was held in common. The industrious man would have to give the fruits of his labor to drunkards and rascals. The rabble would say that those who had property were not Christians: "Therefore, let's do away with them and seize their goods." [73]

The equivocal attitude of the early Anabaptists was also well reflected in statements made by brethren at Sorga in Hesse. Of the thirteen couples that were interrogated, three denied that a Christian could have property: they did not regard anything as their own. The others accepted private property with qualifications: the Christian should own property as if he did not own it and use it to supply the poor and needy. [74] The Hessian chancellor could not find anything wrong with these views. Indeed, these Anabaptists were not really concerned with the problem of private property versus community of goods. They rejected property insofar as it bound man to this world; they accepted it insofar as it enabled the believer to provide for his family and for the poor. The overwhelming mass of Anabaptists at Bern, Augsburg, Esslingen, Regensburg, and Passau, and in Württemberg, Franconia, Hesse, and Thuringia, took generally the same view with slight variations. [75]

Though most Anabaptists kept their property and made only voluntary contributions to the welfare of others, the authorities and the wealthy remained uneasy all through the sixteenth century. [76] The doctrine that among Christians the individual owned nothing had strange undertones. Did it not condemn the wealthy as unchristian? The Anabaptists seemed to suggest that the existing class structure was basically wrong when they said there could be neither rich nor poor among true Christians. Some Anabaptists sensed the concern of the well-to-do, claiming that the rich disliked and suppressed their movement because they feared that they might have to share their property. An Anabaptist butcher at Strasbourg even raised the most dangerous of all questions: where did the wealth of the rich come from? [77] Very few Anabaptists spoke or even thought explicitly along these lines, but the implications were easily drawn.

In practice the Anabaptists took the obligation of helping their poor fellow believers very seriously. A peasant near Ansbach who had only one child sold a meadow for 96 florins to aid needy fellow believers who had many children. Since he then lacked fodder for the animals, he also sold three oxen, seven cows, and three horses. When aid from individual believers proved insufficient, the brethren organized help for the poor by setting up common funds. Such a fund existed at St. Gallen in 1526, among Hut's followers at Uetzing in Franconia in late 1526 or early 1527, and at Augsburg in 1527. At Augsburg contributions were dropped into a hat or box passed around during meetings, for sometimes when the minister reminded his congregation at the end of a meeting to make contributions, he was scarcely heard over the noise of the departing brethren. In 1527 the fund at Augsburg amounted to not less than twenty florins. It was difficult, however, to find a purse bearer to administer this fund, for it had the appearance of a communistic experiment or an unauthorized way of raising taxes and was thus likely to alarm the authorities. This problem was one of the reasons why the Augsburg fund so often changed hands,[78] even though it was still in existence in 1531. It does not appear that the believers at Augsburg attached vital importance to the fund. Perhaps some were too proud to accept help. Anna Salminger, the wife of the imprisoned leader, said in 1528 that she knew nothing of a collection box.

We know that there were common funds in the early congregations at Esslingen, Strasbourg, Kaufbeuren, Passau, and in the Tirol, and possibly also at Appenzell, Zurich, and Basel.[79] Various ordinances related to support for the poor: Scharnschlager ordered that during the meeting the vorsteher or an older believer should remind the congregation of the needy, but he rejected the demand of "certain sects" that contributions be made obligatory.[80] Though most believers at Augsburg could afford only small donations, the merchant Lucas Miller gave not less than ten florins, and Lucas Kreler gave one florin. In later years the congregation of Horgen near Zurich even owned a farm worth 700 pounds; they also used their money to buy a supply of grain.[81]

The orphans of poor brethren were brought up with the help of the congregation's property. When a brother lacked clothes or tools, he was given money to purchase them. For example, an Anabaptist of Augsburg was supported by his fellow believers at "Pach" in Switzerland while he learned the weaving craft. The Anabaptists also seem to have patronized the shops of their fellow believers. At Strasbourg a butcher was called an Anabaptist because only Anabaptists bought meat from him.[82]

Hostile observers maintained that the Anabaptists lured people into their sect by offering them material help. A poor woman at Augsburg who did not have more than a petticoat was promised clothes by the armful if she had herself baptized.[83] The Anabaptists made certain, however, that believers received help only if they had not wasted their property and had conducted themselves with propriety. The idle and lazy were expelled.[84] Also, the amount of material help given should not be exaggerated. Some poverty-stricken brethren were openly told to bear their lot with patience.[85]

Inevitably some renegade Anabaptists thought they had been exploited by the brethren. One man in the area of Bern bitterly complained that as long as he had had wine, flour, bread, lard, and meat in his cellar, the Anabaptists had been glad to lend him money: he was their brother Ulrich. But when his supplies were exhausted, he was called brother Übrig—"Finished." It seems that after his defection they refused to help him, though he and his children suffered miserably in the winter. They demanded that he hand his children over to them, and he of course declined.[86]

There was nothing revolutionary about the help provided by the Anabaptists for needy fellow believers. The poor were also supported by the community in Lutheran, Zwinglian, and Calvinistic cities and territories. Why, then, was Anabaptism associated with communism, not only in the sixteenth century but even up to our own time? Because there were indeed Anabaptists in Austria, the Tirol, Thuringia, and especially Moravia who insisted that private property was incompatible with the Christian faith.

Communistic Anabaptists

By 1527 Anabaptists in upper Austria were already telling the government officials that all property should be held in common.[87] Outstanding among these communistic Anabaptists was Wolfgang Brandhuber, leader of the congregation of Linz, who in 1529 advocated community of goods. Although Brandhuber realized that it was impossible to practice communism in Austria, he suggested that all members of a household who were united in their faith, whether they were lord or servant, mistress or maidservant, should work together for one fund. Though everyone should be paid his wages, love should compel him to put the money into the fund. Brandhuber was soon opposed by some brethren—"false prophets" as he called them—who disliked the idea that the Christian should reveal the size of his property and share it with others. These conservative Anabaptists even preferred the charity of the individual believer to the setting up of common funds.[88]

In the Tirol community of goods and property became a fundamental doctrine. We do not know whether Hutter, the outstanding Tirolese leader, developed these communistic ideas himself; he may already have been advocating community of goods before his first visit to Austerlitz in 1528. In any case, it is certain that he preached this doctrine after his return. Of course, the Hapsburg government would never have tolerated the establishment of communistic communities in the Tirol. But community of goods seems to have been practiced to a certain degree. The believers contributed money to buy large quantities of food; a cobbler worked full time to make shoes for needy brethren; a large quantity of cloth was bought.[89] Then the emigration of hundreds of people had to be financed. The Tirolese brethren contributed not just a few pennies, like the brethren at Augsburg and Esslingen, but most or even all of their property.[90]

We also find communistic views among Anabaptists in central Germany: in 1531 at Reinhardsbrunn, in 1533 at Berka, in 1534 and 1535 at Halberstadt. Even a prince would have to share his property if he joined their brotherhood, the Anabaptists said.[91] We do not know whether these communistic ideas had been preached by the first leaders in the border area of Hesse and Thuringia, such as Melchior Rinck, Jakob Schmid and Jörg of Staffelstein, or by the Hutterite missionaries Georg Zaunring and Christof Gschäl in 1532 and 1533.[92]

The most radical advocates of community of property were the Hutterites. Their unusual stand was defended in the writings of several Hutterite leaders, perhaps most elaborately in the *Grosse Artikelbuch*, written in 1577 probably by Peter Walpot.[93] The Hutterites argued that according to both human and divine law all things should be held in common. As air, rain, snow, water, and the sun, were common to all, so was the right to use whatever was created. Private property was the result of malice, envy and avarice. If people could lay hold of the sun, the moon, and the elements, they would turn them into private property and sell them for money. The Hutterites never entertained the thought that one could own private property without being avaricious. Private property, they said, was the cause of all wars, quarrels, and bloodshed. Furthermore, it had led to an absurd inequality in society: one man starved while the other burst with abundance; one man ran around in rags while the other amassed more and more clothes, only to have them be devoured by vermin. Wherever private property existed, people forgot to work with their hands. Instead they fought over food, harassed their neighbors, practiced usury, demanded payment, and shouted at one another like drunkards in an inn. The Hutterites scoffed at the claim of Catholics and Protestants that they too formed a community of believers in which nobody suffered want. Why, then, were there so many Catholic and Protestant beggars shouting themselves hoarse in the streets for alms? Any Catholic or Protestant would gladly grab everything for himself if he could: then he would spend a few pennies or talers on alms, hoping thereby to raise his prestige, and afterward to make ten times as much money by exploiting the poor. The Lord, however, had commanded that there must be no poor: "Dear lords and government of the Palatinate," one Hutterite said, "if you had lived in poverty like Tytes, your former fellow citizen of Alzey, I would have no worry that you, too, might admit the necessity of community of property." Private property, then, must have no place among Christians. Only one who was "gelassen"—entirely free of creaturely love—would find God. Whoever was unable to give up temporal goods would never find Christ, whether he was a collector of gold or of dirt.

Community of goods was also an expression of love. Repeatedly the Hutterites quoted the word of the Lord: "Love thy neighbor as thyself," and "Love one another as I have loved you." How was it possible for a man to love his neighbor and yet take advantage of him, increasing his own profit at his neighbor's expense? The Lord's Prayer, the confession of faith, baptism, and the Lord's Supper also clearly pointed to community of goods: one did not pray "Give me this day my daily bread," but "Give us this day our daily bread."

The Hutterites supported their demand for community of goods with a mass of quotations from the New Testament. In addition, they quoted passages from the fifth letter of Clement, from Pythagoras, from Augustine, and from Chrysostom, all of which they found in Sebastian Franck's *Chronica*. They cited the *Theologia Deutsch*, the *Ecclesiastical History* of Eusebius, and two writings of Philo. The Hutterites were so interested in the pseudo-Clementine epistles that Leonhard Dax, one of their ministers, even translated them into German.[94]

Quite apart from the first congregation at Jerusalem, the Hutterite Chronicle pointed to two other examples of community of goods: the heretic Fra Dolcino who, influenced by the

Franciscan Spirituals, preached and practiced community of goods with his followers in or around 1300, and the Fraticelli themselves, who had led a life of voluntary poverty. The Hutterites even had a translation of the *Postilla in Apocalypsim* of Olivi.[95] There is no evidence, however, that the founders of the Hutterite communities had been directly influenced by the Franciscan tradition.

No doubt Hutterite communism had a predominantly religious basis. Its purpose was to free man from entanglement with the world and eliminate every incitement to self-love. Yet the Hutterites may also have been following the example of revolutionaries who had already rejected private property and advocated community of goods a few years before the Hutterites began to practice their own communism. The Hutterites were part of a larger movement for social revolution, though they were the only ones to realize their program successfully. This background in turn seemed to confirm the authorities' fears that they were facing a truly revolutionary movement.

Commerce

The great trading companies, such as those of the Fugger and Welser families, which dominated commerce, banking, and mining and accumulated enormous sums of capital, were bitterly resented by the common man in sixteenth-century Germany. The imperial diet of 1523 yielded to public opinion by outlawing all trading companies that had capital of more than fifty thousand florins. During the uprising of 1525 the peasant leader Friedrich Weigand even proposed the dissolution of trading companies with more than ten thousand florins. Apparently merchants were especially mistrusted in the Tirol. In 1525 the Tirolese estates demanded that merchants be forbidden to cover their stalls on the marketplaces to prevent them from cheating their customers in the dim light. The Tirolese peasant leader Michael Gaismaier even demanded in his Ordinance of 1526 that all commerce be abolished.

These antimercantile tendencies may also have affected the early Anabaptists in Austria and the Tirol. In 1529 Wolfgang Brandhuber, leader of the congregation at Linz, angrily condemned all trade, noting that the Lord had cried, "Woe be to all merchants, whether great or small, not one excepted, who have whored with the great whore of Babylon." [96] The early Hutterite leaders, who came predominantly from Austria and the Tirol, also rejected all commerce, refusing to allow trading and peddling in their communities. Riedemann, the outstanding Hutterite theologian, cautioned that a merchant or trader was of necessity a sinner,[97] for he bought products and resold them at a much higher price, thus grabbing the bread from the mouths of the poor. Riedemann rejected the argument that the poor man also profited from the exchange of goods. Of course, the Hutterites did not reject all buying and selling. They bought whatever they needed for their crafts and sold the finished products. But they objected to a system whereby a man might make a huge profit by simply exchanging goods without producing anything himself.

As far as he knew, nobody had ever taught such nonsense, commented Father Christoph Fischer, a Jesuit. One might say that the Hutterites reflected the economic thinking of the peasants or craftsmen who worked for the local market, characterizing as genuinely Christian their own particular phase in the economic development. Of course, Luther also held these traditional economic views.

Strangely enough, the Swiss Brethren in Hesse, who opposed the Hutterites on other issues, also declared in 1578 that the children of God should earn their living by honest manual labor rather than by idle tricks of commerce.[98] They were the only group in our area other than the Hutterites to reject trade. Some Anabaptists were quite definitely merchants: the Pilgramites in Moravia engaged in commercial transactions,[99] and Anabaptist tradesmen attended the annual fairs at Frankfurt.

The problem of trade was raised several times, however,

during the leaders' conferences. The question was not whether
a believer should engage in trade, but to what extent. The fifty
leaders who in 1557 met at Strasbourg were broad-minded: the
brethren should act according to local conditions, they said,
avoiding whatever was "annoying and offensive." In 1568 the
leaders decided that "no brother should engage in buying or
building or any great commercial transaction without the advice
of the brethren and elders." Was this an attempt to restrict business activity, or was it an attempt to keep brethren out of
dangerous business ventures? During the following years the
Anabaptist leaders did view the increasing business activities of
Anabaptist merchants with concern. In 1591 they issued a warning that the freedom allowed to merchants aroused worldly
desires. They nonetheless considered it impossible to stipulate
how much business every merchant should do and how much
profit he should take.[100] Evidently the leaders had realized that
they could not halt the economic development of their age.

Usury

The early radicals at Zurich, such as Grebel, Stumpf, and
Castelberger, strongly condemned the charging of interest. If
a man lent one hundred florins, he should not expect to get back
more. If a man chased a poor fellow from house, farm, fields, and
meadows for not paying rents and charges, he was worse than a
thief and murderer.[101] In 1527 the governments at Zurich, Bern,
and St. Gallen accused the Anabaptists of refusing either to pay
or to accept interest and charges. This accusation was not quite
true. A Christian, the leader Heini Seiler explained in 1529,
would pay whatever was demanded of him, but he would not
accept interest, tithes, or usury. If he did, he had better watch
out.[102]

At the public debates at Bern in 1531 and Zofingen in 1532,
the Anabaptists defended their prohibition of interest at length.
First, interest was clearly forbidden in the Old and the New
Testament.[103] Only recently had it been authorized by the popes,

and without any scriptural basis. Second, usury contradicted the commandment of Jesus: "Love your enemies and do good and lend, expecting nothing in return." A creditor should be motivated by love: one who demanded more in return than he lent obviously had his own interests at heart. But, the Zwinglian pastors asked, could the debtor not show his gratefulness by making a small payment? No, came the answer, for it was written in I John 3:17: "Whoso hath this world's good and seeth his brother have need, and shutteth up his bowels of compassion from him, how dwelleth the love of God in him?" Third, if the creditor could afford to lend money, then he could also afford to lend it without demanding interest. Conversely, a Christian would ask for a loan only when he was in dire need, not to close a fast business deal or live in luxury. Of course, not all Anabaptists were in total agreement. At the Bern debate the vorsteher Pfistermeyer rejected interest on money loans but admitted that it was right to pay interest on "ground," for unlike money the ground yielded a yearly profit to the person who occupied it. In other words, Pfistermeyer accepted the census, or Zinskauf, as it was called.[104]

Interest and charges were similarly rejected by some of the earliest Anabaptists in Germany, such as Hubmaier at Nikolsburg, Römer in Thuringia, and Hans Wolf at Strasbourg.[105] A memorandum sent to Bucer in 1529 by an Anabaptist of Strasbourg, Fridolin Meiger, a public notary, enables us to see why these financial operators were hated. Meiger pointed out that many loans that were to be repaid with wine were fraudulent because the interest was outrageous. Some usurers demanded securities worth twice as much as the loan; thus if a debtor was unable to pay, the usurer doubled his investment. But the peasants, too, had learned to cheat, borrowing from two, three, or four usurers on the same security even though they would swear that the security was free property. When the usurers demanded payment, the whole swindle would come to light. Sometimes a man would flee with his wife and children, leaving behind house and property. In the diocese of Strasbourg a whole village had been deserted by debtors. Sometimes a debtor had to pledge all his property as security. Then if his house burned down or if the Rhine river changed its course, ruining his fields, the creditor would go to court and demand the remaining property as payment. No court would decide against the usurer. God might die and the usurer still be sure of his profit.

Much was amiss, too, with leaseholds sold to peasants by chapter houses, monasteries, noblemen, and rich burghers. Both parties tried to cheat each other as much as possible. Sometimes the yearly payments were so exorbitant that the peasants could not live on what was left. Some contracts stipulated that even if hail, fire, war, bad harvest, or poor weather prevented the peasant from making any profit at all, he was still required to pay the charges. The landlords defended this practice by arguing that in such arrangements the property was leased at cheaper rates. Meiger commented, "O impietas! I see your arguments, dear Junker, God knows them, God sees them, God lives!"

Though he did not approve of the later excesses, Meiger admitted that the peasant uprising of 1525 had not at all saddened him. He had thought God was performing a miracle to free the earth of usury and put an end to tyranny. "God will do it, but I am afraid not until the Last Day." [106] Meiger's views were shared by many people in both town and country, and not just by the Anabaptists. Nonetheless, this man, who had so much practical insight into the financial evils of his time, had already joined the Anabaptists in 1526. Perhaps he was depending on the Anabaptists to bring about a more thorough reformation.

In Hesse the Anabaptist leader Schnabel condemned the practice whereby the churches charged 5 percent interest, not to mention 10 or 12 percent. In the 1540s the brethren at Esslingen and Strasbourg also openly condemned the receiving of interest as unchristian, although the payment of interest was perfectly acceptable. The Anabaptists remained firm on this point. At Frankenthal in 1571 and in Hesse in 1578, the Swiss Brethren emphasized that the children of God should not engage in usury but lend their money freely, expecting their reward in heaven.[107]

Anabaptists did indeed grant loans. In the Grafschaft Leiningen, they lent money to people who promised to intercede on their behalf with the authorities. Others went still further. One brother in Hesse had no qualms about buying an annual rent of half a florin. An Anabaptist in Solothurn is said to have invested his money, though whether or not he expected to realize a profit is unknown.[108] Naturally enough, Anabaptists who lent money sometimes ran into problems. What were they to do if a debtor did not repay his loan? The Discipline of 1568 decided that "if a brother or sister had debts in the world, he might let the authorities set a date [for payment], but not allow anything to be confiscated." Furthermore, "if a brother or sister had money or valuables and wished to entrust them to someone, he should entrust them to the brethren and sisters, and not to the world." [109] Were the Anabaptists as mistrustful of the world as they sounded, or did they prefer to keep the money within the congregation as a loan fund?

Theologians who had to deal with large numbers of Anabaptists were often embarrassed by the question of interest. Fearing criticism from the Anabaptists, Bucer, for one, avoided investing his money in Strasbourg and looked for opportunities of making profit, at 4 or 5 percent, in Constance. The irony of the situation is that interest had also been condemned as usury by both Luther and Zwingli. Indeed, the Lutheran preacher Jakob Strauss went far beyond the Anabaptist position, calling it unchristian even to pay interest. Luther was willing to recognize the census, however, as long as the productivity of the piece of land was taken into account and the payments did not exceed 4 to 6 percent of the yield of the harvest. Zwingli thought of doing away entirely with the perpetual census, although he was willing to recognize the redeemable census in the form of payments of fruit that would vary from year to year with the yield of the land. Seen against this background, the attitude of the Anabaptists does not appear very revolutionary. Why, then, were the Anabaptists repeatedly asked by the authorities whether a Christian "could buy interest, rents, and property with his money"? [110]

The main reason is that neither Luther's nor Zwingli's views on usury were accepted by their churches. On this issue the Lutheran theologians followed Melanchthon, who accepted interest and Zinskauf as they were practiced at the time—an example of the common-sense approach of the Lutheran and Zwinglian churches as opposed to wishful religious thinking. During the famous quarrel over usury at Rudolstadt in 1564, the adversaries of Luther and Strauss prevailed. The interest of 5 percent stipulated by imperial law in 1530 for the Zinskauf was also applied to ordinary loans, a practice recognized by imperial law in 1600. Thus the needs of a growing mercantile economy simply swept aside Luther's biblical thought. Unlike the Lutheran and Zwinglian churches, the Anabaptists continued to condemn all interest right up to the outbreak of the Thirty Years' War, thus providing the governments with one more reason for continuing to distrust them.

Marriage and Divorce

A still further accusation leveled at the Anabaptists—that they subverted the principle of monogamy—hardly comes as a surprise. Heretics were traditionally suspected of unchastity, and indeed, the doctrines of Nikolaus Storch, the ecstatic group near St. Gallen, the Dreamers, and the Bloodfriends indicate that extreme spiritualism may easily lead to the lifting of restrictions on sexuality. Austrian brethren were said to have advocated polygamy on the ground that a man should not have sexual relations with his wife while she was pregnant. At the Council of Augsburg in August 1527, two Anabaptists allegedly proposed that wives be considered common property.[111] In several places in Switzerland and in south and central Germany, Anabaptists were said to have actually practiced promiscuity.[112]

Some early Anabaptists may indeed have questioned existing forms of sexual morality, just as they also questioned the institutions of government, property, commerce, and finance. The Anabaptist doctrine of Christian community, in which all believers shared their belongings, could easily be applied to sexual relations. There is no evidence, however, that the Anabaptists in Switzerland, Austria, and south and central Germany ever thought of abolishing monogamy. Since the New Testament contained no explicit commandment or example in which women were considered common property, the Anabaptists could not very well advocate polygamy or promiscuity. The brethren at Strasbourg even banned the bigamist Claus Fry and his "wife" Elisabeth Pfersfelder.

Some Anabaptists had unusual views on marriage nonetheless. A few either rejected marriage completely or were very hesitant about it. An Austrian brother, Hans Sturm of Freistadt, who was himself married, pointed out in 1529 that Christ had not been married and that God had punished the world because Adam had brought lust into marriage. Marital obligations were therefore sinful. Those who accepted the sign of the covenant and did not pollute themselves with women would rise on the Last Day in white dresses.[113] Sturm's view, however, was by no means characteristic of the Austrian brethren in general.

Some brethren in Hesse and Thuringia, too, uncertain that marriage had been instituted by God, thought it would be preferable to remain single. One should marry only in order to avoid fornication.[114] In 1564 the Thuringian leader Christof Rudolph maintained that there were two kinds of marriage: spiritual marriage, which was the union of Christ with His bride, the Church; and worldly marriage, the union of man and woman, which was fleshly and had not been sanctioned by God. Possibly Rudolph was rejecting marriage not as such but as it was practiced in the world, for some of his followers openly recognized the divine origin of the institution. Many Anabaptists in Thuringia and elsewhere valued marriage highly, believing it had been established by God.[115] Some Austrians even maintained that marriage was the only sacrament.

There were also believers in Thuringia who strongly empha-

sized the spiritual side of marriage. Three Anabaptists from
Eisenach, for example, said in 1539 that one should speak not
of the estate of marriage (*Eestand*) but of an eternal estate
(*Eewigstand*), for marriage was a spiritual matter. External cohabitation without spiritual unity was unity in the flesh only.[116]
Since the spirit was all-important, some brethren of northern
Thuringia quite naturally depended on spiritual guidance in
choosing a spouse. When a brother thought of getting married,
he would say to a woman, "Dear sister, if it should be the will
of God almighty that you should become my wife for His
honor's sake, please do so." Both would then fast nine or ten
days, earnestly imploring God for guidance until He revealed
His will during their sleep or in some other way.[117]

The strong emphasis on the spiritual side of marriage was
largely limited to Thuringia and Franconia, where it contributed
to the aberrations of the Dreamers and Bloodfriends. Other
Anabaptists took a more sober view. Scharnschlager, Marbeck's
disciple, said bluntly that one should marry only to avoid fornication, that is, for sexual reasons. He sharply criticized women
who married for the sake of material security, and scoffed at
those who claimed they had married in order to have someone
they could trust to show them the path to God. "Why,"
grumbled Scharnschlager angrily, "do these sisters distrust other
members of Christ?"[118] The Hutterites, too, held the sober view
that the only purpose of marriage was sexual gratification and
procreation; they even arranged marriages arbitrarily.

The first Anabaptist couples in Switzerland may not have
gone through any sort of marriage ceremony. Blaurock told a
man and woman of Grüningen that since they wished to live
together, they were already married in the sight of God.[119] Soon,
however, the Anabaptist leaders were performing marriage ceremonies; one was held, for example, in 1538 in a forest between
Asenheim and Weitersheim in Hesse. For that matter, numerous
brethren told the authorities they had been married in the
forest church.[120] In the 1540s the Swiss Brethren of Appenzell

were insisting that a believer need not publicly confirm his marriage before the authorities or in a church.[121] Occasionally pastors discovered Anabaptist couples in their parishes whose marriage had never been confirmed before the altar. Johann Marbach, president of the Church Council at Strasbourg, explained why Anabaptist marriages could not be recognized: even though marriage had been made in heaven, it was not a spiritual estate but a secular matter subject to the laws of the government. If an Anabaptist wished to be legally married, then, he should obey the laws of the city. In keeping with this principle Marbach refused in 1567 to recognize the marriage of a recanting Anabaptist. The marriage was acceptable insofar as it had been concluded with the permission of both parents, but it lacked public confirmation because the Anabaptist congregation was not recognized as a church. If the Anabaptist wished to legitimize his children, he should be married in church. In this particular case, the pastor of one of the Strasbourg churches was told to perform the wedding ceremony as quietly as possible at the early morning prayer.[122]

Some Anabaptists recognized the government's authority over marriages. Georg Probst of Augsburg, a friend of Marbeck's, thought a believer could confirm his marriage before the preachers, before the government, or before the public, for the authorities had been instituted to punish adultery.[123] His viewpoint was exceptional, however. At the opposite extreme, the Thuringian Anabaptists declared that marriage in the world was not really marriage but fornication. Worldly marriages were concluded for the sake of flesh and blood, prestige and property: they were swinish and bestial. The members of one very small sect simply asserted that all those outside their group were whores and fornicators! [124]

Most Anabaptists maintained that marriage was impossible between believers and unbelievers. This doctrine had two consequences. First, it obviously meant that the Anabaptists had to marry within their own group, as many of them did.[125] The

Discipline of 1568 strictly enjoined believers to marry only "in the Lord," with the advice of their minister and elders and the knowledge of their parents; otherwise they would be excluded from the Lord's Supper.[126] In practice it was difficult to enforce marriage within the sect because there were very few Anabaptists in most areas. We know that some Anabaptists in the Palatinate were married to Calvinists. In 1540 Scharnschlager was already cautioning believers against intermarriage, which he said had led to the fall of many brethren and sisters.[127]

Some Anabaptists rejected on principle the command to marry only within the sect. Georg Probst, the *enfant terrible* of Augsburg, told the Swiss Brethren that this restriction contradicted the advice of Saint Paul. Probst may have thought of Saint Paul's discussion of mixed marriages in his letter to the Corinthians (I Corinthians 7). Second, there was the problem of what should be done when one spouse joined the Anabaptists but the other did not. Some of the early Anabaptists in Switzerland simply took their departure. Between 1528 and 1531 the matrimonial court at Zurich dealt with several cases of desertion by Anabaptist wives, finally concluding that the Anabaptists did not respect the bond of marriage.[128] Whether or not the Swiss Anabaptists continued this practice in later years is unknown.

As usual, extreme views were advanced in Thuringia. In the 1530s the leaders Heinz Kraut and Jakob Storger taught that there could be no marriage when the spouses did not agree on the Word. As a sheep could not live with a wolf, a believer could not live with an unbeliever: in such a case cohabitation was plain whoring.[129] Kraut and other Anabaptists in the Harz Mountains accordingly left their original spouses and took new ones. One woman announced that she had no intention of returning to her husband unless he converted to her belief.[130] Divorces on the ground of differences in belief occurred in various places in Thuringia, eastern Hesse, and Franconia.[131] But the views of Kraut and Storger aroused sharp opposition in the area of Mühlhausen, especially from the Anabaptist leaders Claus Scharf,

Ludwig Spon, and Christof Rudolph.[132] Scharf and his followers were even called "Scharf's sect." In 1537 Storger and his followers at Mühlhausen censured Scharf for continuing to live with his unbelieving wife. Scharf replied that according to Christ's Word, no man could leave his wife except on the ground of adultery.

By and large the Anabaptists in south and central Germany did not advocate divorce on the ground of differences in belief. This doctrine was condemned by Georg Schnabel, the Hessian leader, in 1538, by the Swiss Brethren of Hesse in 1578, and by various brethren of Württemberg, Augsburg, Esslingen, and even Thuringia in 1564.[133] The Strasbourg Discipline of 1568 counseled believers who had been "driven out" by their unbelieving husbands to pray to the Lord for help.

The radical position, meanwhile, was taken over by the Hutterites. They distinguished between a marriage of believers that was true and could be divorced only on the ground of adultery, and a marriage that could be annulled on the ground of faith. If an unbeliever allowed his wife to live according to her faith, then she might stay with him. But if he sought to dissuade her from her belief, if he grumbled or shouted at her, or if he beat and maltreated her, then she might leave, for the covenant of God was a thousand times more valid than the covenant of marriage. When the theologians replied that according to Christ man should not sunder those whom God had joined together, the Hutterites riposted that those who married in the world had not been united by God. In some cases people married because the bride was carnally attractive. Like whores and lechers, many couples first copulated and only afterward had their union confirmed by the priest, who was usually also a lecher. In other cases people who otherwise would not look at each other through a fence married for the sake of money. They had been united by avarice, not by the Lord.

If an unbeliever did not want to be divorced, the Hutterites said, he should follow his spouse to Moravia. If he changed his

life and allowed his wife to live according to her faith, the marriage could remain intact. The Hutterites would allow such
couples to live close to their communities so long as they were
assured that the believer's faith was not impaired. The believer
was not obliged to return to Germany, however, even if the unbelieving spouse promised to let him live there according to his
faith.[134] The Catholic priests Christoph Erhard and Christoph
Fischer maintained, citing several examples, that Hutterites who
had left their "heathen" spouses were allowed to take new wives
or husbands in Moravia.[135] The Hutterites did not explicitly say,
however, that a believer who had left an unbelieving spouse
might remarry in Moravia.

However pious the Hutterites' purposes may have been, their
views on divorce, being based on the premise that God's law
superseded positive law, had highly revolutionary implications.
The Hutterites unilaterally introduced a ground for divorce
that was totally new to Christian Europe, and that threatened
to cause wild havoc wherever it was applied. Under the Hutterite
doctrine a Catholic, Lutheran, or Calvinist spouse had no rights
whatsoever. He might be a pious, good spouse from a legal point
of view, but the Hutterite still had a right to leave him. Let the
unbeliever take care of himself! While the Hutterites loudly
condemned the use of force, did they not in a way use force
here in a very sensitive relationship? Their system did not even
require a formal divorce in court: the pious Hutterite simply
took to his heels. If the Hutterites had been consistent, they
would have admitted that Catholics, Lutherans, and Calvinists
might use the same justification for divorce. If a man became a
Lutheran, he could leave his Catholic wife. If a woman became
a Calvinist, she could leave her Lutheran husband. A Lutheran
who followed Melanchthon would have been obliged to leave
a spouse who adhered to the rigid position of Flacius. In short,
there would have been general chaos. No wonder the governments feared that the Hutterite principles would undermine the
very institution of marriage.

The Hutterites did not hesitate to put their doctrines into practice. Numerous people in Württemberg, Hesse, and the Tirol left their unbelieving spouses and went to Moravia.[136] Hutterites in Württemberg deserted their spouses so often that the property and matrimonial rights of the deserted party had to be regulated by law. Some zealous Hutterite missionaries seem to have applied these doctrines even to children, leading them to Moravia without the permission of their parents; or a woman might leave and take her children without telling her husband.[137]

Understandably, such principles made bitter enemies for the Hutterites. The missionaries were accused of being child robbers and divorce mongers. Philip of Hesse, usually a mild ruler, ordered that Anabaptists who led away wives, husbands, children, or servants be put on trial even if their heads were to be cut off. A theologian in Württemberg also proposed in 1570 that the Poena Plagii, the punishment for kidnapping, be employed against the Hutterite missionaries. Thanks to the Hutterites, for that matter, all Anabaptists were indiscriminately accused of adhering to the pernicious doctrine of divorce for divine cause.

The Position of Women

Revolutionary as Anabaptism was in some respects, the sect showed no inclination to grant women a greater role than they customarily had in sixteenth-century society. Only the Hutterite doctrine of divorce for the sake of faith may have had the effect of equalizing the sexes: all believers, whether men or women, had the same right to desert their spouses. But such an effect was incidental, the aim of the doctrine being to ensure the salvation of the believer and not the equality of the sexes in society.

Conrad Winkler, an Anabaptist leader from the Zurich area, said in 1529 that women were prohibited from teaching and preaching.[138] They could not be elected as leaders, nor according to Anna Salminger, wife of the Augsburg leader, could they

even take part in the election of leaders or the commissioning of
apostles.[139] Indeed, the Anabaptists took a most traditional view
of a woman's role. In his instructions on the Lord's Supper,
Hubmaier advised women to remain quiet in church. If they
had any questions, they should ask their husbands at home. An
Anabaptist woman of Strasbourg even maintained that she had
to obey her Anabaptist husband because he was her superior.[140]

There was discussion and disagreement among the Anabaptists
about a husband's disciplinary powers over his wife. Around
1550 the Swiss Brethren at Appenzell and St. Gallen denied that
a husband could punish or beat his wife, even if she was guilty
of serious failings. Georg Probst of Augsburg argued, however, that a husband could chasten his wife as a father chastened
his child, for according to Paul woman was subordinate to
man.[141] In all likelihood this question was current not only
among the Anabaptists but in the rest of sixteenth-century society as well.

The social doctrines of the Anabaptists were of a complex
nature. They were the expression of a literal Biblicism, as we
have seen, and at the same time, some of them reflected revolutionary programs of the late Middle Ages. If realized on a large
scale, the Anabaptist doctrines on property, commerce, finance,
and marriage and divorce would have changed sixteenth-century
society radically. The Anabaptist political doctrines, in condemning all governmental office, all courts of law, and all use of
force as unchristian, went far beyond any of the specifically
revolutionary programs of the fifteenth and sixteenth centuries.
They threatened to destroy sixteenth-century society altogether
as, indeed, they would have threatened any form of civilized life.

To say that Anabaptism threatened civilization itself may
sound preposterous, for even the largest concentration of Anabaptists, the twenty thousand Hutterites in Moravia, led a peaceful life and never obstructed the functioning of government.
They did not weaken the defenses of Moravia by refusing to

pay "blood taxes" during the Hapsburg wars, for the Moravian government recouped its losses by simply confiscating their property. In evaluating the impact of the social doctrines of the Anabaptists, however, we have to keep in mind that even a group like the Hutterites formed only a small part of the population in Moravia, and the number of Anabaptists in Germany was still smaller. What were 129 Anabaptists in Württemberg compared to a population of 400,000 in 1570? In other words, the potential effects of Anabaptism were never really able to work themselves out in our area. But what if all 400,000 inhabitants of Württemberg had accepted rebaptism and announced that thenceforth they would live without government and law, depending only on Christ's command of love to guide them? Surely it is inconceivable that a society of 400,000 people, pious as they might be, could exist without government and law enforcement. The evidence of human psychology and history suggests that such a society would soon have degenerated into chaos.

Social doctrines do not exist just to be believed in. Their purpose is to be realized in society. Fortunately the political doctrines of the Anabaptists were never fully applied in reality, for the historian, after thinking through their practical consequences, can only conclude that these doctrines would have resulted in disaster. As it was, they resulted in disaster for Anabaptism itself. Hubmaier, who desperately urged his fellow believers to abandon their irresponsible political doctrines, must have foreseen that the brethren were condemning themselves to sterility as a sect. He knew the mass of burghers and peasants would never be able to accept such outlandish notions—and they never did.

8

The Hutterites

A Historical Overview

The Hutterites in Moravia and the Anabaptists in Germany, Austria, and Switzerland were linked by strong ties. Most of the Hutterites had lived in Germany, Austria, or Switzerland before their emigration to Moravia. They also held the same basic doctrines. And yet, some doctrines of the Hutterites were so unusual and their way of life so distinctive that they merit separate discussion.

How was it that Moravia became a haven for the Anabaptists? Why, in 1526, should Hubmaier have hastened from Zurich all the way to Nikolsburg rather than going to Strasbourg like Reublin, Gross, and Sattler? Having been a priest at Regensburg, he probably knew that the Hussites and the Bohemian Brethren had established a tradition of religious tolerance in Bohemia and Moravia.[1] He may even have been in contact with the counts von Liechtenstein. Such a contact would have been encouraging, for the Moravian nobility insisted on religious independence as one of the liberties of the Moravian Estates. It enjoyed more power on the local level than the nobility in German territories, where a centralizing bureaucratic government was already in full development in the early sixteenth century. In all likelihood, too, the Moravian nobility was aware of the economic advantages it would derive from the settlement of ruined towns and villages. In later years at least, the nobles were anxious to have Anabaptists work for them.

The group that later was to practice full communism can be traced back to Jakob Widemann and Philip Jäger, both of

whom had come from upper Austria in 1527 and joined Hans
Spittelmaier's congregation at Nikolsburg. They soon disagreed
with Spittelmaier over the organization of the community and
over the questions of war and bearing arms, and established their
own community. Although the exact form of this community is
not known, there is no evidence that property was held com-
munally at the beginning. On March 2, 1528, Leonhart von
Liechtenstein expelled Widemann and Jäger and their two
hundred followers from Nikolsburg. Stopping at a nearby village to discuss their situation, the believers pooled their belongings to help the needy. If this measure had been prompted only
by the emergency, it would have been abandoned after Widemann and his group had settled at Austerlitz. Instead, the principle of communal property for its own sake must have been at
work, for it became an integral part of the group's life. Widemann may have been influenced by such Anabaptist leaders as
Brandhuber at Linz, who demanded community of goods among
Christians.

By late 1530 the community at Austerlitz numbered no less
than six hundred men and women. But soon quarrels arose over
the privileged position of the leaders, marriage customs, and the
education of children. On January 8, 1531, Georg Zaunring and
Wilhelm Reublin, together with 150 followers, separated from
Widemann and settled at Auspitz on the estates of the abbess of
Brünn. After Reublin had been deposed by the brethren for secretly retaining his own money and Zaunring for punishing his
wife's adultery too lightly, Sigmund Schützinger headed the
community at Auspitz from Easter 1531 until 1533, when Jakob
Hutter wrested the leadership from him.

When the Kingdom of Münster seemed to reveal the true
menace of Anabaptism, the Moravian Estates yielded to the
demands of King Ferdinand and in mid-February 1535 ordered
all Anabaptists to leave the country by April 23. Unlike other
Anabaptist groups, such as the Philippites, the Hutterites did not
leave Moravia but hid in mountains and forests until, in 1536,

certain noblemen again allowed them to found communities on their estates. Thanks to the tolerance of these nobles and to the continual arrival of refugees from Germany and the Tirol, the Hutterites had no less than 31 communities by 1545. In 1546 they also began to settle in Slovakia.

King Ferdinand had no intention of accepting these conditions. On March 26, 1546, he ordered that all Anabaptists living in communistic communities must leave Moravia by July 25, 1546, and all other Anabaptists by April 23, 1547. The victory of Emperor Charles V in the Smalcaldic War allowed Ferdinand to put strong pressure on the Estates. Though the order to expel the Anabaptists was not rigorously executed either in Moravia or in Hungary, many brethren had to flee to the Polau Mountains, where they hid in caves. Slowly events turned in their favor. In 1550 the Moravian nobles, angered by Ferdinand's interference, fiercely rejected his claim to the right to change the religious conditions in their country. Differences with the emperor over the succession to the imperial crown forced Ferdinand to adopt a more flexible policy toward the Estates, and as a result the persecution of the Anabaptists slackened.

In 1551 and 1552 the Hutterites again started to lead a regular community life. The number of communities rose rapidly, even though the Hutterites were occasionally forced to leave a community, and missionary work in Germany and Switzerland was intensified. The Hutterites themselves referred to the years from 1554 to 1565 as the "good period" and to those from 1565 to about 1590 or 1595 as the "golden period." The emperors Maximilian II and Rudolf II did not bother the heretics in Moravia.

Difficulties began when in the last third of the sixteenth century some Moravian magnates such as Adam von Dietrichstein at Nikolsburg initiated a rigorous counterreformation with the help of Jesuit priests. Worse still, the Austrian and Turkish wars inflicted increasing hardship and suffering on the brethren between 1596 and 1608. After his victory of 1620 over the Bohemian and Moravian Estates, Emperor Ferdinand II firmly resolved to rid the country of heresy once and for all. A mandate of September 28, 1622, ordered all Anabaptists to leave Moravia within four weeks. In mid–October 1622 the Anabaptists were driven out of their last 24 communities. Most of them fled to Hungary, where the magnates allowed them to settle on their estates. Thus Hungary became the second homeland of the Hutterites for the following 150 years.

The Hutterites and the Tirolese Anabaptists

Although Moravia and the Tirol are separated by hundreds of miles, the Hutterites maintained a special relationship with the Tirolese Anabaptists for years. This link was forged by the Tirolese leaders Jakob Hutter and Simon Schützinger, who in 1528 visited Austerlitz and took the unusual step of uniting with the congregation of Jakob Widemann in the name of the brethren in the Tirol. After their return to the Tirol, Hutter and Schützinger sent one group of believers after another to Austerlitz; in one of these groups was the leader Georg Zaunring. The complaints of these Tirolese brethren about conditions at Austerlitz were a major factor in the separation of Zaunring and Reublin from Widemann and the founding of the community at Auspitz in 1530. Now the ties between Moravia and the Tirol came into play: both the Austerlitz and the Auspitz groups dispatched messengers to the Tirol asking the brethren there to arbitrate the quarrel. When in 1531 the congregation at Auspitz had lost all its leaders they again turned to the brethren in the Tirol, asking them to send a servant of the Word. Accordingly Schützinger was appointed head of the entire congregation in 1531, and Hutter in 1533.

Such a close connection between the Tirolese and Moravian congregations is striking. Although the Anabaptists of Switzerland and Germany had connections with those in Moravia,[2] no Swiss or German congregation, however, formally united with the groups of Austerlitz and Auspitz, was asked to settle disputes or provide the emigrants with leaders. More people emi-

grated to Moravia from the Tirol—as many as two or three
thousand—than from any other territory. In addition to predominating by sheer weight of numbers, the Tirolese brethren
held many important positions in Moravia. Hutter is said to have
fully organized the communal life. Two other Tirolese, Peter
Walpot and Hans Kräl, were elected bishops, and no less than
27 were elected servants of the Word between 1530 and 1618.
In point of fact, more Tirolese than Swabians, Bavarians, or Hessians seem to have been elected servants of the Word in the
sixteenth century. Thus it is understandable that the Hutterite
leaders felt a special responsibility for the believers in the Tirol,
and sent more missionaries there than to any other area of the
Empire.

The Emigration
Selection and Assignment of Missionaries

The Hutterite mission was an unusual phenomenon in the sixteenth-century Empire. Catholic, Lutheran, and Calvinist authorities never for a moment entertained the idea of sending
missionaries into other territories, an act that would have undermined the Religious Peace of Augsburg. Naturally enough, they
were angry at discovering Hutterite missions on their own home
ground. Who, they irately asked the Hutterites they captured,
had given them authority to establish churches in their territories? One missionary explained to the indignant superintendent
at Alzey that the power to preach had been given to the first
church of the apostles and the last church of Christ, that is to
say, the Hutterites—and indeed, the missionary zeal of the first
Hutterites might have been related to their eschatological expectations. The Hutterites also considered it an obligation "to visit
the ignorant nations, to preach to them the counsel and will of
God . . . so that the number of the saints will be filled." [3]

The Hutterite Chronicle calls the missionaries "God's messengers," "prophets," "shining stars to light up the firmament,"
"preachers of penance," "fathers of belief," and "servants of

Christ." Even so, the missionaries did not occupy a superior position in the communities but were subject to the servants of the Word. In reality, the servants selected the missionaries, although according to the Hutterite Chronicle, the decision to send missionaries out was made "in the council of the Lord and by the whole congregation of the children of God." [4] Erhard reports that around Whitsun the Hutterites appointed a committee of several experienced former missionaries who designated the areas missionaries were to visit. [5]

Many missionaries were Hutterite leaders. Between 1530 and 1618, 33 servants of the Word and five servants of temporal needs were sent on missionary trips. Since in general these people are mentioned in the Hutterite Chronicle only if they were arrested, died, or otherwise got into trouble during their journey, the actual number of servants sent out was undoubtedly higher. One observer indicated that every confirmed servant was sent out as a missionary. [6]

From at least the mid-1530s, a missionary was accompanied by one or more companions, and sometimes by as many as twenty. The companions were told to obey the missionary, to return to Moravia immediately after they had finished their task, to report on their work, and to account for the money they had spent. Brethren who were often sent to Germany with missionaries complained that they were held in low esteem in the Hutterite communities. Perhaps their standing was low because they had to be given money and were absent whenever people were needed for work.

Frequently it happened that ordinary Hutterite Brethren appeared in Germany who were not working under the direction of a principal missionary. Some were sent to convey letters or messages and at the same time look around for people who might be willing to emigrate. Others went for strictly personal reasons. For example, sometimes brethren in Moravia had received messages from relatives in Germany that they might collect their possessions if they came personally to do so. Before making such a trip the Hutterite Brethren had first to ask their leaders' permission, which seems to have readily been granted. This policy of permitting the brethren to go on journeys was a wise one, for it avoided a prisonlike atmosphere in the Hutterite communities: an individual believer knew he could visit his family if he wanted to. In addition, these brethren served as elusive and ubiquitous missionaries: inevitably they spread Hutterite ideas and attracted new believers to Moravia, even if they were not sent abroad expressly for those purposes. Of course, some brethren just as inevitably lost all desire to return to the community of saints in Moravia once they reached Germany.

Most Hutterites who appeared in Germany were ordinary brethren. Whereas only eighteen of the 82 Hutterites who went to the Tirol between 1530 and 1618 were servants of the Word or servants of temporal needs, 56 held no particular office. (Who the remaining eight were is unknown.) Seventeen brethren sent to Germany either alone or as companions of missionaries were later elected servants of the Word, however. They must have shown such resource on the journey that they were judged worthy of a higher position. Most companions to missionaries remained ordinary believers.[7]

Usually missionaries could both read and write. The Hutterite Chronicle considered it worthy of special mention that two missionaries, Jörg Fasser and Niklaus Geyerspühler, were illiterate. The Hutterites did not send out women missionaries, not only because missionary work was considered hazardous for women but because women did not occupy a leading position in the spiritual life of the Hutterite communities. On a few occasions, however, leaders were accompanied by their wives.

Erhard accurately reports that before leaving for Germany the brethren visited various communities looking sorrowful and delivering farewell sermons. The Hutterites themselves complained that these brethren took their time in making the rounds of the communities, asking for money as they took their leave. Sometimes they carried off considerable sums—as much as ten, twenty, or even thirty florins. The Hutterite leaders countered this practice by ordering that only the *haushalter* or "buyer" was to give such brethren money. One brother sent to the Tirol in 1585 said each person in his party had received four and one-half florins for expenses.[8] The brethren were then warned not to indulge in rich repasts, as if the Hutterites had plenty of money.

Frequently brethren who went to Germany received money from fellow believers to buy them cloth, soft hides, furs, or other goods there. In 1587, for example, a Hutterite asked a missionary who was going to visit his parents in Hesse to buy him a piece of fustian with blue stripes for a bedcover, some linen, a coverlet, and at Nuremberg, a razor of superior make. When the missionaries returned empty-handed, as they often did, they caused disappointment and resentment. All such commissions for purchasing were therefore forbidden. The missionaries also collected letters from other brethren for relatives in Germany before they departed. In several known cases believers explained in their letters that they were writing in great haste because the missionary was about to leave.

The actual departure of a missionary was a serious occasion. The missionary would rise to his feet at a meeting and announce to the believers that he was one of those selected to visit foreign countries, and that much as he hated to leave, he would obey the congregation. He would exhort his fellow believers to receive in friendship any newcomers he might send and ask the congregation for their prayers and their forgiveness for any wrongdoing of his. A member of the congregation would then praise these men, who were leaving to go like sheep among the wolves. In 1568 a special hymn was even written for departing missionaries.[9] As in the time of the apostles, the congregation would accompany them to the town gate. There was good reason for solemnity: in 1532, for example, all of the twenty missionaries sent out were caught and executed.

A defecting Hutterite said in 1597 that missionaries were sent out during the middle of Lent, that is, the week before Laetare

Sunday. They were sent off sometimes before and sometimes after the annual celebration of the Lord's Supper. In Württemberg they would arrive about May. In the Tirol it was noted as an exceptional event when, in 1562, Hutterites arrived as early as February. Before their departure from Moravia the missionaries received express instructions to make a timely return to the congregation. In a letter dated August 2, 1584, a missionary in Switzerland wrote that he hoped to be back by September 29. Gschäl returned from Styria in early November, Riedemann from Hesse in early December. In other words, the missionaries were active from late spring until autumn, when meetings could be held in the open air and before muddy roads and frozen rivers rendered travel impossible. Not all missionaries returned within the year, however. Occasionally a missionary would find some employment and stay for a year or two in Germany, all the time secretly spreading his faith.

Often the Hutterites sent out several missionaries during the same year. In 1540, for example, missionaries were sent to the Tirol, Styria, Carinthia, Hesse, and lower Swabia; in 1570, to the Tirol, the Rhine valley, Bavaria, Silesia, and Slovakia. While generally a missionary visited only one area in a given year, a few traveled widely within a few months. In 1539 Riedemann first visited a congregation in upper Austria, then the home village of Hans Amon in Bavaria, and then Lauingen, the Neckar valley, and Hesse. Several missionaries worked in various areas in the course of several years. If we assume that the missionaries who were repeatedly sent out were those who were particularly efficient, then Griesinger, Riedemann, Gschäl, Hans Gentner, Hans Schmid, and Wolf Zuckenhammer must rank as the most successful.

Did the Hutterites have particular reasons for sending a certain man to a certain area? In 1527 they sent Jörg Fasser to Pöggstall in Austria because the believers there had asked for him. Frequently the missionary or at least his companion was a native of the area to which he was sent. Most of the missionaries who

in the second half of the sixteenth century were sent to Württemberg had originally lived there. Of course, it was advan-
tageous for a missionary to work in an area with which he was
familiar. He knew who might be receptive to his message; relatives and friends would come to his meetings; and above all, he
was more secure among people who knew him than he would
have been among strangers. Though it was strictly forbidden to
receive Hutterites, Simon Kress of Gündelbach in Württemberg
was sheltered by friends and relatives in the neighboring village
of Horrheim. Later he was betrayed not in the area of Gündelbach but about 25 miles away, at Urbach. Sometimes a missionary was sent repeatedly to the same region, having become
familiar with it by missionizing there previously. Gentner, for
example, was sent to Württemberg in 1539, 1540, 1541, and
1543. Of course, being well known in an area could also be
dangerous for a missionary. In 1592 one missionary who preached
in the area of Baden in Switzerland, his native country, was
recognized by a priest. While the priest's cook engaged the missionary in a discussion, the priest called the officials.

The Life and Work of Missionaries

How did the missionaries fare in areas that were foreign to
them? Generally they were safe in villages from which some
people had already emigrated, for the villagers would not betray
the fellow believers of their own relatives or friends. When in
1588 three Hutterites came to the village of Natz in the Tirol,
the women passed word at the well of where the missionaries
were staying. Nobody informed the officials. A peasant allowed
the Hutterites to sleep in his barn and even sent them a bowl of
soup. They stayed in at least five more houses and received from
various villagers gifts of meat and pancakes.[10] One Hutterite
leader explained that there were many hundreds of persons in
the Tirol who sympathized with the Anabaptist faith, though
they did not have the strength to accept it fully. As long as
weather permitted, some missionaries slept and cooked outdoors,

in mountain forests or brushwood. One Hutterite admitted he had not had a warm meal for eight days. A woman of Natz said that her Hutterite guests would arrive in the morning and leave at nightfall. Indeed, in the Tirol the Hutterites frequently traveled at night, and not on the common roads but high up along mountain paths, avoiding towns and villages.

On being captured Hutterite missionaries were invariably asked who had sheltered them. No torture was spared, but the missionaries almost never betrayed a believer or sympathizer. While being questioned at Taufers, Hans Kräl asked the judge and councilors whether they would think it right for him to betray them if they had done him a good deed. Perplexed, the councilors looked at each other and said no. The judge exploded with rage, however, and demanded whether Kräl was accusing the honorable council of soliciting betrayal.[11]

The ordinances advised the missionaries not to stay long in one place, whether it be one inn or one forest. Mobility was the best safeguard against arrest. For its part, the government spared no cost or effort in catching these dangerous ringleaders, as they considered them. Even before the missionaries arrived in the spring, the district officials in the Tirol were ordered to keep close watch on places known to be frequented by Anabaptists. The officials would suddenly raid suspect houses, search all rooms, thrust their swords or lances into ovens, wardrobes, hay, and straw, and throw peasant women they suspected of having sheltered Anabaptists into the cellar. In towns and villages secret guards were hired to eavesdrop at walls and windows, to spy in bathhouses, at town gates, crossroads, bridges, and embankments. Ferrymen, boatmen, and fishermen were forbidden on penalty of death to take Anabaptists across rivers. On being sent into the area of Zurich in 1583, Benesch Köhler reported that he and his companions were safe, but that "skirmishing and fighting are not absent, with worries, trouble, and work day and night." Many people had been fined because they had given them lodging or food and drink, or had attended their sermons. Alerted by an official's wife, one missionary had barely run out of the house into the forest when the officers crashed into the house.[12] When it was too risky for a missionary to walk into a village, he would send a messenger, such as the village shepherd.

In addition to being in constant danger, a missionary who had to spend months in a foreign country far away from his fellow believers inevitably suffered from loneliness. Benesch Köhler left no doubt in 1584 how forlorn he felt in Switzerland, that uncouth, rugged, mountainous, woody, watery, and uncivilized country. "O my God, if I were only in the congregation!" To fight his loneliness he wrote letters to the leaders in Moravia. He had already written to Mathis Binder so often, he said, that he feared Binder might tire of his epistles. In fact, letters were an important link between the brethren in Moravia and the missionaries.[13]

As we have seen, some Hutterite missionaries were caught in spite of all precautions. Some betrayed themselves by ostentatiously praying before and after meals at inns. Others refused to lie when asked by officials whence they came and what their business was. Sometimes fellow passengers on boats denounced them. When a ship carrying Lienhart Sumerauer rammed a bridge at Burghausen, the drunken sailors shouted they had an Anabaptist on board who had brought them bad luck. Some people were tempted by government rewards offered for the arrest of Anabaptists. Occasionally the officials also employed ruses to catch the missionaries. At Pöggstall in lower Austria the district official himself came to a meeting, feigning interest in the Anabaptist doctrines. He had carefully placed his men, who at a wink arrested the leader. Two Hutterites were recognized when they protested stormily against the rape of a feeble-minded woman by a "Sodomite crowd" in an Austrian inn. Sometimes the leaders simply had bad luck: in 1590 Hans Schmid was caught near Welsheim by "an evil man, an enemy of the pious." Sometimes they were careless and ignored warnings. Although Mathis Binder assuredly knew that the Württemberg authorities were searching for Hutterite missionaries, he foolhardily went to the bailiff at Neuffen, identified himself as a Hutterite who had been sent to collect the property of fellow believers, and was arrested on the spot.[14]

Of course, most missionaries were never caught. How did they approach people? Occasionally they might have engaged people in religious discussions on the roads or in the inns, but this course entrusted their safety to strangers. The Hutterites had better methods. In 1577, for example, the missionary Zuckenhammer visited one Steffan Hantaller in the area of Tittmoning to bring him regards from his brother, who several years earlier had emigrated to Moravia. Zuckenhammer used this opportunity to admonish Steffan also to join the brethren, mentioning that 26 persons would shortly be leaving for Moravia.

Zuckenhammer's method—to approach someone who already had a certain connection with the Hutterites—was frequently used. After returning to Moravia, a missionary would give his successor the names of prospective believers. Werner Scheffer, for example, who in 1587 was sent to Hesse, received from his predecessor a "register of zealous people in the lands of Hesse, Fulda, and Thuringia for whom hope exists, and where money can be expected." The list contained the names of persons in fourteen villages and towns. In addition he was given six memoranda in which believers in Moravia had jotted down the names of relatives and acquaintances in Hesse whom he should visit and admonish. He also received a list of people in five villages who were willing to hand over inheritances due to their relatives in Moravia. Finally, he carried letters from believers in Moravia to relatives in six villages.[15] Coming to Hesse, Scheffer thus knew which villages to visit first. These initial contacts would probably then lead to others. As soon as his message reached a large circle of men and women, he could be sure that some would start thinking about joining the movement.

Once they had met people, how did the missionaries try to convert them? The Hutterites must have pondered this problem carefully, for before their departure the missionaries were given a written directive on how to talk to "unbelieving people." [16] In practice there were many variations. A maidservant in the area of Kempten was approached by a relative and one Jakob Miller, a missionary, while she was working. Here, they said, people lead godless lives: they sing, jump, dance, and sin. They also told her that her parents had already consented to her emigration.

This was a somewhat clumsy approach, however. Though he virulently hated the Hutterites, Erhard credited them with more skill. They would appear as saintly men, with "downcast eyes, simple dress, staff in their hands, a false, friendly smile, and feigned patience." Often they would address themselves to poor, simple-minded peasants shortly after Kermess, when people were tired of reveling. They would ask for a night's lodging in the straw or hay, and say that they had been sent in particular to those who lived in a lonely place, to the poor and simple-minded. They would pray in an unusual manner, throwing their hands in a strange way across their breasts or over their heads, and read from their Zwinglian New Testament whatever related to their social doctrines: that a man should help his neighbor by making him concessions and loans, and that all goods should be enjoyed in common; that men should not harm one another but live together in friendship and brotherhood; that instead of one man's having dominion over others, all should be brothers and sisters on equal footing. As Erhard commented, the poor were only too pleased to hear that princes and lords should share their riches with them. As soon as they had won the hearts of the common people, who were always most receptive to innovations, the missionaries would begin to inveigh against priests in the most bitter and violent fashion, and to attack the Catholic Church in general. To prove their charges they would point to a corrupt priest in some nearby village whom they had heard about from conversation with the peasants. Then they would talk for days in a diabolic manner, Erhard said, *a particulare ad universale,* until the peasants turned against the priests.

Then came the decisive point: "I invite you with all my heart, dear cousin Liendl, dear cousin Thomel, and dear cousin Ursula, to join us in Moravia, the promised land which God has given us. There you and your children will not have to labor and suffer poverty; there you will always have food, clothes, and a bed, and your children will have schooling and schoolmistresses; there you will have no cares to vex you." [17] Though Erhard's description is viciously hostile, the Hutterite missionaries might indeed have emphasized their egalitarian type of society, criticized conditions in the Church, and promised material advantages in Moravia. At times, however, the missionaries saw that their teachings met with no response, and simply returned to Moravia.

The Organization of Emigration

Whenever the presence of Hutterite missionaries was reported, local officials knew that people would soon start leaving for Moravia. And yet they were surprised when those who had been under no suspicion suddenly made off. Peasants who only a few days earlier had carted manure to their fields were gone from one moment to the next. A man who walked with sickle on shoulder through the village was never seen again. Parishioners who had regularly attended church left overnight. Fearful of being reprimanded for carelessness, the pastors protested that they could not read anybody's mind.

How was the emigration organized? Whereas the principal missionary was engaged in making converts, his companions were charged with leading the converts to the promised land. Sometimes a meeting was held to discuss the practical problems of the journey. At a meeting held by candlelight at Birmensdorf near Zurich on August 4, 1584, Benesch Köhler, the missionary, told the converts when to leave, which route to take, and what to expect in Moravia. Naturally the emigrants tried to take with them as many of their belongings as possible. One family in the Puster valley left with two horses, eighteen goats, bed sheets, and some twenty to twenty-five florins; a couple in Lucerne took two feather beds, two pillows and one hundred kronen. Some distributed among friends and neighbors the effects they could not carry with them to Moravia, such as iron-hooped wheels, heavy chains, beams, tubs, ropes, and so on. Since the journey to Moravia was rather long, many emigrants left in small groups, though it also happened that a pious man traveled all the way by himself. In 1534 there were reports from Schwäbisch Hall and Dinkelsbühl of groups of emigrants numbering ten to twenty persons.[18]

Quite a number of emigrants were unmarried, and some emigrant groups consisted only of single people. Naturally there were also many couples with children. We also find old emigrants who wished to spend their last years with their children, already in Moravia, or who genuinely regarded the Hutterite life as the fulfillment of their wishes. Sometimes a man would go to Moravia first by himself to see what life there was like, and have his wife and children join him later. Or Anabaptists left their small children behind on their farms. In 1529 the officials in the district of Kitzbühel had to take care of forty to fifty children whose parents had left.[19] Other emigrants entrusted their children for a while to friends and relatives, giving them money and clothes. This practice became so frequent that in 1533 the Tirolese government forbade the fostering of children without the express permission of the authorities. After a while the Hutterites would come secretly to fetch the children. In July 1533, 23 children of emigrated or executed believers who had been placed with other families in the area of Gufidaun mysteriously disappeared. There is no doubt that they were taken to Moravia.[20] Occasionally one member of a family stayed behind while his parents, brothers, and sisters emigrated, perhaps to preserve the family property.

To avoid arrest many emigrants left at night. Sometimes the villagers wished them a good journey, or the emigrants woke up their neighbors and blessed them. Sometimes a leader blessed the departing brethren: "Leave now; the Lord bless you, the Lord guide you, the Lord be with you." [21] Often the parting was sad. Villagers might accompany their friends and neighbors for some of the way. Sometimes the emigrants had to leave in great haste because the authorities had received word of their impending departure. But there were also officials who allowed the villagers to say their good-byes: the officials at Herrenalb declared that their own lives would have been in danger if they had tried to prevent the emigration. In one village the emigrants' houses were plundered before the official could make an inventory.

Many emigrants traveled by horse and wagon, especially if they had children; obviously they could not move fast. It was nevertheless rare for officials to catch up with them, even though officials in the Tirol were specially empowered to arrest heretics in districts under other jurisdiction. How did the Hutterites get away? They did not rely on speed. Instead, hiding places were usually arranged where they could disappear for a time. For example, when around Easter 1544 believers emigrated from the Wipp valley, one of the leaders had arranged hiding places along the old "Salt Road." For some of the emigrants the first stop was a solitary farm, the Grundwalterhof; for others, a blacksmith's house in Aldrams. On the third day the emigrants reached the Volderer Forest, where they rested for several days. Brethren brought them food and drink.[22] The missionaries had lists of places where the believers could stay between the Tirol and Wasserburg in Bavaria, and between Wasserburg and Moravia.[23] Believers from several towns or villages usually assembled in a specific house or forest, such as the Volderer Forest in the Tirol in 1533. When in 1584 a group of emigrants failed to appear at Guntmadingen near Schaffhausen, as they had been instructed, the missionary Köhler became nervous and sent a brother to Schaffhausen to see what had happened. The brother found the emigrants safely on a ship. The next day the group arrived at Guntmadingen, and Köhler hired a wagon and sent them off to Ulm.[24]

Most emigrants were not able to sell their property before their departure, and many did not have much in any case. How, then, could they afford the trip to Moravia? The example of a group that emigrated from Kaufbeuren in 1545 tells us how the Hutterites financed the emigration. After gathering at the appointed meeting place, the believers handed over all their money to the leader, Hans Klöpfer. Hans Staudach gave 50 talers and two florins; his cousin Blasius Staudach, 60 florins; Georg Lang, as much as 76 florins; the widow of Christof Strobel, 34 florins; and the widow of Leonhard Klein, eighteen.[25] After all, community of goods was the basic requisite of Hutterite life. Klöpfer then returned to each emigrant a small amount. The widow of Leonhard Klein, who had given eighteen florins, received five. Klöpfer gave eight florins of her money to another woman and apparently reserved the remaining five for some other emigrants. Of course, this procedure gave the leader much flexibility: he could even use extra money from one emigrant group to help another, if its collective funds were insufficient.

Sometimes the believers had to take care of themselves. One Hutterite missionary advised emigrants from the Wipp valley that the authorities were looking out for them on the way: they should therefore buy their food only at Rattenberg in the Tirol, where they boarded boats, and at Krems in Austria, where the trip on the Danube ended. On a few occasions a man handed over his money to the leader but then decided not to leave after all and demanded it back. As a matter of principle the Hutterites did not return money. When one Tirolese did not get his two hundred talers back, he shouted angrily that he would rather starve with his wife and children on a mountain ridge than have anything to do with these leaders. In fact, the leader might already have distributed the money among other emigrants or sent it directly to Moravia. Prompted by bad experiences of this kind, the Hutterite leaders decided that the missionaries should discontinue taking money from unbaptized persons, leaving them to pay their own expenses.

We know the routes taken by many emigrants from the Tirol,

Württemberg, and Hesse, either directly to Moravia or to towns situated on the rivers.[26] In 1586, some time after he had emigrated, one man wrote that the longer the journey had lasted the slower his horse had walked. To make things worse his wife had fallen ill on the way, having drunk bad water.[27] Sometimes the emigrants could not avoid staying in public inns. The Lutheran town councils of Schwäbisch Hall and Dinkelsbühl let them eat for their money and insisted only that they left afterward. There were zealous Hutterites who did not miss this opportunity to spread their belief.

Most emigrants did not travel all the way on land, but used convenient waterways, such as the Inn and Danube rivers. In 1544 twenty Tirolese emigrants boarded a ship at the Volderer Bridge and sailed to Passau, where they changed boats and sailed to a place six miles from Krems, and then finally to Krems itself.[28] Frequently the leaders had arranged these trips with the ship owners before the emigrants arrived. Of course, the Tirolese government tried to prevent the Hutterites from using the rivers, ordering in 1532, 1533, and 1542 that no ships were to be allowed past the customs at Rattenberg until the passengers had been examined. When the emigration continued in spite of these orders, the government in 1544 forbade all fishermen, boatmen, and raftsmen to transport anyone who did not have a sealed passport. A few months later the first boatman was put on trial for having taken Hutterites on board or having sold them riverboats. Further government orders in the same vein were issued in 1560 and 1565. The bureaucratic machinery of the sixteenth century was nevertheless too clumsy to enforce these laws. Also, the poverty and greed of the boatmen made any prospect to earn money far too irresistible. After completing four missionary trips to the Tirol, Niklaus Geyerspühler told the Tirolese officials in 1566 that all emigrants were picked up by boatmen on the Inn River: "As long as you pay the fare, they do not inquire into your affairs." [29]

Many south German and Swiss emigrants embarked from

Augsburg, Donauwörth, and Ulm, staying at inns near the river until a boat or raft departed. Although in 1543 the governor of Neuburg was already complaining to the Ulm town council of the Hutterite traffic, the emigration via Ulm continued for years. When Hutterites were repeatedly arrested in Austria, Archduke Ernst voiced a strong protest at Ulm in 1579, whereupon the town council forbade the raftsmen and boatmen of the town to transport emigrants. As a result the emigrants simply went to the other nearby towns on the Danube, such as Lauingen, where the raftsmen were only too willing to profit by them. The Ulm town council's protests at Lauingen were to no avail. Finally, under strong pressure of the guild of raftsmen, Ulm again opened the emigrant traffic in 1588.

How much did the trip cost? In 1544 Leonhard Glockl paid the raftsman Hans Petz 23 florins to take seven adults and eleven children from Augsburg to Krems, or 77 kreuzers per person. The following year Hans Petz was again paid 23 florins to take fourteen persons from Augsburg to Grafenwörth in lower Austria, or 97 kreuzers per person. More than forty years later, in 1587, Michael Schwartzman, a raftsman at Ulm, charged nine batzen (36 kreuzers) per person, a much cheaper rate than Petz had charged.[30] One man wrote to his son in Württemberg in 1614 that in order to cross cheaply he should take his four children to a certain boatman at Ulm and let them work on the raft.

The emigrants disembarked at Stein or Krems and then traveled by wagon through Laab to Schakwitz or Znaim. Some emigrants brought a letter from the missionary with them. Sometimes Hutterites in Moravia went to meet relatives from Germany shortly before they arrived in the community. Of course, not all emigrants reached their destination. A few fell ill and died during the journey. Some had second thoughts and turned back. In 1538 a group under the leadership of Michael Widemann was caught at Reuten in the Allgäu. Whereas Widemann was executed, the other members of the party were permitted to return home. Altogether, more than 25 groups of Anabaptist emigrants are known to have been apprehended on their way to Moravia.[31] Four groups were arrested at Ingolstadt, two at Stein, and two at Ybbs in Austria. Even so, considering that most emigrants from south Germany, the Tirol, and Switzerland traveled on the Danube, and that the customs officials had been alerted to watch for them, it is surprising that more Anabaptists were not arrested. Some emigrants later said that nobody had molested or questioned them, not even at the customs stations at Linz and Stein.

According to one report newly arrived believers were sent from one community to the next until they finally came to the bishop, who assigned them to various communities.[32] Believers from one area were not kept together but dispersed over several communities. In the 1580s, for example, emigrants from Hesse could be found in eighteen communities, and from Württemberg, in not less than 22.[33] People from a single village, Urbach, were living in seven different communities.

Many emigrants were never heard from again in their homeland: they were considered "missing." Others kept in touch with their relatives through an occasional letter carried, as we have seen, by fellow Hutterites who returned to Germany for one reason or another, and who were referred to as "brother letter carrier" or "messenger." In many of these letters emigrants exhorted their wives, husbands, parents, and children to join them. Sometimes the recipients were asked to receive the missionaries in their houses and treat them well. Some letters dealt with property questions. All of them, of course, contained personal greetings. One woman wanted to know what had become of her husband, and where her father was having his meals now.

Conversely, relatives in Germany or even local officials sometimes sent messengers to Moravia to settle property questions. Messengers sent by noblemen to the imperial court also took letters to the Hutterites in Moravia. In the 1590s one Maisenhenslin traveled every year from Württemberg to Moravia, at the same time taking emigrants with him, until he was finally apprehended by the authorities.

Since private property had been abolished in the Hutterite communities, one might think the emigrants would not have worried about their belongings and inheritances. But the reality was quite to the contrary! Before leaving their villages the Hutterites sold as much of their property as possible and called in all the money they had lent. A man at Storndorf in Hesse, for example, started selling his animals and belongings in the fall of 1586, planning to emigrate the following Easter. Being barred by official law from taking their property with them, emigrants from Württemberg used a trick: their parents arranged to give them their inheritance in cash, while houses, fields, and animals went to those of their brothers and sisters who stayed at home. The government in the Tirol accordingly became concerned over the loss of currency. In 1560 the authorities asked the missionary Hans Mändl how much money had actually been taken to Moravia. He replied proudly that he had not come to the Tirol for money's sake but for the sake of his dear fellow believers. In fact, the amount of money taken out of the country was small, but it represented a continuous drain. In 1561 the officials kept getting reports that four Anabaptists had taken among them 250 florins; one man, 79; another, 128; and a third no less than 1,600.[34]

Even after they had settled in the Hutterite communities, the emigrants did not forget their property at home. Again and again brethren wrote letters asking relatives to send them their inheritance. In 1587 a Hutterite at Moskowitz complained in a letter to his father in Hesse that since her marriage, his sister was said to be grabbing his property; naturally he felt that his father should not allow her to.[35] Not surprisingly, however, some relatives refused to hand over the inheritance, either because they feared to break the law or because they were interested in the property themselves. Sometimes brethren returned to their native village, feigning repentance, but hurried back to Moravia once they had their money.

Why did the Hutterites betray such concern over property they could not in any case enjoy within their communities? Their leaders may have encouraged this concern on the ground that the community could use all the money it could get. Possibly, too, individual believers wished to be able to contribute something to the community. Occasionally emigrants were reproached when they brought nothing at all.[36] Basically, then, it was self-esteem, a state of mind the Hutterites hardly wished to foster, that made these emigrants ask for their property.

In territories where the property of sectarians was sequestrated or confiscated by the governments, their relatives usually made every effort to secure it for themselves. Indeed, the missionaries occasionally promised that the relatives might have it; but the authorities predictably took quite a different view.

The Extent of Emigration

Between 1530 and 1618 there were 161 known Hutterite missions to south and central Germany, Switzerland, and Austria. Almost eighteen hundred persons definitely emigrated. Another three thousand are said to have emigrated from the Palatinate in the 1550s, and six hundred from Bavaria in the 1580s. In any case, the total number of emigrants was undoubtedly higher than eighteen hundred, for in the second half of the sixteenth century, the total number of persons in the Hutterite communities was between seven and twenty thousand.

Three criteria can be used to indicate the extent of emigration from the various areas: the number of missions sent to an area; the number of actual emigrants from an area; and the number of believers from an area who were elected servants of the Word. As Table 3 shows, the Tirol and Swabia were the areas most strongly affected by the Hutterite emigration according to these criteria. Here we find the greatest number of missionaries and

Table 3. Emigration from Germany, Austria, and
Switzerland, 1525–1618

Area	Missions sent *	Emigrants	Leaders from
Switzerland	19	179	4
Rhine valley	18	165	5
Swabia	27	667 (95) †	15
Tirol	41	531 (86)	28
Austria	10	6	5
Southeast	20	102	8
Franconia	3	30	1
Thuringia	2	8	0
Hesse	21	165	2

* Number of years in which Hutterite missionaries appeared
in an area.
† Emigrants suspected of having joined the Hutterites.

emigrants, and in turn believers from the Tirol and Swabia were
most frequently elected servants of the Word. In Hesse, the
Southeast, Switzerland, the Rhine valley, and Austria, we find
fewer missionaries and emigrants, and relatively few believers
from these areas were elected servants of the Word. Except for
some Hutterite activity in the border area of Hesse and Thuringia in the early 1530s, Thuringia and Franconia were hardly
touched by the emigration.

In general the tide of emigration was strongest during the
1530s and 1540s, and during the 1570s and 1580s. There were
variations from area to area, however. In Switzerland emigration
was at its height from the 1570s to the early 1600s; in the Rhine
valley, probably during the 1550s; in Swabia, from the 1530s to
the 1550s, and again from the 1570s to the 1610s; in the Tirol,
from the 1530s to the 1560s; in Austria, during the 1530s and
1540s; in the Southeast, during the 1530s, and from the 1550s to
the 1580s; and in Hesse, during the 1530s and 1540s, and again
from the 1580s to the 1610s. Whereas in the Tirol emigration

was largely over by the 1590s and in the Rhine valley by 1600, in Swabia, Hesse, and Switzerland it continued until shortly before the Thirty Years' War.

Causes of Emigration

Why should so many people have left their property and families to set off for Moravia, a distant country most of them knew little or nothing about? For one thing, Moravia might have played a role in the eschatological thought of some early leaders, since Hut had exhorted believers to flee to five cities before the Last Day, naming Nikolsburg as one of them.[37] Indeed, some of his followers took refuge at Nikolsburg in March 1527. For another, many Anabaptists, especially in the early years, were driven to Moravia by persecution and expulsion. Rather than yield, almost the entire village of Sorga fled to Moravia in 1533. Once the Hutterites had developed their doctrine of true community, emigration to Moravia became a necessity for the Hutterite believer, for no government or town council in Germany or Switzerland would have tolerated anything like a communistic way of life.

People who accepted the Hutterite belief must have had a strong craving for salvation. Among Catholics and Protestants, conversions affected only the spiritual and moral life of a person and not his property and social status, unless he should take holy orders. For the Hutterites, however, conversion led to a change of all social values. Property, social status, and even family suddenly became less important. To be sure, the sixteenth century was a religious age. But people were surprised nonetheless when without apparent reason, rich peasants suddenly left their farms, or couples separated.

How were the emigrants emotionally able to tear themselves away from their customary environment? The answer is that their environment suddenly appeared to them in a new light. It was a horrible, godless, shameless world, burdened with all sorts of sin and injustice. Those who did not leave this godless life could only expect damnation. The Hutterites repeatedly warned their listeners against the example of the foolish virgins, of Noah, of Sodom and Gomorrah: "Renounce the world or face eternal damnation." [38] They also put strong emphasis on Christ's exhortation to forsake all in His name, admitting that to leave their homes had not been at all easy for them: "I and my brother . . . did not consider this a small matter, but we abandoned everything and departed for the sake of our salvation." [39] A mother admonished her son, "Let nothing stand in your way, but turn to God and join His people." [40] What she meant was emigrate to Moravia, for only in Moravia could the believer live in a Christian society. The brethren therefore called Moravia the "blessed land," the "promised land," the "pious land." Nothing could better indicate the immense strength of religious faith in sixteenth-century Germany than the emigration of the Hutterites to Moravia.

This intense desire for sanctification affected both rich and poor. Many a wealthy peasant emigrated: at Michelsburg in the Tirol, every person with a large inheritance was said to have emigrated in 1543. It was the view of one Hessian official that the missionaries sought especially to entice people of property rather than the poor. Yet material considerations also played a weighty role in the emigration of some. In 1557 a woman in the area of Kempten, the wife of Michel Heyse, asked the missionaries to take her two daughters, who were maidservants, to Moravia. She would follow soon with her young son because her husband was a good-for-nothing: drunk every day, abusive, and foulmouthed. A relative who had emigrated three years earlier had urged her to come.[41] In Swabia, Hesse, and the Tirol poor people repeatedly entrusted their children, sometimes illegitimate, to the Hutterites. As soon as the children had left, however, some parents bitterly regretted their decision and did all they could to get them back.

In the duchy of Württemberg many emigrants declared that they had left for Moravia because of great poverty, lack of food, and rising prices, or because the vineyards had not borne fruit. Several small farmers assured the officials that they did not emigrate for religious reasons but because they were burdened with great debts.[42] These statements were not merely excuses. Württemberg's population grew enormously during the sixteenth century, in spite of high infant mortality and plagues. Since handicrafts were not greatly developed in the countryside, a peasant's economic future was largely determined by his inheritance. In lower Swabia a man's land was usually divided equally among all his children, a custom that by the sixteenth century had led to an excessive subdivision of fields. In all likelihood the children and grandchildren of small winegrowers and farmers had sunk to the status of wage laborers. It was from this area, where inheritances were divided equally among all children, that the Hutterites drew the largest number of emigrants.

Poverty might also have been a factor in the Tirol, another area from which a great number emigrated. Though little statistical evidence is available, we know that in nine communities in the districts of Landeck and Landeck-Ried, the population more than doubled between 1427 and 1615, rising by 122 percent. Here too, the intense population pressures resulted in the subdivision of larger farms into two, three, four, or even ten or twelve small farms that often could not support a family. In the sixteenth century, as later in the seventeenth and eighteenth centuries, houses or even rooms in houses might be shared by several families. Areas where mining had declined in the course of the sixteenth century were strongly affected by increasing poverty.[43] Indeed, the Hutterites endeavored to attract poverty-stricken Tirolese with promises of material help.[44]

The poor were also badly hit by the tremendous rise in the price of food, which accelerated in the 1560s and turned into a veritable price revolution in the early seventeenth century. Since food prices rose much higher than prices for products of craftsmanship, the real income of the master craftsman and journeyman decreased. At Augsburg, for example, the prices of rye and barley rose by 300 percent from 1550 to 1618, whereas the wages of bricklayer's hands, bricklayer journeymen, and carpenter journeymen rose by about 200 percent.

In some years prices rose unusually high owing to bad harvests. In south Germany the worst famine occurred during the years 1570 to 1574, when for four consecutive summers the grains and to some extent the grapes were destroyed by heavy rains and hailstorms. Immediately the prices of rye, barley, and wheat shot up. In the markets of Munich, Augsburg, and Würzburg, grain prices reached their highest point of the sixteenth century in 1571. The smaller winegrowers, who used to offer the coming wine harvest as security for loans, got no advances at all. The wage laborers could not find work and could not pay the high food prices. But even the well-to-do could not get any grain. Groups of hungry laborers wandered begging from village to village. The district officials reported on the threat of starvation in their villages. There was talk, here and there, of an uprising.

In Württemberg the government and parliament hesitated to impose maximum price limits. When representatives of parliament or of communities at last succeeded in buying rye or wheat at Strasbourg or Amsterdam, they could not transport it to Württemberg before March or April, for in winter the rivers were frozen and the roads in the Black Forest and the Alb were blocked by snow. When the snow and ice melted, the roads turned into muddy swamps, and swirling floods made it impossible to transport goods of any kind on the rivers. Meanwhile, weak from hunger, the people succumbed all the more easily to the plague.

It was not only physically, however, that the lower and middle orders suffered. They were also haunted by the fear of being degraded to the class of propertyless laborers and servants. When during the famine the communities, hospitals, and relief boards distributed soup, vegetables, flour, and money, the propertyless laborers, journeymen, and beggars immediately accepted the help. The artisans and small winegrowers, on the other hand, did not, "for they were ashamed to receive alms." Rather than join the dregs of society, they sold their clothes and furniture, and hungered at home.

During the same years the Hutterite communities in Moravia flourished as never before. Was this not a sign of God's blessing? The missionaries hinted at the material advantages of emigrating: Christoph Hirzel preached in Switzerland that anyone would be supported by the community, whether he had contributed property or not.[45] The brethren also wrote to relatives in Germany and Switzerland of how inexpensively one could live in Moravia.[46] Unlike the wealthy merchant or rich landowner, the poverty-stricken journeyman or farmhand was hardly deterred by the communistic character of the Hutterite communities. Were not inequalities of fortune and social differences basically unjust? The poor man had nothing to lose by joining the Hutterites. In 1545 one woman at Augsburg explained she had joined the Hutterites because "they lived their lives in common, did not yell at each other, and owned all property in common." [47] Moravia became the aim not only of the genuine religious converts but also of those who wanted to escape from debt, poverty, and hunger.

Although religious motives still played an important role in emigration, then, the misery in which the poor lived may have further prompted some to leave their native land. Thus strong waves of emigration frequently coincided with years of high prices and famine. In Württemberg emigration was strongest during the 1570s. About one-third of all emigrants in the district of Maulbronn, a center of Anabaptism, left between 1570 and 1577, during or immediately after the great famine. In the summer of 1573 many servants emigrated from this district to Austria and Alsace, where life was said to be cheaper. A similar phenomenon can be observed in the Margravate of Ansbach: when prices rose in 1574 following the poor harvest of 1573, large numbers of people from the district of Münchberg followed the missionaries to Moravia. In 1573 many Swiss came to the communities. Expecting that more would arrive in 1574 and 1575, the Hutterites sent missionaries to Switzerland to make sure that the emigrants knew what the Hutterite faith and life were like. Many more examples could be given.[48]

The Hutterite leaders were aware that some of the emigrants were not believers. The missionary Köhler reported from Zurich in 1584 that a group he had sent off were "rather insolent rabble." There was not a single believer among them, but they had promised to do their best. In 1587 the missionary Hirzel said at Ulm that many of the emigrants who followed him had joined him at Schaffhausen of their own accord. He had not incited them to emigrate, but they had left with the permission of the authorities because of the great famine. The Hutterite Chronicle confirms that in 1586 hundreds of Swiss came to the communities, many of whom had left on account of the famine but desired to accept the faith and change their lives. Hoping they would do so, the Hutterites admitted them for a trial period.[49] That these Swiss emigrants admittedly came for economic reasons indicates how indifferent many common people were to the religious divisions of their time. They obviously thought that the disagreements between Zwinglians, Lutherans, and Anabaptists were exaggerated by the pastors. Were there not good and pious Christians in all churches? If the Hutterites offered them food, they were as good as the others. It does appear, however, that poverty was a more important factor in emigration in Protestant Switzerland, Württemberg, and Hesse than it was in the Tirol, a Catholic region where Anabaptists faced the death penalty.

The hospitality of the Hutterites had its limits. When one man who had joined the Hutterites because of his poverty informed the leaders he would leave, they told him sharply that he should not have come in the first place. He and his little daughter were evicted.[50] In order to prevent incidents of this sort, the servants of the Word finally forbade the missionaries to preach of the abundance and the good and peaceful times that were to be had in Moravia. People who were not interested in their faith, the servants decided at last, should not be encouraged to come. They also issued warnings against indiscriminately sending out invitations to come to Moravia, for some people kept such invitations for years and came only after they had wasted their inheritance.

There were still other reasons why people emigrated. Some went to visit relatives in Moravia and stayed on. Some were simply adventurous or curious. Some left because they were unhappily married—a woman because she had a spendthrift husband, a number of men because they had had illicit relations with sisters-in-law or maidservants, or because their families were socially frowned on. A shepherd ran off because he had been ill-treated by his master. One emigrant was even said to be a murderer and a thief.[51] People who held a grudge were heard to mumble angrily, "I wolt' gen Märn"—"I wish I could go to Moravia."[52]

It is not likely that such people were accepted by the Hutterites once their motives became known. Some missionaries simply rejected certain people. The servants also ordered them not to send any more people who were too old to understand the true faith or to change their minds. Nor should they send mentally retarded children who did not have a father or mother in the communities. Despite these measures there was undoubtedly a decline in the number of true believers among the emigrants in later years. The Hutterites complained that after 1600 "few good people came to them anymore."[53]

We can assume that the emigrants were received in a friendly manner—"cordially and humanely," as one emigrant put it. The leaders advised them to think no more of the Egypt they had left behind, but to listen to the Word of God and pay heed to how the pious lived. But it took time for the newcomers to adapt themselves to the unusual communal life, and to a certain extent unpleasant incidents were unavoidable. The Hutterite leaders therefore reminded the brethren to be friendly to the new people. If they did not immediately grasp what work they should do, it was not right to yell right away, "Oh, you stupid Swiss, you know-all of a Rhinelander, you sullen Hessian!" [54]

In later years the leaders complained that some people who came without religious motivation were told by their friends how to procure themselves clothes and goods but were not instructed in the faith. Formerly, in times of great suffering, many sterling folk had been obliged to wait a long time before they were admitted. According to the Hutterite ordinances, new arrivals were to be carefully observed by various officeholders who had to deal with them daily. If a divine spark was seen in them, it was to be cultivated. If not, a leader was to talk to them about their intentions. The missionaries were forbidden to promise anyone in Germany that he would be allowed to stay in Moravia once he had arrived. Indeed, as a precaution the belongings of newly arrived people were stored separately. No servant of temporal needs was allowed to receive strangers on his own initiative. The Hutterites granted admission, or claimed that they granted admission, only after they had advised the postulant to be sure of what he was doing and not to hurry into any commitments.

As we have indicated, not all those who joined the Hutterite communities stayed. Some left after a few months, others after a few years. Here and there in the small towns in Moravia up to thirty or forty defectors could be found. Other defectors returned to their native country. In the duchy of Württemberg 75 persons are known to have returned, or 5 to 10 percent of all who emigrated from that area. Some returned to assist their aged parents, without rejecting the Hutterite faith. Most of those who returned, however, were disappointed with Moravia. Some of the inhabitants of Urbach in Württemberg appear to have gone to Moravia in times of famine without any real intention of staying. After a year or two they simply returned home.

Citing legal, theological, and practical reasons, the Hutterite leaders refused to return to defectors property they had contributed to the brotherhood. In the first place, if someone acting in full possession of his senses and under no coercion made such a donation, the leaders said, he could not the next day claim that this gift was still his property. Second, it was not in their power to return something a believer had handed over to the Lord and His people. Heaven and earth and all believers had been witnesses when the person had made a covenant with the Lord at the time of his baptism. The person might break this covenant, but the leaders could not do so. Third, the congregation of God was not a "Pfründhaus" that sold benefices. The contributed money was immediately spent on clothes and food. Often not a single penny was left, for the number of believers who brought little or no money was much greater than the number of those who contributed a considerable sum. If the latter were to receive receipts, then one would also have to present bills to those who had not contributed anything, and who had often brought children, orphans, or widows, or arrived weak and ill. Who was going to reimburse the congregation for these expenses?

The Hutterites would nevertheless consent to give the defectors a few pennies for food, or at least the leaders said they would. In point of fact, some defectors were not given so much as a mite and had to sell their clothes in order to pay their way home. Needless to say, the defectors were furious. Some returned home as paupers and were by no means received with open arms in their native country. In Württemberg their religious views were carefully investigated before they were allowed to stay. In 1531 the Tirolese government ordered the local officials to keep watch in the valleys and mountains for returning Hutterites. Sensing trouble, one man first wrote to his former priest, asking him to intercede on his behalf. Some defectors carried certificates from the Moravian or Austrian authorities stating that they had abandoned their heretical beliefs. The genuineness of the seals was frequently questioned, however.

A few years later some regretted their decision to defect and approached the Hutterite missionaries again. In 1584 a man who had left the community at Protzka in 1577 and a woman who had left in 1582 asked the missionary Köhler, near Zurich, to take them back to Moravia. Since they desired from their hearts to do penance, Köhler sent them to Moravia. Indeed, the Hutterites are known to have readmitted defectors, once they had done penance. We even hear of a man who emigrated to Moravia for the third time.[55] And Catholic writers admitted that it was rare for defecting Hutterites to regain their loyalty to the Catholic Church. The reason: they had been bewitched.[56]

Number and Size of Communities

The communistic community was the distinctive mark of Hutterite Anabaptism. During the entire period from 1531 to 1622, there were 102 known Hutterite communities in Moravia, and there may have been thirteen more. Before the persecution of 1547, as Table 4 shows, there were already 31 Hutterite communities. When around 1550 the Moravian nobility again allowed the Hutterites to settle on their estates, the number of communities rose steadily, reaching 68 during the golden period, 1565 to 1592, and 75 during the years 1593 to 1622, even though many communities had to be vacated during the devastations of the Hapsburg Wars. In Slovakia there were at least five communities in the sixteenth century, and possibly more.

Some contemporaries estimated that there were thirty to sixty or even seventy thousand Hutterites in Moravia. But where could these people have come from? Though children are not included in the figure of eighteen hundred emigrants known to us, it is unlikely that only one out of every thirty or forty emigrants should have been noted in the records. Naturally the communities varied in size.[57] According to one estimate about three hundred persons lived in the average community, one-third of them children.[58] Although some of the larger communities may have numbered three hundred, there is no firm evidence that the average community was so large. Even a community of one hundred would have been a large crowd. Let us assume that between one hundred and three hundred people lived in most

Table 4. Hutterite communities in Moravia, 1531–1622

Period	No. of communities		Period	No. of communities	
	Certain	Possible additional		Certain	Possible additional
1531–35	4	0	1593–1622	75	7
1536–47	31	1	Time uncertain	1	6
1550–64	38	1	1531–1622	102	13
1565–92	68	2			

communities, and also that a new generation of Hutterites appeared every thirty years.[59] Some 3,100 to 9,300 people, then, lived in the 31 known communities from 1531 to 1550, as Table 5 shows; 6,800 to 20,400 in 68 communities from 1565 to 1592; and 7,500 to 22,500 believers in 75 communities from 1593 to 1622. In other words, in any given year during the second half of the sixteenth century, there would have been roughly 7,000 to 20,000 Hutterites in Moravia. The total number of Hutterites from 1531 to 1618 would have amounted to somewhere between 17,400 and 52,200, or if we take the average, 34,800.[60]

Table 5. Estimated number of Hutterites

Period	No. of communities	No. of Hutterites *
1531–50	31	3,100–9,300
1565–92	68	6,800–20,400
1593–1622	75	7,500–22,500
1531–1622	102	17,400–52,200

* Assuming that one community numbered one hundred to three hundred inhabitants.

Legal Arrangements

Among the Hutterites all property—buildings, tools, raw material and finished products, animals, food stores, movable property, cash—was owned not only by the individual community but by the entire brotherhood. When the brethren

settled on a lord's estates, at least in later years, a contract would
be drawn up: for example, a contract in respect of the brethren's
settlement at Sobotiste was signed and sealed on April 23, 1613,
by the lords von Berencs and specified, among other things, the
houses and fields the brethren were to occupy, the payments and
services they were to render, their rights to use wood from the
land and to brew and sell beer, their freedom from all religious
oppression, and their right to leave, sell their houses and fields,
and take their belongings with them.[61]

Around 1581 Hauptrecht Zapf began to write his *hausbuch*—
a register of buildings, vineyards, fields, meadows, gardens, and
fishing waters of the community at Neumühl. The *hausbuch* lists
when each of these possessions was bought, by whom, and from
whom, and how much rent was to be paid. Sometimes the purchase price was also listed. The location of real estate and houses
was carefully indicated.[62] The idea of keeping such records was
nothing new. Practically every village in sixteenth-century Germany had a book that described the property and obligations of
every farmer.

Inevitably the Hutterite communities had to pay taxes. In
1570 the Moravian Estates imposed a tax on them of twenty
florins per one thousand florins' worth of property. Additional
taxes were levied during the following years. Yet the Hutterites
were never legally recognized as Moravians. No doubt the indigenous population regarded them as strangers, and in the end
they were simply driven out. At the same time the Hutterites
were fortunate in escaping serfdom, which was onerous indeed
in Moravia.

The Hutterite leaders never went to law courts. Sometimes
their contracts specifically stated that the lord was obliged to
represent the brethren in court. Their Catholic enemies maintained that by pandering to the higher officials the Hutterites
never failed to get whatever they wanted.

The Hutterite Leaders

Referring to Jethro's advice to Moses in Exodus 18:12 to appoint leaders over groups of a thousand, a hundred, fifty, and ten people, the Hutterites established a hierarchy of leaders. At the top were the bishop and servants of the Word, and under these the servants of temporal needs. The servants, especially those of the Word, were also called "Elteste," or elders, in the Hutterite Chronicle.[63]

The Number of Leaders

Between 1530 and 1618 the Hutterites had a total of ten bishops. Usually only one bishop headed the brotherhood, though on two occasions there were two. The bishops and their periods of tenure were as follows: Georg Zaunring, 1530–31; Sigmund Schützinger, 1531–33; Jakob Hutter, 1533–35; Hans Amon, 1536–42; Peter Riedemann, 1542–56; Leonhart Lanzenstil, 1542–65; Peter Walpot, 1565–78; Hans Kräl, 1578–83; Claus Braidl, 1583–1611; Sebastian Dietrich, 1611–19.

The number of servants of the Word during the first ten years is uncertain. The Hutterite chroniclers reported the election and death of leaders with care, but only from about 1539 onward. Between 1539 and 1618, 150 men were elected servants of the Word in the Hutterite communities. Since four of them were relieved of their duties shortly after their appointment, however, the number was 146 for all practical purposes. But the important question is how many servants of the Word were active at a given time. In 1550, as Table 6 shows, there were fifteen servants of the Word in the Hutterite communities; in 1560, 23; in 1570, 31; and from 1575 to 1618, about thirty in any given year. This figure raises a problem. If there were 68 Hutterite communities in Moravia between 1565 and 1592, and 75 between 1593 and 1622, the Hutterites had twice as many communities as servants of the Word in any given year during those periods. The figures given for the Hutterite communities may be

Table 6. Servants of the Word, 1545–1618

Year	No. of servants *	Year	No. of servants
1545	9	1585	34
1550	15	1590	33
1555	14	1595	32
1560	23	1600	33
1565	23	1605	32
1570	31	1610	29
1575	33	1615	27
1580	35	1618	32

* Neither bishops nor servants whose period of activity is uncertain are included.

too high, or some servants of the Word may not have been listed in the Hutterite Chronicle. But it is also possible that a servant of the Word headed not just one but two or three communities.

Between 1537 and 1618, as Table 7 shows, 186 men were elected servants of temporal needs—that is, 36 more than were elected servants of the Word. The exact number of servants of temporal needs in any given year cannot be established, however.[64] We know only that in 1545, 31 servants of temporal needs were active, apparently one for each of the 31 communities the Hutterites had by 1547. Presumably every community had its own servant of temporal needs in later years, too.

Table 7. Servants of temporal needs elected, 1537–1618

Period	No. of servants	Period	No. of servants
1537–39	12	1580–89	15
1540–49	22	1590–99	24
1550–59	24	1600–09	34
1560–69	35	1610–18	13
1570–79	7		

The Qualifications of Leaders

The qualifications for Hutterite leaders were the same as those for Anabaptist leaders in general. Not only the servants but their wives were expected to lead exemplary lives. In 1534 Griesinger was dismissed from his position because his wife had committed a sin, probably a serious one.

A few Hutterite leaders seem to have received a good education. Joseph Hauser knew Hebrew, Greek, Latin, and French. Some knew Latin,[65] others more than one language.[66] We may also assume that those who had formerly been priests, such as Leonhard Dax, were educated men. But the vast majority of Hutterite leaders were craftsmen; they knew how to read and write and were acquainted with the Scriptures and the Hutterite literature, but that was all.

Catholic writers did not miss the opportunity to poke fun at these straw cutters, vinedressers, cloth nappers, blacksmiths, weavers, soap boilers, and carpenters who presumed to rule over twenty thousand people. Claus Braidl has never learned anything but how to make shoes, said Erhard: "How can he be a bishop? How can Gilg, a lumberman, be a preacher, unless his wide, well-brushed, and ugly beard qualifies him for this position?" That Christ's apostles had been fishermen, net knitters, and carpet makers, as the Hutterites pointed out, made no difference as far as Erhard was concerned, for the apostles had studied in the school of Christ, the "archdoctor." The Hutterite leaders, Fischer said, were better qualified to select a solid pitchfork or a plow or a good sister than to preach on the sacraments, on the true church, or on baptism. Educated people in Moravia regarded them as *frates ignorantiae*.[67]

There might be an element of truth in these charges. Thus it is all the more remarkable that despite the efforts of Sir Thomas More and other learned visionaries of social reform, these uneducated craftsmen were the only group in sixteenth-century Europe who successfully established a new type of society based on community of goods.

The Election of Leaders

The first Hutterite bishops were appointed in unusual ways. Hutter designated his two predecessors, Zaunring and Schützinger, and his successor, Amon. It is possible that these choices were then confirmed by the congregation. After Hutter had thrown out his rival, Schützinger, in 1533, he held such strong sway over the congregation that they thanked God in their prayers for his very presence, calling him a "gift of God." No leader after Hutter ever enjoyed so much power.

Hans Amon did not designate a successor. Until a new bishop was elected, Leonhart Lanzenstil, assisted by Hans Gentner, directed the congregation's affairs. Finally the elders of the congregation, that is, the servants of the Word, unanimously decided that Lanzenstil and Riedemann should share the office. The reports on the elections of the following bishops, Walpot, Kräl, Braidl, and Dietrich, give more insight into the actual procedures. On his deathbed the old bishop might summon some of the servants and entrust the care of the congregation to them, but designation was no longer practiced. As Walpot said, it was safer if not just one man but God and the congregation appointed the new bishop. Before the election, held in the main community, such as Neumühl, prayers were said in all communities. The electors included all servants of the Word and of temporal needs, together with a number of ordinary brethren. Of course, only men could vote. After discussion and prayers the assembly would decide unanimously that God had chosen this or that man, always a former servant of the Word. Kräl and Braidl asked to be spared this duty, but were finally prevailed upon to accept it. After the election the servants and the brethren would promise obedience to the new bishop, and on at least one occasion, they all shook hands with him.

The accounts of the Hutterite Chronicle leave some questions unanswered, such as the size of the electoral assembly. The servants of the Word and of temporal needs together numbered about a hundred in the second half of the sixteenth century, but it is not known how many ordinary brethren took part in the election. Nor is the actual election process clearly described. Presumably several possible choices were discussed, but how did the servants and brethren recognize unanimously that God had chosen a certain man? They may have drawn lots or actually voted, or they may have used the same method as that used in banning sinners: a brother was proposed as bishop and the assembly expressed its approval by refraining from raising objections, that is, by silence.

From 1535 onward the Hutterite Chronicle scrupulously reported all occasions when a brother was "elected into the service of God's Word" or "into the service of household or temporal needs and presented to the congregation." A servant of the Word or of temporal needs was elected not by the brethren of the community he would serve but by the assembly of elders, that is, servants of the Word, in the main community. There is no evidence that ordinary believers of various communities took part in the election of the new servant, as they did in that of the bishop. Riedemann said that the believers should pray to God to reveal whom He had chosen for His ministry. If several men were "recognized through God's counsel to be suitable," one of them should be selected by lot. If, however, only one or as many as were needed were revealed, then the lot system was unnecessary. After his election the newly chosen servant was presented to the Gemein. What was the Gemein? The term Gemein had two meanings in Hutterite literature. First, it referred to the Hutterites in Moravia as a group, having the same abstract meaning as "church." Second, it referred to a concrete assembly whose decisions expressed the view of all Hutterites. It was the Gemein in the latter sense, a common assembly, to whom new servants were presented. Of whom was this common assembly composed? Certainly it did not include all Hutterites. Nor was it, as far as we know, an assembly of representatives of all Hutterite communities. It is more likely that the Gemein included all baptized men either of one of the main communities, such as

Schakwitz or Neumühl, or of a specific community, assembled for a special purpose. In the thinking of the Hutterites, such a community spoke for all Hutterites.

As a rule, this common assembly accepted the decisions of the servants. We do not hear of a single occasion where the presented servant was rejected by the Gemein, or common assembly. Sometimes the bishop and servants transferred a servant from one community to another, again without consulting the communities involved. In other words, the election of Hutterite leaders was in no way a democratic process: the leaders constituted an elite that coopted its members. The Hutterite hierarchy was authoritarian and centralized, as opposed to the democratic and decentralized organization of Anabaptists in Germany and Switzerland.

Like the minister of the Swiss Brethren, the Hutterite servant of the Word was first placed on probation. He could not yet baptize, receive new members, or exclude sinners, and he had to preach "without books." [68] Most servants worked thus on probation for two or three years, more or less. Between 1539 and 1618, however, six are known to have had their appointment confirmed on the same day as their election.[69] The confirmation was performed by the existing servants of the Word. By the laying on of hands the new servant received the power to bind and absolve. Servants of temporal needs were reportedly confirmed in 1544, 1552, and 1558. After 1558, however, the practice seems to have been discontinued.

Frequently three to five servants of the Word were elected at a time, less often only one or two. Servants of temporal needs were almost always elected in groups, generally of three to five, sometimes of six to twenty, and on two occasions of even more than twenty. Whatever the reasons for these group elections, the practice clearly demonstrates that the individual community was considered not a separate entity but part of a larger congregation.[70] On at least 27 occasions the Hutterites elected or confirmed servants of the Word or of temporal needs at Neumühl,

on six occasions in Niemschitz, and on five occasions at Schakwitz. In other places elections were held only once or else very
rarely. Neumühl was indeed the center of the Hutterite
brotherhood.[71]

January, February, and March were the months when the
Hutterites generally elected or confirmed their new servants,
though on a few occasions they did so in April, September, or
October. By far the greatest number of servants of the Word
were elected and confirmed on Sundays. Twenty-seven servants
were presented on Sunday Oculi, and 32 confirmed. But there
were also many other elections on other Sundays in January,
February, and March. Why these particular months were
favored is unknown.[72]

Between 1537 and 1618, 21 servants of temporal needs, after
several years of service, were elected servants of the Word. We
may assume that these men had shown such outstanding intellectual qualities that they were deemed worthy of higher positions.[73]

The Privileges of Leaders

When in 1528 Wilhelm Reublin joined Widemann's community at Austerlitz, he noticed to his indignation that leaders
such as Franz Intzinger lived like noblemen. While the ordinary
brethren were given only peas and cabbage, the leaders and their
wives were served roast meat, fish, poultry, and good wine.
Reublin never saw the wives of the leaders at the common dining
tables. An ordinary brother was refused shirts and shoes, but the
leaders had an abundance of fine pants and coats and warm
furs.[74]

Although the Hutterites later spoke with great contempt of
Widemann's congregation at Austerlitz, their leaders also lived
in a conspicuously different style than ordinary brethren. Defecting Hutterites, Antitrinitarians from Poland, a visitor from
Venice, and various Catholic writers expressed their astonishment at the inequality in the Hutterite communities.[75] The Polish

Antitrinitarians reported that the Hutterite leaders kept "one table, rich and abundant, for themselves, and another for the rest of the community. While they filled their bellies with fish and meat and wine, they starved the ordinary brethren on food boiled in water, without butter or any other fat, and a pig's trotter or a hen's leg thrown into for sustenance; they did not give them beer but only water to drink."

Two defecting Hutterites, Hans Jedelhauser and Johann Eysvogel, confirm that there were two kitchens in the communities. In the one, wholesome-looking and neatly dressed women prepared meals for the leaders; no one was allowed to remonstrate with them. The leaders—the servants of the Word and of temporal needs, the barber-surgeons, and the stewards—and their wives were served two square meals of the best beef, geese, pork, poultry, and deer. They also had wine, cooled on ice. The common brethren, on the other hand, had to be content with barley, turnips, cabbage, and sour beer. Erhard and Fischer maintained that the servants distinguished themselves by their fat paunches, their broad, fat, pudding faces, and their long, well-combed, shining beards. Did the servants get that way from living on water, bread, cabbage, and turnips like the common brethren? they asked.

According to Jedelhauser and Eysvogel even sick brethren and sick leaders were treated differently. A simple believer might have contributed a thousand florins to the community, but if he fell sick he was told to be patient, and received only cheese soup and a sip of sour wine even when he was fighting death. When a servant or his wife fell ill, the barber-surgeon and pretty sisters would tiptoe in and out, hold his hand, and say sweetly, "Eat and be well, dearest brother." There would be no end to flattery, caresses, refreshments, and sweets. When an ordinary sister found herself with child, she would receive only seven and a half quarts of wine during the six weeks of childbed.[76] When the wife of a servant gave birth, however, everyone would visit her, bringing food and wine.

Leaders also dressed differently than the common brethren. They wore long coats and round hats, and Erhard claims that their own wives bought the finest silk at the fairs, even though the Hutterites condemned the whole world for wearing damask and satin. Even the assistants of the barber-surgeons walked around proudly and well groomed in their smart and smooth pants and boots made in Cordoba style. The ordinary believers, for their part, were expected to content themselves with simple, thick, unfulled cloth.

Trying to refute the supposedly egalitarian character of the Hutterite communities, Erhard, Fischer, Jedelhauser, and other writers greatly exaggerated the inequalities between servants and ordinary Hutterites. Indeed, some of their descriptions come close to being caricatures. The Hutterite servants hardly enjoyed so many comforts as these authors claimed. Nor was the life of the ordinary Hutterites so depressingly wretched and ascetic. And yet, there is no doubt that the life of the ordinary Hutterite was much harder than that of the servants, for the Hutterite Chronicle itself reports that the inequalities between servants and believers led to dissension within the communities. In 1540 two believers, Herrmann Schmid and Hans Edelmair, criticized the leaders for preaching community without practicing it: the leaders did not work, but were nevertheless given the best wine. Schmid and Edelmair were evicted, but other believers also began to murmur and grumble. As a result a large meeting of the common brethren was called in 1540 to discuss the problem in the absence of the leaders. The assembly rejected the critics and affirmed its loyalty to the servants. Meanwhile, deeply disturbed, Riedemann wrote from his prison in Hesse that it was Satan's plan to destroy the congregation by attacking its leaders. The epistles of Saint Paul and the sacrificial practices of the Old Testament were proof that the servant should always receive special treatment. Even if the leaders objected, the congregation should not allow them to go without their privileges.

Riedemann's letter was read to the congregation, although it is uncertain whether the reading took place at the meeting of 1540 or later. Edelmair retracted his criticism and was readmitted. The privileged position of the leaders remained a burning question nonetheless. In 1551 and 1552, and in the seventeenth century, brethren again accused the leaders of preaching doctrines they themselves did not keep. The ministers refused to yield: their privileged position had been instituted by God, laid down by Christ, and ratified by the congregation a hundred years earlier. For the rest, the leaders said, these privileges were not as wonderful as some brethren seemed to believe.

The question arises whether it was only the Scriptures that suggested the practice of granting special privileges to the leaders. Because of the communal way of life among the Hutterites, the early leaders in Moravia faced a problem their fellow leaders in Switzerland and Germany had never encountered: how to maintain authority in a society without using force. The privileged position of the Hutterite leaders emphasized and strengthened their authority by distinguishing them from the common brethren. From a psychological standpoint the method was effective, but from a social standpoint the Hutterites had clearly reestablished the specially privileged class of priests that the early Anabaptists had so fiercely rejected.

In general the Hutterite Brethren seem to have respected their leaders: the high position of the servants in the communities is reflected in the Hutterite Chronicle, which sometimes reads like a chronicle of Hutterite leaders. During Zuckenhammer's trial in 1597, one brother demanded that Zuckenhammer be excluded because he had insulted "the elders, our fathers." [77] But the Hutterites did not hesitate to rise against leaders who committed unjust acts, as shown by Zaunring's exclusion in 1531. Servants were reprimanded by the bishop and the prominent leaders for minor, but nonetheless annoying, abuses.

The Dismissal of Leaders

Twenty-one servants of the Word and of temporal needs were relieved of their duties or deposed. These dismissals were due to a variety of failings, such as erroneous doctrine, partiality toward wives, abuse of power, serious negligence, stubbornness, arrogance, and immorality. One man asked to be released because he had nagging headaches, another because he did not feel equal to the task.

The misconduct of a servant was first investigated by the bishop and servants of the Word, who summoned the accused and heard the testimony of witnesses. Whether all servants of the Word or only some of them took part is unknown. At any rate, even if the bishop and the servants decided that the charges were well founded, they did not have the right simply to depose the accused. This grave decision could be made only by the Gemein, the common assembly, which we have already encountered. If the bishop and the servants dropped the charges, the brethren could request that the case be taken up again. Gschäl was tried by the Gemein at Schakwitz in 1542, Zuckenhammer in his community at Protzka in 1597, Ludwig Dörker and Georg Riedel at Neumühl in 1606 and 1612. Apparently the bishop and servants of the Word were the only representatives from outside communities to attend these trials: at least, there is no evidence to indicate otherwise.

When a servant of the Word was found guilty of immorality, he was not only deprived of his office but excluded from the congregation. Servants who did not repent or even accused the congregation of injustice were also excluded. If he made the express request, an excluded servant might avoid physical eviction from the community buildings. Indeed, some of these servants were old men who had no place to go. If an excluded servant did penance, he was allowed to rejoin the congregation, though not in his former capacity.

Government

The Hutterite communities were a theocracy in which the
powers of decision lay with the bishop and the servants of the
Word, that is, the Hutterite equivalent of pastors. The bishop
probably had general supervisory functions. He might have
called the meetings of the servants. Charges against a servant
were brought to him and investigated in the meeting of the
servants. Letters of missionaries were addressed to him, and he
also represented the Hutterite brotherhood to the outside world:
for example, it was to the bishop that the governor of Moravia
(*landeshauptmann*) sent his demands for loans and taxes. Although the functions of the office remain vague, it is safe to
assume that the bishop might not act on his own but only on
the advice of the servants. Erhard tells us that twelve servants
were specially assigned to the bishop at Neumühl and would
be convened by him within hours of any assembly of the Moravian Estates. This may well have been so. The bishop and some
of the servants repeatedly discussed legal suits and loan requests
of the Moravian authorities.

Despite the prominence of the bishop and a few of the servants, important decisions on the organization of the brotherhood, appointments, economic activity, the purchase of houses,
and relations with the outside world were made by an assembly
comprised of all servants of the Word. (The duties of the servants of the Word as heads of individual communities will be
discussed later.) Moreover, the bishop and servants of the Word
were intelligent enough not to monopolize all power. Servants
of temporal needs repeatedly participated in meetings that
issued important ordinances, particularly in the economic sphere.
Sometimes only some of the servants of temporal needs were
present, but more often all of them attended.

Not only servants of the Word and of temporal needs but
certain ordinary brethren attended some meetings in which

weighty matters were decided, such as the choice of the bishop, the granting of loans to the emperor, or the payment of ransom for abducted brethren. Obviously the leaders wished to draw support from the whole community, but who these ordinary brethren were is not precisely known. They may have been the oldest or most respected members of the community, or they may have been elected or specially delegated for the occasion. Maybe they were the elders mentioned by Riedemann in his description of offices in the congregation, but the Hutterite Chronicle does not call these ordinary brethren elders. It is also possible that everyone was invited to attend certain meetings, but then we must ask why only a few ordinary brethren actually came. Decisions were made by unanimous vote; again, this custom probably meant only that no dissensions were voiced.

Finally, as we have seen, some questions were decided by the Gemein, the common assembly, frequently represented by one of the main communities. It was the Gemein to whom new servants were presented and by whom they might be dismissed, and it was the Gemein who expelled offending brethren. There is, however, no evidence that the Gemein was anything like a legislative assembly to whom the bishop and the servants were responsible or which enacted laws. The Hutterites did not have a democratic form of government. The real power was wielded by the bishop and the servants.

It cannot be said with certainty whether or not during the first half of the sixteenth century one particular community predominated as the center for elections and important meetings for the entire brotherhood. If any community had this role, it was probably Schakwitz.[78] During the second half of the century, Neumühl seems to have had central importance.[79]

The Hutterites compared their communities to a clock in which one wheel is geared on the next or to a beehive where all the bees carry wax, water, and honey, producing not only for themselves but also for humans. Indeed, visitors to the communities were amazed at the orderly way in which things were done. The Hutterite leaders carefully regulated life and work in their communities through ordinances. The servants of the Word, the missionaries, the servants of temporal needs, the *weinzirl,* who was in charge of agriculture, and the heads of the various crafts all received detailed instructions. The ordinances were issued by the assembly of the servants of the Word and of temporal needs, obviously in collaboration with the officials of the crafts concerned. They stipulated in fine detail the duties of the various officials, the failings to be avoided, and the relations to be maintained with the outside world. The ordinances for the crafts contained a mass of technical detail on the kinds of products the Hutterite craftsmen were allowed to manufacture, how work was to be organized, and the purchase of material and sale of products. While most ordinances dealt with one type of official or with one craft, a few were of a more general nature: one issued in 1612, for example, concerned certain serious faults like extravagance in apparel, travel on Sunday, drunkenness, and unchastity.

The ordinances bear witness to the organizational ability of the Hutterite leaders. Without ordinances the leaders would hardly have been able to maintain basic uniformity among some twenty thousand people living in roughly a hundred communities dispersed all over Moravia. In a sense, the ordinances also reflect the immense legislative activity that can be observed in all German territories of the sixteenth century. The strong religious orientation permeating the Hutterite ordinances, however, is not so conspicuous in the general laws passed in Catholic and Lutheran territories.

In 1640, seeking to restore the original purity of Hutterite life after the exodus to Hungary, the Hutterite bishop Ehrenpreis assembled and reissued excerpts of various ordinances. Ehrenpreis' collection contains altogether thirty items, the oldest of which dates from 1561. Whether or not ordinances were issued before that date is unknown, but it seems likely. At least twelve of the thirty ordinances, and probably four more, were issued in the sixteenth and early seventeenth centuries.[80] Most, if not all, of the remaining fourteen were issued after 1618.

Community Life

The individual community was headed by the servant of the Word and the servant of temporal needs. Though the relationship between the two offices is not entirely clear, the servant of the Word held the superior position, being the spiritual head of a basically religious community. He might be compared to an abbot in a monastery. As pastor he was charged with preaching the Word of God and visiting believers employed on noblemen's estates. In order to maintain their authority, servants of the Word were cautioned not to be too familiar or jocular in their dealings with the people. At the same they were not to be too austere, especially toward servants of temporal needs. It would be an impossible situation if the servants were heard yelling at each other in the streets. Some servants of the Word occasionally did light manual work, such as raking loose hay and leaves in October.

The servant of temporal needs, or *haushalter*, was in charge of the practical administration of the community. Since his position was a powerful one, he was cautioned to avoid overconfidence, to heed the servants of the Word and to render clear decisions. The brethren, for their part, were told to accept his orders peaceably. The servant of temporal needs had many duties. Above all, he administered the finances of the community. He received all income and at least in theory approved all expenditures, keeping careful records of income and expenses, debts and loans. He collected the earnings of the artisans every two weeks, and an assistant, the *kellner*, evidently administered cash for current expenses. The servant of temporal needs was admonished to be cautious: money saved was money earned. Savings were sent to the central communities and stored in treasuries.

Together with the weinzirl, the servant of temporal needs

directed the community's agricultural business. He arranged
with the lords what work the brethren would do, and he also
went to fairs and markets. Furthermore, he was responsible for
the well-being and safety of the community, for fireplaces,
candles, food supplies, and so on. Another of his duties was to
provide newly arrived believers with clothes and beds. Finally,
it fell to the servant of temporal needs to settle disputes within
the community. The ordinances enjoined him to decide such
matters quickly to minimize their harmful effects. A defecting
Hutterite later said that the servants of temporal needs were
like village judges, busy with interrogations and accusations.

The Hutterite leaders were well aware of the importance of
this office. As one ordinance noted, the negligence of a single
servant of temporal needs could have very harmful results for all
Hutterites. Every servant, the ordinance continued, should have
two qualities above all others: prudence and loyalty. He should
not allow himself to think that the work of other officers, such
as the weinzirl, did not concern him, for the entire community
was in his care. He should always be on call, refraining from
reading in bed or in secret places (privies?) when no one knew
his whereabouts. When necessary, he and other officeholders
should take turns guarding turnip fields or kitchen gardens at
night.

Hutterite communities were frequently situated in or near
a village. At Neumühl, for example, the community occupied the
southern and eastern part of the village.[81] The Hutterites had six
units of farm buildings, or *hofstätten*, at Neumühl by 1589. The
principal hofstatt comprised the great dining room and assembly hall; the kitchen, storeroom, and bakery; the bathhouse;
the stable; the barber-surgeon's quarters; and presumably bed-
chambers for the believers. A nearby hofstatt contained the
printing press, the forge, quarters for women in childbirth, the
hatters' workrooms, the fishermen's hall, and a school for older
children. The coppersmiths were housed in another building,
and the weavers in a fourth adjacent to the stockyard, next to

which was a farm with granary and oxhouse. The sheep enclo-
sure was placed at the end of the village. To some visitors such
communities looked like monasteries. People wishing to enter at
night after the gates had been locked had to disclose where they
had been. The community was guarded by watchmen at night
because of the danger of fire.

Whereas unmarried people slept in large rooms, couples had
little rooms containing only a bed, a chamber pot, and a white
towel. The Polish Antitrinitarians who visited the brethren in
1568 or 1569 indignantly reported, however, that there was only
a sheet hanging between the beds on which married couples
slept. Father Erhard states that there were forty or more beds
in one room so that every sound was audible. But these charges
are plainly no more than slander. The Hutterite leaders, in accord with their privileged status, had separate apartments. The
Poles complained that nobody was allowed access to these rooms
except the few who had been raised to the lower ranks of the
hierarchy. In the middle of the sixteenth century there was
violent protest after the discovery that some of the leaders slept
on feather beds. Ordinary believers slept only on bulrushes.

In theory the believers had no personal property, receiving
clothes, bed linen, and whatever else they needed from the
community. But there is evidence that at least toward the end
of the sixteenth century, the believers were allowed to have
certain objects for personal use, such as sheets, blankets, and
razors.[82] Even so, the principle of community of goods was not
really in danger of being abandoned until the Hutterites were
expelled from Moravia.

The community decreed at what time believers were to rise
and go to bed. Like all sixteenth-century people, the Hutterites
were early risers; the girls who did the spinning got up at 4 A.M.
in winter. Hutterites also dressed alike, as visitors to Austerlitz
noticed. Erhard said that they wore the dress of the peasants
in the Tirolese mountains, Salzburg, Bavaria, Swabia, and
Silesia in an effort, or so he claimed, to impress the native Mora-

vians with their outlandish attire: Silesian carter's hat, close-fitting Bavarian breeches, and long and crafty German beards.[83] To the Mennonites of Prussia the Hutterites looked as shabby as gypsies. Brethren sent to Germany were sometimes recognized by their attire, presumably because it was not fashionable.

The servants of the Word observed with misgiving that vanity also appeared in their communities. In 1605, therefore, they drew up scrupulous regulations for tailors: sleeves of ordinary jackets must not be longer than four and a half viertel, tail coats were not to exceed half an ell, breeches were not to be caught in at the knee or to be baggy or trimmed with ruffles—a fashion of the time. Useless things were the root of all evil, the servants warned. In 1612 they angrily criticized the headmen of the crafts for wearing such clothes as coats lined with fur, costlier apparel than that worn by the servants. The Bohemian type of hat was also forbidden.[84] The Hutterite faith had indeed produced strange forms of legalism.

Meals were taken in common in Hutterite communities. At Neumühl the brethren were wont to eat in the tailors' workshop, probably in a large room. They said grace both before and after meals. Every community had a complete kitchen staff whose duties were carefully described in the ordinances: there were the Haushälterin and her maids, who did the milking and supervised the kitchen and laundry; the storekeeper, who administered the supplies; the cook and her assistants; the food carriers, the bread cutters, and the woman who washed the dishes. The servant of temporal needs had the final responsibility, however. Periodically he himself had to taste the food prepared for the sick, the young, and the aged, as well as for the healthy.

An ordinance issued in 1569, at a time of famine, indicates that the Hutterites were well fed, though their enemies claimed the opposite. As long as the famine lasted, the common brethren were to receive a hot breakfast, some bread at noon, and another hot meal in the evening. They were to have meat on Wednesday

and if possible also on Sunday. Those who did heavy physical
work, such as blacksmiths, were to receive meat twice a week
and in addition a piece of cheese in the afternoon. During the
seventeenth century the brethren had meat every evening and,
when possible, several times a week in the morning as well. Every
day they received two portions of wine. They ate plain bread,
except when they celebrated the Lord's Supper and at Easter,
Whitsun, and Christmas, when special treats were baked.

A visitor to the communities noticed that men and women
were never seen together. Indeed, men and women worked
separately, sat at different tables during meals, and presumably
sat apart during religious services. Even marriage seems from
the outset to have created a problem in the community life of
Moravia. Since there were many single people in the community at Austerlitz, Widemann put pressure on the younger
sisters to get married, for otherwise he would have to marry
the brethren to heathen women. According to Reublin, Widemann simply forced the girls to marry "without the will and
consent of their hearts." As a result four girls separated from
their husbands when it came to consummating the marriage.

Riedemann provided the theological justification for the extraordinary marriage customs that were to evolve in the
Hutterite communities: in choosing one's partner one should
not follow the inclinations of the flesh, which might desire
beauty, youth, or money, but the decision of God as communicated through the servants.[85] Men and women who had
informed the servant of the Word of their wish to get married
were called to one of the principal communities in May or in
the autumn. After a religious service the pairing began.

The reports vary in their descriptions of what actually happened. Stephan Gerlach, a Lutheran theologian from Württemberg was told by his own sister in Moravia that men and women
were placed facing one another and that each girl was given a
choice among three men. Though she was not obliged to take
any of the three, she was not supposed to challenge the de-

cision of the servants either. Gerlach's sister told him frankly that she had not really wished to marry her husband.[86] Another visitor reported that each man was given a choice of one out of three girls. In fact, a combination of these two methods may have been used. According to Erhard and Fischer, the pairing was done largely by the leaders. Those to be married would file into a room, the men on one side, the women on the other. The servant would then tell each man the name of his wife, and each woman the name of her husband. Whatever the method, the personal factor was eliminated in this most personal of all relationships. The leaders made sure that the prospective couples did not already know each other by taking them from different communities. Reportedly there was sometimes much embarrassment because a young fellow might be paired with an older woman or a girl with an elderly man. Those who rejected the match offered them were obliged to wait until the next pairing.

Of course, those who accepted the match were married before the congregation. The traditional Hutterite marriage sermon dates from 1585; it was based on Ephesians 5:12-33 and lasted about two hours. After the service there would be a meal, during which men and women sat separately, as always. Then the couples would leave for their communities, where they were assigned a room. If Hutterite weddings were not celebrated with feasting and entertainment, they were nonetheless considered major events. In 1597 a brother made a point of including in his letter to a missionary in Germany news of the weddings that had been celebrated since the missionary had left.

Erhard contended that the pairing procedures caused much discontent and ill will among the Hutterites. Many believers, he said, simply left the community on not being given the woman they wanted. Such a reaction seems likely enough. To be sure, most marriages in the sixteenth century were arranged by parents and relatives, but the parents were anxious to ensure their children's happiness and took great care to find the right partner for them. Sometimes negotiations with a prospective spouse lasted weeks or even months. Above all, the final decision rested with the young person. In the Hutterite communities, however, the choice was either made by the leaders, who could not know the temperament and character of a young man or woman as well as the parents knew it, or the person arbitrarily chose between three prospective spouses who were unknown to him. Why did the Hutterites devise this bizarre system? They may have been trying to discourage erotic relations among believers by eliminating love as a factor in marriage, and they certainly were trying to ensure that a believer did not become engrossed in his marriage. Since marriage served only to avoid fornication and produce offspring, a mechanical way of arranging marriages was considered sufficient. Anyway, husband and wife were together only when they went to bed, for there was no place for family life in the Hutterite communities.[87] That such drastic changes in marriage customs were actually carried out reveals the fantastic power wielded by the servants of the Word.

The Hutterites also had radically different methods of rearing children. Women giving birth were put together in one room. The newly born babies were taken care of in another room, which according to a visitor's account had nothing but cradles in it. Only widows took care of the mothers and children. Having thus been born in common, at least as much as possible, the children were then educated in common. In his pamphlet "On the Great Transformation," Johann Hergott insisted that in the new society, all children should be educated in common from the age of three or four. If the Hutterites were not acquainted with Hergott's proposals, their attempt to create a classless society led them to similar conclusions. Between 1528 and 1531 the congregation of Austerlitz was already taking care of all the children. When he stood up against Widemann in January 1531, Reublin claimed that no fewer than twenty small children had died because they had received only solid food, with no milk. After the exodus to Auspitz the brethren bought a house at the Rossmarkt, where the children were educated by a man and several women. At night they stayed with their parents, however. During the years that followed, the Hutterites developed their new system of education. In particular, it appears that Hieronymus Käls of Kufstein was the father of the Hutterite school system.

Most, though not all, communities had a "small" and a "great" school. All children had to be placed in the small school at the age of two or three; after a few years they advanced to the great school. These schools were not similar to the ordinary schools that existed all over Protestant Germany, however, or to modern kindergartens, for in the Hutterite system the children no longer lived with their parents. As many as four hundred children were in the school at Schakwitz in 1544. The records also speak of schools with four hundred children around 1600. Children of newly arriving families were not all placed in the same school: in 1558 one man had two of his children in the school at Lundenburg and four at Deckenwitz.[88]

Every school was headed by a schoolmaster and a school-mother. They in turn had several women helpers, such as the *betterin*, who was in charge of the beds. The servants reminded those who ran the schools of their great responsibility: they must be present at all times. The schoolmaster and the school-mother were not allowed to introduce innovations without the permission of the servants.

Erhard claimed that the schoolmother and her helpers were irascible women who beat the children without love, restraint, or pity. There may have been an element of truth in this charge. According to one ordinance some parents refrained from beating their children because they would be beaten enough at school. In their instructions to the educators, the Hutterite servants repeatedly emphasized moderation: those in charge of the children should treat them as if they were their own, preferring leniency to severity. Realizing that children were not alike, the Hutterite leaders recommended different educational methods: one child might be won by friendly words; another with a present; a third only by severity. Children who were to be punished for lying, stealing, or unchastity should be spanked not secretly but in front of all the others. Detailed regulations were given on how to take care of the children: the temperature of the water for their baths, the clothes and shoes they wore, their beds, and their toilet. The children were not to sit with their elbows on the table or reach their hands into their bowls. At night the women had to make sure the children did not catch colds. Once a week the lice must be picked from their clothes.

The children were divided into three groups: the youngest, the "Tafelkinder," and the oldest. The oldest girls rose at five in the morning, and the oldest boys at six; then the Tafelkinder would get up, and finally the very young children. In winter the children went to bed at six, in summer at sunset. The ordinances required that they be taken on daily walks to gardens, fields, and forests. Erhard, however, reports that only once every two weeks were the children driven up the hills, like flocks of geese. The older boys and girls helped in the community, cutting bread, carrying water, making the smaller children's beds, sweeping floors, and nursing the sick. How long the children stayed at school is unknown. On leaving school they slept in the dormitories with the unmarried believers.

Instruction centered on religion. As soon as the little ones began to talk, the teachers taught them to recite prayers. In the morning when they got up and in the evening before going to bed, all boys and girls were called together to kneel down and raise their hands while a boy recited a prayer. Once or twice a week the schoolmaster would preach to the children, though without "straining them with long sermons, many scriptures and quotations." The older children attended the regular services in the community on Sundays.

Boys were taught to read and write. Girls were taught to spin and sew, though they also received some instruction in writing. The basis for instruction was provided by the Ten Commandments, the Twelve Articles of Faith, and the children's catechism. The intellectual level of the education the Hutterite children received was elementary and can at best be compared to the primary education in Protestant Germany; certainly the Protestants educated girls better. The foremost aim of Hutterite education was to accustom the children to life in a community and to instill in them strong religious and moral principles.

Actually, Hutterite children behaved like children everywhere: at least there were complaints that in the evening they would run up and down in front of houses and around courtyards, disturbing the adults. But Erhard claimed that the Hutterite children lacked color and looked puffy and sickly: hardly one out of fifty, he said, ever grew up to be a strong and healthy adult. Although Erhard's figure was greatly exaggerated, infant mortality seems to have been high in the communities. One Tirolese woman lost her four children within six weeks after her arrival at Schakwitz in 1543. Three of the four children of a couple from Württemberg died in 1559.[89] This high mortality rate may have been caused by poor hygiene in the schools. The Hutterites recognized the danger and dealt with it in a strict ordinance of 1568: new children were to be examined, and those who had scabs, syphilis, or other diseases were to sleep and eat apart. Their linen, brushes, and combs were also to be kept separate.

Erhard further said that many Hutterite children later became rather strange. For example, they avoided company. Even the Swiss Brethren in Germany thought that the extreme moralism imposed by the Hutterites on their children produced a morbid sensitivity: nobody could carry a pitcher of wine across the street without being condemned.[90] The Hutterites themselves admitted that their system had flaws, for many of their children were poorly educated and developed into unstable people who would run off into the world. Some even turned out to be evil and came to a bad end.[91]

Clearly the Hutterite educational system imposed a great sacrifice on parents by separating them from their children. For this reason the ordinances enjoined upon them strictly to give up their children at the age of two rather than wait until they had to be taken away. Rigid rules were laid down concerning visits and gifts: parents had to ask permission even to take their children for a walk. The Hutterites mitigated the rigor of this system by allowing parents to have their children during the day for four weeks in the year. Some women could not endure the separation and returned with their children to Germany.[92] One mother simply took her sick child out of school. The leaders rebuked her for her disobedience, but let her nurse him. When the same woman subsequently fetched her other children, she was expelled from the community.[93]

Of course, boarding schools were not unknown in sixteenth-century Germany. The houses of the Brethren of the Common Life had already offered lodging to pupils before the Reformation. The convent schools in Württemberg and the prince's schools in Saxony were also boarding schools, but the boys entered them at the age of fourteen or fifteen, not at two. Obviously the Hutterite boarding schools were aimed at destroying the special bonds between parents and children, for such bonds were incompatible with life in a Hutterite community. People who reared their own children would naturally consider the interests of their children first and think of the community only afterward. They might even try to provide for their children's future by amassing property. As a result the old class distinctions would reappear. In the Hutterite community, by contrast, both parents and children would be emotionally attached only to the congregation—at least that is what the leaders hoped. They even went so far as to bury children without notifying their mothers. However extreme their doctrines, it must be admitted that the Hutterites were consistent. Ultimately the institution of the family may very well not be compatible with the principles of a classless society.

Although 73 of the 102 Hutterite communities were located in towns and villages where only Slavic dialects were spoken, the Hutterites preserved their German language. But the dialects of emigrants from the Palatinate, Hesse, Württemberg, Switzerland, the Tirol, and Austria differed greatly. According to Erhard, the leaders therefore tried to impose the Tirolese peasant dialect on all. Whether they succeeded is doubtful, however: in all likelihood a variety of dialects was heard in the communities, especially among first-generation emigrants. The Hutterite Chronicle was written in "early new High German" with many words of upper German and particularly of Bavarian-Austrian origin.

Sometimes a believer asked for permission to live in another community. The servants frowned on these requests, for did not such a person reveal that he still clung to the world? The servants of temporal needs were not permitted to accept people who had left another community. To be sure, whenever communities were situated in close proximity, such as those of Wischenau, Teikowitz, and Stiegnitz, the Hutterites freely went from one to the other. But as a rule they had to confine their lives to one community. The believer was not allowed to leave his community even temporarily without permission, which was not readily granted. Inevitably some Hutterites grew weary of this isolation and simply walked away on Sundays and feast days, forgoing religious services. There were brethren who went to the markets and brethren who watched public executions of criminals. The servants discovered to their chagrin that some brethren conversed with defectors or people of the world: even the servants of temporal needs socialized with the local noblemen and their officials, thus divulging the affairs of the communities to the outside world.

Of course, the servants of the Word had to travel frequently to visit believers in the "wilderness" or attend conferences with the bishop. While simple Hutterites walked on foot with a walking stick, the servants traveled by horse and carriage. These trips eventually drew severe censure, for the leaders not only took their wives and children with them but also loaded coaches with clothes and bed linen.

If the ordinary brethren did little traveling, there were people who came to see them, such as noblemen on their way to the imperial court at Prague, messengers from Germany, relatives, or people who were simply travelers for one reason or another. The ladies of the Moravian nobility preferred the clean houses of the Hutterites to the Moravian village inns. While offering hospitality, the Hutterites yet remained cool and reserved. The Polish Antitrinitarians complained that an escort had dogged their every step, as if they were Tartars. When Stephan Gerlach, whose relatives had joined the Hutterites, came to Wischenau in 1578 and asked a fellow he met whether there were any people from Württemberg and especially Knittlingen in the community, the brother answered very slowly and reluctantly that there were. He refused to give any names, however, until he realized that he was talking to his own brother-in-law. He then took Gerlach to the dining hall and served him and his companion meat, wine, and beer, as the ordinances prescribed. Gerlach's sisters were overjoyed to see their brother and showed him the Hutterite school. One zealous servant of the Word did not fail to explain to him that the Lutheran doctrines of church and community were all wrong.

As one might expect, the Hutterite Chronicle records that piety and strict morality reigned in the communities. Curses and blasphemous talk were never heard. Dancing, gambling, and excessive drinking were unknown. Only Christian hymns were sung, and never infamous "bawdy songs," by which was meant folk songs. With prayers and thanks the believers went to bed, and with prayers and thanks they rose again. Some people who had left the communities took a different view, however. One

Tirolese woman said in 1544 that the practice of denouncing sinners to the leaders led to many quarrels among the brethren.[94] Jedelhauser also reported that there was much quarreling, grumbling, spite, disobedience, and lying in the communities. He himself had witnessed a carter and a weinzirl assailing each other with sharp, cutting words. Although they did not come to blows, their looks were fierce and vicious. When Jedelhauser expressed his shock at this episode to the servant of temporal needs, he was told: forget it; it will pass; do not think badly of them.

Apparently the leaders of the communities did sometimes give rather gay parties. At one of these feasts, held by the schoolmaster of Malspitz, fire broke out at one o'clock in the morning, leveling eighteen houses.[95] Erhard and Fischer claimed that some Hutterites were alcoholics: how often during the previous summer had the leaders left the local nobleman's castle blind drunk and later been found lying in the cornfields! [96] The ordinances did indeed warn the leaders to be careful in this regard. Their breath should not smell of brandy in the morning or of wine during the day. Nevertheless, drunkenness seems to have been a problem for only a few, and the punishment for excessive drinking was severe: one drunkard is known to have been expelled.

Citing specific examples, Erhard, Fischer, and Jedelhauser all maintained that promiscuity was widespread in the Hutterite communities. There is no proof that sexual transgressions were more frequent among the Hutterites than in other communities of ten to twenty thousand people. But as usual, the charges are not completely groundless. The destruction of several communities and the unsettled conditions during the wars from 1596 to 1608 might have led to a relaxing of discipline. It may be, too, that religious fervor had fallen off after the first two generations of believers had died. Whatever the reason, in 1612 the servants were appalled by the "gross and inhuman unchastity" in the communities and ordered severe punishment for sinners. To avoid rumors the servants of temporal needs were to be accompanied only by the housekeeper and no other woman when they traveled to the market. They were not to laugh and joke with the women of the congregation or let them lie too long in bed, for soon the servant would start to play and be intimate with them.[97] A later ordinance warned that at first everything looked quite harmless: a brother would take to sitting and talking at wrong times and of wrong things and then at the first opportunity put his arm around the woman's neck and other parts.[98]

The Hutterites brought with them from Germany the custom of building bathhouses, which soon were very popular in Moravia. On Saturdays, indeed, their bathhouses were packed with villagers. The ordinances sharply reminded the barber-surgeons of their great responsibility. They were told to study dispensatories, to collect herbs and roots, to keep their instruments clean, and to be extremely careful with their prescriptions. Actually, Hutterite physicians such as Georg Zobel, Balthasar Göller, Sebastian Dietrich, and Conrad Blösy enjoyed a good reputation. Nikolsburg seems to have been the seat of Hutterite medicine. Possibly the early Hutterite barber-surgeons had met Paracelsus, who paid a lengthy visit in 1537 to Johan von Lepnick, on whose estate the Hutterites had a community. But we do not really know how the Hutterite barber-surgeons learned and practiced medicine, and hence the basis for their renown. In any case, their services were certainly much in demand with the nobility and burghers in Moravia and Austria: Georg Zobel was even summoned to Prague to help the emperor Rudolf II in 1582 and 1599. Like modern missionaries the Hutterite physicians tried not only to cure bodies but to save souls, with the result that Archduke Ferdinand ordered their arrest in 1612. But the Austrian nobility tended to ignore his orders. In 1613 the abbot of Admont himself issued a safe-conduct for a surgeon of Nikolsburg.

Though the Hutterites spent practically all day working, had no family life, and did not even enjoy harmless pastimes such

as playing games, they were generally healthy. One visitor noticed that they seldom fell ill, and said he had seen more really
old people among the Hutterites than elsewhere. To be sure, the
community took care of its sick and old: the Hutterites tried
to make sure that nobody died alone.

Unlike the Anabaptists in Germany and Switzerland, the
Hutterites were able to establish their own cemeteries. In 1544,
however, one Tirolese woman claimed that the Hutterites had
buried her three dead children somewhere in the fields. When
her fourth child also died, they had refused to bury him: she
had taken him out of school without their permission, and now,
they said, she could also bury him herself.[99] Similarly, Erhard
said that the Hutterites used to bury their deceased fellow believers like old dogs or criminals, throwing them into a hole in
a vineyard or meadow, "sine lux, sine crux et sine deus." In
reality the Hutterites had cemeteries at least in the second half
of the sixteenth century. In one community the dead were
buried between a fish pond and a grove. In 1589 the brethren
at Neumühl reserved part of a field near the river Theya as their
burial ground.[100] Although in 1582 a defector said that the dead
were buried without any ceremony, burial sermons have been
preserved.[101] Even so, there is something strange about these
Hutterite burials. One man claimed in 1557 that his deceased
wife and another woman had been buried in the same grave,
and that he had not been allowed to attend the burial.[102] In the
seventeenth century the brethren became so irreverent at burials
that an ordinance was issued expressly enjoining them to bury
the dead with devotion and decency, not with laughter and
gossiping.[103]

Religious Life

Clearly, religion dominated Hutterite thought, but little is
known of the actual religious life of the Hutterites. Did they
read the Bible daily? According to the Antitrinitarians, the servants thought the brethren should read Riedemann's confession

of faith rather than the Scriptures. Even Catholic writers admitted, however, that these uneducated peasants and craftsmen had a phenomenal command of the Bible.

The Hutterites recited prayers several times a day. In 1582 a defector said that in the morning they prayed, "May God the Father protect me"; at noon, "May God the Son protect me"; and in the evening, "May the Holy Ghost protect me." The same man recited the beginning of a prayer he must have heard frequently: "Lord, I thank you for giving me food and drink. Lord, I thank you for giving us house and home."

As in the Zwinglian and Lutheran churches, the life of the congregation centered on worship, baptism, and the Lord's Supper. In the community at Austerlitz services were held three times a week between 1528 and 1531. According to Reublin this congregation stopped saying the Lord's Prayer. The Hutterites did not have churches, chapels, or altars, but met simply in a large room, such as the community dining room or spinning room.

We have already seen that some German Anabaptists considered Sunday an ordinary day like any other. Riedemann's view was that believers should observe one day of quiet on which they read the Word of the Lord. Since it did not matter which day was chosen, they might as well designate Sunday out of consideration for their neighbors. Toward the end of the sixteenth century, however, the Hutterites worked on Sundays: on Sunday, September 21, 1586, for example, Erhard saw Hutterites dyeing cloth and firing clay bricks. Fischer also reported that the Hutterites simply abolished Sunday and other feast days. These accusations are corroborated by the Hutterite ordinance of 1651, which expressly ordered the overseers of crafts to make sure that the young people came to their workshops on Sundays and feast days.

During the sixteenth century the Hutterites held services twice a week: on Sunday before seven in the morning and on Wednesday late in the evening when, according to Erhard, the tired brethren would have preferred to go to bed like other people. Believers who did not live in the communities but in mills or on noblemen's farms made great efforts to come to the services, walking on dark nights through mud and snow or waiting in the wind by lakes and rivers for the ferry. Obviously the services meant much to them—spiritual comfort and an opportunity to meet their fellow believers. The Hutterites were told to come to the services in decent dress: the men should be sure to wear coats, and the women, veils.[104]

The order of the Hutterite service is known only from the 1620s onward. But it is likely that in the seventeenth century the tradition-minded Hutterites only codified the form of service their forebears had already practiced in the sixteenth century. First the congregation sang a hymn, and then the servant of the Word preached a short sermon (*vorred*) dealing with a biblical passage or a specific subject. After a prayer the servant would deliver a second, longer sermon (*lehr*) that sometimes interpreted an entire chapter of the Scriptures. The service ended with another hymn. According to Fischer the believers did not kneel or stand during the service but seemed to be nailed fast to the benches. During the middle of the seventeenth century, under the direction of Bishop Ehrenpreis, the Hutterites began to write down all the vorred and lehr. From that time on, the servant read only these sermons during the service. Altogether some eighty to one hundred vorred and two hundred fifty to three hundred lehr have been preserved; of course, they are still being used in the Hutterite services. Presumably most of these sermons date from the time of Bishop Ehrenpreis.[105] The Hutterites also had collections of lehr for specific events such as weddings, elections and confirmations of servants and bishops, departures of missionaries, baptisms, and even exclusions. In addition to their collection of sermons, from the seventeenth century onward the Hutterites used a religious calendar in which books or chapters from the Bible were prescribed for every Sunday and feast day. It seems quite likely that the

Hutterites were already following such a calendar before their expulsion from Moravia.

Baptism was a very important part of the Hutterites' religious life. Children born in Hutterite communities were baptized at the age of twelve. As for emigrants, some had already been baptized in their native countries; others were baptized during the journey to Moravia, for example at Donauwörth or Dillingen or during a halt near the Brenner Pass. In 1576, however, a brother by the name of Ott Niederländer severely criticized this practice of baptizing people who had not even seen the community in Moravia. Having been led to expect a peaceful and lovely life, they later were dumbfounded when they encountered quarrels, dissension, spite, backbiting, and vanity. Of course, many believers were not baptized until they reached Moravia. One man was baptized two months after his arrival, others three months after their arrival.[106] Niederländer also reproached the leaders for browbeating people into having themselves baptized, thus making it all the more likely that they would run away. One fellow who just did not want to be baptized had to clean the stable.

It seems that believers of several communities often assembled in one community to be baptized. This custom explains why as many as seventy believers were sometimes baptized in one community on the same day.[107] The ceremony is described in detail by Riedemann. During the second half of the sixteenth century, probably between 1565 and 1578, the Hutterite leaders gave the proceedings their final form. The actual baptism was preceded by instruction (Taufunterricht), held on the Friday and Saturday evenings and the Sunday morning before the service. This instruction consisted of two parts: first, there were three lessons (Taufreden) lasting about two hours and preceding prayer services. Second, there were three sermons (Tauflehren) delivered during the prayer services on Friday and Saturday evenings and during the main service on Sunday.

The baptism on Sunday also consisted of two parts: a private

meeting of the believer and the servants,[108] and the actual ceremony. At the meeting the servants first inquired whether the
believer had committed any punishable offenses in the world
and whether he had promised marriage to a woman not of the
community; if the answer to either was yes, the congregation
would not stand up for him. Then the servants told the believer
that those who entered the service of God would have to suffer
persecution; that he must be willing to submit to punishment
at the hands of the brethren and "let himself be used in the
countries," or on missionary trips; that he must give up all property; and that the congregation was not obliged to return any
property to him if he should leave.[109] The actual ceremony of
baptism was similar to that performed by other Anabaptists.
The believer had to recite a confession of faith and answer
questions about baptism. Then the kellner, servant of temporal
needs, or weinzirl brought a pitcher of water which the servant
of the Word poured over the believer's head, saying, "Your
faith has saved you."

Like other Anabaptists the Hutterites valued the ban very
highly as a way of dealing with sinners. First two or three believers approached the sinner and admonished him. If this step
proved fruitless, they would report to the servant of the Word,
who in the presence of two or three believers would interrogate
the sinner and hear witnesses. As the Hutterites discovered,
however, brethren were frequently reluctant to testify against
one another.[110] Then the matter was brought before the congregation during the church service. After the sermon and before the prayer, the servant of the Word would order the
sinner to step forward, disclose his wrongdoing, and ask the
congregation how he should be punished. Contrary to the practice in the German and Swiss congregations, only the most
prominent brethren would speak: first the servant of temporal
needs or an old brother, then the kellner or the weinzirl or the
headmen of the crafts. Ordinary believers merely listened to the
proceedings—another example of the authoritarian character of

Hutterite Anabaptism. Afterward, the minister would summarize
what kind of punishment the majority of the speakers had
recommended and invite the congregation to express their approval by silence. Then the decision would be formally announced to the sinner.

There were two types of penalty: "renunciation of the
peace" and outright expulsion. In the first, the lighter punishment, the sinner was forbidden only to give or receive from
another the Lord's Peace, that is, the Hutterite form of greeting.
He would stay in the community, do his usual work, eat with
the others, and sleep in his old bed. He would several times be
summoned before the congregation until he was finally pardoned and again be allowed to give and receive the Lord's
Peace. As a sign of his readmission, he would shake hands with
several witnesses and say, "The Lord be praised." The second
penalty, expulsion from the Hutterite community, was of course
reserved for serious offenses. Not only did the expelled person
have to find lodging and work elsewhere, but his believing spouse
was forbidden to have conjugal relations with him until he had
shown "real fruits of repentance." In other words, like the
Mennonites, the Hutterites practiced strict avoidance.

If the expelled sinner was willing to do penance, he had to
come to the sermons every Wednesday and Sunday, standing
at the window or door. After three or more weeks, he would be
summoned before the congregation and told to bear the punishment still longer. He might be summoned again after two more
weeks, and yet again after another week. At last the servant of
the Word would allow him to return to the community for ob-
servation. In the community he had to do hard, unpleasant work
such as loading manure or digging. He would eat by himself
at the stove or a separate table and sleep on hay and straw in
the stable. The brethren would not greet him or shake hands
with him. This stage of the punishment could last three or even
six months. Finally the servant of the Word would call upon
the congregation to discuss the matter. A few prominent

brethren would recommend that the sinner be pardoned and that the congregation express its approval by silence. The minister would lay his hands on the kneeling sinner and readmit him to the congregation. Through the sinner's readmission, all suspicion and complaints against him were considered to have been swept away. Even those guilty of fornication might be readmitted, if they had done penance. People who did penance only on their deathbed, however, were not readmitted.[111]

If a sinner did not do penance, the Hutterites would give him a few pennies and tell him to leave. A woman was not obliged to leave the community and follow her unrepentant husband into the world, but if her husband was willing to stay near the community, the servants might allow her to live with him. Their children had to attend the Hutterite schools, of course. If a sinner left for good, his spouse who remained in the community could not simply remarry. Only if the sinner remarried, thereby dissolving his first marriage, could the believing spouse also marry.

The Hutterites celebrated the Lord's Supper only once a year, at Whitsun or possibly Easter, and only in the larger communities, such as Neumühl, Schakwitz, Pribitz, Stiegnitz, and Austerlitz. This was the only time when the believers were allowed to leave their own community—like prisoners leaving their prison, Erhard commented. At Schakwitz not less than seven hundred men and women gathered in 1545, and we even hear of gatherings of two or three thousand: sometimes the streets of the small towns and villages were filled with Hutterite men and women. For two or three days the servants delivered sermons—vexatious and drowsing sermons, according to Erhard, that made the people fall asleep. One former Hutterite, however, said that the sermons consisted of sharp admonitions.

During the seventeenth century the manner in which the Lord's Supper was to be celebrated was finally specified. Two services were held on Easter Sunday: the morning sermon, dating from 1585, was based on Exodus 12; the afternoon ser-

mon, dating from 1629 and lasting from three to three and a half
hours, was based on I Corinthians 10. On Monday the Supper
was celebrated in a service lasting about four hours. The sermon,
based on I Corinthians XI, dated from 1629 or earlier. For the
Resurrection service on Tuesday, seven different sermons have
been preserved.[112]

The ceremony of breaking the bread was quite simple. Plates
of bread slices and pitchers of wine were placed on the tables.
After the sermon the believers would go to the tables singing
Riedemann's hymn, "Wir glauben an einen Gott und lieben
in vom Hertzen." Then they would break the bread and afterward sing Hut's hymn, "Wir danksagen dir, Herr gott der
eeren." Having drunk from the chalice, they concluded with
the hymn "Do ward der Fels geschlagen." The ceremony ended
with a brief exhortation.

The celebration of the Lord's Supper was also a happy
occasion when the Hutterites could see their relatives, friends,
and countrymen who lived in other communities. For once the
Hutterites indulged in some carousing. Erhard reports that during these three days, they carried on as if they were at a
country feast, consuming several oxen, cows, calves, pigs, and
sheep: "This is what they call celebrating the Lord's Supper,"
the priest sighed.

When during the early seventeenth century discipline in the
communities slackened, some shocking episodes occurred. The
Hutterite leaders angrily noted in 1612 that people got drunk
on brandy at a time when the sweet memory of the Lord was
celebrated. In one community several buckets of brandy were
distributed among the guests. In the morning when the believers
went to the sermon, they heard these drunkards bawling at
one another in the chambers and workshops. Some went from
room to room guzzling three or four cups of brandy at a time.
They slept through most of the sermon, while the air reeked
of brandy. Horrified, the servants resolved that brandy should
no longer be made available except for medicinal purposes.[113]

Economic Life

Idleness was not tolerated in the Hutterite communities. Even former priests, such as Leonhard Dax, and former government officials of noble birth, such as Michel Veldthaler, were expected to do their share of physical labor. The Polish Antitrinitarians who visited the communities in 1568 and 1569 were dismayed when some of their educated young men were straightaway sent to thresh rye and chop wood. The individual believer did not choose his work; it was assigned to him. The Poles remarked how humbly the brothers and sisters carried out even the most unpleasant of the servants' orders.

Agriculture

There was a considerable amount of farming in the Hutterite communities. By 1610, for example, the community at Neumühl had not less than 95,587 square yards of vineyards, fourteen square plots of fields, two meadows, three gardens, and three ponds stocked with fish.[114] These vineyards and fields did not lie in the same stretch of land but were divided up into small parcels scattered among the vineyards and fields belonging to the local lords and villagers. The community at Neumühl also had sheep, oxen, and other animals, probably cows. The Hutterites must have seemed prosperous, for at times they were accused of impoverishing the native Moravian population by renting large tracts of arable land and vineyards.

There were difficulties, however. At Auspitz during the 1530s the followers of Zaunring and Reublin felt wretched at having to do heavy work, to which they were not accustomed, in the vineyards. Like the majority of the early Anabaptists in Germany, Austria, and Switzerland, most early Hutterites were probably craftsmen. In later years, too, many newcomers avoided farm work insisting that the missionaries had promised them work in the crafts. Making knives or earthenware was obviously more interesting than carting manure or plowing fields. Since the

Hutterite leaders were short of people to work in the vineyards, feed the animals, cut wood, and administer farms, they forbade the missionaries to make any more such promises. Actually we do know of emigrants who worked as farmers and vinedressers.[115] There were so many vinedressers in the communities that one missionary even addressed an epistle to them.[116] The Hutterites sold wine to the native population until this practice was forbidden in 1590 by the Estates.

Farming was under the general direction of the servant of temporal needs. He was responsible for seeing that the grass was cut before it sprouted into ears, that the straw cutters and mowers did a good job, that the grain was harvested in time, and that the animals had enough straw and hay. He himself had to inspect fields and vineyards, barns and stables. Whenever extra hands were required for farm work, he would make arrangements for craftsmen to be released from the workshops. He also made certain that all the farming equipment—plows, plowshares, wheels, wagons, hoes, and ladders—were placed under the roofs and kept in good condition.

It was the weinzirl, as the Hutterites called the foreman, who supervised the actual work. He assigned people to such tasks as mowing, threshing, and preserving cabbage in jars, and saw that the work was done quickly and well. He was also responsible for preventing the pilfering of fruit, wine grapes, and cider. Actually, morale was high among the Hutterites: even if a boy chanced to knock down some grapes, he would not eat them. Finally, the weinzirl had to see that the work was done peacefully. Despite these responsibilities the weinzirl could take no action except on the advice of the servant of temporal needs. He could not go to bed without consulting the servant about the work to be done on the following day; on this matter the servant seems to have had the final word. The weinzirl was forbidden even to reveal any differences of opinion he might have had with the servant of temporal needs.

The Hutterites knew their farming quite well. They took care to analyze the soil—sand, loam, or clay; lumpy, hard, or fine; dry or humid—and then made the appropriate arrangements for manure and irrigation. They used teamwork: on one occasion 23 young women were working in one field during the harvest. At harvest time, too, the straw cutters and mowers and other workers in the fields were required to get up an hour earlier, but were allowed an hour's rest at noon and rations of bacon and wine. A group (*zug*) of threshers threshed three *muth* (one muth is equal to about 50.7 bushels) of grain in a week; a mower cut a cartload (*fuder*) of hay in one day.[117] No wonder the Hutterite farms flourished. Their enemies protested that they had the best fields, meadows, and gardens. In their cattle sheds they had plenty of fat oxen, pigs, and sheep, and the horses they bred were in great demand. When the Hutterites were finally driven out of their last 24 communities, they left behind more than 800 muth of barley, 478 muth of oats, 133 muth of buckwheat, 300 barrels (*fass*) of wine, 130 cows, 70 oxen, 150 horses, and 655 pigs.

All the same the Hutterites were not self-sufficient but had to buy large quantities of grain, lard, and oil. On one occasion they bought grain worth not less than 2,200 florins. They liked to buy grain directly from the peasants at a lower price. The Moravian Estates finally prohibited such purchasing and ordered the Hutterites to buy at the public market, with the result that they were accused of ruining the local markets by buying up all the grain. Much of this grain was not immediately used but stored. Thanks to their large supplies of grain, flour, and foodstuffs, and to the mutual help among the communities, the Hutterites were much less affected by bad harvests and famine than the Moravian population in general. The terrible famine of 1600 caused them hardly any difficulty at all, and they were even able to help the Moravian villagers.

Craftsmanship

Although the Hutterites farmed extensively, craftsmanship
seems to have played an even greater role in their communities.
The Hutterite Chronicle enumerates 36 crafts that were practiced by the brethren in addition to the spinning and weaving
done by the women.

The buyers for the communities were in charge of regulating
the supply of raw materials. No doubt mutual cooperation among
the buyers of the various communities helped the Hutterites turn
price fluctuations on the Moravian markets to their advantage.
The buyers were warned not to trust the merchants, butchers,
and Jews, who allegedly had already cheated the brethren. Although the exact relation of the buyers to production is not
clear, they seem to have bought and distributed the raw
material and to have made sure that the work was well done and
fairly priced. Since the buyers handled considerable sums, they
were told never to entrust any money to their wives, but only
to the servant of temporal needs or reliable brethren.

Each of the 36 crafts was headed by a headman, a *fürgestellte*,
who accepted orders, assigned and supervised the work, and
sold the products. The servants enjoined upon all craftsmen,
especially the saddlers, leather cutters, and smiths, to repair used
articles before producing new ones. Also, they were to work
first for the congregation and only afterward for outsiders:
apparently such a rule was necessary because the craftsmen
preferred to make the more challenging and intricate products
that were sold to the outside world. The headmen were forbidden to ask for expensive working tools.

At least in theory, the headman had nothing to do with
financial matters. Within a week or two weeks at the most, he
was supposed to hand over all the money he had received from
sales to the servant of temporal needs. But some headmen could
not resist the temptation to dispose of the money otherwise.
such as by giving cash to missionaries or granting loans to

outsiders. The headmen were also forbidden to lend or borrow from one another, for no money was to be exchanged within the community: if one headman gave another some material, he should not expect to reap a profit. Headmen who needed money were expected to request it from the servants. Evidently the Hutterites experienced difficulties in separating money from production, however, and in centralizing the financial administration in the hands of the servant of temporal needs. Of course, the headmen were subordinate to the servants of temporal needs and servants of the Word. Without the permission of the servant of temporal needs, for example, a headman could not go to the markets to buy wine, oxen, sows, pigs, spice, or crockery, nor could he commission anyone else to go. All purchases were ultimately controlled by the servant of temporal needs. Nonetheless, since the headmen controlled production, they occupied a powerful position in the communities.

In addition to the raw material available in the communities, such as hides, the Hutterites bought large quantitites from outside. On one occasion as many as twenty wagon loads of leather arrived at Protzka. The leaders ensured that only good material was bought: though Silesian and Hungarian iron was cheaper than Styrian iron, they bought the Styrian iron for its superior quality. Sometimes they did not have much choice, however: they preferred to buy their wool in Hungary, but a law passed by the Moravian Estates obliged them to buy it in royal towns and in villages owned by nobility. Still, Hutterite cloth was of high quality. Already in 1534 the cotton spinners produced such fine cotton yarn and gauze that ascetically inclined brethren raised an outcry of indignation. The women spinners worked together in a large room: one visitor saw no less than a hundred distaffs in one room. Though they worked long hours, in winter until eight in the evening, they seem to have been a happy lot, singing while spinning.

The craftsmanship of the Hutterites was well known. Knives produced in the communities, with sheaths of mother-of-pearl, ivory, and sandalwood, were often presented as gifts. Hutterite pottery, with its elaborate decorations in yellow, blue, and white, found its way into the gardens and houses of numerous noblemen and burghers in Moravia and Hungary. Coaches, furniture, metal beds, and clocks made by the Hutterites were ordered through Moravian intermediaries by princes of the Empire and even cardinals. Hutterite seamstresses are known to have made shirts for Moravian noblemen. The brethren also made glass windows.

The houses built by the Hutterites were unusually solid. The walls were made of unfired clay. The thatched roofs, which sloped upward from the top of the first floor, consisted of several layers of a special mixture of brick clay and straw and were supposed to be fireproof. There were relatively large rooms on the ground floors, and numerous small attics. On the inside the floors, walls, and roof were covered with layers of fired white clay and brick clay.

The diversity of Hutterite craftsmanship was partly due to the fact that in Germany, Austria, and Switzerland artisans of no fewer than 123 crafts joined the Anabaptist sect. Those who emigrated to Moravia pooled their knowledge. In general, too, the technical skill of German craftsmen was higher in the sixteenth century than ever before or since. Assured of a secure livelihood, the Hutterite craftsman could devote great care to his work.

Catholic critics accused the Hutterites of destroying the independence of the native craftsmen by forcing them to work for their communities in order to survive. No independent craftsman, they claimed, could be found within five or six miles of a Hutterite settlement.[118] In all likelihood the native craftsmen were forced out of the market by the low price of Hutterite products. For one thing, the Hutterites bought their raw material in large quantities and hence at a lower price. For another, their production costs were lower because they did not have to pay markup on half-finished products. For example, Hutterite spinners would send yarn to the weavers, who in turn would supply the clothmakers and tailors. Similarly, at Altenmarkt the Hutterites had a big tannery and leather factory. But there may not have been much division of labor within a craft anyway. Perhaps a more important factor in keeping production costs at a minimum was simply that Hutterite craftsmen were paid no wages.

There were certain things the Hutterites refused to make. They did not produce swords, spears, muskets, or other weapons, for unlike knives, hoes, and axes, weapons only served to kill. Nor did they produce items of finery that might give rise to vanity and pride, such as elaborate braiding and frogging, or passion flower and other embroidery work. Thus religious considerations clearly restricted the economic activity of the brethren.

Relations to Nobility and Prelates

A large number of Hutterites did not work in the communities but were employed by lords and burghers. Hutterite craftsmen built mills and breweries, dug wells, laid water pipes, and built stoves particularly in Moravia but also in Austria, Hungary, and Bohemia. They managed mills and farms for one-third or one-fourth of the produce or for wages—whichever was customary or considered more to their advantage. Hutterites were also in charge of sheep farms, wineries, malt mills, fish ponds, orchards, pleasure gardens, and brickyards. Many ladies of the Moravian nobility employed Hutterite women as midwives, wet nurses, and nurses, or to work in their milk room, laundry, and kitchen. No doubt the nobles considered the Hutterites excellent employees: they were more skillful than the Moravian population, and thanks to their preoccupation with religion and morality and their status as a small, persecuted minority, they were hardworking and conscientious.

The Hutterite leaders drew up ordinances for those who worked in the outside world, or the "wilderness" (einöde), as it was called. Needless to say they were still considered part of the communistic economy: they had to hand their wages over to the servant of temporal needs. One defector in Swabia described how he had worked all week as a bricklayer only to have his wages taken away on Saturday. But of course, he was also provided for by the community.

Catholics such as Erhard and Fischer bitterly castigated the lords for being so dependent on the Hutterites. The lords trusted their secrets to the Hutterites, they charged, more than to anyone else. The Hutterites entered the lords' chambers unannounced, while noblemen had to wait for hours. One prominent lord had entrusted all his wine to the Hutterites without even demanding an account of it. The lords visited the Hutterite communities, raised their hats when they saw the brethren, addressed them with the kindest of words, stayed overnight, celebrated the Lord's Supper with them, used their bathhouses, called on them when they were sick, and entrusted the education of their children to them. Hutterites who worked for lords received higher wages than Catholics. They also insisted on being paid promptly, while Catholic workers often had to wait a year.

This picture is one-sided. The Hutterites were careful when it came to working for the lords: for example, the ordinances bade the servants of temporal needs to write down carefully how much work they agreed to do, and with good reason. On several occasions the Hutterites collided with the lords over wages, payments, and services. In 1581 Count Franz Thurn chased the brethren out of their community at Wostitz because they refused to help prepare for wedding celebrations. In 1609 the Hutterite bishop Claus Braidl threatened to recall all Hutterites working for Ulrich von Kaunitz unless their wages were raised by September. There was the danger, too, that the lords might exploit the Hutterites, who were helpless against them. Many lords asked the Hutterites for a farm manager, and if their request was denied, they threatened the brethren in various ways until they finally sent someone. In 1614 the Catholic lords even tried to reduce the Hutterites to the status of serfs, a move that was thwarted, however, by the Protestant noblemen and the governor, Karl von Zierotyn. Most noblemen would have agreed with Ulrich von Kaunitz, who in his testament of 1613 advised his sons not to permit the establishment of new Hutterite communities, but not to chase the brethren out of their old communities either: it was difficult to live with the Hutterites, but even more difficult to live without them.[119] Thanks to the reciprocal advantages, indeed, the relations between the Hutterites and the lords were on the whole quite good.

Fischer claimed that the partiality of the nobility for the brethren had a harmful effect on the native Catholic population. Seeing the Hutterites prosper, Catholics either began to wonder whether there was not some value in the Hutterite doctrines or simply left the country to seek a better living elsewhere. According to Fischer, too, some Hutterites behaved with great insolence toward Catholic peasants and craftsmen. If they spoke to the Catholics at all, they spoke curtly indeed. As managers and overseers the Hutterites treated the Catholic workers like enemies. Even allowing for Fischer's bias, there may be an element of truth in his charges, for the brethren regarded the Catholics as heathens.

In 1535, when following the Kingdom of Münster persecution of believers increased violently, the Hutterites decided they would have no more to do with the "scribes and Pharisees"—that is, the priests, nuns, and "belly preachers." They immediately informed the abbess of Brünn, who in 1531 had graciously allowed them to settle on her grounds at Auspitz, that they would no longer work for her. Furious and embittered, the abbess told them to leave her property. In 1545 the Hutterites reiterated their determination not to render services or payments to priests or have commercial transactions with them. In later years they modified their position in order to retain their communities: in 1599, for example, they confessed themselves ready to work for Franz von Dietrichstein as far as his person was concerned, but not in his capacity as bishop and cardinal.

Wealth

Visitors in the second half of the sixteenth century were surprised at the affluence of the Hutterite communities. The Hutterites grew wealthy mainly from their extensive craftsmanship. The wages they received from the lords could hardly have amounted to large sums, and their farms did not even produce enough to feed their own people. The total value of their property—houses, fields, vineyards, meadows, workshops, barns, stables, mills, tools, produce, animals, and cash—is not known, but it was undoubtedly a large amount. According to one estimate, in 1618 the Hutterites had fifty or sixty thousand florins in cash alone. In 1621 hidden treasures of cash totaling some thirty thousand florins (old value) were confiscated by imperial officials.[120] When in 1624 the Hutterites were expelled from their last 24 communities in Moravia, they were allowed to take with them as much of their movable property as they could transport. According to their own estimates they still left behind property worth some 364,000 florins.[121]

In spite of their wealth the Hutterites disliked lending money. In his native country, they reasoned, the individual believer would have disliked lending his property; in the community he did not even have the right to dispose of property that had been given to the Lord. This view was confirmed by some bad experiences: Hutterites had lost money when headmen of crafts had died or left without informing the community of loans they had granted. Occasionally the Hutterites had borrowed money from outsiders, who in turn had borrowed it from another Hutterite community. The Hutterites concluded that the unbelievers should be left to their own devices, and they were serious in this decision. Subsequently they turned down a request for a loan from the governor of Moravia, and in 1596 even one from Emperor Rudolf II. If they ever did agree to advance a loan, it had to be repaid within two weeks.

The Individual and Community

It is questionable whether the thousands of emigrants who went to Moravia really knew what kind of life they would lead there. In the Hutterite community a person was no longer his own master. He had to do whatever work he was ordered to do; he had to work long hours without any form of personal reward; he was not allowed to choose his own spouse or to rear his own children; he could not even visit friends or relatives in another community without asking the permission of his superiors. The most innocent enjoyments, such as talking with friends over a glass of wine, were forbidden.

The Hutterite leaders wished to free man from his ceaseless preoccupation with the world—a preoccupation that prevented him from loving God and his neighbors. Realizing that it was impossible to eliminate all earthly desires and aspirations, they devised institutions that at least reduced their effects to a minimum. In the Hutterite communities it was impossible to chase after money or women, to aspire to social distinction, or even to grow very attached to one's own children.

The Hutterites were aware that they imposed heavy sacrifices on the individual believer. They warned prospective converts that leaving the world would mean mortifying the flesh and blood: the door to the kingdom of heaven was also called the "door of death"; whoever left the world would suffer the Cross. Then, they continued, the flesh would at once demand, "Who can live and suffer like this?" And God would answer, "Whatever you are not able to do, I can do." [122]

The extraordinary and almost incomprehensible fact is that not just a handful of zealots and eccentrics but thousands of people accepted this way of life that appears so bleak. Of course, for some emigrants it would have been difficult to leave the communities: anyone who had contributed his property stood to lose everything by leaving. Most emigrants, however, had been forced to leave their property at home and could generally expect to have it restored to them if they returned to their native country. Yet the majority stayed in Moravia, and some for as long as fifty or sixty years.

The few letters that chanced to survive reveal that the writers were indeed happy in the communities. A physician of Göppingen in Württemberg who had recently joined the brethren at Pribitz wrote to a friend in 1597 that he carefully looked about him, observing the leaders in particular. But, he added, "I have already conceived such a love for these people that I would be willing to give my life for them." Naturally there were some uncouth brethren but the majority led decent, sober lives. "I must say in truth," he continued, "that from my youth until this hour I have never had happier days." Other emigrants were equally elated: "God in heaven be praised that as a father He has led us here. This I know in my heart. If we stayed day and night on our knees, we could not thank God sufficiently. I have never regretted a single step. I would not leave, even for a kingdom." [123]

Of course, there were also those who left. The Hutterites took this problem quite seriously. Whenever someone talked of leaving, they would ask him why he wanted to return to the godless life of the world. Why, indeed, should a believer have wished to leave? We have already seen that some found the school system intolerable. Others were upset at being separated from their loved ones in times of illness. One man became disillusioned when the leaders refused to let him see his wife who was near childbirth. When they finally allowed him to come, she was dying. There were those, too, who could not stand the food in the communities. They had come from different areas, such as the Tirol, Württemberg, and Hesse, with different cooking procedures. When in 1534 a Swabian group complained of the strangely prepared food, Jakob Hutter arranged for them to have their own cook and kitchen, but they laughed and left the community. One defector complained that having worked hard he had been given nothing better than abominable soup made of cheese or with large root vegetables floating in it whole.[124] Others seem to have disliked the whole idea of communal life; after their return they told horrible stories about it. One man complained that the Hutterites had begun by promising him a great deal but had kept none of these promises, and that he had suffered hunger and deprivation.[125] It should be remembered, however, that those who left constituted only a small minority.

Conclusion

The Hutterite community was a place of religion where the Hutterites tried to live as true disciples of Christ. In order to make such a truly Christian life possible, they eliminated or nearly eliminated some of the most basic institutions of European society—private property and family life. The only important institution they did not touch was monogamy, though they limited the purpose of marriage to the bare task of procreation.

Are religious motives really sufficient to explain these profound social changes? The man of religion is primarily concerned with God, man's salvation, and perhaps also the outward forms of the church. Like Luther or Calvin, he is also interested in the problems of society, but this interest is subordinate to his religious concerns. After all, society is transient, whereas the eternal questions of God and man's salvation are unchanging. The man of religion hardly demands a complete overthrow of society. If, however, a man rejects the most fundamental institutions of society, then he may be said to be motivated by not only religious but social considerations.

The early Hutterite leaders were naturally concerned with man's soul, but they also thought deeply and searchingly about the institutions of sixteenth-century society and concluded that these institutions were incompatible with God's Word. And since God's Word was the only truth, society must be changed.

Hutterite Anabaptism must be seen against the background of

revolutionary tendencies in the Germany of the 1520s. The Hutterites were not the first to advocate community of goods. During the uprising in 1525 the peasant armies of the Black Forest and Tauber valley had tried to establish a new society consisting of peasants and burghers with no nobility. Michael Gaismaier in the Tirol had even envisaged a classless peasant society without towns. A few years later the Hutterites founded their communities in which, apart from the leaders, all were equal and all had to do manual labor. It appears most likely, then, that the early Hutterite leaders were influenced by the social criticism of their time.

Whatever the Hutterites' motives may have been, their new form of society amounted to a revolution. The fact that, unlike Thomas Müntzer and the Münsterites, they did not impose their social system by force but withdrew to Moravia does not diminish the revolutionary character of their communities. In fact, the Hutterites achieved the most radical and successful social revolution in sixteenth-century Germany.

It might be argued that the Hutterites did no more than put into practice tendencies inherent in Anabaptism that the Anabaptists who stayed in Germany could not fully realize. To be sure, the notion of withdrawal from the world and of the establishment of a truly Christian community already permeated the Schleitheim Articles of 1527. Doubts about private property and the division of Christians into rich and poor were widespread among Anabaptists. As we have seen, some Anabaptists even criticized marriage as it was practiced in the world.

Yet it is very unlikely that if the Anabaptists in Switzerland and Germany had enjoyed a tolerant reception from their governments they would also have established communistic communities. There were regional differences in Anabaptism from the beginning. Müntzer's legacy was strong in Thuringia; Hut and his disciples influenced Anabaptism in Franconia, Bavaria, Austria, and possibly also the Tirol. And it was from Austria, the Tirol, and perhaps Thuringia that early Hutterite Anabaptism received its formative influences—not from Switzerland or the Rhine valley.

After the Hutterites had fully developed their institutions, they had almost become a movement of their own. It may be asked whether the Hutterites should primarily be classified as Anabaptists, for what chiefly characterized them was not the baptism of believers or the rejection of governmental office but their communistic community life. Their communism separated them from the Anabaptists in Germany as well as from the Catholics, Lutherans, and Calvinists. From the perspective of the social historian, indeed, there is a gulf between the Hutterites on the one hand and all other churches and Anabaptist groups on the other.

9

The Appeal
of Anabaptism

As we have seen, Anabaptism advanced strongly in some areas, but not at all in others. Whereas in some towns Anabaptist congregations flourished for ten or twenty years, or even longer, in others they collapsed after only two or three years. Obviously an element of chance was always involved. Hut and his friends, for example, visited certain towns and villages because they had relatives there. The success or failure of the leaders was also influenced by local conditions, such as the popularity of the local pastor. These local conditions varied widely from town to town and even village to village, and cannot be reconstructed. More to the point here are basic factors that affected the advance of Anabaptism in several areas. These factors fall into three categories: those that influenced the geographic expansion of Anabaptism; those that determined the reactions of the various social classes; and finally, those that might have influenced individual persons to become Anabaptists.

Geographic Expansion
Areas of Different Religion

The area where Anabaptism appeared in the sixteenth century was characterized by great religious diversity: the Hapsburg lands and Bavaria were Catholic; the Swiss territories were Zwinglian; the southwest German cities were both Zwinglian and Lutheran; Württemberg, Ansbach, and Saxony were Lutheran; and the Palatinate was Calvinist. Did the prevailing religious conditions play a role in determining where Anabaptist ideas took root? Duke William of Bavaria certainly saw a relationship between Lutheranism and Anabaptism: the Anabaptist apostles, he remarked in 1527, approached only those who had already accepted Lutheranism.[1] On the other hand, the Protestant city council of Strasbourg pointedly told King Francis I of France that the disaster of the Anabaptist Kingdom of Münster would never have taken place if the bishop of Münster had allowed the preaching of the gospel.[2] A look at the distribution of Anabaptism in Catholic and Protestant areas might show which of these views, if either, was correct.

During the first five years, 1525 to 1529, the appearance of Anabaptism seems to have been related to the spread of Protestant ideas. As Table 8 shows, some 31 percent of all persons who joined the sect lived in territories where the Catholic Church clearly dominated but Protestant doctrines had been preached, as in parts of the Tirol, and in Austria, Bavaria, Würzburg, and Bamberg. Another 12 percent lived in cities and territories that nominally were still Catholic but had very strong Protestant movements, such as Basel, Bern, or Worms. Another 32 percent lived in areas that had accepted the Reformation and were in the process of establishing a new church, such as Zurich after April 1525. Ten percent of the converts, finally, lived in cities where Catholic and Lutheran or Zwinglian services were openly conducted, as in Augsburg, or in territories where the parishes were allowed to chose their form of worship, as in Appenzell or Graubünden. In other words, 85 percent of all Anabaptists during the years 1525 to 1529 came from areas that had been affected by Protestantism, whereas only 15 percent came from areas that were still strictly Catholic.[3]

In territories that were basically Catholic and only lightly touched by Protestantism, the Protestant preachers might have prepared the ground for the Anabaptists. In the early 1520s, for example, the Lutheran doctrines were proclaimed with great success by Stephan Agricola, Jakob Strauss, Urbanus Rhegius,

Table 8. The religious background of the Anabaptists

Background	1525–1529 No. (%)	1530–1549 No. (%)	1550–1618 No. (%)	Total No. (%)
Catholic area	542 (15.1)	1,748 (47.7)	774 (20.4)	3,064 (27.8)
Protestant area	1,126 (31.5)	1,264 (34.4)	2,738 (72.3)	5,128 (46.5)
Catholic area with strong Protestant movement	443 (12.4)	182 (5.0)	40 (1.1)	665 (6.0)
Catholic area with light Protestant movement	1,099 (30.7)	323 (8.8)	140 (3.7)	1,562 (14.1)
Protestant area with Catholic group	23 (0.6)	23 (0.6)	13 (0.3)	59 (0.5)
Catholics and Protestants coexist	346 (9.7)	82 (2.2)	33 (0.9)	461 (4.2)
Interim	0 (0.0)	45 (1.2)	49 (1.3)	94 (0.8)
Total	3,579	3,667	3,787	11,033

Note: The religious background of 142 Anabaptists cannot be determined.

and others in the Tirolese mining towns of Rattenberg, Schwaz, and Hall. Though these pastors were expelled by the Innsbruck government, they had aroused angry dissatisfaction with the church among the miners, many of whom were of Saxon origin. This may be one of the reasons why a few years later the Anabaptists found their largest following in the mining districts of Schwaz, Rattenberg, Hall, Kitzbühel, and Sterzing.

The relation between Protestantism and Anabaptism is more evident in areas that were nominally Catholic but where the Lutheran or Zwinglian doctrines had given rise to strong popular movements. In Switzerland, for example, laymen and pastors had preached the new doctrines at Zurich, Bern, Basel, St. Gallen, Appenzell, and Schaffhausen before the Anabaptists appeared in 1525.[4] By 1525 a large number of burghers had accepted the new doctrines but the ceremonies of the Church, especially the mass, were maintained. In none of the Swiss cities had the Reformation been officially introduced at the time when the Anabaptists began to preach, and several months or even years passed before the mass was officially abolished.[5]

A strange interregnum existed in these areas where the Anabaptists appeared before the Reformation. The pastors who proclaimed the new doctrines were tolerated or even protected by the government. In individual churches the mass was no longer celebrated. But if there was no doubt that episcopal authority would not be reestablished, there was as yet no comprehensive reform in progress. It appears that this atmosphere of uncertainty made people receptive to the radical doctrines of the Anabaptists.

Once the Anabaptists had gained a foothold, even the adoption of an official reform by the authorities could not stop the advance of the movement. Anabaptism continued to spread, for example, in the villages and small towns of the territory of Zurich in the late 1520s, although the mass had been abolished in April 1525. It took the Protestant pastors and officials many years to halt the growth of the sect. Indeed, the largest bloc of converts, 32 percent, lived in territories and cities that were passing through the tumultuous period when the old Church was torn down and a new one established. Luther's and Zwingli's defiance of the hierarchy, doctrine, and practice of the Church had broken down old inhibitions and roused the desire for change. Once five of the sacraments had been thrown overboard, it was not difficult to question the remaining two: indeed, all doctrines might now be questioned. People might also have been favorably impressed by the fact that the Anabaptists advocated a thorough reform along biblical lines independent of the governments.

A strong Anabaptist movement failed to develop, however, in cities and territories such as the Electorate of Saxony, Nuremberg, Reutlingen, and Schwäbisch Hall, where a thorough reform had already been effected before the Anabaptists appeared. The Anabaptists found few followers here, if any, for the desire of the populace for a revolutionary change had already been satisfied. Nor were the Anabaptists very successful in areas where the authority of the Church had never been questioned, such as the inner cantons of Switzerland—Uri,

Schwyz, Unterwalden, Zug, and Freiburg. The devoutly Catholic farmers of these areas were not interested in religious revolution.

In territories where religious conditions had been uncertain, a definite decision was made by the 1530s or 1540s at the latest: either the government strictly enforced Catholicism or it introduced Protestantism. During the years from 1530 to 1549 about half the people who became Anabaptists had a Catholic background, owing to the amazing appeal of Anabaptism in the Tirol. Some 67 percent of all Anabaptists in Catholic areas between 1530 and 1549 were Tirolese. From the middle of the sixteenth century onward, however, the percentage of Anabaptists in Catholic territories began to diminish. Only in the Tirol and Solothurn did the Anabaptists still attract relatively large numbers of people. By the 1570s only about 20 percent of all new brethren had a Catholic background, and by 1600 a mere 5 percent.[6]

The decline and disappearance of Anabaptism in most Catholic territories were due to extremely severe persecution. Only in the Tirol did Anabaptism survive mass executions, possibly because there the Anabaptists offered the only alternative to the hated Catholic clergy. There was no establishment of the Lutheran church in the Tirol, for the government forcibly suppressed all Protestant tendencies and the Tirolese peasants had lost confidence in the foreign Lutheran preachers who had played such a prominent role during the disastrous peasant uprising of 1525. Ultimately the success of Anabaptism in the Tirol remains a puzzle. In any case, by the middle of the sixteenth century, Tirolese Anabaptism was also on the decline, and by the end of the century it had largely died out.

By contrast, in the Protestant territories of Württemberg, the Palatinate, Hesse, and possibly Zurich, the number of converts to Anabaptism remained relatively high until the Thirty Years' War.[7] From 1550 to 1618 the vast majority of all Anabaptists, some 73 percent, came from Protestant areas. Why was it that the Anabaptists scored such a success in territories where the Reformation was firmly established? The times when religious uncertainty and confusion had reigned in these territories were long past: articles of faith and church life were minutely regulated in the church ordinances, and the ecclesiastical hierarchy was again firmly established, though it was now Protestant rather than Catholic. Of course, it must also be remembered that compared to the whole population, the number of Anabaptists was still very, very small. But even though these territories were decidedly Lutheran or Calvinist, the Anabaptists there received relatively light treatment. Very few Anabaptists were executed, and many were not even imprisoned. Sometimes months or even years passed before an Anabaptist was expelled. In the Palatinate the order to leave the country was sometimes never given at all. Thus the main reason for the Anabaptists' success in Protestant territories seems to have been the absence of a policy of violent suppression. The examples of Lutheran Saxony and Catholic Speyer confirm that persecution decisively influenced the development of the sect. In Lutheran Saxony obstinate Anabaptists were executed and the movement stamped out at its very beginnings. By contrast, the prince bishops of Speyer, who refused to execute after the 1530s, had many Anabaptists to contend with in the second half of the sixteenth century.

Possibly, too, the preoccupation of the Protestants with Bible reading helped stimulate sectarian thinking. When people read the Bible at home regularly, it was only to be expected that they would conceive their own interpretations. The Catholic authorities were well aware of this danger. In 1582 a recanting Anabaptist of Catholic Lucerne had to promise to refrain from reading the Bible. Yet the availability of the Bible in Protestant areas cannot have been a decisive factor in determining the advance of the sect, for otherwise Anabaptism would have flourished at the very heart of Lutheranism, that is, in Saxony. Similarly, the argument that moral standards were low in the

Protestant territories and that people therefore turned to the purer life of the Anabaptists does not hold up in the case of Saxony. Even the premise of this argument seems faulty, for the visitation transcripts do not indicate that moral standards in the Protestant churches were low.

Were the various Protestant groups affected by Anabaptism to different degrees? During the first ten years, 1525 to 1534, most Anabaptists of Protestant background lived in areas that were part of the Zwinglian or upper German branch of the Reformation. The reasons for this are obvious: the movement had originated in Zurich and first spread to other parts of Switzerland and to the southwest German imperial cities. In the 1530s, however, the proportion of Anabaptists with a Lutheran background increased, and from the 1540s onward most Anabaptists lived in Lutheran areas. From 1550 to 1618 about 75 percent of the Anabaptists in Protestant areas had a Lutheran background, and only 25 percent a Calvinist one.

These figures might not reflect the actual conditions, however. Documentary material for Swiss Anabaptism during the second half of the sixteenth century is not yet available, but Anabaptism was probably much stronger in Reformed Switzerland than is generally assumed. Furthermore, in the Lutheran territory most strongly affected by Anabaptism, Württemberg, the church service was much more sober and intellectual than it was in Saxony, where many vestiges of Catholicism remained.

It is striking that some uncompromisingly Lutheran territories and cities with no Zwinglian or upper German influence—the Margravate of Ansbach, the upper Palatinate, and the cities of Schwäbisch Hall and Reutlingen—should hardly have been touched by Anabaptism at all. If Anabaptism did appear it was quickly suppressed, as in Electoral Saxony, Nuremberg, and Windsheim, or it remained insignificant, as in the Duchy of Neuburg or the city of Heilbronn. Apparently the only strictly Lutheran territory with a fairly strong Anabaptist movement was Pfalz-Zweibrücken, which may have felt the influence of

Anabaptism in the neighboring Electoral Palatinate. Quite possibly, then, territories that adopted a Reformed type of Protestantism or where Lutheranism was at least influenced by tendencies of the Zwinglian Reformation offered greater receptivity to the Anabaptist doctrines than strictly Lutheran ones.

Urban and Rural Areas

During the first five years, from January 1525 to December 1529, people from urban environments dominated in the Anabaptist movement: about two out of three Anabaptists were burghers, or to be more exact, some 62.4 percent lived in cities or towns and about 30 percent in villages or on farms, as Table 9 shows. During the following years the movement changed greatly in this respect. In the 1530s and 1540s Anabaptism was already attracting more villagers than burghers. During the period from 1550 to 1618 the proportion of villagers even rose to 73 percent, whereas that of urban Anabaptists dropped to 16 percent. Clearly, then, Anabaptism had changed from a movement that was largely urban into one that was largely rural. But if the center of Anabaptism shifted from the towns to the coun-

Table 9. Urban and rural Anabaptists

Place of residence	1525–1529 No. (%)	1530–1549 No. (%)	1550–1618 No. (%)	Total No. (%)
Imperial city, Swiss city	822 (22.7)	517 (14.0)	212 (5.5)	1,551 (13.8)
Capital, large town	525 (14.5)	441 (12.0)	50 (1.3)	1,016 (9.1)
Small town	900 (24.9)	483 (13.1)	355 (9.2)	1,738 (15.5)
Village	1,069 (29.6)	1,673 (45.4)	2,811 (72.6)	5,553 (49.7)
Farm	10 (0.3)	63 (1.7)	27 (0.7)	100 (0.9)
Residence unknown	291 (8.0)	510 (13.8)	416 (10.7)	1,217 (10.9)
Total	3,617	3,687	3,871	11,175

try, it was not because the absolute number of Anabaptists in villages had increased: the number of Anabaptists dropped both in towns and in villages from 1535 onward. The decline was simply much greater in the towns than in the country.

The gradual transfer of Anabaptism from the urban centers to the country is also reflected in the shifting percentage of Anabaptists in cities and small country towns. Up to the middle of the sixteenth century there were almost twice as many Anabaptists in the larger cities as in small country towns. Indeed, the largest Anabaptist groups were in the imperial cities of Augsburg, Esslingen, and Strasbourg, and in the Tirolese towns of Kitzbühel and Rattenberg. The picture changed completely during the second half of the sixteenth century, however. After the 1570s hardly anyone in the larger cities accepted Anabaptism. Most Anabaptists of urban background now lived in small country towns such as Pfeddersheim, Heppenheim, Lörrach, Göppingen, Knittlingen, and Schorndorf.

The greatest actual number of urban Anabaptists lived in Swabia, the Tirol, and the Rhine valley. As far as the relative strength of urban and rural Anabaptists is concerned, however, Austria and the southeastern area (Bavaria, Passau, Salzburg, and Neuburg) had the greatest percentage of urban Anabaptists: 73 percent of the Austrian and 68 percent of the southeastern Anabaptists lived in towns. Why was this so? Anabaptism spread strongly in these areas only during the 1520s, when congregations were forming in towns. There was no forceful Anabaptist movement in Austria and the southeastern territories after the 1530s, when in other areas the sect shifted to the countryside. The Tirol, the Rhine valley, and Swabia also had a relatively high percentage of urban Anabaptists: in the Tirol, 59 percent of the Anabaptists lived in towns; in the Rhine valley, 47 percent; and in Swabia, 41 percent. In the Tirol the urban character of Anabaptism was due to the great success of the Anabaptists in the mining towns; the Rhine valley and Swabia simply had highly urbanized populations. By contrast, Hesse had a lower proportion of urban Anabaptists than any other area, a mere 17 percent. This figure is hardly surprising, since there were no large towns in the Landgraviate of Hesse.

Why did large congregations develop particularly in cities such as Strasbourg and Augsburg during the 1520s? For one thing, some of these cities, being situated on important waterways such as the Rhine or the Danube River, were particularly accessible to leaders spreading Anabaptist doctrines. Perhaps more important, the cities, as centers of learning and book printing, were the centers of the greatest religious turmoil. Important Reformers were at work there—for example, Wolfgang Capito and Martin Bucer at Strasbourg, or Urbanus Rhegius at Augsburg. Cities like Strasbourg were thus markedly tolerant of religious innovation during the 1520s. Reublin, Gross, Hut, and the other apostles must have reckoned that they would quickly find followers under these conditions. Conversely, Anabaptism soon disappeared in towns that executed and imprisoned the sectarians, such as the Catholic towns of Schwäbisch Gmünd, Munich, and Passau, and Protestant Zurich. Only in those Protestant cities that treated the sectarians mildly did Anabaptism survive longer—at Esslingen until 1544, Augsburg until 1573, and Strasbourg until 1605.

Of course, Anabaptism finally disappeared from Protestant cities too. In the long run, Anabaptist conventicles could not remain unnoticed within the confines of a town, where lodgers in the same house or neighbors might observe the brethren. Sometimes the Anabaptists betrayed themselves by refusing to render the annual oath of allegiance. Once they had been discovered, the Anabaptists were made to submit to instruction by town pastors, who unlike village pastors were in general talented men. If the Anabaptists remained obdurate, they were ordered to leave the city. Unlike village bailiffs, town officials could not ignore the orders of the town council, and actually led the sectarians to the city gates. Thus the Anabaptist circles in the cities became smaller and smaller. Once Anabaptism had removed to the villages, the inferior status of the villagers also diminished its appeal: burghers were not attracted by the religious gatherings of uncouth peasants.

At the same time, sociological factors facilitated the advance of Anabaptism in the country. The church authorities usually employed the less gifted pastors in villages. As a result, many honest village parsons were simply no match for the eloquent Anabaptist apostles. Whereas there were several pastors and deacons in a town, there was only one in a village. If a village pastor failed because he was incompetent or indolent, the villagers received insufficient religious instruction. If he quarreled with his parish, the result was even more disastrous: the peasants would stop going to church altogether. The superintendent might admonish the pastor, but it was difficult simply to dismiss or transfer him. While in a town the parishioners might attend one of the other churches, in a village they did not go to church at all. Under such conditions the peasants might instead attend the meetings of an Anabaptist preacher—their only alternative. And since they had received little or no religious instruction in their own church, they would find it difficult to counter his arguments.[8]

The external conditions and the attitude of the population also made it more difficult for the officials to discourage Anabaptism in the country. First, it was hard to discover the Anabaptists. Meetings held in mountainous forests or in lonely mills or barns were hardly ever noticed, and often the peasants did not report Anabaptists. If the sectarians were discovered, there were considerable practical obstacles to instructing them. For example, whereas the authorities at Augsburg had to deal with about thirty Anabaptists in the town during the 1550s, the Church Council of Stuttgart in 1570 undertook to instruct 103 Anabaptists in 33 villages and towns dispersed all over the duchy. Inevitably there were numerous delays. Often, too, the local officials tolerated the brethren in their villages, but even when Anabaptists were obliged to leave the villages, they would find work on the estates of neighboring noblemen. Thus the sect persisted for decades in the villages of Württemberg, the Palatinate, and Hesse, and to a certain degree also in the Tirol.

The Reactions of the Social Classes
The Social Background of the Anabaptist Leaders

Even in areas where the Anabaptist preachers were successful, the social classes reacted differently to their message. Before analyzing the reaction of the various social classes, let us consider the background of the leaders who shaped the intellectual and moral world of the Anabaptists.

We know the social background of 167 of the 257 leaders of the first five years (1525–29), that is to say, of 66 percent. Fifty-nine of them, a fairly large proportion, had an intellectual background, as Table 10 shows. Most of the intellectuals were pastors, but there were also schoolmasters, clerks, students, artists, physicians, and scholars among them. As a matter of fact, seven of the nine most prominent early leaders of 1525 and 1526 had an intellectual background: Grebel, Manz, Blaurock, Reublin, Hubmaier, Denck, and Sattler. Only Gross and Hut were craftsmen. Relatively speaking, many intellectuals were active in Switzerland, Austria, and the Tirol; fewer in Swabia and the Southeast; and only very few in the Rhine valley, Franconia, Thuringia, and Hesse. It may have been Hut's eschatological views that kept the intellectuals in Franconia and Thuringia from joining the new movement.

From the start uneducated people also played a leading role among the Anabaptists. In 1525, seventeen of the 34 leaders in Switzerland were craftsmen or peasants. Altogether 108 of the 167 leaders up to 1529 whose background is known, or 64 percent, were uneducated. Although intellectuals such as Grebel and Manz had evolved the new doctrines, it was among common men that they quickly found their most numerous and enthusias-

Table 10. Professions of Anabaptist leaders in Switzerland,
Germany, and Austria

Profession	1525–1529	1530–1549	1550–1618
Intellectuals			
Clergymen	38	5	1
Schoolmasters	8	3	1
Clerks (*schreiber*)	6	0	0
Students	3	1	0
Others (artists, physicians, scholars, booktraders, "corrector")	4	3	2
Subtotal	59	12	4
Nonintellectuals			
Craftsmen	76	38	22
Peasants	19	12	1
Farm laborers, servants, shepherds	7	5	1
Tradesmen	2	0	1
Innkeepers	0	1	0
Others (collector of customs, gauger, horseman, sexton)	4	0	0
Subtotal	108	56	25
Grand total	167	68	29

Note: This table does not account for all Anabaptist leaders, since the
professional background of a considerable number is unknown.

tic apostles. Among the uneducated leaders, craftsmen formed
by far the largest group. There were also some peasants and a
few farm laborers.

From 1530 to 1549 the uneducated leaders played an even
greater role, at least relatively speaking. Of the 68 local leaders
and missionaries whose background is known, only twelve were
intellectuals; the remaining 56 were craftsmen, peasants, and
laborers. Although the uneducated Anabaptist leaders were now
clearly in the majority, it is true that some of the most influential leaders of these years, such as Marbeck and Griesinger, had
received a formal education. We know the background of only

29 local leaders and missionaries during the final period, 1550 to 1618. Of these only four were educated, and 25 were common people. In all likelihood most of the leaders who were active during these years were craftsmen.

Thus the social background of the Anabaptist leaders was quite different from that of the pre-Reformation humanists, such as Erasmus, who has been credited by some with influencing Anabaptist theology; the humanists were all intellectuals. The Anabaptist leaders also differed from the Lutheran and Zwinglian Reformers, who were almost always clergymen. Lay leaders such as Christoph Schappeler at Memmingen and Kessler at St. Gallen were exceptions in the Protestant establishment. There was no room for a leadership of craftsmen in the official churches. Not surprisingly, the university-trained pastors looked down on the Anabaptist ministers, who typically had learned only to repair boots, make wine barrels, or weave baskets. But the brethren were not at all embarrassed by the humble position of their leaders, reminding the theologians that Christ had hidden the secrets of God's kingdom from the learned and revealed them to the poor, the young, and the simpleminded.

In summary, then, the intellectuals played a powerful role among the leaders up to the year 1529, though they were never in the majority. Their numbers subsequently dwindled until hardly any remained. During the later years of the movement, practically all Anabaptist leaders were craftsmen, and a few were peasants. This shift in the social background of the Anabaptist leaders indicates that the various social classes not only reacted quite differently to the sect but reacted differently at different periods.

The Nobility

In 1528 an Anabaptist in Franconia said that there were "poor and rich people, noblemen, monks, and priests in their league." [9] Actually only 24 nobles are known to have accepted the Anabaptist faith. Most of them lived in the Tirol, Austria, Bavaria, and Swabia. Two members joined in Franconia, two more in Hesse, and none in Thuringia. In general, the nobility was not interested in the Anabaptist sect.

Some noblemen, such as Eberhard von der Tann, castellan at the Wartburg, believed that the Anabaptists were revolutionaries like the peasants of 1525. Having experienced the fury of the peasants during the Peasants' War, the nobility could hardly sympathize with these new revolutionaries. Then, too, the Anabaptist leaders, mostly common craftsmen and peasants, had no contact with the circles of the nobility. Finally, joining the Hutterites would have entailed heavier sacrifices for the nobleman than for the craftsman or peasant. The latter would lose his property but not his accustomed way of life: he would continue working as a craftsman or peasant in Moravia or wherever he went. The nobleman, however, would not only forfeit fief and title but be forced to earn his living by manual labor. In a Hutterite community his noble birth would mean nothing: he would do the kind of work his servants had formerly done for him. Joining the Anabaptists thus implied social degradation for the nobleman.

The Urban Upper Class

We do not know the total number of wealthy burghers in the cities of south and central Germany, Switzerland, and Austria who adopted the Anabaptist faith, for the tax records for most towns are lost. It is certain that 109 wealthy burghers joined the sect. Well-to-do people found their way to Anabaptism particularly in the imperial cities of Augsburg, Esslingen, Heilbronn, and Ulm, and to some extent in the towns of upper and lower Austria and the Tirol.

Though at Augsburg and Esslingen wealthy burghers were among the first to be baptized, conversions among the upper class soon became relatively rare. Of the 109 rich Anabaptists on record, 67, or about 61 percent, joined the movement during the first years, from 1525 to 1529; another 23, or 21 percent, joined during the 1530s, and only nineteen joined during all of the following decades.[10] Nor did the wealthy burghers play a significant role in the history of Anabaptism. Only two outstanding leaders came from their ranks: Grebel of Zurich and Marbeck of Rattenberg. Langenmantel at Augsburg might have had some influence through his writings; Lienhart Lutz and Joachim Fleiner at Esslingen had only local importance. There can be little doubt that Anabaptism was not a rich man's movement.

It is easy to see why the interest of the wealthy in Anabaptism was greatest during the 1520s: the unsettled religious conditions in many cities during these years affected rich and poor alike. But once the Lutheran and Zwinglian churches had been established or the exclusive dominance of Catholicism reaffirmed, the preoccupation with religious problems and new doctrines subsided. Ordinary class interests, which had been overshadowed by the intense religious turmoil, again dominated the thinking of the wealthy burghers, and such class interests had nothing in common with the Anabaptist teaching. The aesthetic culture of the wealthy burghers of Augsburg and Zurich was strongly condemned by the Anabaptists: the elegant houses and fountains, the sculptures and paintings, the fashionable dress, necklaces, and rings, the organ music in the churches.

A rich burgher of Augsburg elected to the town council might be motivated by personal ambition, but he also felt responsible for law and order. How was he to take any group of people seriously who condemned as unchristian such elementary civic duties as taking an oath? An Augsburg merchant whose trading connections covered the whole of Europe was not impressed by Hutterite missionaries who vociferously condemned private property, commerce, and finance. Wealthy burghers were also aware that if they supported a proscribed sect of religious fanatics, they would be ruining their own chances of being elevated to the nobility or their children's chances of marrying into prominent families.

Intellectuals

Intellectuals are loosely defined here to include university professors, pastors, lawyers, syndics, Latin schoolmasters, architects, artists, and musicians—in other words, all those whose income derived from intellectual work rather than from agriculture, craftsmanship, trade, or rents. Of course, some intellectuals invested money, bought real estate, and might even have done some farming, but these activities were not their main occupation. All those who at some time pursued university studies are counted here as intellectuals, although some intellectuals, such as schoolmasters, had not attended a university.

The number of intellectuals who joined the Anabaptist movement was small. The records show that 176 Anabaptists, or about 1.6 percent, had an intellectual background. Nevertheless, intellectuals played an important role in formulating Anabaptist doctrine in Zurich. Who were these intellectuals? More than half of them were former pastors or monks—not a surprising proportion, for clergymen formed the largest group of intellectuals in the sixteenth century, and they would also be interested in any new religious movement. Some of them, such as Schiemer and Salminger, were actually no longer priests but had learned a handicraft; naturally they would be attracted by religious circles of lay people. Schoolmasters formed the second largest group, numbering 34 persons. Fourteen clerks of cities, law courts, and mines, and sixteen physicians joined the brethren. At the universities only one magister and six students became involved with the sect. Most of the 176 Anabaptist intellectuals were men of modest ability, with the exceptions of Hubmaier, the theologian; Denck, the philosopher; Wendel Dietrich, the architect; and possibly Ludwig Hätzer, the translator.

Like the wealthy burghers, the intellectuals were interested in Anabaptism primarily during the early years of the movement. By 1529, 110 intellectuals had joined, and another 31 joined during the 1530s. In the course of the following eighty years, however, only 35 intellectuals became Anabaptists. The scarcity of Anabaptist intellectuals was so conspicuous that a Hutterite even wrote a tract entitled "On the Absence of the Learned from the Congregation." Some have maintained that it was because of the elimination of the early Anabaptist intellectuals such as Manz, Grebel, and Hubmaier that Anabaptist thought did not evolve after the 1520s. Of course, nothing prevented intellectuals from joining the movement after the 1520s. Why did their interest wane?

Erasmus' reaction to Anabaptism may be indicative of the feeling among the enlightened intellectuals of the time. Living at Basel, he was aware of the success of the Anabaptists in Switzerland. He may even have felt a little sympathy for the brethren, who were suppressed not only by the Catholics but also by Protestants. He mentioned in his letters of 1528 and 1529 that the Anabaptists were praised for their pure and innocent lives. Where, however, he cautiously added, could there be purity of life if the soundness of faith had been corrupted? Erasmus may have sympathized with the Anabaptist position on baptism. In 1533 he remarked that the practice of baptism should be continued in the church as always, but he added that perhaps the parents should be permitted to decide whether a child should be baptized immediately or only after he had been given instruction in doctrine and morality. In 1528 and 1529 Erasmus may even have doubted that the Anabaptists were really revolutionaries. He knew that the princes hated them more than any other sect, but he commented, somewhat skeptically, that the Anabaptists had not so far usurped the rights of government or defended themselves by force. In the following years, however, he became impatient, accusing the Anabaptists of disobedience and communism: Anabaptism must not be tolerated under any circumstances. In 1534 he described the Anabaptists as madmen bent on their own destruction, and

expressed astonishment that in spite of the absurdities taught
by the Anabaptists the common people were rushing into the
sect as if obsessed by an evil demon.[11] Erasmus was plainly
worried by the advance of the sect, soon to culminate in the
tragedy at Münster.

Most intellectuals did not even share the cautious sympathy
Erasmus had shown during the 1520s. The largest group of
intellectuals during the sixteenth century, the clergymen, were
strongly indoctrinated against Anabaptism during their theological training. In Württemberg, for example, students of theology
attended interrogations of Anabaptists. After all, one of a pastor's professional duties was to refute the Anabaptists, and a
pastor also knew that if ever he should evidence sympathy for
this sect, he would immediately be dismissed. Like the schoolmaster, then, the pastor had to reject Anabaptism simply in
order to keep his livelihood. In any case, it was unlikely that
pastors, who were bitterly reviled by the Anabaptists, would
have warm feelings toward them.

The contempt shown by the Anabaptists for any form of
higher education annoyed and alienated the intellectuals. No
doubt some Anabaptist leaders were intelligent, eloquent, and
thoroughly familiar with the Scriptures. More than one famous
theologian found himself in an awkward position when arguing
with the brethren. But Anabaptist thought turned almost exclusively on the question of salvation, and the brethren were
most certain that they were the elect: the Hutterite missionary
Glock, for example, was convinced that only the twenty thousand Hutterites in Moravia would be saved, while the rest of
mankind was cursed and damned. He also felt intellectually
superior to all theologians. Recounting an occasion when the
theologians jumped to their feet in indignation after he had
called them godless and accursed villains, he commented, "This
is how I finished them all off." [12] Another Swabian brother also
claimed after his interrogation at Stuttgart that he had van-

quished all the theologians: they could not even answer without looking into their books.[13] The theologians might have been amused or angered by this show of arrogance, but they were hardly converted.

While to the Anabaptists all teachings were contained in the Scriptures, the lawyer, physician, pastor, or Latin schoolmaster had at the university been taught of things that had nothing to do with religion—philosophy, logic, ancient poetry, mathematics, astronomy, Roman law. It never occurred to the intellectual to condemn these disciplines because Christ or the apostles had not taught them. The lawyer or theologian who had studied natural law could only smile when these pious farmers and seamstresses tried to reduce all political philosophy to the Sermon on the Mount. In 1535, at the height of the Kingdom of Münster, Erasmus' friend Vigilius Zuichemus maintained that if Anabaptism were allowed to continue, religion, letters—indeed all humanity—would come to a certain end. Later in the sixteenth century the intellectuals simply ceased to be impressed by the intense religious orientation of the Anabaptists. Pedagogy, alchemy, astrology, witch-hunting, and the like were the favorite topics of the time.

It may be wondered why no intellectuals arose from within the Anabaptist ranks. During the sixteenth century one received an education at the Latin school and the university. Most Anabaptists, however, were simply too poor to attend Latin schools, and they had no use for the studies pursued at the university— usually theology or law, and less often medicine. As far as the brethren were concerned, ministers had to be taught by the Holy Spirit, not by professors; and since they rejected the legal system, they had no reason to study law. Furthermore, they deeply distrusted higher education as such. "We have had universities for fifteen hundred years," Ascherham exclaimed, "but they had only prevented people from finding their salvation." Hans Hut, a brilliant man who had never been formally educated, cursed the universities of Wittenberg and Paris as dens and murder caves. One Hutterite missionary even boasted, "I study with hoe and flail." [14]

Hostility toward learning was inherent in Anabaptism from the beginning, as Hut's example shows. After the elimination of the intellectual leaders of the early years, this hostility was reinforced by the low educational background of the new generation of leaders. A certain cultural primitivism became a dominant characteristic of the Anabaptists. For example, even after his return to Lutheranism, a former Anabaptist condemned all books and writers, insisting that one should read only the Bible. Since they themselves were uneducated, the Anabaptists concluded that only the uneducated could truly be pious. Any form of higher intellectual life was condemned as wordly vanity. It took the German Anabaptists more than two hundred years to overcome this hostility, which was ultimately a rejection of modern civilization.

Craftsmen

Some 1,165 Anabaptists are known to have been craftsmen, or 1,458, if Anabaptist women whose husbands were craftsmen are included as members of the class. Undoubtedly the real figure was higher. Is it possible to classify all Anabaptists in towns as craftsmen, unless they are known to have been intellectuals, or noblemen, or to have practiced other professions? The problem is that in the smaller towns numerous burghers were also farmers (*Ackerbürger*). Such an assumption seems safe enough, however, in the case of Anabaptists who lived in imperial cities, capitals, or the larger territorial towns, for it was here that the crafts were concentrated. By adding this figure to the number of Anabaptists in small towns and villages who were definitely craftsmen, we reach a total approximation of 3,160 Anabaptists who belonged to the class of craftsmen, or about 28 percent of all Anabaptists. If, however, we assume that most Anabaptists in small towns were also craftsmen, then the figure would rise to 41 percent. In all likelihood the correct figure lies somewhere between 28 percent and 41 percent (see Appendix C below). Of course, an analysis of the various crafts must rely on actual data rather than estimates. Although the data available are incomplete, they cover the entire area of our study. Also, since 1,458 persons constitute a considerable number, the analysis should reflect the actual conditions with reasonable accuracy.

Anabaptists were to be found in 123 crafts, or if Anabaptist women whose husbands were craftsmen are included, 133—a surprisingly high figure. They were very unevenly distributed among these crafts, however. There were no more than three Anabaptists in each of 78 crafts, that is, 63 percent of all the crafts involved (or if Anabaptist wives of craftsmen are included, the figure is again 78 crafts, or 59 percent of all crafts); and there were no more than ten in each of 102 crafts, that is 83 percent (including Anabaptist wives, 94 crafts, or 71 percent)—and this in the course of a century. Actually, Anabaptist craftsmen were concentrated in four crafts: there were 160 Anabaptist weavers, 133 tailors, 103 shoemakers, and 69 millers. Since these particular crafts were the least specialized, there is no basis for the Marxist theory that highly specialized craftsmen, who were sensitive to changes on the markets, joined the sect in particularly large numbers. But why did so many members of the basic crafts become Anabaptists, and so few specialized craftsmen?

One explanation may be that their working conditions made the weavers, tailors, shoemakers, millers, and also the blacksmiths especially susceptible to Anabaptist influence. In the case of weavers, tailors, and shoemakers, the quiet sedentary routine of their work may have encouraged brooding on religious problems. Millers and blacksmiths, for their part, had contact with a larger number of people than most craftsmen. Peasants and merchants came constantly to the mills to have their grain ground, and the mills, frequently situated outside the villages near rivers and creeks, could not be easily observed by officials. Similarly, there was much coming and going in the blacksmiths' shops, where peasants brought their horses to be shod. Millers and blacksmiths, then, might have been more exposed to new ideas than craftsmen with only a few customers. It is possible that such conditions prepared the terrain for sectarian influence, although there is no definite proof.

Another explanation is much simpler. Those who worked in the unspecialized crafts were naturally more numerous than those who worked in the more specialized and sophisticated ones: if there were more weavers, tailors, and shoemakers than, say, cardmakers or silversmiths, there would naturally be more Anabaptist weavers, tailors, and shoemakers than Anabaptist cardmakers or silversmiths. There were more Anabaptist weavers in the great textile centers, such as Swabia, than in the Tirol, where weaving was not such a prominent occupation. Since tailoring, shoemaking, and grain grinding were practiced everywhere, there were relatively many Anabaptist tailors, shoemakers, and millers in all areas. And since copper and silver mining played such an important role in the Tirol, there were many Anabaptist miners there: the real number, indeed, was definitely higher than the 32 miners (or 37, including wives) known to us.

Though the high percentage of weavers among the Anabaptist craftsmen has been mentioned, the weavers' role should not be exaggerated, as it frequently is. At Augsburg, where the crafts of most Anabaptists are recorded, there were 61 weavers among 403 Anabaptists between 1526 and 1573, or 84 if Anabaptist wives of craftsmen are included. Though they formed the largest contingent of craftsmen, the weavers still constituted only 15 percent of all Anabaptists at Augsburg, or 21 percent including their wives. Even these figures are exceptional, weaving having been a much more prominent craft in Augsburg than in most other areas. In general, the percentage of weavers among the Anabaptists was smaller. In the textile crafts as a whole, there were 402 Anabaptists (or 502, including Anabaptist wives). Again this figure is not surprising, for textile production occupied the largest number of craftsmen in sixteenth-century Germany. The second largest group of Anabaptist craftsmen were metalworkers, and the third largest were occupied in the preparation of food.

From January 1525 to December 1529, 693 craftsmen (including Anabaptist wives) joined the Anabaptist sect. This figure amounts to 47 percent of the total number of craftsmen who were to convert to Anabaptism by 1618. During the 1530s only 342 craftsmen became Anabaptists, that is, half as many as during the first five years. By 1539, 71 percent of the 1,458 known Anabaptist craftsmen had already joined the sect. The number of Anabaptist craftsmen, then, was highest during the first fifteen years of the movement. From the 1540s onward Anabaptism lost its attraction to craftsmen. Only twenty to at the most eighty craftsmen became Anabaptists with every decade. There was an increase in the number of craftsmen in the 1570s, corresponding to the general increase in the number of Anabaptists during these years. But though the craftsmen constituted only a small group in the Anabaptist congregations, many Anabaptist leaders came from their ranks.

Some 46 percent of the Anabaptist craftsmen lived in the imperial cities, capitals, and larger towns of the territories, and 19 percent lived in small towns. In other words, 65 percent of the Anabaptist craftsmen were town dwellers, whereas 29 percent lived in villages. The residence of the remaining 6 percent is not known. As Table 11 shows, the chronological distribution of craftsmen in towns and villages also differed considerably. While the number of craftsmen in both towns and villages was highest during the first years of the movement, the decline from the 1540s on was much greater in towns than in villages. From 1550 to 1618, almost twice as many village craftsmen as urban craftsmen (202 as opposed to 120) became Anabaptists. Only at Augsburg was there a large group of craftsmen continuing up to 1573, when the Anabaptist congregation finally dissolved. These figures suggest that the decline in the number of craftsmen was due not to the rejection of Anabaptism by the craftsmen but to the persecution and elimination of Anabaptists in towns. In villages Anabaptism continued to attract craftsmen. Since craftsmanship played a very minor role in the country, however, the number of village craftsmen among the brethren remained small.

Table 11. Anabaptist craftsmen in cities, small towns, and villages

Period	Imperial city, capital, large territorial town	Small country town	Village	Uncertain	Total
1525–29	427	152	102	12	693
1530–39	153	59	99	31	342
1540–49	29	12	23	5	69
1550–59	21	8	17	1	47
1560–69	19	7	44	9	79
1570–79	14	27	55	13	109
1580–89	4	9	30	4	47
1590–99	1	5	18	3	27
1600–09	0	4	22	1	27
1610–18	1	0	16	1	18
Total	669	283	426	80	1,458

Peasants

In estimating the number of Anabaptists engaged in agriculture, we should bear in mind that during the sixteenth century almost all those who lived in villages were engaged in farming, whether as owners of farms, farmhands, or maidservants. Many burghers of small towns were also farmers. Of the 6,870 rural Anabaptists living in villages and isolated farms, 614 were not farmers but craftsmen, noblemen, or intellectuals, or were employed in other occupations. This leaves 6,256 Anabaptists, or 56 percent of all Anabaptists, who were engaged in farming.

If we add to village farmers those of the small towns who were not craftsmen, noblemen, intellectuals, or otherwise employed, then 7,647 Anabaptists would have been engaged in agriculture, or 68 percent of all Anabaptists. Thus farmers constituted between 56 percent and 68 percent of all Anabaptists—definitely a majority.

This figure is an average, however. During the first five years of the movement, 1525–29, farmers were probably in the minority, constituting between 33.5 percent and 53.1 percent of all Anabaptists. But from 1530 onward this percentage rose rapidly. During the period 1530–49 farmers were already in the majority, constituting between 55.8 percent and 66.7 percent. The percentage continued to increase: between 1550 and 1618 some 77 percent to 84.3 percent of the Anabaptists were engaged in farming. Anabaptism had largely become a movement of peasants.

Conclusion

More than 98 percent of all Anabaptists were common people, earning their livelihood on farms, in workshops, and by other forms of manual labor. Less than 2 percent were intellectuals or noblemen. Peasants formed the largest group within the sect, between 56 percent and 68 percent, and craftsmen constituted between 28 percent and 41 percent. As we have seen, these figures do no reflect the changes in the social composition of the movement. Whereas craftsmen formed the majority of the believers during the first five years, from about 1530 onward, Anabaptism turned increasingly into a sect of farmers. In spite of these changes, Anabaptism was never a sect of craftsmen only or peasants only. Both groups were strongly represented from 1525 to 1618.

Though the Anabaptists were common folk by and large, they were not necessarily poor. There were wide differences of social position both among craftsmen and among peasants. Which group did Anabaptism attract—the prosperous craftsman or the indigent journeyman, the wealthy farmer or the impoverished day laborer?

Rich and Poor

To establish the exact social position of the Anabaptists, we shall analyze the social composition of three representative Anabaptists groups: the large congregation at Augsburg, the biggest city in the Empire; the congregation of Munich, the relatively small capital of Bavaria; and the prodominantly rural Anabaptist movement in the duchy of Württemberg.

Augsburg

Between 1526 and 1529, 300 inhabitants of Augsburg joined the Anabaptists. We can establish the social position of 212 of these 300, that is, 71 percent. As Table 12 shows, 127 of them, or 60 percent of those whose position is known, belonged to the lowest class: 37 were journeymen, day laborers, or servants; 23 were maidservants, and not less than 67 were listed as having

Table 12. The social position of Anabaptist converts in Augsburg

Period	Day laborer, servant, journeyman	Maid-servant	Poor without property	Propertied (by property value in florins)				
				1–50	51–150	151–500	501–1,000	Over 1,000
1526–29	37	23	67	24	5	28	11	17 *
1530–39	8	13	11	1	0	0	1	0
1540–49	0	3	4	0	2	1	0	1
1550–59	0	2	3	1	1	1	0	1
1560–69	6	1	1	0	0	1	0	0
1570–73	0	0	2	0	0	2	2	0
Total	51	42	88	26	8	33	14	19

* Of these, eleven had between one and three thousand florins; two had five to ten thousand; three had ten to twenty thousand; and one had twenty to thirty thousand.

no property. Another 11 percent had a modicum of property worth up to fifty florins. In reality, they too formed part of the very large class of poor people at Augsburg. Thus 71 percent of the Anabaptists in Augsburg from 1526 to 1529 were poverty-stricken. Another 2.3 percent had limited means of 51 to 150 florins. Twenty-eight Anabaptists, or 14 percent, owned medium-sized property of 151 to five hundred florins. Another 24 Anabaptists, or 11 percent, were well-to-do, with property worth between 501 and ten thousand florins. Finally, 2 percent of the Anabaptists were very wealthy, with property worth ten thousand to thirty thousand florins. The Anabaptists at Augsburg, then, came from all social classes, though the poor were most numerous.[15]

Those leaders of the congregation who were natives of Augsburg rose from among the poor. Hans Leupold and Augustin Bader, who in October 1527 were elected ministers, had no property. In March 1528 two journeymen were elected ministers by the congregation. It would nevertheless be erroneous to say that the proletariat dominated the congregation. The chronicler Sender observed in 1527 that there were journeymen and maidservants, rich, moderately rich, and poor people among the Garden Brethren, as the Augsburg Anabaptists were called. Since there were 28 wealthy people among the Anabaptists of Augsburg, they cannot really be termed exceptions. Four of these wealthy Anabaptists were merchants with more than ten thousand florins' worth of property; thirteen were prosperous craftsmen with property ranging from a thousand to ten thousand florins. Particularly annoying to the town council was the presence of two guild masters who were also town councilors, and three high officials of the guilds, the *zwölfer*, among the congregation.

Nor were the wealthy and the moderately rich at the periphery of the movement. The first to accept baptism at Augsburg in 1526 were propertied people. The three brethren who in 1527 were elected purse bearers were moderately rich craftsmen. Two of the four brethren chosen as purse bearers in 1528 were wealthy; a third had a very small property; the social position of the fourth is not known. It was not by chance that the Anabaptists tended to elect men of property to administer the common fund: they wished to counter the charge of communistic tendencies. Among the seven Anabaptists who in October 1527 were characterized by the town council as "captains" of the Anabaptists, we find the patrician Langenmantel, two guildmasters, two craftsmen with medium properties, and only two poor people. If the poor dominated numerically, people with property were nonetheless the backbone of the congregation.

Though the Anabaptists were supposed to regard each other as brothers and sisters, class distinctions did not disappear among them. To be sure, in 1527 well-to-do and poor Anabaptists alike gathered at meetings.[16] In March 1528, however, a strange split appeared among the Augsburg brethren. The leaders Nespitzer and Bader had lately been holding meetings outside the city in nearby forests, gravel pits, and quarries. Soon they noticed that nine believers were not attending these meetings. Four of these nine had also refused to act as purse bearers. When Nespitzer asked them to join the congregation outside the city, they flatly refused. What was the reason for their refusal? Some of these Anabaptists, arrested in 1527, had promised to stop attending Anabaptist meetings. It was their impression, however, that the town council would have no objection to their gathering in small circles to read the Bible. Although they held to the Anabaptist doctrines, then, they also tried to obey the council's orders.

It is striking to note that five of these nine Anabaptists were wealthy people. They may have disliked associating with so many poor, whose actual intentions were not altogether clear. The mass of brethren that gathered outside the city walls were offended at this conduct. Angry words were heard: the wealthy were obviously ashamed to associate with the poor and preferred to have their own meetings, but the brethren would eventually make sure that the rich would also come.[17] The wealthy Anabaptists avoided large meetings even within the city: few of them attended the large gatherings in the houses of Barbara Schleifer and Susanna Doucher. Honester Crafter, a very wealthy widow, openly stated that she and her two daughters had been baptized "in the absence of the mass of people", and had left the meeting on Easter morning because too many people had been present.[18]

The antagonism between rich and poor brethren lingered on even after almost the entire Augsburg congregation had been rounded up by the town council in 1528. A weaver protested that only the poor were expelled from the city, whereas rich men such as Lucas Kreler and Lucas Miller were allowed to stay. A cobbler asked why the wealthy were not tortured, as he was.[19] Most well-to-do Anabaptists of Augsburg who had hesitated to expose themselves were quick to abandon their belief.

The arrests of 1528 did not completely eradicate Anabaptism at Augsburg, for from 1530 to 1573, 105 Augsburgers accepted the Anabaptist doctrines. We know the social position of 69 of these 105 Anabaptists, that is, of 66 percent. As Table 12 shows, the proportion of poor Anabaptists seems to have increased. Fifty-four Anabaptists between 1530 and 1573, or 78 percent, were journeymen, day laborers, or servants, or had no property. One man, for instance, received alms from the city at one time. Another 3 percent had a modicum of property worth up to 50 florins. In other words, 81 percent of the Anabaptists from 1530 to 1573 belonged to the lowest class, as compared with 73 percent during the years 1527 to 1529. Naturally the number of Anabaptists with property was smaller. Three had limited means of 51 to 150 florins; only five had a medium amount of property; and another five were well-to-do. The wealthy had obviously lost interest in the sect after 1528: even these five well-to-do Anabaptists cannot truly be described as wealthy, since none of them had more than three thousand florins.

Munich

In Munich also, the congregation was largely composed of poor people. We know the social position of 21 of the 38 Anabaptists at Munich from 1527 to 1530. Sixteen of them had no property whatsoever, paying an annual tax of only two shillings. Four had very small property, worth between 51 and one hundred florins. One, Jörg Schachner, later an Anabaptist leader who finally joined Kaspar Schwenckfeld and his followers, had a little more than 150 florins. He was the son of a rich weaver who sat on the Munich town council from 1519 to 1532. Similarly, in such cities at Steyr and Enns in Austria, and Strasbourg, Anabaptism spread mainly among poor and lowly people, such as the employees of craftsmen.[20]

Württemberg

In the towns and villages of the duchy of Württemberg, the social position of 471 Anabaptists can be established.[21] During the period 1527–1619, as Table 13 shows, 111 of them, or about 24 percent, were farmhands, maidservants, day laborers, or journeymen who held property worth not more than twenty florins, if any. Another 71 Anabaptists (about 15 percent) held small property worth 21 to fifty florins, but they, too, were employed by others. Another 120 (about 25 percent) were small farmers or craftsmen with property worth only 51 to 150 florins. Though they might have been independent, they suffered bitterly when crops failed and prices rose. Some 145 Anabaptists in Württemberg (31 percent) had property of medium size (151 to 500 florins). This figure includes 46 Anabaptists whose exact property is not known, but who either were characterized as rich or served as officials in towns and villages. Twenty-four (6 percent) had more than 500 florins, but none were as wealthy as the rich brethren at Augsburg.

Table 13. Social position of Anabaptist converts in
the duchy of Württemberg

Period	Servants	Poor	Propertied (by property value in florins)				
			0–20	21–50	51–150	151–500	Over 500
1527–29	0	0	2	3	0	2	4
1530–39	0	1	6	4	20 *	20	4
1540–49	1	0	0	4	7	6	3
1550–59	1	2	0	4	13	20	3
1560–69	0	7	2 (2) †	11 (1)	8 (11)	22 (25)	2 (6)
1570–79	20	6	3 (0)	23 (8)	35 (37)	40 (51)	5 (10)
1580–89	5	5	5 (3)	8 (4)	16 (14)	13 (17)	2 (6)
1590–99	0	3	9 (5)	3 (4)	10 (9)	11 (12)	1 (4)
1600–09	2	19	1 (0)	4 (2)	5 (6)	0 (2)	0 (0)
1610–19	5	6	0 (0)	7 (3)	6 (5)	11 (16)	0 (0)
Total	34	49	28 (18)	71 (37)	120 (122)	145 (171)	24 (40)

* Seven of these twenty had houses worth 25 to 40 florins. Thus they are
classified in this category, though the exact value of their property is unknown.
† Figures for Anabaptists between 1527 and 1559 are based on tax rolls of
1544, but for Anabaptists after 1559 we have to rely on inventories of property
values. During the second half of the sixteenth century, however, the value of
real property rose immensely owing to inflation. There is evidence that the
price of real property in France rose by 150 percent between 1550 and 1600,
and in Germany, by at least 100 percent (Abel, 63–67). Statements made by
local officials in Württemberg in 1607 also indicate that the price of real
property and houses had doubled within the preceding thirty to forty years.
Thus it has been assumed here that during the period 1560 to 1618 the price
of a given piece of land was twice as high as it had been before 1560; the
property groupings are wide enough to allow for smaller inaccuracies. The
figures in parentheses, then, are the original figures before changes were made
to adjust for inflation.

Thus the majority of the Anabaptists in Württemberg, about
64 percent, had property worth less than 150 florins, if they
had any at all. Even so, a substantial minority of 37 percent
were either moderately well-to-do or rich farmers and craftsmen.

We find among the Anabaptists in Württemberg only 15
village officials. However, not less than 96 families of rich
farmers and officials in 59 villages of the duchy had at least one
Anabaptist member. In villages with a large Anabaptist popula-

tion usually a number of well-to-do peasants were also among the believers. In some villages the rich farmers were even the first to be converted and then spread their belief among their neighbors. In a very few villages only one or two rich families accepted baptism, while the rest of the village population had nothing to do with the sect.

Anabaptism, then, did not attract just one class, such as the proletariat. It is true that paupers and people with little property were very numerous, constituting 72 percent of the brethren at Augsburg, 76 percent at Munich, and 64 percent in Württemberg. But about a third were propertied: 28 percent at Augsburg and 36 percent in Württemberg. As at Augsburg, however, in Württemberg a decline can be observed in the social standing of the Anabaptists during the sixteenth century. Until the middle of the century, the number of Anabaptists possessing no property or only up to 150 florins was about equal with the number possessing a medium or large property (more than 150 florins). From the 1570s onward, the proportion of poor farmhands, journeymen, and small farmers with up to 150 florins clearly predominated. In the early seventeenth century, finally, most of the converts to Anabaptism were poor.

Why were most Anabaptists either poor or nearly poor? One reason is obvious: since the mass of the general population was poor, the Anabaptist leaders were likely to find most of their followers among the poor. The social background of the Anabaptists by and large reflects the social structure of cities, towns, and villages in sixteenth-century Germany. At Augsburg in 1527 the Anabaptist group was even slightly better off on the whole than the general public. Yet there is no compelling reason why most Anabaptists should have been people of little or no property. Schwenckfeld, for example, had many followers among the wealthy burghers of Augsburg and the nobility in Swabia. There must have been a reason why the Anabaptists appealed in particular to the lower classes.

Could the political doctrines of the Anabaptists have attracted the poor? The peasant uprising of 1525 had very little effect on the Anabaptist movement. The revolutionary groups in Thuringia and possibly in Franconia and Esslingen were not characteristic of early Anabaptism and were limited to the years 1527 and 1528. The political radicalism that appeared among the genuine Anabaptists in Thuringia may have impressed some former rebels, but the Anabaptists in Thuringia never attracted many people. Nor do we know whether or not the Thuringian Anabaptists were particularly poor.

The ordinary political doctrines of the Anabaptists probably did not repel the poor as much as they conceivably repelled the well-to-do. The indigent craftsman or peasant was hardly shocked by the Anabaptist doctrine that a Christian could not hold political office. Poor people like him did not even have the right to vote and were certainly not elected into the town council or law court. Since they never held positions of responsibility, the poor might not have realized the consequences of the Anabaptist doctrines. In times of war it was usually the peasant who suffered most: his farm might be burned down, his livestock stolen, and his family massacred. Hence he did not object to the condemnation of war as unchristian. Nor was the poor laborer or journeyman vexed when the Anabaptist leaders condemned fashionable dress, luxury, and an easy life.

The relation between political doctrine and social structure is still more evident in the case of the Hutterites. The decline in the social status of the Anabaptists in Württemberg during the second half of the sixteenth century coincided with a strong increase in the number of Hutterite emigrants. Whether or not the poor were attracted by the communistic and egalitarian character of the Hutterite communities is not certain. But it is certain that numerous journeymen and landless laborers in south Germany and Switzerland joined the Hutterites in Moravia because they suffered great misery in times of famine and high prices.

The democratic trend in Anabaptism might also have appealed to the common people. The Anabaptist leader was
elected by the congregation. He had no mysterious powers, nor
was he a university man; he earned his living by manual labor.
His language, dress, tastes, and behavior were those of the
craftsmen and peasants. Often the Anabaptist leader preached
in colorful language that suited the common man. What distinguished him was not his educational background or social
prestige but his leadership qualities, intelligence, eloquence,
knowledge of the Bible, and exemplary way of life—his
charisma.

In the Catholic Church, the ordinary believer was only a
passive recipient. One man said that since the mass was in
Latin, he could not know whether the priest was cursing or
teaching wholesome doctrine.[22] Even in the Lutheran and
Zwinglian churches the parishioner was only the recipient of
pastoral care. But in the Anabaptist meetings everyone could
speak up: for example, all members voted on the exclusion of
sinners. Neither Catholics nor Protestants ever thought of doing
away with social distinctions: in the village church the nobleman and wealthy peasants had their prominent pews. The Anabaptists, on the other hand, tended to eliminate class differences.
They addressed one another as brother and sister. A rich Anabaptist woman dressed as modestly as a poor one. The secret
nocturnal meetings linked the believers much more closely
than the service in the village church on Sunday morning. Yet
the example of the Augsburg congregation showed that class
differences sometimes persisted among the brethren.

The Anabaptists made great efforts to help the needy in
their midst. When a brother was expelled, fellow believers
would employ him or help his wife on the farm. The poor, who
knew what it was like to go hungry, appreciated the help
offered by the brethren much more than did the rich.

Their strict Biblicism might also have helped the Anabaptists attract common people. The craftsman or peasant knew

nothing of the non-Christian classical civilization—of Aristotle's political philosophy or of Roman law, subjects the intellectual would have studied at the university. The uneducated man, distrusting the devious interpretations of both lawyers and theologians, was receptive to the Anabaptist view that the Scriptures alone, especially the New Testament, contained God's explicit teaching on faith, church, and society.

When the Anabaptists attacked the practice of infant baptism or the doctrine of the Real Presence of Christ's body in the elements of the Lord's Supper, they often appealed to common sense and daily experience to support their views. Arguments of this kind may have had a particular appeal for simple folk who were used to taking things as they were without attaching to them any mystical significance, as monks or theologians might be inclined to. Of course, the opposite could also be argued: uneducated people often tend to be superstitious.

The Anabaptist criticism of the immoral conditions that prevailed in the Catholic and Protestant churches and their emphasis on the pure life may also have impressed the common people. Whereas the educated man looks primarily to the intellectual content of a religion, the common man is inclined to judge a religion by its effect on his everyday life. It could be argued that the Anabaptist emphasis on church discipline reflected the ethical concern of the poorer class of people. The wealthy burghers in many Protestant cities were opposed to a strict church discipline because they did not want to be supervised by ambitious and revengeful pastors who might even have risen from the lower orders of society. Thus at Esslingen the church discipline of 1533 was never fully applied. The poor man, who by pure accident of birth had been condemned to a life of drudgery and misery, thought that a man's worth was revealed in his personal life, not in the size of his house or the number of his fields. He would thus approve of rigorous moral supervision. Of course, this factor would have attracted people to Anabaptism only in Lutheran and Catholic areas, for the

Zwinglian and Calvinist churches maintained strong church discipline.

It must be emphasized that though some or all of these factors may account for the large percentage of poor Anabaptists, there is no real evidence to prove that they do.

Personal Factors

Reactions of Men and Women

A striking characteristic of the Anabaptist movement is that there were more than twice as many men as women in its ranks. During the entire period from 1525 to 1618, as Table 14 shows, 68.4 percent of the Anabaptists were men, and 31.6 percent women. Of course, the proportion of men to women was not constant all through the sixteenth and early seventeenth centuries. But on the whole men constituted more than 65 percent and women less than 35 percent. The preponderance of men can be observed in all areas, Catholic or Protestant. A study of individual congregations confirms this result, though there were

Table 14. Men and women Anabaptists

Period	Men No. (%)	Women No. (%)
1525–1529	1,767 (70.0)	758 (30.0)
1530–1549	2,187 (68.9)	987 (31.1)
1550–1618	2,125 (66.7)	1,062 (33.3)
Total	6,079 (68.4)	2,807 (31.6)

Note: The sex of only 8,886 Anabaptists can be determined. Repeatedly the sources tell us only that a certain number of people joined the Anabaptists, without specifying their sex.

variations. At Augsburg from 1526 to 1529, about 57 percent of the Anabaptists were men, and 43 percent women. At Munich between 1527 and 1530, 68 percent were men, and 32 percent women. At Esslingen in 1527 and 1528, fully 71 percent were men, and only 29 percent women.

Naturally it would be wrong to call Anabaptism a male movement. Some of the three thousand women believers were to be found in every Anabaptist congregation, and they were just as zealous in their beliefs as the men, if not more so. A woman at Strasbourg engaged Wetzel von Marsilien, a town councilor, in a discussion on the incarnation of Christ. Another at Heilbronn challenged the reformer Johann Lachmann to a disputation. In Thuringia, the Tirol, and Styria women were very active in spreading their belief. A few wrote hymns. Some men said quite frankly they wished they were as pious, learned, and intelligent as this or that sister. Many women were also extremely courageous, preferring to endure long imprisonment or exile rather than abandon their faith. Some 164 women Anabaptists are known to have been executed.[23] And yet the fact remains that only about one-third of the Anabaptists were women. Several factors appear to have discouraged women from joining the sect.

The bad reputation of the early Anabaptists might have deterred some women from attending their conventicles. It was said that some Anabaptists were promiscuous and had sex orgies. In Franconia it was rumored that during the ceremony of baptism both men and women stripped off their clothes and obeyed the words "Be fruitful and multiply."[24] Then there were Hut's menacing eschatological predictions, which appeared to aim at another uprising. This might explain why the percentage of women Anabaptists was lower in Franconia than in any other area. The charges of obscenity and subversion were leveled against the brethren especially during the first years of the movement. Indeed, the proportion of women among the Anabaptists was especially low from 1525 to 1529. Generally speaking it rose during the period 1530 to 1549 and even more after 1550.

Of course, all through the sixteenth century such apprehensions and suspicions remained alive. Laws, books, and sermons characterized the Anabaptists as sinister heretics who held suspicious gatherings at night in desolate places. Since the Anabaptists did not preach or meet openly, a certain stigma was always attached to them. As late as 1588 a Tirolese woman said that though she had frequently seen Anabaptists, she had avoided them because they were "wild people." [25]

Women may also have been deterred more than men by the danger of persecution: the prospect of imprisonment, banishment, the confiscation of their property, and even execution may have been particularly frightening to them. Furthermore, women might have found it more difficult to subordinate their natural feelings to the demands of ideology. A man might be willing to sacrifice everything to his salvation—his family, home, and property. When one Anabaptist was reminded of the sorrow he had caused his wife and child, he coldly replied, "Nobody is as dear to me as my own salvation." [26] A man might agree that for ideological reasons it was preferable to take children away from their parents at the age of two or three, as the Hutterites did. But it was undoubtedly harder for a woman to part with her children, even for the sake of saving her soul. Of course, this factor should not be exaggerated. Many women did not hesitate to make great sacrifices for their belief.

Individual Motives

Why did people choose to become Anabaptists? There certainly was ample opportunity for people to be exposed to the Anabaptist beliefs. Some learned about Anabaptism from relatives. For example, a woman at Kaufbeuren said her niece had asked her to renounce all evil and listen to the brethren. More often people met Anabaptists at work. A journeyman at Strasbourg was reproved by a fellow worker for his loose morals. A carpenter at Ansbach was convinced by his journeyman that Christ had never preached infant baptism. Indeed, the Anabaptists tried to disseminate their ideas wherever they could.

Straw cutters and well-diggers would talk of serious matters with the farmer's family. The brethren approached shepherds or peasants as they harvested flax in the fields or carted onions to town. One Anabaptist talked religion in the public bath-house. Sometimes people walked inadvertently into religious conventicles. A man who took honey to a neighbor's house, another man who went to buy or sell cloth, a woman who went to fetch some milk—each on arriving found an Anabaptist preaching and stayed to listen. Occasionally village parsons who raged against the sect achieved the opposite of what they had intended: the peasants became so curious that they went to see what Anabaptists were like.

People who came across Anabaptists in one way or another must have been surprised. Far from being the dangerous here-tics, revolutionaries, or even criminals against whom the pastor had warned his flock, they turned out to be harmless and devout. Even so, most people who were exposed to Anabap-tism did not become Anabaptists. No doubt many did not want to break the laws of their country. Most probably thought, too, that one could also be a good Christian in the official church. Yet there were always some who felt drawn to the brethren, for a variety of reasons. Here we shall indicate only those motives the Anabaptists and the authorities recognized. Deeper motives, which could only be guessed at, must remain hidden. The categories presented here do not always appear in a clear-cut way in the transcripts, however; there were also Anabaptists who cited several reasons.

A frequent motive mentioned by the Anabaptists was the realization of their own sinfulness. People overcome by the awareness of their sins sometimes break entirely with their past. They might take holy orders, as Luther did. In Protestant countries they would join sects and revivalist groups that de-manded greater religious and moral efforts. In January 1525 one of the first brethren, Jörg Schad of Zollikon, stated that he had spent all his life in vice and sin and that in deep despair he had asked for mercy and the sign of baptism. One man was reminded by the leader that he was old and near death; another became conscious of his great sinfulness during a severe illness.[27] Some believers said they had experienced an inner conversion: God Himself had spoken to them.[28] Such an experience could provide the strongest inducement to join the brethren, and it was very difficult to dissuade such a believer from his faith.

The publication of Luther's translation of the Scriptures also stimulated sectarian thinking. Many common people were overwhelmed by the Bible's depth and richness; formerly they had heard only bits and pieces of the Bible without being able to read it for themselves. Soon they had their own interpretations of Christ's teaching, which appeared very clear to them. He had never heard the gospel at Passau, the leader Nespitzer said: when the government had forbidden anyone to buy or sell Luther's New Testament on pain of death, he had begun to wonder about it. At that time Hut had come to Passau and read from the Old and the New Testament, especially from Exodus 28 and from Matthew 28, where Christ sends out His disciples to teach all nations the Gospel of All Creatures and baptize them. As a result Nespitzer and his wife had been induced to accept baptism. Indeed, Christ's injunction that only believers should be baptized played a great role in the process of conversion. When in 1533 nineteen men and women at Berka in Hesse were asked why they had joined the sect, all of them mentioned the role of baptism.[29]

Whether it was the consciousness of sin, or the conviction of having been called by God, or the impression made by the New Testament, most Anabaptists joined the movement for religious reasons. Rarely is there an indication of a political motive.[30] Fridolin Meiger, a notary at Strassbourg, could have spoken for many brethren when in 1529 he told the story of his conversion. He had really tried at first to live according to the beliefs of his ancestors, but when Erasmus and Luther had appeared, he had followed what seemed to him the better way. When the new preachers had started to quarrel with each other, he had been greatly disturbed. At that time the brethren—who were known as Touffer—had come and preached a middle way between popery and Lutheranism. They had directed him to a good and virtuous life.[31]

Apparently preachers who proclaimed the Day of Judgment managed to terrify some into becoming Anabaptists. In 1529, for example, one Veltin Romeis of Grossenbach in Fulda stated that when he was working on a building a fellow worker, Otto Haunmoller, had spoken to him of the Anabaptist doctrines, but he had not been interested. After the job was done, Haunmoller had reminded him on three occasions that the whole world would soon be destroyed. Though Romeis began to feel apprehensive and scared, he still hesitated. Five weeks later Haunmoller informed him that an Anabaptist leader had again predicted the terrible end of the world. Alarmed, Romeis went to hear the leader, who described to him the imminent punishment: "Whosoever did not believe and have himself baptized would be eternally lost." Stricken by fear, Romeis now accepted baptism.[32]

Here and there we come across still other reasons why people became Anabaptists. Several people in Thuringia and in the Tirol explained that the steadfastness of the brethren at their execution had made them wonder about this sect.[33] Others said that they had been appalled by the ugly strife and disputes between Catholic and Protestant pastors, and within the Protestant camp, between Lutheran and Zwinglian pastors. One woman stated in 1528 that during four years of attending the sermons at Augsburg, she had heard one pastor preach this, and another that: one called the Sacrament a sign; another called it flesh and blood. She became so confused that she had finally decided to hear also the Anabaptist leader Hans Leupold.[34] Frequent religious changes ordered by various princes also seem to have had an unsettling effect. In 1609 inhabitants of Grafschaft Leiningen explained that having been first Catholics, then

Lutherans, and then Calvinists, they had become disillusioned and turned to Anabaptism.[35]

It might well be wondered whether all these reasons were accurate explanations of conversion to Anabaptism or whether they were simply rationalizations after the fact. After all, millions of Christians who were equally conscious of their sins, who let themselves be guided by the Holy Spirit, who read the Bible daily, and who were quite aware of the immorality of their neighbors stayed in the official church. The music, the devotional literature, and the loyalty shown by many Protestants and Catholics to their faith in times of adversity testifies to the vitality of the official churches during the sixteenth century. There was an undeniable strangeness about people who separated from the official church. Did those who became Anabaptists yearn to be better than other people? Was their sensitivity so great that they could not tolerate the physical presence of unrepentant sinners? Were they attracted by the nonviolence of the brethren? Or was it that they preferred a life of suffering to a normal life? The historian can give no answer.

At a loss to understand the sudden conversion of their neighbors to Anabaptism, some contemporaries also searched for underlying reasons. One man suggested that the position of the constellations in the firmament was instrumental in these conversions.[36] Shrewd peasants, Freudians *avant la lettre*, surmised that a certain Anabaptist must have been "a real eunuch . . . otherwise he would not have adopted these views." [37]

Conclusion

The most important factor determining the geographic expansion of Anabaptism seems to have been the religious conditions already prevailing in a territory or city. The diffusion of Protestant ideas in Catholic areas encouraged the spread of Anabaptism: in territories where people were dissatisfied with Catholicism but did not have Protestant leaders to turn to, the Anabaptists sometimes attracted a good part of the population.

Even the subsequent Reformation could not stop the sect once it had spread in an area. Anabaptism was unsuccessful, however, in areas where the Reformation was thoroughly established before the Anabaptists appeared. Similarly, in staunch Catholic areas the Anabaptists were also unsuccessful.

A second important factor was government persecution. Most governments that vigorously executed Anabaptists suppressed the movement at an early date. Wherever governments used milder measures such as expulsion, the sect flourished until the Thirty Years' War. Thus Anabaptism soon disappeared in most Catholic areas, where it faced stern official measures, but continued to gain adherents in Protestant ones. The degree of government control over the population seems to have been a third factor. Since the city governments exercised relatively great control over their citizens, the movement collapsed early in the cities. Lack of strong administrative control in the countryside explains why Anabaptism was never fully suppressed in some rural areas. The amazing development of Anabaptism in Moravia was due to the fact that the feudal lords could disregard the orders of the Hapsburgs.

As we have seen, the appeal of Anabaptism was largely limited to two social classes, the craftsmen and the peasants. The Anabaptists inevitably evoked hostility or indifference among the upper classes and intellectuals, for most of their leaders were uneducated craftsmen who angrily condemned as unchristian the urban economy and social conventions of the sixteenth century and rejected any form of higher education. While there is no evidence that political considerations brought craftsmen and peasants to Anabaptism, numerous poor laborers and artisans followed the Hutterite missionaries to Moravia because they suffered bitter economic misery at home.

The success or failure of Anabaptism under various conditions can thus be attributed to a number of different factors, several of which may have been at work in a given area at once. Unfortunately, however, historical and sociological anal-

yses do not fully explain religious phenomena. They tell us why
the nobility distrusted the Anabaptists, why the upper class and
the intellectuals showed little interest, and why craftsmen and
peasants constituted the majority of the movement. But they
do not explain why any one craftsman or peasant should have
joined the sect, for even among those social groups that were
most receptive to Anabaptism and strongly exposed to Anabaptist preaching, such as the village craftsmen and peasants
in the Calvinist Palatinate, only an exceedingly small fraction of
the population ever embraced Anabaptism. Though certain
trends can be discerned among large social groups, the reasons
for each Anabaptist conversion ultimately lay within the convert himself.

10

Anabaptist Literature

Although most Anabaptists were illiterate, their leaders, especially during the early years of the movement, produced a considerable body of literature, including both hymns and prose. Here we shall not attempt to offer an interpretation of Anabaptist literature but only to indicate the extent of Anabaptist literary activity.

Hymns

If Conrad Grebel had had his way, no hymns would have been sung at Anabaptist meetings, for the New Testament contained no commandment to sing. Other leaders such as Hubmaier and Riedemann, however, declared that to sing spiritual hymns was pleasing to God.[1] Even the first Anabaptists in Switzerland disregarded Grebel's disdain for hymns. When at the end of January 1525 Johannes Brötli, one of the first radicals, had to leave Zollikon, he sang happily, as he himself later wrote. Blaurock also sang on his way to prison at Grüningen in October 1525. What did the early Anabaptists sing? In March 1525 one of the brethren of Zollikon, imprisoned in Zurich, asked his wife to send him the Easter hymn, "Christ ist erstanden." The early German Anabaptists sometimes sang psalms, and at other times, Latin and German hymns.[2] Strange as it may seem, as late as 1535 the Anabaptists of Thuringia sang the hymns of Luther.[3] These Saxon brethren apparently did not know any Anabaptist hymns.

In fact, a substantial body of Anabaptist hymns was already in existence by 1535. Some of the great martyrs of Anabaptism

in 1527 and 1528, such as Manz, Kellermann, Hut, Leupold, Hubmaier, Schiemer, and Schlaffer, as well as many simple believers
had expressed their faith, hopes, and anguish in hymns. The
Anabaptists of south Germany wrote a great number of hymns
during the first half of the sixteenth century. After the publication of their hymnbook, however, their creativity waned.
The Hutterites in Moravia, by contrast, continued to write
hymns until the early seventeenth century.

Most Anabaptist hymns were written by one person, though
at times several persons contributed a stanza each, as did Martin
Zehentmaier and his fellow believers in the dungeon at Schwäbisch Gmünd. According to the Hutterites, many of their
hymns had also been written in prison, though Erhard doubted
it: those in prison, he said, were mostly illiterate, and they
were certainly too sad and terrified before their death to do
any hymn writing. At any rate, the Hutterites seem to have
used hymns written by their martyrs to spread their faith. In
the Tirol, for example, they distributed copies of a song on the
execution of Andreas Büchner, hoping thus to arouse sympathy.

Some early hymns were published in single sheets, but most
seem to have been preserved in manuscripts or simply committed to memory. Finally, by the middle of the sixteenth
century, the Anabaptists collected and published their hymns:
at least as far as we know, the first hymnbook of the brethren
in south Germany appeared in 1564,[4] though an earlier edition
is not impossible. The book contains 53 hymns written between 1535 and 1540 by Philippites imprisoned in the dungeon
of Passau. The hymns were evidently smuggled out of the
prison and carefully preserved. The most prolific of the hymnists at Passau were Hans Betz and Michel Schneider. Whereas
the hymns written by Betz are of a doctrinal character, those
by Schneider usually express a mystical devotion.

During the public debate at Frankenthal in 1571, the Calvinists referred to a book of spiritual songs, *Der Aussbund*.
When this songbook first appeared is unknown, but it evidently

existed by 1571. The earliest edition extant is dated 1583.[5] The book is in two parts, the first of which contains 80 hymns written between 1524 and 1570. Among these are hymns composed by some of the early Anabaptist leaders, such as Manz, Blaurock, Leupold, and Hut. Five hymns were contributed by Hans Büchel, leader of the Swiss Brethren in the Neckar basin in Württemberg. Who collected these hymns is not known, but it may have been Büchel himself. The second part of the *Aussbund* consisting of 51 hymns, is identical with the collection that had appeared in 1564. A new edition of the *Aussbund* appeared in 1622. It remained the hymnbook of the brethren in south Germany and Switzerland until the eighteenth century.

At about the same time the Swiss Brethren published their first hymnbook, the Mennonites in the Netherlands and the Anabaptists in northwest Germany were also publishing hymns. The Dutch Mennonites published three hymnbooks during the second half of the sixteenth century. The first hymnbook of the northwest German Anabaptists appeared before 1565.

Some Anabaptist hymns of the sixteenth century may have been forgotten, never having appeared in print. Manuscripts containing hymns definitely continued to circulate alongside the hymnbooks. In 1583, for example, the two sons of an Anabaptist at Frankenstein in Leiningen copied Anabaptist hymns in books and tried to distribute these among acquaintances. In 1598 a woman at Urbach in Württemberg had both a printed and a handwritten hymnbook. That same year the authorities discovered that six persons at Urbach had Anabaptist hymnbooks. The officials surmised that there were more copies hidden in the village.[6] Since Menno Simons' *Fundament* was also discovered in this village, these might have been north German hymnbooks.

The Anabaptists especially liked a hymn written to commemorate Jörg Wagner's death. One brother at Urbach was heard singing the "Jörg Wagner" at night; another said he had memorized half of the hymn, which consisted of 26 stanzas.[7]

The Anabaptists of Württemberg seem to have enjoyed singing: the villagers of Illingen were much impressed by the fact that a brother among them sang Anabaptist hymns when working in his vineyards.

Unlike the other Anabaptist groups, the Hutterites of the sixteenth century did not publish any hymnbooks. Their hymns were preserved in the form of manuscripts only, and altogether 450 are still extant. Most of these hymns were unknown to Anabaptists outside the Hutterite communities. Peter Riedemann, the most prominent Hutterite hymnist, wrote 47 hymns. Two other prolific writers, Wolf Sailer and Hans Raiffer, wrote 50 hymns and 16 hymns respectively. There was also a host of other hymnists, but none achieved the same depth of thought as these three. Erhard says that the Hutterites thought a great deal of their hymns: anyone who could read, however poorly, had a hymnbook.

There was some interchange of hymns among the various Anabaptist groups. The Hutterites used certain hymns by the early Anabaptist leaders of south Germany and others by the Philippites imprisoned at Passau. The *Aussbund* of 1583 contained eleven hymns from the Dutch hymnbook *Offer des Herren* and another eleven from the north German hymnbook *Ein Schön Gesangbüchlein*, which in turn had been taken from the Dutch. But the differences of doctrines between Mennonites, Swiss Brethren, and Hutterites limited this interchange, and of course the three groups each kept their own hymn collections.

The hymns were generally written in the New High German used by Luther in his translation of the Bible rather than in the south German and Austrian dialects spoken by the hymnists in everyday life. The Anabaptist hymnists preferred stanzas of seven or eight lines, but forms with four, five, nine, ten, and thirteen lines to a stanza were also used. Like the Meistersingers of the cities, the hymnists strove for rhyme frequently at the expense of style. Though the Anabaptists preached separation from the world, the form of their hymns was more closely related to the German folk song than to the liturgical music of the sixteenth century. The technique of the folk song is recalled in hymns introduced by such phrases as "Harken, all ye," or "Now listen." Like the folk songs of the sixteenth century, many Anabaptist hymns have a personal note in the closing stanzas, mentioning the name and occupation of the writer, or a plea to heed his exhortation. Influenced by the Catholic practice of ending psalms, canticles, and hymns with the Gloria Dei, the doxology, some hymnists also ended with a praise to the Trinity or to God. Many Anabaptist writers, especially those of the Hutterite branch, used acrostic techniques, which were highly popular at the time. For example, the initial letters of consecutive stanzas would form the name of the author.

Anabaptist hymns are surprisingly long. Of the 133 hymns of the *Aussbund*, 52 have twenty or more stanzas. The Hutterites in particular wrote long hymns: many of theirs have more than fifty stanzas, especially those devoted to the Old Testament stories. A hymn composed by Wolf Sailer and devoted to the Book of Tobit consists of 130 eight-line stanzas, or 1,040 lines.

A certain pattern can be observed in many of the martyr hymns. There might be a brief introduction, and then the arrest, imprisonment, and trial of the believer would be described. Many hymns included the believer's detailed defense of his faith and an account of his torture and execution. The Anabaptists also wrote metrical paraphrases of a number of psalms, especially those appealing to God for help and expressing trust in Him. There were metrical versions, for example, of the canticles of the Old Testament, the Song of Deborah, and the Song of Hannah. Some brethren wrote outright didactic hymns dealing with such matters as true community, Christian faith, baptism, and the Lord's Supper.

Neither the Anabaptist hymnbooks nor the Hutterite manu-

script collections contain musical notations. But at the top of
the hymn were the first lines of tunes that were to be followed.
Like Luther and other Reformers, the Anabaptists borrowed
tunes that were already well known. Unlike Luther, who made
full use of the abundance of liturgical hymns in the Catholic
Church, the Anabaptists used only two of these. One of them,
"Pange Lingua Gloriosa," seems to have been greatly loved.
It was used by the north and south German Anabaptists and
the Hutterites for hymns about the Passion of Christ.

The Anabaptists adopted a few tunes from pre-Reformation
German sacred songs, but about fifty tunes used by Anabaptists of south Germany and Austria were taken from the rich
treasure of German folk songs. The simple people who joined
the Anabaptists knew these folk songs, one of which, "Ich
stund an einem Morgen," was used for as many as thirty Hutterite hymns and six hymns from the *Aussbund*. The titles of
another 42 tunes suggest folk songs, but the original tunes have
not yet been discovered. Furthermore, the Anabaptists appropriated 46 tunes that had appeared in the growing number of
Lutheran and Moravian hymnbooks. Whether or not the Anabaptists themselves composed any tunes is unknown, though of
course they may well have done so. The most popular tune
among the Hutterites, "O Sohn David, erhör mein Bitt," used
for 32 Hutterite hymns, cannot be traced to any other source.

The Hutterites sang their hymns without harmony and without instrumental accompaniment. Hymns were sung by the entire congregation except at times when an individual person
teaching a hymn, such as a missionary, might sing the hymn
alone first. Frequently the weinzirls were reputed to be good
singers. Riedemann strictly rejected the aesthetic appreciation
of music as sinful, however: the sole purpose of singing was to
express faith. The hymns were called spiritual songs, he said,
because they had been inspired by the spirit. Therefore, they had
to be sung in the spirit of Christ. Those who sang and listened
only for the sweet sound of music sinned greatly against God.

Prose Works

The Writings

The Anabaptists' prose writings are no less impressive than their hymns. They consist of treatises on doctrine, epistles that also generally discuss questions of doctrine, elaborate confessions of faith, exegetical, liturgical, and historical works. The total number of known Anabaptist writers, including authors of epistles and confessions of faith, is 137—69 Hutterites and 68 non-Hutterites. The total number excluding authors of epistles and confessions of faith is 51—13 Hutterites and 38 non-Hutterites. Nonetheless, only 76 Anabaptist works appeared in print, for the great majority of Anabaptist works circulated only in manuscript form.

At least 38 non-Hutterite Anabaptists in Switzerland, Germany, and Austria, then, are known to have written treatises or books on questions of doctrine.[8] The actual number was no doubt greater because several treatises are anonymous. The most brilliant of the early Anabaptist writers was Balthasar Hubmaier. From 1525 until his death in 1528, he produced in rapid succession nineteen treatises on such subjects as baptism, the Lord's Supper, church discipline, and the use of the sword. Michael Sattler, the author of the Schleitheim Articles, is said to have written six short treatises on the Scriptures, the satisfaction of Christ, obedience, and false prophets. There is no definite proof of his authorship, however. Hans Hut's treatise "On the Mystery of Baptism," Schiemer's treatises on "Three Kinds of Grace," "On the Little Bottle," and "On Three Kinds of Baptism," and Schlaffer's works on Christian life and on baptism are pearls of Anabaptist literature. In them Müntzer's theology of the cross was reaffirmed. Langenmantel's writings on the Lord's Supper appear to have been widely read. Hans Haffner wrote a profound little treatise, "On the True Knight of Christ," in the early 1530s. The outstanding Anabaptist writer from the 1530's to the 1550's was Pilgram Marbeck; not less than sixteen of his works have been preserved. During his bitter controversy with Schwenckfeld, he wrote two eminent works, the "Verantwortung" (with Scharnschlager, his disciple, as coauthor) and the "Testamentserläuterung," which contain important clarifications of Anabaptist thought. No other authors of treatises wrote as profoundly or were as influential as these.

Some 28 confessions of faith and 68 epistles are known to have been written by brethren in Switzerland, Germany, Austria, and Italy.[9] In particular, the epistles of the Marbeck group offer vivid insights into the thought and religious life of the brethren. Fifteen treatises by Marbeck and Scharnschlager and fourteen letters of the Marbeck group were collected in the so-called Kunstbuch. Similar collections of tracts and letters may also have been made by other Anabaptist groups. The Anabaptists in Switzerland, Germany, and Austria did not write exegetical works, liturgical literature,[10] catechisms, or historical works. But the early brethren in Switzerland, and also Hut and Marbeck, did compose concordances.[11]

Among the Hutterites are thirteen known authors of treatises [12] and another eleven authors of confessions of faith.[13] The most eminent Hutterite authors were Ulrich Stadler, Peter Riedemann, and possibly Peter Walpot. Stadler's profound writings have a mystical tendency. Riedemann wrote the most important systematic work on Hutterite doctrine, originally intended as a defense of the Hutterite faith for Landgrave Philip of Hesse. Walpot composed several significant treatises on questions of doctrine. Furthermore, 298 lengthy epistles, many written from prison, were produced by more than 58 Hutterites, the most prolific being Hans Schmid, who wrote 36 letters, Paul Glock, who wrote twenty letters and two confessions of faith, and Hans Amon, who wrote seventeen letters.[14]

During the second half of the sixteenth century, the Hutterites produced several exegetical works, dealing particularly with the Old Testament prophets and with Luke, Paul, and the

Revelation of John in the New Testament. At the same time they began their rich collection of liturgical literature, concentrating especially on sermons and formulas for baptism, marriage, the ordination of servants and bishops, the departure of missionaries, and the important Easter service. Various catechisms were also written,[15] and a concordance of the New Testament, presumably of Hutterite origin, has recently been discovered.[16] Almost all these works are anonymous. Further, the Hutterites recorded their history in a magnificent chronicle, begun around 1565 by Caspar Braitmichel and continued by Hans Kräl and Hauptrecht Zapf; smaller chronicles were also compiled. All told, the literature of the Hutterites is more extensive than that of any other Anabaptist group.

Frequently the letters, accounts of faith, and tracts that were most valued by the Hutterites were copied and collected in large codices. The oldest known Hutterite codex, a collection of 1566 of 1,282 pages, contains a very large number of epistles and treatises by 33 brethren [17] and also several anonymous and collective epistles; as many as seven similar Hutterite collections are known.[18] The Hutterites were very careful not to show their writings to outsiders, however. The Jesuit Fischer commented resentfully that exceedingly few people—one in a thousand—were ever allowed to see them. Only four Hutterite writings were printed.[19]

Although the various Anabaptist groups generally disagreed on a number of points, they nonetheless influenced one another on the literary level, as, for example, when Rinck published Bernhard Rothmann's treatise on baptism. The commentary of the Swiss Brethren on the Frankenthal colloquy occasionally follows verbatim the Hutterite treatise "Fünf Artikel darumb der grösst Streit ist." Conversely, the Hutterites had on hand a large body of non-Hutterite literature, such as the Schleitheim Articles, numerous theological tracts, and letters and confessions of faith.[20]

The geographic distribution of literary activity among the

Anabaptists was unusual. In Switzerland, where the movement had begun, only a few Anabaptists, such as Conrad Grebel, Felix Manz, and Martin Lincki, actually produced theological works. The great Anabaptist writers were located in southwest Germany, Austria, the Tirol, and Moravia. In other words, the intellectual center of Anabaptism shifted quickly from Switzerland to the Empire.

The literary creativity of the non-Hutterites was limited to only a few years. It was greatest during the first years of the movement, especially in 1527 and 1528. By 1529 ten of the authors of theological treatises were already dead or in prison, or had recanted.[21] Apart from the writing of Marbeck and his disciples, there was little literary activity among the Anabaptists in Germany from the 1530s on. During the second half of the sixteenth century, only three treatises are known to have been written by brethren in southwest Germany.[22] In striking contrast to this lack of literary expression is the rich and colorful literature of the Hutterites, who during the second half of the sixteenth century were undoubtedly the most articulate Anabaptist group in our area. Most of the theological and historical works of the Hutterites were written after 1550. The earliest exegetical and liturgical works also date from the second half of the sixteenth and from the early seventeenth century. However, the works of such men as Hans Schmid, Peter Walpot, and Joseph Hauser cannot compare with the brilliant writings of a Hubmaier, Hut, or Stadler. Frequently the former were no more than systematically arranged paraphrases of biblical passages.

The lively literary activity of the German Anabaptists during the 1520s was prompted by the need to define, explain, and justify the new doctrines. For example, the deviationist views of spiritualists and libertines had to be combated. Marbeck's principal works in the 1540s were occasioned by his disagreement with Schwenckfeld. The decline of literary activity among the Anabaptists in Germany and Switzerland can probably be attributed to the disappearance of the strong missionary drive of the

1520s and the increasing cultural primitivism that characterized the movement.

But why did the Hutterites continue to write all through the sixteenth century? As we have seen, from a sociological point of view the Hutterites and the Swiss Brethren constituted different movements. Whereas in Germany or Switzerland the Anabaptist lived in a Lutheran or Calvinist village and met with his fellow believers every month or so, in Moravia dozens or even hundreds of Anabaptists lived in a single community. Their communal life was entrenched in religion—in prayers, Bible readings, church services, the selection of ministers, and the like. Much of the Hutterite literature was related to Hutterite concepts of community life; hence so long as the communities remained vital, literary activity continued to flourish. The conviction that they were God's elect may have prompted the Hutterite leaders to record their history in chronicles.

A second factor was the different position of the ministers in the Hutterite communities. Whereas the minister in Germany or Switzerland spent much of his time working as a farmer or craftsman, the Hutterite servant of the Word could devote himself entirely to his spiritual tasks: thus he had time to write. There is also a third factor. It was surely not coincidence that Hutterite literature flourished at a time when, unlike the Swiss Brethren, the Hutterites were making great efforts to spread their belief in Germany, Austria, and Switzerland. Missionary work forced the Hutterites to explain their doctrines both to unbelievers and to other Anabaptist groups.

By the middle of the seventeenth century, however, the Hutterites, too, had ceased to write religious works. Andreas Ehrenpreis, bishop from 1639 to 1662, was the last creative writer of the Slovakian Hutterites. The decline of literary production among the Hutterites may well have been related to their abandonment of missionary work in Germany and Switzerland after they were expelled from Moravia in 1622. It is also possible that the later Hutterites refrained from composing new works out of great respect for the rich literature of their ancestors. From the seventeenth century to our own times, the Hutterites have largely contented themselves with copying the sermons and works of the sixteenth and seventeenth centuries.

Printing

Sigmund Sorg at Nikolsburg in 1526 and 1527 and Philip Vollandt at Neumühl in 1565 were the only printers who openly printed Anabaptist books.[23] All other printers took care not to divulge their identity, considering the undertaking too dangerous. It is known, however, that Philipp Uhlhart of Augsburg printed nine Anabaptist tracts, seven of them in 1526 and 1527.[24] There are indications that Anabaptist books were also printed at Nuremberg, Worms, Strasbourg, and Regensburg.[25] In 1550 at Augsburg an Anabaptist revealed that Pilgram Marbeck and his followers were running a clandestine printing press, though he could not tell where it was. Perhaps Marbeck's *Vermahnung* and *Testamentserläuterung* were printed on this press.[26] Some printers demanded advance payments for the printing of Anabaptist treatises. In 1528 a Franconian Anabaptist said that the sectarians often paid in the neighborhood of three or four hundred florins, a sum they could afford thanks to rich believers. How large were the editions? In 1528 a thousand copies of Freisleben's book on baptism were printed. In 1544 the city of Bern reported that fifteen hundred copies of an Anabaptist book had been printed.

The Anabaptists quickly informed each other when a book was published. In 1528 Freisleben sent word to the brethren at Esslingen and Augsburg to dispatch a buyer to Frankfurt to purchase his newly published book on baptism. The brethren might buy the book for two pennies per copy less than the fixed price. The books were distributed by ordinary book traders. Of course, the authorities were well aware of the threat posed by Anabaptist writings. Repeatedly at Frankfurt, Stuttgart, and Bruck booksellers were arrested for selling Anabaptist literature.

When in 1528 Anabaptist books appeared at Schwaz and Hall in the Tirol, the officials simply closed and searched all bookstores. In 1535 the authorities at Strasbourg forbade the printing or selling of books that had not been approved by the town council. In Württemberg district officials were ordered to examine all books sold at fairs and markets, and booksellers were obliged to submit lists of books they had purchased at fairs. Nevertheless, sectarian books continued to appear in the duchy. The government of Stuttgart feared in 1593 that these "impure sectarian books" might do harm to students at the university, to pastors, and to those who were simply curious. Only those ministers who were engaged in fighting the Anabaptist sect were allowed to buy these books, and even then they could do so only with written permission from the superintendent. Other territories passed similar laws. Augsburg seems to have been less repressive, however, and Anabaptists repeatedly went there to buy Bibles and Anabaptist literature.

Reading

All through the sixteenth century books and manuscripts were discovered in the possession of Anabaptists. The authorities were aware that the Anabaptists were busy dispensing their literature for example bringing printed or handwritten books and long letters of consolation to imprisoned fellow believers. Around 1600 officials in Baden even drew up a list of printed and handwritten Anabaptist books they had confiscated.

At meetings in Augsburg, Uttenreuth, and Iphofen it was customary for the Anabaptist leaders to read aloud. Naturally, the Bible was the book most often read. We hear of leaders who memorized entire chapters of the Old Testament.[27] Some early Anabaptists were greatly attracted by the prophets and psalms. The revolutionary Anabaptist Römer was especially interested in the "old prophetic books"; he suggested they should be translated into German.[28]

In 1527 Lienhart Schiemer exhorted the congregation at Rat-

tenberg to read the Book of Psalms and above all the New
Testament, since it revealed with clarity what Moses and the
prophets had indicated only cryptically. Indeed, the New Testament was the staple reading for all brethren. In 1528 at Passau
the leaders read to the believers the epistles to the Thessalonians
and Corinthians, chapter 24 of Matthew, and the sixth and tenth
chapters of John. Leaders in Thuringia also read the Revelation
of John. The apocryphal Fourth Book of Esdras was highly esteemed by various Anabaptists such as Michael Sattler, the Hessian leaders Tesch and Schnabel, Pilgram Marbeck, and the
Hutterites.

A few educated leaders, such as Hans Stiglitz of Passau, had
copies of the Bible in Latin. Manz is even said to have owned
a Hebrew Bible,[29] but ordinarily the Anabaptists used a German
translation. The Swiss Brethren, Marbeck, the Anabaptists in
Hesse and Strasbourg, and the Hutterites used the Froschau
edition of Zurich.[30] The Worms translation of the prophets
was also used.[31] Some Anabaptists were quite careful to make
sure that any Bible they might buy did not contain pictures of
idols or heretical prefaces.[32] On a few occasions, as in 1528 at
Augsburg and 1614 in Württemberg, Bible concordances are
mentioned in the records.[33]

It is plain that the Anabaptists also studied their own literature. Hut's treatise "On the Secret of Baptism" was read at
Augsburg;[34] Freisleben's book on baptism was read at Esslingen
and Reutlingen; and the writings of Rinck circulated in Hesse.[35]
In 1538 a book was sold at Schwaz in the Tirol that contained
illustrations of the ceremony of rebaptism.[36] In 1531 several
Anabaptist writings were found in the possession of Julius Lober,
a leader who on his way from Bruchsal to Moravia was arrested
at Hoheneck in the Duchy of Ansbach. Lober had with him
three or four treatises by Schiemer, one by Schlaffer, writings of
Hut, a treatise of Christian Hintz, copies of letters of Reublin
and David Schweintz, and two more treatises whose authors are
not known. We may assume that Lober had come by these

works at Bruchsal or elsewhere in southwest Germany. It is surprising that the writings of Hut, who had died at Augsburg in 1527, and of Schiemer and Schlaffer, who had been executed in the Tirol in 1528, should have been circulated in 1531 among the brethren in southwest Germany, who belonged to the tradition of Swiss Anabaptism. The Anabaptists obviously attached great importance to these writings.[37]

The Hutterite leaders encouraged believers to read and copy epistles and confessions of faith. Those who wished to learn reading and writing were given ink and paper. We know that in winter, when little farm work could be done, the weinzirls devoted themselves to reading and writing. In this way the Hutterites acquired the skills necessary to defend their faith if they were arrested by the authorities.

Non-Anabaptist literature also circulated among some brethren. Müntzer's liturgical writings were used by Anabaptists of Sangerhausen in December 1527. In 1533 a Thuringian leader read to believers from a "book on the creation and kings" that discussed the origin of infant baptism. In 1545 Waldensian books were found in the area of Zwickau, where the Anabaptists were also active. Georg Probst, Marbeck's friend, used to read the *Imitation of Christ.* And in 1590 Anabaptists in the area of Zurich were familiar with Bernhard Herxheimer's *Fassnachtsküchlein* and a "Schwenckfelder Täfeli." [38]

Though the literary activity of the Anabaptists was limited, the importance of their books should not be underestimated. Carefully treasured by believers, they kept the faith alive in times of persecution and in the midst of a hostile environment. It is also possible that through their books, the Anabaptists influenced sectarian movements in the following centuries, such as Pietism.

II

Persecution

The first ceremony of rebaptism was performed in defiance of the Zurich town council, which on January 21, 1525, had issued an order for the express purpose of ending discussions at secret meetings on the problem of infant baptism. The movement that developed at Zurich and Zollikon thus violated the law from the beginning, and it was to remain an outlawed movement all through the sixteenth and early seventeenth centuries. Unquestionably the fate of the Anabaptists was hard—very hard. But the persecution they suffered was not simply the expression of blind fury at radical doctrines unacceptable to the pastors; rather it resulted from basic principles of sixteenth-century political philosophy.

Anabaptism could have existed legally only if it had been adopted by the government of a territory or city of the Empire as the official religion. Generally both Catholics and Protestants agreed that the government was obligated to establish and protect the true faith, and furthermore that there could be only one true faith.[1] Of two opposing interpretations of Christ's teaching, it was argued, only one could be correct; the other was therefore heresy. In addition it was considered dangerous on political grounds to tolerate more than one religion in one territory, lest religious differences lead to unrest and even civil war—a prospect, indeed, that eventually did materialize in France and England.

The Peace of Augsburg sanctioned these political principles by ruling that if one faith, Catholicism or Lutheranism, was established by the government of a territory, the other was legally excluded. The governments can hardly be expected to have exempted the Anabaptists, of all groups, from the dominion of widely held principles of political philosophy and law; nor could they have based their policy on principles of religious freedom that were not formulated and accepted by public opinion until the seventeenth and eighteenth centuries. In other words, Anabaptism could have been tolerated only had it become the official religion of a territory.

Of course, for Anabaptism to be accepted as the state religion by any government was an impossibility. First, the Anabaptists, as we have seen, condemned government itself as being unchristian—indeed, as the very enemy of Christianity. Second, no sixteenth-century government would have accepted the Anabaptist views on property, commerce, and finance. But even if Anabaptism had been a purely religious movement, its establishment as the official religion of an area could not have satisfied the sixteenth-century requirement for a state church, for the Anabaptists rejected the very concept of a state church. Thus Anabaptism could never become the official religion of any sixteenth-century territory, and it could never be tolerated by any sixteenth-century government either.

Capture, Interrogation, Admonition, and Recantation

If Anabaptism was to be suppressed, the authorities were obliged to proceed resolutely. A single Anabaptist might disseminate sectarian doctrines throughout his town or village. The Strasbourg pastors were afraid lest an Anabaptist permitted to go free might tell his neighbors that since the authorities had taken no action against him, they obviously were prepared to tolerate his religious views. His neighbors would then have no qualms about attending Anabaptist meetings. There was, in short, no middle way between suppression and toleration of the sect; but there were different methods of suppression.

In order to devise the most effective methods of combating Anabaptism, governments often considered laws used for that purpose by other territories and cities. Theologians and lawyers frequently had to submit memoranda on how to deal with the Anabaptists. The drafts of the mandates against the sect were the subject of long and searching deliberations in the highest councils of government. All through the sixteenth century the imperial diet, the Swiss confederation, the territories, and the cities issued a vast number of laws against the Anabaptists. The mandates explained why Anabaptism was a heretical and revolutionary movement, forbade all subjects to join this outlawed sect or give aid to its members, and ordered the immediate arrest or denunciation of any Anabaptists discovered. Special mandates and decrees addressed to judicial and administrative officials prescribed the steps to be taken against the heretics and the punishment to be given. Sometimes various governments would hold meetings to coordinate their campaigns.

But first the Anabaptists had to be caught. How were the governments able to track down the members of a sect that represented only a very small minority of the population? During the first months of the movement, at Zollikon, for example, the Anabaptists did not hide their views but spread them openly among the population. Under such circumstances the task of the officials was easy. But when arrests began in earnest, Anabaptism quickly became a clandestine sect. To uncover this secret movement was very difficult.

Disturbed by the possibility of an uprising, some authorities, such as the Swabian League and the Tirolese government, mobilized troops to hunt down the Anabaptists. But military patrols were largely unsuccessful. In Bavaria, Württemberg, and Austria special investigators were appointed to pursue the heretics.[2] More effective than either patrols or investigators, however, were paid informants. In June 1532 Ferdinand I himself ordered that trustworthy people should join the Anabaptists in the Tirol and have themselves baptized. For their services they were to be paid sixty, seventy, or even as much as a hundred florins. The Hutterite Chronicle bitterly complains of these spies, who approached believers with some story of not being able to find peace until they joined the brethren. Through the efficient spies in his employ, the district official at Schöneck received the embarrassing news that his own daughter was an Anabaptist. In 1528 the Stuttgart government had an informant among the Anabaptist refugees at Reutlingen.[3] But few other governments used these methods: among the Protestants, only Strasbourg tried to get inside information through spies.[4] Why did the Protestant governments in Württemberg, the Palatinate, and Hesse disdain to employ such methods, of which they were hardly ignorant? Was spying considered a Machiavellian tactic that was contrary to the German honesty these governments prided themselves on displaying?

On April 13, 1528, officials surprised a large meeting in progress in the city of Augsburg; in 1535, one at Kleineutersdorf in Saxony; and in 1562, another in a forest near Esslingen. A few more large meetings were rounded up, but the total number was not very great. At a word from an informant, the Tirolese officials would sometimes rush to a place only to find it abandoned by the Anabaptists, who had also been warned and run away. Needless to say, the governments became impatient with the local officials' failure to trace such meetings. During the winter of 1531 the Tirolese government insisted that Anabaptist meetings could not be difficult to discover, since they would have to be held in huts and houses near the villages as long as the forests and mountains were covered by deep snow.

Sometimes the Tirolese officials took almost desperate measures. When in 1538 a search for Anabaptists was organized in the districts of Michelsburg and Niedervintl, soldiers were stationed at all nearby bridges and passes to cut off the escape routes. Travelers on lonely roads and paths were stopped and questioned about their religious views. In 1553 the local officials received orders to question all travelers about where they came from, where they were going, why they were traveling, and what their religious views were. Did the government at Innsbruck seriously believe that it was possible to stop and interrogate every traveler on the busy roads between Italy and northern Europe?

Common people could not fail to notice the comings and goings of the Anabaptists in their neighborhood. Rarely, however, did they inform the authorities, as demanded by the law. Why should a man betray his neighbor, with whom he had shared both good times and bad, just because he had suddenly joined a strange religious sect? Only occasionally do the records show cases of outright betrayal. Overhearing the conversation of two peasants in front of his shop, a merchant at Brixen realized that one of them was an Anabaptist and immediately ran to the officials. Sometimes denunciations were made anonymously or information was given to the authorities because of personal harm caused by the Anabaptists, as when they induced a man's children to emigrate. Of course, those who were put on oath to reveal what they knew usually did not hesitate to tell the truth.

Some wilier governments knew that money could often persuade people to become informants. In 1527 the Bavarian government was already offering a reward of 32 florins to anyone informing on an Anabaptist. In 1530 the Tirolese government was offering thirty to forty florins. Ferdinand I's last mandate of 1563 specified an additional bonus: anyone who brought about the arrest of an Anabaptist would receive one third of the Anabaptist's property.

On their arrest Anabaptists were always told to give the names of their leaders and fellow believers. Though many refused to divulge these names, a careful interrogator could gather much information by asking the prisoners who had informed them of the time of their meetings, where they had gathered, who had read the Scriptures, and so on. Some Anabaptists gave this information only after they were subjected to torture or lengthy imprisonment.

The pastors began to register baptisms as a means of discovering parents who had not had their children baptized. The pastor at Hinwil in Switzerland started recording baptisms on July 3, 1525, one day after Conrad Grebel had preached to large crowds in his village. Less than a year later, in May 1526, the city of Zurich officially introduced baptismal registers.[5]

The most effective method of tracing Anabaptists eventually proved to be the visitation, which in some Protestant territories took place once or even twice a year. The visitator would inquire about parishioners who did not come to church services or to the Lord's Supper. The culprits were summoned and asked why they disobeyed the law. Under such circumstances the Anabaptists made no attempt to conceal their belief but openly explained why they might not associate with the Lutheran or Zwinglian congregation.

The Catholic authorities in the Tirol also tried to introduce controls on the local level. In 1530 the local officials were ordered to visit all houses in their districts three times a year—in February, at Easter, and in July—to question the occupants about when and where they had last gone to confession and communion, and when and where their children had been baptized. In 1553 the episcopal officials at Brixen devised a more practical procedure: confessional registers were to be established in those parishes of the Puster valley that had been particularly affected by Anabaptism.

The governments, especially the city governments, took the arrest of Anabaptists very seriously. The Augsburg town council remained in session for unusually long hours following the mass arrests of Anabaptists in April 1528. During the 1520s, when the Anabaptists were still regarded as revolutionaries, committees of town councilors and government officials rather than priests or pastors were appointed to question the prisoners.[6] At Augsburg, Konrad Peutinger, the famous humanist and syndic, conducted the interrogations in 1527 and 1528.

Before the interrogation began, long lists of questions were drawn up to ferret out every aspect of this revolutionary movement. At Augsburg, Hans Hut was subjected to as many as eight interrogations. At his first interrogation, on September 15, 1527, he was obliged to answer more than eighty questions. Detailed transcripts of the interrogations were kept. In later years lists of questions were frequently included in mandates designed to instruct the local authorities how to proceed against the sectarians. In Württemberg, for example, the ordinances of 1558 and 1571 contained two long series of questions. The first dealt with political matters, such as doctrines on government and property, and was handled by government officials. The second dealt with theology and was handled by theologians. Even so, some Anabaptists complained that they were not interrogated in an orderly manner or allowed to write their answers down in a quiet room by themselves. Only on rare occasions were they given paper and ink to write down their answers.[7]

Sometimes torture was used to elicit information from recalcitrant Anabaptists. The use of torture was greatest in 1527 and 1528, when Anabaptist uprisings were feared. Apart from Saxony, however, Protestant territories resorted to torture only rarely. In Lutheran Württemberg, for example, Anabaptists were sometimes interrogated in the presence of the torture master, but few were actually put on the rack because special permission had to be obtained from the Estates to torture a prisoner.

Some Catholic governments did not waste too much time on the Anabaptists. In 1527 and 1528 Anabaptists at Augsburg and Esslingen were simply thrown out of the city unless they abandoned their heresies on the spot. In vain did the leader of the Esslingen congregation assure the town council that he would abandon his doctrines if anyone could prove him to be wrong. Other Catholic governments, however, applied themselves conscientiously to the task. In 1528 the government at Stuttgart asked the university of Tübingen for suggestions on how the Anabaptists could be persuaded to give up their errors. In later years the Bavarian authorities occasionally even sent priests from Munich to district towns to talk to captured heretics. But though they gave persuasive tactics a trial, these Catholic governments would never have dreamed of letting the Anabaptists go free.

Some Protestant governments also threw Anabaptists into prison or adopted other stern measures to break their resistance,[8] but on the whole most tended to become more lenient than the Catholic governments as the century went on. In Lutheran Württemberg, for example, laws of 1554 and 1557 still ordered the imprisonment of stubborn Anabaptists; indeed, the officials did not hesitate to imprison even old and ailing persons. But a new law of 1566 brought changes. The Anabaptist remained at liberty during instruction first by the local minister and then by the superintendent. Only if he still refused to abandon his views was he to be placed in custody and taken to Stuttgart for a final admonition. The ordinance of 1572 abandoned the use of force almost entirely. The Anabaptist was to be instructed first by his minister "with gentleness," and if this effort failed, by the visitators and then by the superintendent in the district town. If he persisted in his belief at this stage, he was to be summoned to the capital and admonished by members of the Church Council, but not kept in custody. Only after he had rejected all advice would he be put in prison, where the theologians would continue their friendly talks with him. In other words, the Anabaptist remained free during almost the entire process of instruction. In their "Anabaptist calendars," the church officials at Stuttgart recorded carefully whether the sectarian was to be admonished next by the local pastor, by the superintendent in the district town, or by the Church Council, or whether he should be expelled from the country.

This series of instructions was very time-consuming. If after long and useless admonitions by the local pastor and by the superintendent, the Anabaptists were summoned to Stuttgart, they found excuses not to appear at all: some claimed they were ill; others said they were too busy during the harvest. If they did eventually go to Stuttgart, they quite often arrived late or did not report to the officials in the castle at all; then they walked home again. Sometimes, too, the officials were busy with other matters and let the Anabaptists wait all day or sent them home. The evening before a brother was due to go to Stuttgart, fellow believers would visit him to strengthen his morale. Before and after his actual interrogation, he would talk with fellow believers at Stuttgart. Sometimes the authorities dealt with individual Anabaptists over a period of months or even years. When, after lengthy instruction, an Anabaptist finally returned to the Lutheran church and accepted the Lord's Supper, some officials expressed their relief by scribbling in the margin of the report: "So be it," "Deo gratias," or "Pergat sic." [9] Whereas the governments allowed the Anabaptist to decide for himself whether or not he wanted to return to the church and be saved, they sometimes denied him the right to lead his children to perdition. On a number of occasions the unbaptized children of sectarians were baptized at the order of the government.

If the authorities had aimed solely to clear their territories of Anabaptists, they could have expelled the Anabaptists forthwith and saved themselves much trouble. But as Frederick III of the Palatinate remarked, such a policy would have done nothing for the salvation of these people. Occasionally even a ruler, such as Landgrave Philip of Hesse, took the time to talk to an Anabaptist himself.[10] Some of the great Reformers, such as Zwingli at Zurich, Luther and Melanchthon in Saxony, Bucer at Strasbourg and Hesse, and Brenz and Ambrosius Blarer in Württemberg, spent hours discussing difficult questions on baptism, the Real Presence of Christ's body in the communion bread and wine, or the nature of political office with illiterate tailors, wood-cutters and peasant women.

Generally, however, the sectarians were dealt with by the village parsons, who could hardly be described as sophisticated. One lewd pastor of the Bern area shouted in his church that it

were better the Anabaptists should beget dogs and cattle than
leave their children unbaptized. Another was ready to term
the Anabaptists godless traitors and arch-criminals unless they
could prove their views on baptism were correct. Such an
uncouth attitude was hardly likely to win the brethren back to
the state church. Some governments, therefore, issued advice to
the pastors on how to counter the Anabaptist arguments, such
as that provided in 1528 by the city of Nuremberg. Sermons in
which eminent theologians refuted Anabaptist teaching were
reprinted.[11] But sometimes the most patient officials thought
it a waste of time to spend hours with an Anabaptist: an old
wolf could not be tamed. Occasionally Anabaptists who recanted
were asked to talk to their former fellow believers. Peter Tesch,
formerly a leader in Hesse, is said to have persuaded two
hundred Anabaptists to abandon their heresy.[12] This method
did not always work, since many Anabaptists refused to listen to
traitors.

When an Anabaptist was persuaded to see the error of his
ways, he was not simply set free. During the 1520s and 1530s
some governments first punished the former heretics for their
disobedience: at Zurich and Augsburg they had to pay fines;
in the Electoral Palatinate and at Rothenburg signs were burned
onto their foreheads or they were whipped.[13] Even during the
1520s, however, not all governments punished recanting Anabaptists. Later most governments were glad to have Anabaptists
recant at all, and had no thought of punishment. Before an
Anabaptist was released from prison, he had to sign a statement,
the Urfehde, declaring that he had deserved severe punishment
for having joined the Anabaptist sect and promising on oath to
live in the future according to Christian doctrine. The prisoner
also had to pay the costs of his imprisonment if he was able to.

Whereas the government readmitted the former heretic into
civil society, only the ecclesiastical authorities could readmit
him into the church. In both Protestant and Catholic territories,
however, the government rather than the church stipulated how

the recantation was to be conducted—an indication of the dominant role of the government in fighting the sect. In Catholic territories these ceremonies were flamboyant and pompous. In 1527 Ferdinand I ordered the Anabaptists of Horb to appear on a special scaffold set up in the marketplace and swear an oath that they had abandoned their heresy and would obey the church. On seven consecutive Sundays they had to walk before a procession that made its way around the collegiate church. They had to wear woolen robes, with their heads bare and their hair unbound, carry a rod in the left hand and a burning candle in the right, and kneel down in front of the altar for matins, where they would receive absolution.

Who was to grant absolution proved a thorny problem in Austria. Since only the bishop had this power, the priests of upper Austria refused to absolve recanting Anabaptists unless the bishop of Passau expressly authorized them to do so. This procedure was too slow for Ferdinand I. Dietrich von Hartitsch, who in 1527 had been appointed special provost, and his chaplain therefore literally forced the priests to absolve recanting Anabaptists, "violating all justice and fairness," as the bishop of Passau complained. On two occasions Ferdinand I asked the bishop to grant the priests a general authorization, but the bishop refused him outright. Before their absolution, the bishop said, certain Anabaptists had begun to argue with the priests, who were unable to refute their doctrines.

In Protestant Zurich, Hubmaier was ordered to make a public recantation in December 1525, but there is no evidence that all Anabaptists at Zurich had to make formal recantations in the church at that time. The custom was soon introduced, however, for it was being practiced by 1530 at the latest. As always, the Protestant territories had a great variety of ceremonies. In some, such as Ansbach, the Catholic influence can still be detected.[14] At Nuremberg the Anabaptist had to stand beside municipal officials in the church on certain feast days and make a public recantation. At Augsburg some Anabaptists were obliged to read a recantation first before the town council and then in public. In 1531 one weaver asked the town council to excuse him from this humiliating requirement for his children's sake. In Saxony the Anabaptists had to forswear their faith first in the town where they had been imprisoned, then in their home parish; in Pfalz-Zweibrücken they had to recant before the examining commission. At Strasbourg no ceremony is recorded at all. In general recantations were less theatrical in Protestant territories than in Catholic Austria or Bavaria. In all territories, however, the recantation procedures were aimed at impressing on the sinner the seriousness of his offense.

Some congregations were more involved with the fate of the sectarians than one would imagine. When in 1538 Hermann Bastian, a leader in Hesse, spontaneously asked Bucer during a church service at Marburg for readmission to the church, members of the congregation were overjoyed, and tears flowed freely. Inevitably, some Anabaptists changed their minds at the last minute. Putting aside the recantation he was supposed to read, Hubmaier instead defended rebaptism in the pulpit of the Zurich cathedral in December 1525. Zwingli himself had to calm the angry crowd while Hubmaier was led back to prison. "You criminals," one Anabaptist shouted at the priests in front of the whole congregation, "you have forced me through torture and misery to abandon my faith"; then he took up the defense of Anabaptist doctrines. In Catholic territories such a relapse could lead to death. In the Protestant territories, the officials did not go beyond expressing their anger and banishing the sectarian from the country for life.

Many, indeed most, Anabaptists abandoned their faith when confronted with the power of the government. Nevertheless, there were some who refused to yield. What were the authorities to do with them? One Thuringian official resorted to the simple punishment of having some Anabaptist women weed the barley fields, and then let them go free. Such a light punishment was rare, for the territorial state of the sixteenth century did not

tolerate defiance from Anabaptists. More commonly governments invoked the traditional punishment for stubborn heretics:
death, imprisonment, or expulsion.

The Death Penalty
The Number of Executions

Certain evidence exists of the execution of 715 Anabaptists in
123 towns and villages in Switzerland, south and central
Germany, Austria, Bohemia, and Moravia during the years
1525 to 1618, as Table 15 shows. There is reliable evidence—
consisting of Julius Lober's list,[15] chronicles, and documents—of
the execution of another 130 Anabaptists in 27 more towns and
villages. Altogether, these figures indicate that 845 Anabaptists
were executed in 150 towns and villages. According to the lists
of martyrs in the Hutterite chronicles, the number of executions
was well over a thousand, even if one does not count the unlikely
figures of six hundred executions at Ensisheim and three hundred
fifty in the Palatinate. It is possible that the records of the executions of some two or three hundred Anabaptists have been lost.

Table 15. Anabaptists executed, 1525–1618

Area	Certain	Probable *	Certain and probable	Listed in chronicles † Zieglschmid	Beck
Switzerland	30	43	73	28	0
Hapsburg terri- tories	408	5	413	732	706
Southeast	113	9	122	153	124
Franconia	30	5	35	68	38
Swabia	41	46	87	120	81
Rhine valley	22	17	39	75	55
Thuringia and Fulda	71	3	74	19	47
Uncertain	0	2	2	0	0
Total	715	130	845	1,195	1,051

* Probable executions reported by Lober and chroniclers.
† Six hundred alleged executions at Ensisheim and 350 at Heidelberg
are not included.

For the sake of accuracy, however, this study is based primarily on figures that can be documented.

The first execution of an Anabaptist took place on May 29, 1525, at Schwyz, and the last, as far as this study is concerned, on August 4, 1618, in a village near Bregenz. In other words, the Anabaptists suffered persecution even to the point of death from the beginning of the movement right up to the Thirty Years' War. It was during the years 1527 through 1533, however, that the bloodshed was greatest. No less than 679 executions, that is 80 percent of all executions, took place during these years. The bloodiest year was 1528, when 200 Anabaptists were executed, followed by 1529, when 152 were executed. Altogether, 352 Anabaptists, or 41 percent of all those executed, were executed during these two years. Once again it is clear that Anabaptism in our area was already largely destroyed in 1528 and 1529, several years before the Kingdom of Münster. In 1530 the death toll was again high, with 80 executions, but in the following years the number of executions decreased, and from 1540 onward it decreased still more sharply. In Bavaria, the Tirol, and Switzerland, however, executions continued to take place until the early seventeenth century.

The number of executions varied considerably in different areas, from about seventy in Switzerland, to about one hundred twenty in each of southwest Germany, southeast Germany, and the area of Franconia-Thuringia, to more than four hundred in the Hapsburg territories. Relatively few executions occurred in city states. Only 73 Anabaptists, or 8.6 percent of all Anabaptists executed, were executed by city governments in Switzerland, and 61, or 7.2 percent, in the imperial cities. These relatively low numbers of executions are surprising because the Swiss territories of Zurich, Bern, and Basel and the imperial cities of Strasbourg and Augsburg were centers of the Anabaptist movement. In the imperial cities the greatest numbers of executions occurred at Mühlhausen in Thuringia, where twelve died, and in the Swabian cities of Isny (eight), Esslingen (seven), Schwäbisch Gmünd (seven), and Kaufbeuren (five). Most cities were very reluctant to execute Anabaptists. Nuremberg, Augsburg, Regensburg, Schweinfurt, and Speyer executed only one Anabaptist apiece. Many cities, such as Strasbourg, Ulm, Schwäbisch Hall, Reutlingen, Heilbronn, Nördlingen, Donauwörth, and Windsheim, executed none at all. In the towns and villages of various counts and noblemen, there were 49 executions, and in the prince bishoprics, 96, or only 11.3 percent of all executions. Among the areas under ecclesiastical rulers, Salzburg had the most executions, 26, followed by Bamberg, with sixteen; Fulda, with thirteen; Würzburg, with twelve; and Passau, with ten.

The Anabaptists executed in the Swiss city states, the imperial cities, the territories of counts, and the prince bishoprics constituted only 33 percent of all the Anabaptists executed. The overwhelming majority, 67 percent, were executed by secular princes, that is, members of the first and second houses of the imperial diet. One ruler in particular, Ferdinand I of Hapsburg, distinguished himself by the amount of blood he shed in suppressing Anabaptism. Between 1527 and 1618 not less than 419 Anabaptists were put to death in Hapsburg territories, and another 77 in the duchy of Bavaria.

To realize the ghastly enormity of the measures carried out in the Hapsburg territories and Bavaria, one must compare the figures of executions there with those for other territories. Whereas 257 Anabaptists were executed in the Tirol, 109 in Austria, and 77 in Bavaria, only 40 were executed in Bern, 26 in Salzburg, and 21 in Electoral Saxony. The remaining 57 governments executed no more than twenty believers each: of these, 46 executed no more than ten, and 37 executed no more than five.[16] In other words, the governments of the Tirol, Austria, and Bavaria were very much more severe than any other governments in Germany and Switzerland. During the 1520s and 1530s, indeed, Austria and Bavaria were already the protagonists of a violent Counter Reformation.

Of the governments in our area that executed Anabaptists, a strong majority, 38 out of 56, were Catholic. Indeed, all the larger Catholic territories resorted to executions to stamp out Anabaptism. By contrast, many Protestant governments, such as Hesse, the Palatinate, and Württemberg, resolved not to use capital punishment in the case of Anabaptists; in fact, only eight Protestant governments did use it. In eleven cities and territories where Anabaptists were executed, however, the religious conditions are unclear. At any rate, Catholic governments were responsible for 709 executions, whereas Protestant governments were responsible for only 81, or 10 percent of all executions. Of these 81 Protestant executions, 40 were carried out by Zwinglian Bern, and 21, ironically enough, by Lutheran Saxony. In general, then, the number of executions in Protestant areas was very small. Another 55, that is 6 percent of all executions, were carried out in areas where religious conditions were unsettled and which were not clearly Protestant at that time. Even the latter two categories combined would account for only 16 percent of all executions, whereas Catholic areas would account for 84 percent.

The manner of execution is known in the cases of 420 Anabaptists: 97 were burned at the stake, 234 were beheaded, and 89 were drowned. Only Catholic governments executed Anabaptists by burning at the stake, which was the medieval punishment for heretics; and whereas the Austrian, Tirolese, and Bavarian governments burned numerous Anabaptists, other Catholic governments avoided this type of execution. Even in Austria, the Tirol, and Bavaria, burning was largely limited to the 1520s and 1530s. Only three executions at the stake occurred in the second half of the sixteenth century. Those who were burned were generally leaders, though sometimes they were ordinary Anabaptists. Usually ordinary Anabaptists and sometimes even leaders who refused to abandon their belief were executed by decapitation. Protestant governments usually executed Anabaptists by decapitation, whether they were leaders or not. Burning at the stake was obviously considered a custom of the past.

Burning and decapitation were largely reserved for men: 68 percent of the Anabaptists burned and 88 percent of those beheaded were men. Death by drowning was, on the whole, the punishment for women; only a few governments beheaded or burned women. At least 26 men, most of them in Switzerland and parts of Thuringia, were also executed by being thrown into the river. Presumably this unusual type of punishment was occasioned by local legal traditions.

Legal Basis

Three legal bases for the execution of Anabaptists can be distinguished: the violation of civil laws; rebellion; and heresy and rebellion. Though sometimes two of these charges are contained in the same mandate or death sentence, the emphasis is ordinarily on just one point. Most Anabaptists executed in Protestant Switzerland were charged with violating civil laws. To be sure, the mandate issued at Zurich on March 7, 1526, stipulated the death penalty for all those who were found after that date to have rebaptized others, but this provision was aimed at Anabaptists who after their release simply went back on their oaths and resumed the practices of their sect. This act of disobedience was considered detrimental to government, the commonweal, and true Christianity. Four of the seven Anabaptists executed at Zurich had broken their oaths and promises to return to the official church. But this was not the only accusation. At least six were also charged with belonging to a sect that opened the way to rebellion and uprisings and to the overthrow of Christian peace.[17] All of those charged were considered ringleaders. The death penalty was not imposed on ordinary Anabaptists in Zurich.

Similarly, at Bern, Basel, and Schaffhausen Anabaptists were not executed because they had accepted rebaptism but because they had violated an obligation that, properly speaking, had nothing to do with religion: the obligation to leave the country if so ordered by the government. It might be argued that since these people enjoyed the protection of the laws of their society, they were obliged to obey those laws. The Anabaptists were convinced, however, that the government did not have the right to expell anyone because of his belief in the first place; hence the order expelling them was invalid. In this sense the Anabaptists were ultimately sentenced to death in Protestant Switzerland for their beliefs.[18] In Germany there were only two cases, at Augsburg and Speyer, in which death sentences were given on similar grounds.[19] A few early Anabaptists at Königsberg, Nuremberg, Ansbach, and Erfurt were charged with outright rebellion, but only at Erfurt can the charge be called truly valid.

In only a small number of cases were Anabaptists charged with violating civil law or outright rebellion. Most executions were based on the charge of heresy or of both heresy and rebellion. These accusations were already contained in the imperial laws that served as a basis for some of the territorial laws against the Anabaptists. The imperial mandate issued on January 4, 1528, declared that the Anabaptists were guilty not only of rebaptism but also of the attempted suppression of all political authorities and civil order. The death penalty was stipulated on the basis of laws passed in the late Roman Empire against the Donatists.[20]

A new imperial law of April 23, 1529, tried to end all doubts concerning the punishment of the Anabaptists by ordering that all rebaptized men and women were to be executed by fire, sword, or the like, without prior ecclesiastical inquisition. Those who recanted, did penance, and accepted punishment might be pardoned by their government as the circumstances indicated. But leaders, stubborn Anabaptists, and all who had already recanted once were not to be pardoned on any account. Those who had been pardoned were not to be expelled, nor were Anabaptist refugees to be tolerated by other governments. Evidently recalcitrant Anabaptists were not to be expelled under any circumstances. The law of 1529 was confirmed in 1544 and 1551. In 1544 an important procedural change was introduced: in territories where arrests could be made only after a denunciatory trial, the authorities were given the right to arrest Anabaptists without prior denunciation—a measure also used in the prosecution of witches. Actually, it is strange that this measure was adopted only after the Anabaptist danger had largely subsided.

The Empire might pass general laws, but it was the individual territory or city that in fact prosecuted the Anabaptists. The question, therefore, is which charges and procedures were used by the individual governments, and particularly by the Catholic governments, which were responsible for the majority of the executions. The first trial of Anabaptists in a Hapsburg territory was that of Michael Sattler and five codefendants at Rottenburg in May 1527. The legal basis of the proceedings was the Edict of Worms of 1521. Sattler and the five others were accused of rejecting the Catholic doctrines of baptism, the sacraments, Extreme Unction, the Virgin Mary, and the saints. They were also charged with rejecting the swearing of oaths and the obligation to fight in war. Sattler was sentenced to death at the stake; four others were sentenced to execution by the sword; and Sattler's wife was sentenced to be drowned. Similar trials for heresy were held at Steyr and Freistadt in upper Austria in November 1527.

In the meantime, on August 20, 1527, Ferdinand had issued the first of several important mandates. Anyone who violated the Twelve Articles of the Christian faith and the doctrines of the seven sacraments would be punished as a heretic "in body and life." It was not simply as heretics that Ferdinand regarded the Anabaptists, however. The watchwords of the last great uprising, he declared, such as community of goods and suppression of all government, were again being advanced by those who had not yet had their fill of blood. Indeed, toward the end of 1527 the Austrian government evidently was deeply disturbed by the revolutionary character of Anabaptism. These fears were kindled not by the Anabaptist view of government alone but by the chiliastic doctrines of Hans Hut and his followers. There appeared to be strong evidence that the Anabaptists planned a new uprising for 1528. The violent suppression of the Anabaptists in 1527 and 1528 must be seen against this background.

Because of the threat of "rebellion, uprising, and bloodshed," Dietrich von Hartitsch, the special provost in lower Austria, was ordered to proceed against obstinate Anabaptists "without the solemnity of the law." The local courts were suspended. The traditional trial for heresy as it was practiced in 1527 at Rottenburg, Freistadt, and Steyr was replaced by the summary court of jurisdiction that had been in use during the peasant uprising of 1525. Hartitsch soon acquired a reputation for hanging and beheading Anabaptists: at Neulengbach he ordered the execution of eighteen persons on a single day. It is not correct to say, however, that the charge against the Anabaptists changed from heresy in 1527 to rebellion in 1528.[21] In 1528, too, Anabaptism was considered both a heretical and a rebellious movement. Furthermore, in the Hapsburg territories of southwest Germany, the Anabaptists were accused not only of being heretics and rebels, but members of criminal gangs that made signs on crossroads, churches, and wayside shrines, set sheaves on fire, burned down entire villages, and even murdered people. There is no hard evidence that these accusations were justified.[22]

When Ferdinand I ordered the authorities in the Tirol not to put the Anabaptists on trial but simply to deal with them according to the law of August 20, 1527, the government of Innsbruck and the courts rejected such a procedure as contrary to ancient tradition and the liberties of the country. They warned that even if Anabaptists were not publicly put on trial according to criminal law but sentenced "behind closed doors in summary courts of jurisdiction," the jurors would still be divided on the meaning and application of the mandate; furthermore, they criticized the principle that even recanting Anabaptists should be sentenced to execution. Finally, they pointed out that many Anabaptists who lived in the mountain districts had never heard of the mandate of August 20, 1527, and therefore could not very well be held responsible for failing to obey it.

Yielding to this criticism, Ferdinand issued new mandates in February and April 1528 that gave all Anabaptists until April 26, 1528, to surrender; if they then recanted, they could be pardoned. Leaders and stubborn or relapsed heretics, however, should be sentenced to death.[23] These mandates became the basis for general policy in the Hapsburg territories.[24] Both in lower and upper Austria and in the Tirol, Anabaptists were tried by courts that often consisted of representatives of several towns. Summary executions, as practiced by Hartitsch in 1528, were exceptions. The common criminal law did not apply to Anabaptists, however, for their heresy was considered more serious than an ordinary crime. The courts had to proceed in direct accordance with the imperial mandate of 1529.

Ferdinand admitted in 1534 that most Anabaptists did not hold revolutionary views. But this was so, he said, because they had not yet been taken into confidence by their leaders, who realized that they would not be able to attract converts if they revealed their true intentions. Though the charge of rebellion was still repeated in later mandates, the policy of the Austrian government became more lenient. When in 1535 and 1548 the influx of Anabaptist refugees from Moravia was expected, the local authorities were ordered only to expel these people. This relatively mild tactic would have been unthinkable in 1528. Toward the end of the sixteenth century, the authorities in lower and upper Austria almost never sentenced Anabaptists to death. In 1601 Emperor Rudolf II merely ordered that all Hutterites working in upper and lower Austria leave within three weeks. In the Tirol, however, persecution remained severe: around 1600 brethren who refused to abandon their beliefs were still being executed. The charge of rebellion was no longer used, however. The Hapsburg government also ordered that houses where Anabaptists had met be razed to the ground or at least closed.[25] The land was then confiscated by the government. But there is no evidence that this practice was continued in the second half of the sixteenth century.

Summary courts of justice were also used in the bishopric of Salzburg and the duchy of Bavaria. In Bavaria the mandate of November 15, 1527, expressly reserved to Duke William the right of pronouncing sentence; the sentence was then simply announced to the heretics.[26] These sentences were very severe: in 1528, 1531, and 1533 Anabaptists were executed at Munich, Landsberg, Burghausen, and Ingolstadt, even though they had recanted and taken the sacrament. Andreas Pernöder, Duke William's secretary, justified these executions by saying that "the secular law did not stipulate anything in these cases."[27] Clearly the governments of Salzburg and Bavaria hoped to stamp out Anabaptism by exemplary punishment. Duke William was genuinely convinced that he acted rightly. At the end of a letter in which he urged his brother Ludwig to take strong measures against the Anabaptists, he added in his own handwriting, "Dear brother, consider this matter in all seriousness; you owe it to God and your own soul."[28]

Not all recanting heretics were sentenced to death, however. In 1527 some former Anabaptists were pardoned at Salzburg, and in 1528 others were pardoned at Munich, Aibling, and Rosenheim. On April 27, 1530, a new Bavarian mandate prescribed the death penalty for all Anabaptists, men and women, whether they abandoned their heresy or not. It is doubtful whether this mandate was consistently applied beyond a few cases. A new mandate of 1544 reflected the practice in Bavaria: the death penalty was made compulsory for leaders and for stubborn or relapsed Anabaptists, but ordinary Anabaptists who had recanted might be pardoned. During the following decades the government seems to have been willing to spare even captured Hutterite missionaries if they recanted;[29] they generally remained inflexible, however, and paid with their lives. There is no evidence that in later years formal trials were held. The decision to execute an Anabaptist was still made by the duke or the government, and the judge merely announced the decision to the prisoner.[30]

Like Austria, Salzburg, and Bavaria, the Swabian League was determined to wipe out the new heresy by force. The federal assembly decided on February 27, 1528, that Anabaptist men should be beheaded if they recanted, and women drowned; both men and women were otherwise to be burned. Clearly there was no regular trial. Berthold Aichelin, the widely hated provost of the Swabian League, wasted no time in killing Anabaptists: in 1531 he burned down a farmhouse, the Mantelhof, with twenty Anabaptists inside whom he had surprised during a meeting. The owner of the farm had already been hanged.

Unlike the governments of Salzburg, Bavaria, and the Swabian League, the elector of the Palatinate tried in 1528 to maintain legal forms and immediately ran into difficulties. For one thing, his councilors could not agree on a basis for convicting the Anabaptists. A memorandum from the elector's chancellor, Florenz von Venningen, urged the view that the Anabaptists were guilty of rebaptism and liable to capital punishment according to both imperial and canonical law. Venningen did not even mention the charge of rebellion. Nonetheless, the mandate issued on March 5, 1528, characterized Anabaptism as a continuation of the peasant uprising, aimed at the overthrow of all forms of authority. The mandate also mentioned that rebaptism was an offense against God and the Christian faith. On the basis of the imperial mandate of January 4, 1528, it said, death at the stake was the punishment for Anabaptists. The courts did not share this view, however. When twenty Anabaptists were imprisoned at Alzey in 1528, the elector summoned a court consisting of representatives of eight towns. The court first refused to pass judgment without a prior ecclesiastical inquisition. When the episcopal inquisition found the Anabaptists guilty of heresy, the court claimed lack of competence to pass sentence. Neither Venningen's memorandum nor the mandate of March 5, 1528, impressed the judges. In the end the elector seems to have pronounced the death sentence himself by executive order based on the imperial mandate of 1528.

Some Catholic governments remained obdurate even during the second half of the sixteenth century. In 1571 one Alexander, a leader, was beheaded at Bühl in the margravate of Baden, even though he had recanted. As we have seen, in some Catholic territories executions continued until 1618.

How was it that Anabaptists also died in Protestant Saxony, the homeland of Martin Luther? Had not Luther, in his early treatises "To the Christian Nobility" and "Secular Authority" clearly rejected the use of force in matters of faith? In fact, the events connected with Müntzer and the peasant uprising, the practical difficulties of organizing the new church, and the appearance of Anabaptism led to a gradual revision of Luther's views during the years 1526 to 1530. At Luther's urging the elector stipulated in the Instruction to the Visitators in 1526 that in order to prevent rebellion, sects, and separatism, only one doctrine would be tolerated: those who held different views would have to go elsewhere. Even so, Luther held in 1528 that hell was sufficient punishment for the Anabaptists.

When Anabaptism began to spread in Thuringia, Melanchthon and Luther grew sterner. Melanchthon pointed out in 1530 that though the Anabaptists appeared quite harmless, they still violated one or the other of their civic duties; leniency would encourage them to promote rebellion. Anabaptism, he said, was part of the movement that had begun with Storch and revealed its full fury in Thomas Müntzer. Thus not only rebellious but also blasphemous Anabaptists should be punished with the sword. Luther also adopted this position in 1530.

In 1531 Melanchthon distinguished three types of Anabaptists. First were the instigators, who should be executed. Second were those who rejected government and oaths as unchristian, demanded community of goods, planned to exterminate the godless, rejected interest as usury, and repudiated the church; if they remained obstinate, these Anabaptists should also be executed. Finally, there were the simple-minded Anabaptists who had erred only through misunderstanding and who should be re-

admitted into the church once they recanted; if they did not
recant, they should be banished or sentenced to a lighter punishment than death. Luther approved of Melanchthon's arguments,
adding that although it seemed cruel to punish the Anabaptists
with the sword, it was even crueler to condemn the ministry of
the Word and destroy secular government.

In a memorandum of 1536 Melanchthon reiterated that both
Mosaic and Roman law justified the death penalty for blasphemy. The blasphemies of the Anabaptists consisted of the
rejection of infant baptism, the denial of original sin, special
revelations, the Hofmannite doctrine of incarnation, and the
view that there was no forgiveness after death. Luther added
that since the Anabaptists did not keep their recantations, they
deserved death. Yet unlike Melanchthon he was never quite at
ease in advocating the death penalty for Anabaptists. By 1540
he apparently thought that Anabaptists who held heretical but
not seditious views should only be banished.[31]

That the views of the Reformers influenced Saxon legislation
is shown in the law of April 10, 1536. But enforcing these mandates was a different matter. When in 1536 the Aulic Court
(Hofgericht) condemned an Anabaptist to death for blasphemy,
the elector would not ratify the sentence but asked why it was so
severe. In his reply Chancellor Brück suggested that the Anabaptist be sentenced to death for blasphemy, heresy, and acts
conducive to rebellion. The final death sentence referred to
heresies and the imperial law of 1529. In other words, the charge
of heresy alone was not considered sufficient.

In 1536 two other prominent Protestant theologians, Urbanus
Rhegius and Ambrosius Blarer, approved of the death penalty
for Anabaptists, at least in principle.[32] Their views had no practical effect however: there were no Anabaptists in Brunswick-
Lüneburg, and no Anabaptist was executed in Württemberg
after the reformation of the duchy. Nor did a memorandum of
1557 by Melanchthon and five other Lutheran theologians advocating the death penalty for seditious and blasphemous Ana-

baptists change the policy of the Protestant governments.[33] Aside
from Electoral Saxony, Pfalz-Zweibrücken was the only Lutheran territory that retained the death penalty for Anabaptists,
and it never executed so much as one. In other Protestant territories the death penalty was stipulated only for expelled Anabaptists who returned illegally.

Criticism of the Death Penalty

The Anabaptists and various independent thinkers like Sebastian Franck strongly rejected the use of force in religious matters, but since they spoke to their own interests they could hardly
influence the councils of government. It was of greater significance that numerous Germans who had not renounced the state
church objected to the execution of heretics. Possibly Luther's
original views regarding freedom of faith had left their mark
on public opinion. Even Catholic princes were concerned about
their public image: such considerations prompted Elector Ludwig of the Palatinate to ask as many as eight universities for
their opinion on the memorandum by his chancellor, Venningen.
Doubts about the death penalty for rebaptism were greatest in
Lutheran cities and territories. Repeatedly the town council of
Nuremberg ordered its theologians and jurists to submit memoranda on this question. Regensburg and Rothenburg asked
lawyers of other cities for their views. By 1529, indeed, the question was already giving rise to a lively controversy.

Among those who rejected the death penalty for Anabaptists
on principle were theologians and jurists, and one ruler. The
underlying conviction of these men was that the secular authorities wielded the sword to punish offenses against society, not
errors of belief. The latter should be corrected by the word
rather than by the sword. Out of such a conviction Capito and
the pastors of Strasbourg condemned the execution of Sattler
and other Anabaptists at Horb. There were soul sicknesses, they
said, that could not be healed all at once but only by patience.
Capito thought that the Anabaptist doctrines on rebaptism and

political matters were not really vital points of belief. In all essential doctrines the Anabaptists agreed with other Christians.[34]

There were circles of Lutherans at Nuremberg during the 1520s who questioned the right of the authorities to use force against any religious group, whether they were Catholics, Zwinglians, Anabaptists, Jews, or heathens, unless the group had disturbed the public peace. If in 1529 the theologians at Nuremberg were still divided on whether the death penalty should be used against the Anabaptists, they clearly rejected it in two memoranda in 1531. Some theologians even objected to the imprisonment of obstinate Anabaptists, for "assent to truth should be free, without terror, through the Word of God." Obstinate Anabaptists, they said, should simply be expelled from the country.[35]

The Lutheran theologians in the neighboring margravate of Ansbach even argued that Anabaptist leaders or ordinary believers who did not advocate blasphemy or revolution should be allowed to stay in the country as long as they did not preach.[36] In his treatise "Whether Secular Authorities May by Divine and Common Right put Anabaptists to Death at the Sword," Brenz, the famous Swabian Reformer, also denied that the government had the right to execute Anabaptists. He compared the Anabaptists' demand for community of property to monastic practices and their rejection of political office to the canonical stipulation that a priest might not pass judgment on matters of life and death.

For lawyers it was much more difficult to disregard the imperial laws. Johann von Schwarzenberg, the author of the important criminal code of Bamberg and an outstanding Lutheran statesman, rejected the death penalty on two grounds. First, the inner court of conscience, as he called it, did not allow him to sentence anyone to death for his views on baptism and the Lord's Supper. Second, it was contrary to the teaching of Saint Paul and the canon law to use force in matters of belief.[37] In 1529 another lawyer, Ludwig Hierter at Speyer, used the argument already advanced in the trial at Alzey: the law required only the civil death of the Anabaptist, that is, banishment, and not physical death.[38] Landgrave Philip's approach to the question was based more on common sense than on theological or legal arguments. He observed that scriptural passages could be interpreted in more than one way. Consequently, different people could have different views on the Sacrament and other matters of faith. Even among true believers there would be differences of opinion.[39]

It can be said, then, that those who rejected the death penalty for the Anabaptists were mainly men of strong Lutheran background who occupied positions of high responsibility. They were not merely free-lance literati like Sebastian Franck, nor were they members of a proscribed sect. Their protests against the death penalty were not in vain. Landgrave Philip of Hesse and the authorities in several Protestant imperial cities, such as Strasbourg, Heilbronn, and Ulm, executed not a single Anabaptist. Some governments that either were Protestant or had strong Protestant leanings, such as those of Augsburg, Nuremberg, Regensburg, Speyer, and Ansbach, executed one Anabaptist and then determined not to execute any more. The city of Nuremberg, for example, executed Wolfgang Vogel on March 16, 1527, primarily for plotting rebellion. In August 1527, however, the Nuremberg town council informed the Augsburg authorities that it would not execute Anabaptists in the future. Finally, there were territories and cities, such as Württemberg and Esslingen, that put a stop to all executions after they adopted Protestantism.

The Protestant governments that refused to execute Anabaptists were violating the imperial law of 1529. This was not a matter to be taken lightly, particularly for the imperial cities. The Smalcaldic League accordingly declared on June 11, 1531, that no general law against sectarians could be passed, since there were many differences between the sects. The imperial law of 1529 had been adopted too hastily, without the full knowledge of all governments, and should be modified by each government individually. The sectarians should be punished for their offenses, not their faith.[40] In other words, the Protestant governments in denying their obligation to observe the mandate of 1529 did not reject the death penalty altogether. They could still justify the execution of Anabaptists by referring to the law of 1529, as Saxony later did.

The decision of the powerful Smalcaldic League allowed its members to disregard the imperial law, paying no heed to protests from king or emperor. The city of Regensburg did not belong to the Smalcaldic League, however, and had to explain its failure to execute Anabaptists to King Ferdinand in the most submissive terms. It is only fair to add that from about 1535 onward certain Catholic governments, such as those of the bishoprics of Passau and Speyer, also stopped executing Anabaptists.

Imprisonment and Expulsion

A government that rejected the death penalty for Anabaptists had only two other ways of clearing the country of them: imprisonment or banishment. The Zurich town council first resorted to banishment, decreeing on March 11 and 25, 1525, that all persons who had rebaptized or accepted rebaptism must leave the territory. By 1525, however, the council was already doubting the wisdom of its choice, and some Anabaptists who refused to recant were kept in prison. By March 1526 the Zurich authorities were definitely convinced that imprisonment was a more effective measure than banishment. Eighteen men and women were sentenced on March 7, 1526, to stay in prison on bread and water until they recanted or died. In the following years only foreign Anabaptists were expelled; subjects were thrown into jail.

Whereas a few Protestant governments in Germany, such as that of Strasbourg, expelled all Anabaptists whether they were leaders or not (except Melchior Hofmann), others realized very soon that it was absurd to let the leaders, the most zealous and gifted agitators, continue to propagate their doctrines. Augsburg, Nuremberg, Hesse, and Württemberg therefore kept leaders in prison. A primary purpose of imprisonment, then, was not to punish the Anabaptists but first to eliminate the most active propagators of Anabaptism from the population and second to break the leaders' resistance. The Anabaptists were released as soon as they abandoned their heresy. Gross, Dachser, and Salminger were set free at Augsburg in 1531 after they had recanted. Rinck in Hesse and Hofmann at Strasbourg died in their dungeons because they refused to give in. Riedemann, by contrast, was finally expelled by the authorities at Nuremberg, who got tired of the situation after four futile years of keeping him in prison. In the case of the Hutterites some governments did not demand even a recantation but only a promise that they would not return. Those who refused to give such a promise remained in custody for years—Mathis Binder for four years, Paul Glock for as many as nineteen.

The hardship of imprisonment varied. Some brethren suffered greatly. "For five weeks you have kept me in darkness on straw, giving me bread soaked in water," one Anabaptist accused the town council of Rothenburg. "If God had not strengthened me, I would have gone mad or frozen to death." [41] The agony of solitary confinement sometimes produced hallucinations: one Hutterite thought the devil was tempting him by appearing in the form of a virgin who tried to embrace him. When he knelt down to pray, the devil would appear in the form of a woman who lay down on his bed. Actually, the officials played a cruel joke on this poor fellow by chaining him to a young and handsome Anabaptist woman. But the two were decent and godfearing and did not let themselves be tempted.[42]

Sometimes imprisonment was not so oppressive. Paul Glock, imprisoned for years at Hohenwittlingen, wrote in 1566 that he had promised not to run away and therefore was no longer locked in his cell. He was allowed to visit the family of the district official and even had a meal with them. He fetched them

fruit from their orchards, helped with the harvest, carted manure
to the fields, repaired fences, cut grass, and took rakes to the
market. Years later, and still angry, the theologians grumbled
that Glock had not been so much confined to a prison as given
a sinecure. Whenever a pastor had come to exhort him to recant,
Glock had not been in his cell but out carrying messages across
the country.[43]

Riedemann was secretly let out of his dungeon at Wolkersdorf
in Hesse when his warden discovered that they were both cob-
blers. Riedemann now worked for the warden in a room in the
tower, and in return the warden allowed brethren from Moravia
to visit Riedemann and stay overnight. Later Riedemann and
his fellow prisoners were even allowed to eat with the castellan.
Riedemann regarded this leniency as a temptation put to him
by the devil, and a sign that he and his followers had to be all
the more careful. When they were allowed to walk freely about
the castle, they were extremely wary of the servants. He would
rather lie in prison than listen to their dirty talk, Riedemann
lamented.[44]

Numerous Anabaptists, especially Hutterites, wrote epistles
in jail. Schiemer at Rattenberg in 1527 received ink, paper, and
quill from the prison official, who was severely reprimanded as
a result by the government. Others were given ink and paper by
sympathizers or visitors. Their epistles tell of their interrogations
and suffering, and their steadfastness or the defections of weak
brethren. It is surprising how many of these letters were smuggled out of the jails. Emigrants sometimes took them to Moravia.

When several brethren lay in the same prison, they comforted
and encouraged one another. It was precisely for this reason that
some governments preferred to put Anabaptists in different jails,
whatever the cost. When they were in the same prison but different cells, they kept in touch by singing hymns at night at the
windows. Sometimes, too, Anabaptists shared their dungeons
with common criminals, who cursed and ridiculed them.

In Protestant territories as a rule only leaders and Hutterite missionaries were imprisoned for long periods of times; ordinary Anabaptists who refused to recant were banished.[45] In 1527 and 1528 Augsburg and Esslingen ordered the Anabaptists to leave forthwith. Some governments, however, gave the Anabaptists a final period of grace, a month or even half a year, to think matters over before the order of expulsion was pronounced.[46] Even after the order had been pronounced, several governments gave the sectarians time to prepare for their departure. Some granted only three days, and others up to 45.[47] The spouses of banished Anabaptists were generally allowed to remain. At Colmar, however, the wives of banished Anabaptists were also expelled, especially if they continued to give their husbands shelter, money, or food.[48]

In the city states it was the town council or a commission that pronounced the order of expulsion. In some of the larger territories, such as Württemberg and Ansbach, the decision was made by the government or even the ruler himself. In Württemberg the district official then announced the decision before the court of justice. At Lauingen, Anabaptists were simply seized in their houses or workshops, taken straight to the town gates, and without formal sentence ordered to leave.

Expelled Anabaptists frequently had to swear an oath or at least promise never to return, and they were warned that they would be treated as perjurers if they did. In Hesse, Anabaptists who refused to swear were whipped or branded on the face. In cities officers took the Anabaptists to the city gates. In the country districts the beadle might chase the sectarians out of the village with a whip. When Anabaptists obstinately refused to leave, Württemberg decided in 1584 not to spare any costs: special guards were ordered to take the sectarians to the frontiers of the duchy. Sometimes, however, the guards were not familiar with the complicated frontiers. On one occasion two heavily armed guards took their prisoner right into the territory of Ulm, thus evoking angry protests from the city fathers there.

Occasionally the Anabaptists endured other punishments in

addition to expulsion. In the Grafschaft Fürstenberg they also
had to pay a fine of twenty florins. At Augsburg sectarians were
sometimes whipped; or some of their fingers, the ones usually
raised in the swearing of oaths, were cut off; or their cheeks
were branded; or their tongues were cut out. The Anabaptists
given these additional punishments had committed special offenses, such as announcing meetings or permitting them to be
held in their houses, offering other Anabaptists food and shelter,
refusing to swear not to return or returning in spite of their expulsion, or going back to Anabaptism after a previous recantation. Those whose tongues were cut out usually had made some
infamous allusion to the Lord's Supper or other remarks considered evil and seditious.[49] Though these punishments seem atro-
cious, they were not considered unusually cruel in the sixteenth
century. Mutilations and similar punishments had been traditional for blasphemers and perjurers in the Middle Ages. Anabaptists who were merely obstinate did not usually suffer these
punishments.[50] In 1570 theologians in Württemberg warned that
Anabaptists should not be whipped—a punishment considered
degrading—lest people thought the Anabaptists were being
whipped because of their faith.

Did the policy of expulsion really eliminate Anabaptism from
an area? In 1540, to be sure, the town of Steyr declared that
through banishment the sect had been eliminated; but banishment could never be more than a partial solution. After all, the
Anabaptists had to go somewhere. As we have seen, the great
development of Anabaptism in Moravia resulted directly from
the persecution Anabaptists suffered in Germany and Austria.
Officials in south Germany may have felt relief when these
troublesome sectarians fled to Moravia, but they were hardly
very pleased when these same people returned a few years later
to spread their doctrines as missionaries. Some Anabaptists did
not even go as far as Moravia but appeared in such towns as
Strasbourg or Augsburg. Ultimately the expulsion policy simply
transferred Anabaptists from one community to another.

In 1535 the theologians of Strasbourg expressed the opinion that neither imprisonment nor expulsion really served any purpose and suggested forced labor instead. A high government official in Hesse likewise proposed that the Anabaptists should be set to work: they might be sent to the iron mines, for example, as the convicts in Prussia were. But no government ever followed this advice.

Occasionally governments disregarded their own laws when the professional services of an Anabaptist were considered too valuable to sacrifice. Although his Anabaptist views were well known to the town council, Marbeck was allowed to stay at Augsburg from 1544 until his death in 1556 because he administered the city's magnificent water supply. Sometimes alchemists and physicians were also allowed to remain in the country.

Expulsions were not considered permanent: those who abandoned Anabaptism were generally allowed to return. But the authorities were incensed if Anabaptists returned without recanting. No government during the sixteenth century would tolerate this sort of insubordination. The Protestant cities in Switzerland, particularly Bern, executed many of such lawbreakers. The German Protestants were a bit more lenient: at Augsburg and Ulm Anabaptists who returned without permission were whipped, imprisoned for a while, perhaps even tortured, and finally banished again; in Leiningen they had to pay a fine. The governments of Württemberg, Baden-Durlach, Hesse, and the Palatinate decreed that returning Anabaptists must be brought to justice and condemned to death, not because of their religion but because of their contempt for the law.[51] Such bloodthirsty threats were never carried out in any of these territories, though Anabaptists continued to return.

The authorities soon learned that the policy of expulsion had still more flaws. Württemberg farmers whose wives had been expelled complained that they could not take care of the children and the household. Therefore it was decreed in 1584 that obstinate Anabaptist women might stay in their houses and do their housework, but that they must be kept in chains to prevent them from spreading their doctrines in the village.

A third form of punishment should be mentioned, though it was applied only on rare occasions: service in the galleys. Proposed to Ferdinand I in 1539, it was employed in 1540. Ninety Anabaptists were taken from castle Falkenstein in lower Austria to Triest for this purpose; there, however most of them escaped. During the following years a few stubborn Anabaptists from the Tirol who were not leaders were punished this way, and Zurich used the same method in 1613.[52]

Following an old legal tradition,[53] a Tirolese law of April 1, 1528, ordered that the property of expelled or executed Anabaptists be confiscated. Usually the property was used to rear the former owner's children, but they could not lay claim to it. In 1536 Ferdinand I changed this policy: the property of Anabaptists was no longer confiscated but handed over to the heirs or the next of kin. Ferdinand justified this change by referring to public opinion: the impression had been created that Anabaptists were persecuted not because of their beliefs but because of their possessions. The officials remonstrated that now the Anabaptists would be even more inclined to emigrate, since they knew their property would be handed over to their children; furthermore, the government needed the confiscated property to defray the costs of keeping Anabaptists in prison. But Ferdinand remained firm: he would rather show mercy to widows and orphans, he said, than punish them for the offenses of other people. Despite Ferdinand's admirable intentions, the law was modified in 1542. The property of an emigrated Anabaptist was confiscated, and it could be delivered to the owner's heirs only when the government had received reliable reports that he had died. This policy was continued in the Tirol. In other Catholic territories policies varied: some confiscated Anabaptist property, but others only administered it in the owner's absence.[54]

Most Protestant states, such as Württemberg in 1535, 1538, and 1571, the Electoral Palatinate in 1564, Baden-Durlach in

1570, Baden-Baden in 1578, and the city of Heilbronn in 1557, also prevented a banished or emigrating Anabaptist from taking his property with him.[55] His property was not confiscated permanently, however, but only sequestrated, to be returned if he recanted.[56] Thus the temporary confiscation was a means of bringing pressure to bear on the Anabaptist to abandon his sectarian beliefs.

Some Anabaptists managed to sell some of their fields and vineyards secretly, or received part of their inheritance in cash from their parents, or assisted by their fellow believers took their furniture, animals, or other belongings with them. A woman of Colmar sent her Anabaptist son her silver, finest jewels, money, and the titles to their land. But these cases were the exception: most Anabaptists left their property behind, where it was carefully administered by the government according to law. By 1606 the Anabaptist property confiscated in Württemberg was valued at 55,300 florins. In 1610 the Zurich officials administered property worth 10,501 florins. In Württemberg the proceeds from the sale of Anabaptist farms, mills, and other property were sent to the chancellery, which used these funds to grant loans. The resulting interest payments were used to defray the prison costs of poor Anabaptists and for such charitable uses as the construction of hospitals or the payment of hospital dues for the poor. Pressed by growing debts, however, Frederick II in 1606 appropriated 55,000 florins to cover the government's expenses. This grave violation of the law prompted an investigation by the Estates, which led to the execution of the highest official involved, the *landprokurator* Esslinger.

Two Protestant territories, Hesse and Leiningen, did not agree with the policy of confiscating Anabaptist property. Philip of Hesse had already ordered in 1528 that banished Anabaptists might sell whatever they owned—house, farm, fields, rye, barley, fruit, or animals—and take the money with them. If the Anabaptists were not able to sell their possessions within two weeks, the district official would do it for them after their departure.[57]

Anabaptists in other territories, such as Württemberg, did not fail to remind the authorities that in Hesse no Anabaptist was deprived of his property. But the Anabaptists in Hesse had only Philip to thank for this leniency. His successors pursued a policy of sequestrating Anabaptist property.[58] When the government at Leiningen first allowed the Anabaptists to sell their property is unknown. At any rate, in 1584, 1598, and 1609, they were told to sell their belongings and get out.

As a rule, expelled Anabaptists were permitted to take their children with them. Only the Palatinate (in 1564) and Baden-Durlach (in 1570) forbade the Anabaptists to take with them children who had not joined the sect yet.[59] It is very doubtful whether these provisions were ever put into effect.

Disputations

The Anabaptists did not always face the theologians just as prisoners. On at least 23 occasions formal disputations were held during which both sides freely presented their views: sixteen disputations took place in the Zwinglian towns of Switzerland, one in Waldshut, three in Bucer's Strasbourg, one in Lutheran Hesse, and two in the Palatinate, which was Calvinist.[60] Of course, disputations with heretics were out of the question in Catholic territories, for there doctrine had already been defined by the Church. Either the Anabaptists accepted it, or they were eliminated as heretics. But why were there not more such public debates in Lutheran territories and cities? The reason may have been partly political. The Anabaptist disputations at Zurich grew out of the already established practice of discussing proposed reforms in public debates before they were adopted by the town council; for example, such disputations were held in Zurich in January and October of 1523. German territories or cities had no similar custom.

Of course, disputations were common during the sixteenth century. Luther himself had defended his new ideas in public debates at Heidelberg and Leipzig. To the Anabaptists a public disputation offered an excellent opportunity to present their views and refute false rumors. Accordingly the Anabaptists of Strasbourg asked several times for permission to defend their doctrines in public. Of the 23 disputations known to have been held, eight had been requested by the brethren. For their part, the authorities hoped to achieve two aims in disputations: first, to stem the tide of Anabaptism by proving in public that the Anabaptist doctrines, even when presented in their most persuasive form, could not prevail against an intelligent discussion; second, to counter the claim that the Anabaptists were not convicted by the Bible but were suppressed without even being heard. The preachers were particularly sensitive to this charge: at least five disputations are known to have been held on their initiative. If the preachers at Strasbourg had had their way, more disputations would have been held, but the town council often rejected their requests or permitted only an exchange of memoranda on disputed doctrines. On at least one occasion—at Basel in 1585—the Anabaptists turned down the opportunity of a disputation on the ground that they were not sufficiently learned to represent the Anabaptist views.

In general it was the government that called and organized the disputations and discussion. When the Strasbourg preachers held a disputation with Denck in December 1526 without even informing the town council, they were curtly told that in the future the permission of the town council was required. The disputations were publicly announced in the churches. At Frankenthal in 1571 all Anabaptists, native or foreign, including even those who had fled or had been expelled, were offered safe-conducts extending from two weeks before to two weeks after the disputation, though they were forbidden to preach or baptize in the Palatinate during this period. To prevent anyone from claiming that poverty had kept him from attending, the active participants were offered free board and lodging at Frankenthal. Sometimes the authorities even brought Anabaptists from the prisons to disputations.

Disputations were usually presided over by the town council, or a commission, or representatives of the prince. At Bern in 1527 four town councilors presided; at Frankenthal the elector himself presided during the opening session, and his officials took over in the following meetings. In Switzerland the public was generally allowed to attend disputations. At Strasbourg the the disputations with Denck and Hofmann were held in public, whereas those with Marbeck were held only before the town council. A crowd of four hundred attended the disputation between Bucer and Denck at Strasbourg, but the disputation at Marburg in 1538 seems to have had only a small audience: the pastors of the town, the rector of the university, the town council, two representatives of every guild, some prominent burghers, and persons who were suspected of leaning toward Anabaptism. The disputations were held in town halls, guild houses, churches, and former monasteries. Some lasted only a day or two, but the one held at Frankenthal lasted three weeks.

The churches were always represented by preachers or theologians, while the civil authorities were supposed to act as impartial judges, though naturally they never were. Generally the Anabaptists had two or more speakers. At Zurich in November 1525, Grebel, Blaurock, and Manz faced Zwingli, Judd, and Megander. At Marburg, Bucer argued with three Anabaptists, one after the other. At Frankenthal there were fifteen active Anabaptist participants, though two of them did most of the talking.

At Bern in 1527 the Anabaptists suggested the topics for the disputation. In general, however, the theologians made up the agenda. If they formulated the premises carefully, they had already won a great advantage. Prior to the Zofingen disputation in 1532, Heinrich Bullinger advised Berchtold Haller that the Anabaptists should first be urged to accept two basic hermeneutic principles: that all disputed questions should be decided on the basis of both the Old and the New Testament; and that passages in the Scriptures should be interpreted according to other clear statements in the Scriptures, in a nonliteral manner, and with faith and love as guidelines. Bullinger even offered a line of arguments the Bernese pastors should use. Once the Anabaptists had accepted these hermeneutic principles, he said, they would find it difficult to maintain their doctrines.[61]

At some disputations, such as the one at Frankenthal, a wide variety of subjects were discussed: the relation of the Old and the New Testament, the Trinity, incarnation, original sin, the church, justification, marriage, community of goods, government and oaths, and finally baptism and the Lord's Supper. Often genuine discussion took place, though on some occasions the opposing parties did no more than read lengthy justifications of their views and rebuttals of the other side's position.

Now and again the records mention events that took place during the disputations: for example, that an Anabaptist spokesman looked for a while at the books and notes in front of him or was cautioned by a fellow believer not to carry an argument further than he could justify. A high Bavarian official who was present at the disputation of Frankenthal was amazed to see how quickly these uneducated craftsmen and day laborers, pure idiots as he called them, quoted scriptural passages and defended their doctrines.[62] Sometimes a friendly atmosphere prevailed. At the end of the Zofingen disputation of 1532, both sides thanked each other and asked forgiveness for impolite words. The Anabaptists generally refrained from making insulting remarks, though at Basel in 1529 the Anabaptist spokesman forbade a guildmaster to call him brother unless he did penance and resigned from his office. Even so, the theologians were not always content. Denck's "admirable obscurity" annoyed Bucer and the Strasbourg preachers: among one hundred persons, hardly any had understood what he meant by free will or sin. At Frankenthal the presidents sometimes ordered the Anabaptists to give clear answers, or to stick to the issue. Only rarely did Anabaptist spectators interrupt the proceedings. When Zwingli's book on baptism was read during the St. Gallen disputation of May 1525, however, the Anabaptists shouted from the gallery, "Stop reading; tell us God's word, not Zwingli's word." [63] And at Zurich in November 1525 a group of Anabaptists stormed into the hall shouting, "Zion! Zion!" [64]

At the end of the disputation the judges usually decided that the doctrines of the preachers were clearly based on the Scriptures. The Anabaptists were admonished to accept this verdict and abandon their sectarian errors. Naturally, the Anabaptists refused to comply. As far as they were concerned, they were the ones who had proved their doctrines to be based on the Bible.

During the disputations one or more clerks kept transcripts. At the Frankenthal disputation, Frederick III received his copy daily. Intent on showing the whole world that the Anabaptists had been vanquished by the pastors, some governments hastily published these transcripts, which the Anabaptists inevitably declared to have been falsified. In fact, some Swiss transcripts devoted pages to the arguments of the theologians and only a few lines to those of the Anabaptists. Other governments were more scrupulous. In 1538 the authorities at Bern asked the Anabaptists to examine the transcript before it was published. At the end of the Frankenthal disputation, the Anabaptists took part in the editing of the whole transcript. As far as we know, the most reliable transcripts are those of the disputations at Zofingen in 1532 and at Bern and Marburg in 1538, and above all, the huge transcript of the disputation at Frankenthal.

Undoubtedly the disputations helped both the theologians and the Anabaptists to see their differences more clearly. But the authorities' hopes that the Anabaptists might recognize their errors were rarely realized. To be sure, after the disputation at Marburg in 1538, four Anabaptist leaders abandoned their faith —an event that triggered the collapse of Anabaptism in Hesse. But since these leaders had never differed from Bucer on decisive matters, such as government, military service, war taxes, and oaths, the situation in Hesse was not typical at all. After the disputation at Zurich in November 1525, only thirteen Anabaptists

in the district of Grüningen abandoned their belief, whereas
more than ninety remained unyielding. After the Frankenthal
disputation only three Anabaptists gave up their faith. One observer commented that in spite of the long debate, everything
remained as it had been before. The failure of the disputations
to persuade Anabaptists to abandon their doctrines was no doubt
a major reason why no more disputations were held in Protestant
Germany or Switzerland. Instructing Anabaptists individually
proved much more successful.

The Reaction of the Anabaptists

The persecution suffered by the Anabaptists must have made
a strong impression on their state of mind and way of life. No
one can tell how the Anabaptist movement would have developed if it had been allowed to operate freely. Perhaps under such
circumstances eschatological visions would not have had such a
hold on so many early Anabaptists. Perhaps the Anabaptists
would not have been so adamant in their rejection of public
office and their hatred of pastors.

Of course, the threat of persecution forced the Anabaptists to
carry on their activities in secret. The leaders warned the brethren not to tell outsiders what transpired in the congregation—
better they should lie drowning, with a stone around their necks.
Having suffered grievously because of informants, the Tirolese
Anabaptists seem to have been more secretive and distrustful
than other brethren. New members were not told who had
brought food to the meetings; the brethren did not tell each
other who else had joined the sect; and the leaders went from
place to place without giving the ordinary believers any account
of where they were going.

Threatened by traitors and constantly hunted by officials, the
Anabaptists sometimes escaped arrest only by running through
back doors, jumping over fences, fleeing into forests, or hiding
under staircases and in cellars. Some used disguises. During the
wave of arrests at Augsburg in 1528, a rich lady escaped from

the city by donning a milkmaid's dress and carrying a milk pail. Once caught, however, the Anabaptists did not resist arrest by force, "for one should be gentle and humble." [65] One official took the view that Anabaptists never sought to escape: they were criminals, possessed by the devil, who wanted to die.[66] Certainly the Anabaptists were resigned to persecution. "Whether you kill me or not, life on earth is only a little matter," one woman said. "Do whatever you want; I owe God a death." [67] To the brethren, their suffering had a deeper meaning: God chastised whomever He loved. Repeatedly the Anabaptists thanked the Lord that they were allowed to suffer for His sake; they were not even worthy, they said, to suffer for His holy name. Still, some Anabaptists were not able to submit to the Cross. Fore-warned of imminent arrest, one lady of Augsburg quickly left the meeting.

The Hutterite leaders told brethren who were jailed in Ger-many to run away whenever they could. Many Anabaptists did not let a good opportunity pass; some left only after they had assured themselves in prayer that the name of the Lord would not be dishonored by their escape. One man on the way to prison ran away as night began to fall; another escaped when his guard got dead-drunk at an inn. Sometimes fellow believers smuggled tools into the prison. One man escaped from prison with the aid of a hammer and rope and then, leaving his clothes behind him, swam across a river. Sometimes sympathetic castle servants showed prisoners a secret opening in the walls, and oc-casionally governments even suspected their own officials of complicity. Anabaptist prisoners at Wolkersdorf in Hesse made a hole in the wall, but they did not run away: one or two would leave at a time, visit their families, preach and baptize, and then return to the prison. There were also a few Anabaptists who obstinately refused to leave even though tunnels had been dug into their cells or burghers had promised to lead them to safety. In 1533 a brother was arrested in the Tirol who had written down the accounts of escaped fellow believers.

During their interrogation many Anabaptists refused to divulge the names of other Anabaptists. As they pointed out, the Lord Himself had not answered all the questions put to Him. Others said their conscience and brotherly love would never permit them to deliver anyone to the slaughterhouse. Asked who his friends were, a brother in Thuringia replied that they were God's children and their flesh was of the earth. Where did they live? In God's hand, between heaven and earth.[68] Other brethren, by contrast, willingly disclosed the names of other believers: a Christian should not tell lies, they said. There were also some who broke down and gave a full list of names in order to prove that they were not alone. In some instances it is simply not clear why an Anabaptist betrayed his fellow believers.

Many Anabaptists, especially in Protestant territories, did not bow meekly but spoke up to their persecutors. Sometimes there were horrible scenes when the children of Anabaptists were baptized by order of the government. One irate Anabaptist instructed the pastor to announce in church that neither the father nor the mother wished to have their child baptized. Then, losing his temper, he called the pastor a seducer and murderer of souls, to which the enraged pastor responded that the Anabaptist was the devil's spawn.[69] Some interrogations turned into violent and noisy brawls. Melanchthon was appalled by his experiences at Jena, where angry Anabaptists stormed and vituperated. In others the believers brushed aside all questions concerning baptism and the Lord's Supper, saying that as scribes and Pharisees, the pastors themselves should know the answers. When in 1601 one pastor in the Palatinate tried to admonish some brethren, they only shouted: "Do you not hear, do you not hear? We want none of you; we have not sent for you; we have our own teachers who are much better than you! How often must we tell you this, when you already know it!"[70] Some pastors would not tolerate such insolence and cut off the discussion. There were Anabaptists who did not even attend visitations, sending word through the beadle that they were resolved to remain outside the church. One brother simply tore up the summons: "Return these pieces to the bailiff." On being forbidden to use the common water and pasture, he only laughed: "That is nothing to me, for I eat no grass and relish no water." [71]

The Anabaptists bitterly castigated kings, princes, and town councilors for trying to usurp God's powers. Only God, they said, could grant faith, and not the worldly authorities: the prince elector of Saxony, who placed his orders above those of God, was a "foreign God." "There is another little God," an Anabaptist said, pointing to the town bailiff of Zwickau.[72] The brethren asked sarcastically what sort of Christianity it was that threw people into prison without refuting their belief with the Scriptures and ordered the beadles to force them to attend church. God had sent His Son into the world to preach, but where in the Scriptures had He said, "If they do not listen to you and refuse to accept your teaching, then arrest them, torture them, yea, strangle them until they believe"? [73] When the theologians tried to talk to them in a friendly spirit, however, the brethren became suspicious: "That old snake the devil comes craftily; therefore let us beware!" [74]

Having been subjected to great pressure, some Anabaptists finally agreed to attend church services, but they left no doubt that they were not interested in what was going on. Some read books during the service; others smilingly checked scriptural passages quoted by the pastors; still others looked at each other in a mocking manner or expressed their approval or disapproval by nodding or shaking their heads.

Those who did recant naturally aroused the wrath of their leaders: they received word that they were damned, or they were openly called traitors. A few fanatics even tried to stone a man who was recanting in the church.[75] Of course, the brethren were even more embittered by the defection of their leaders.

Since some Anabaptists who had recanted returned to the sect,[76] the pastors of Basel accused the brethren of making light of their recantations. In fact, one believer at Basel claimed that the leaders had advised the congregation to swear and do whatever was demanded of them when they were captured, for they were not obliged to keep their word once they were freed.[77] Other Anabaptists contended that the recantation had been forced on them by torture. There were also some who cleverly argued that they had not done anything wrong by rejoining the Anabaptists, for in their recantation they had promised to turn to the Word of God. Others returned after being reproached by former fellow believers: "Dear brother, you have acted against the Word of God by defecting; desist from your accursed and sinful life." [78] Frequently, however, a former believer's return to the sect was due less to the persuasive tactics of other Anabaptists than to his own inner restlessness and bad conscience. Ten years might go by, and still a man might return to the brethren on the spur of the moment. Whatever their reasons for returning, the brethren were not greatly concerned with such earthly matters as the bail put up by friends and relatives guaranteeing their good conduct.

Most Anabaptists who defected, however, never returned to the movement. The Strasbourg Discipline ordered the believers to avoid defectors with discretion and humility. Some defectors, indeed, seem to have turned to the other extreme: there were complaints at Basel in 1533 that former Anabaptists led a particularly loose life, playing music at dances and the like.

Of course, there were also Anabaptists who never yielded to the arguments, entreaties, and threats of the pastors. One Thuringian leader told the theologians coldly that he thought as much of their questions and arguments as he thought of a louse: even if they talked all day, he would rather die than yield. Others argued that they were too old to change their beliefs again. When neighbors advised the brethren in a friendly spirit to give up their sectarian views, they were told to mind their own business. Luther's religious individualism had indeed borne fruit.

The most severe test for the brethren was the death penalty,

and as we have seen, hundreds of Anabaptists submitted themselves to it. That they did so is all the more remarkable because
the Anabaptists were not simply slaughtered like the Cathari
in thirteenth-century France: many of them would have been
pardoned and set free even at the very last moment if only they
had abandoned their beliefs. With the corpses of three fellow
believers lying at his feet, one Anabaptist at Rottenburg still
turned down all exhortations to yield: "If I had seven heads, I
would offer them for Christ." The great number of Anabaptist
martyrs is indeed surprising. Where in recent centuries did so
many people *deliberately* accept a death sentence for the sake of
their Christian faith? These martyrs were not bishops, monks, or
nuns, but ordinary peasants and artisans, the most common people in the world. They did not seek death: some Anabaptists said
frankly that like all living creatures they dreaded death and
wished to live. But there is little doubt that many brethren were
actually in a very different state of mind than most people.
When the judges at Augsburg sentenced one believer from life
to death, he interrupted them: "No, my lords, from death to
life." [79] Strange as it may appear in the twentieth century, the
Anabaptists valued their faith more than their life. But there
was another psychological reason for their martyrdom: as one
official observed, many people found their consciences harder
to resist than brute force.

If the Anabaptists were prepared to die for their belief, they
nonetheless warned the authorities that they were shedding the
blood of innocent people. One Hutterite leader appealed to the
jury to follow their hearts and consciences rather than the law
lest they have biting worms in their hearts. At the Day of Judgment, Christ would show mercy to the compassionate but stern
justice to the merciless. [80]

Erhard reports that on their way to the gallows some Anabaptists were fearful, if not terrified, and depressed. In fact, some
brethren had a very lonely death. Augustin Würzelgruber at
Regensburg was led like a calf from the town hall to the place

of execution. He said nothing, and no one said a word to him. He died, as one chronicler put it, "sine crux, sine lux, et sine deus." [81] Other Anabaptists exhibited an abnormal frenzy during the last moments of their life. Ten believers at Mühlhausen who were taken by cart to the river to be drowned shouted continuously to the bystanders: "Do penance, do penance, you stubborn people of the great crowd; desist from the dog's bath, the pig's bath, and dirt bath of infant baptism." A maidservant called loudly to the people: "O you heretics, you heretics, do penance; turn to us, the few, look how constant we are!" When a journeyman asked her to turn back so that he could marry her, she did not so much as answer him; moments later she was thrown into the river.[82] Sometimes there were little outbreaks of violence: at Ingolstadt one Anabaptist spoke with such vehemence that the Jesuit priest spat at him and the executioner himself had to wipe off the spittle. The brother in turn spat at the cross the priest was holding toward him.

Under immense nervous strain, some of the Anabaptists doomed to die behaved in a most unusual way. All through the sixteenth century Anabaptists were reported to have gone singing to their death. One brother who lost his shoes in the mud along the road did not even look back and went right on singing. A chronicler reports that five Anabaptists who were executed at Kaufbeuren in 1528 appeared to be quite happy; one even embraced and kissed the executioner. This was by no means an isolated incident.[83] Other Anabaptists danced around the place of execution and shouted with joy, referring to their execution as a beautiful wedding.[84] Many addressed the crowd before their death. Fleiner at Esslingen delivered such an "angelic" sermon that people began to cry. An Anabaptist at Innsbruck once more adjured the people to reflect on their sinful lives and not to boast of being Christians: "Woe and eternal suffering," he shouted, "will come to those who murder a Christian." [85] The Anabaptists never failed to say a prayer before the end. One brother in the Tirol turned his face to the east and then with a loud voice thanked God for all the mercy He had shown him. Some Anabaptists also repudiated the bystanders' prayers.

The executions terrified and saddened the Anabaptists, but in a sense they were also a source of strength. The brethren were convinced that their fellow believers could not have borne so much suffering if the Lord had not been with them. Anabaptists of Thuringia told the theologians that since the twelve believers who had been put to death at Mühlhausen had never been convicted by virtue of the Scriptures, there was no reason why they themselves should yield. Catholic and Protestant theologians, for their part, were convinced that the fearlessness of the Anabaptists was inspired by the devil, for even Christ Himself had suffered in His death. A wise government would therefore seek ways to prevent the deaths of these insane people. Only Capito showed more insight. He pointed to the baptismal dogma of the brethren as an explanation of their fortitude. To the Anabaptists, baptism was not simply a ceremony but a solemn testimony that they believed in Christ and had already left the world—a testimony to be confirmed by their blood and their life.[86]

As we have seen, in most Protestant and some Catholic territories the Anabaptists were punished not by death but by banishment. Though banishment caused them great material hardship, some brethren were by no means dismayed at the prospect. An Anabaptist at Heilbronn received the order to get out of the city "with a laugh on his mouth and with all his heart." While descending the stairs at the town hall, "he continuously thanked God that he should suffer persecution for the Lord's sake." But there were also believers who felt dejected: one woman consoled her husband by saying that he should not be afraid, for Christ, too, had suffered this fate.[87]

Some Anabaptists accepted the order to leave with reservations, declaring that God's orders superseded those of the government. As early as April 1525 Anabaptists at Zollikon questioned the right of the Zurich town council to expel them: God had created the earth for the brethren as well as for the lords.[88] The Anabaptists also argued that they had not done anything that would warrant their expulsion. Their views on baptism had nothing to do with taxes, interest, tithes, and other obligations, which they were willing to meet. If the government drove them out it was applying force, not the law.[89] Alternatively, the Anabaptists would ask how the landgrave could tolerate Jews and expel Christians. Eventually God might enlighten the ruler himself, they would say: then he would be glad to have them in the country. Other Anabaptists pointed to their family obligations as a reason why they should be allowed to stay.[90]

Indeed, some Anabaptists did not move from their villages, even though they were ordered to leave.[91] Others would merely go to stay in a neighboring village for a while, cutting straw or spinning yarn there. Some even worked in their fields and vineyards in broad daylight, returning to their village occasionally to sell or buy wine or grain, pick up a sack of wool, and also have a meal in the public inn. After a while they might return permanently. One man whose wife had thus returned told the officials that a dove could be sold or released, but she would still return and the fowler would be glad to let her in.

Some astute brethren in Alsace acquired Strasbourg citizenship and then returned to their village, claiming immunity from local jurisdiction. Others argued that though they had promised to go away, they had not promised to stay away.[92] There were Anabaptists who returned even after being expelled for the second or third time. Understandably, the governments found this sort of insubordination unacceptable. If this "wanton deliberate disobedience" were allowed to go on, the officials warned, the Anabaptists would finally chase the duke himself and his subjects out of the country.

As the Anabaptist leaders realized, expulsion put a great strain on family relations. Scharnschlager pointed out that whereas one spouse might be prepared to suffer want, hunger, thirst, frost, and the cross rather than endanger the salvation of his soul, the other would clamor, "To the devil with suffering. We must have food and drink in the kitchen and cellar: one day we have too little lard, the next too little meat, cheese, wine, bread, and eggs." [93]

There were also Anabaptists who plainly said they would leave the country if ordered to do so by the government, for they owed obedience to the authorities.[94] Some brethren who were expelled in 1578 humbly asked the landgrave to let them settle in a desolate area. Of course, their plea was rejected. Where, indeed, could the brethren go? The Anabaptists who escaped from the Zurich prison in April 1526 jokingly said that they would join the red Indians beyond the ocean—in other words, in America. Many brethren were forced to go into hiding or wander from place to place doing odd jobs.

Even after they had left their home country, the Anabaptists were still pursued by their wrathful governments. In 1527 the Austrian government forwarded to Reutlingen the names of four refugees from Horb, demanding their arrest or at least their expulsion. Some believers had to bear a double burden—the malevolence of the authorities and the bitterness of their families. A Bavarian peasant had a fierce quarrel with his Anabaptist wife, who had fled to Augsburg. Though he came to the city every week, he did not even let her have her clothes.

We quickly lose track of the Anabaptists who fled to villages or small towns. Better information is available for those who took refuge in larger cities. During the early years of Anabaptism, the largest number of refugees flocked to Strasbourg and Augsburg: 73 were discovered at Strasbourg from 1527 to 1535, and 56 at Augsburg in 1527 and 1528. At least 43 of those at Augsburg had come from nearby villages, which for the most part were situated in the duchy of Bavaria. Others had come from Franconia, Austria, and the Tirol.[95] Only sixteen of the refugees arrested at Augsburg on Easter Day had been in the city for more than two weeks. More than half had arrived less than a week before, and three had only arrived the preceding evening. Possibly they had come to Augsburg for the Easter season. Some refugees probably thought that their exile would be temporary. A few refugees from Augsburg returned to the city after a few weeks. Others left Augsburg permanently, however, becoming citizens at Strasbourg.

The refugees assured the authorities they had fled their homeland "solely for the sake of the gospel," because they had "hungered for the divine word." [96] Many had already suffered for their beliefs. One refugee at Strasbourg had been in prison at Pforzheim; one had twice escaped from prison at Lahr; a bricklayer of Worms had been chased out of the city at the end of a leash; another man had been whipped and expelled from Altensteig.

The refugees were not entirely forsaken but received help from their fellow believers. Some were told beforehand where they could find assistance. At Augsburg refugees often went straight to the Rossmarkt to the house of Konrad Huber, one of the earliest Anabaptists, who in 1527 administered the common fund. Anabaptists at Rottenburg, Isny, and Augsburg were given the names of leaders at Esslingen who would help them. Of course, not only the leaders but ordinary Anabaptists helped the refugees. The innkeeper Hans Lauterwein at Augsburg took a sick woman into his house and even hired two nurses to take care of her until she died. Asked why she had opened her house to the Anabaptists, one woman said she had received the Lord; another said that she hoped people would also help her banished husband.

The Anabaptists frequently stayed at inns. At Regensburg, for example, three Austrian refugees, two men and a woman, stayed in the inn of one Alkofer. While the woman did the cooking, one of the men carried the water. To be sure, the authorities strictly forbade the innkeepers to receive Anabaptists, but how were they to know who was an Anabaptist? Fear of arrest explains why the refugees at Augsburg constantly changed their lodgings: one man stayed at a different inn every night, and a woman said she had stayed at six different inns. Some refugees also rented rooms.

Of course, the refugees also had to eat. It was partly to alleviate this problem that common funds were established by the Anabaptist congregations. The believers also helped individually. An Augsburg woman who worked as a cook for the innkeeper Lauterwein once brought the refugees two heads of cabbage, a herring, and a small sum of money. Another woman, whose husband ran a laundry, washed the refugees' shirts. In other cases a rich Anabaptist paid a poor brother's rent or the costs of his imprisonment. In August 1528 the few remaining believers of the Augsburg congregation arranged with an innkeeper that they would send poor and hungry Anabaptists to his inn for a bowl of soup and bread, and pay for these meals afterward.

Inevitably, some refugees went too far in demanding assistance from fellow believers: if you are sister, they told a woman, you won't refuse us help. But the sister threw them out of the house. A critic of the Anabaptists at Strasbourg even maintained that the refugees deliberately fleeced their fellow believers. "They shun work as if it were a heresy and live in comfortable corners at the expense of the poor brethren." When the refugees had sucked their brothers dry, he continued, they left and wandered like gypsies from congregation to congregation.[97] These charges are certainly exaggerated. Sixteen of the 41 refugees arrested at Augsburg on Easter 1528 had been employed—the women as seamstresses, maidservants, and nurses, and the men as craftsmen, weavers, and wage laborers. Some had worked in burghers' fields and gardens, where plowing and sowing had just started. Lauterwein had employed fellow believers in building. Indeed, the Anabaptists preferred to employ men and women of their own faith: in 1568 the Swiss leaders at Strasbourg even made employing fellow brethren an obligation. Farmers who were Anabaptists or whose wives were Anabaptists hired refugees during the harvest and haymaking season. Anabaptists employed as farm managers by noblemen gave jobs to fellow believers: during the 1570s and 1580s, for example, the two farm managers and twelve to fourteen workers and maidservants of the lords von Wittershausen in Württemberg were expelled Anabaptists from nearby villages. Refugees who worked for nonbelievers had to be cautious, however. An Anabaptist tailor working at Augsburg never revealed his faith to his employer.

Having sacrificed a great deal for their faith, if not everything, the refugees were particularly religious, and gathered with fellow believers as often as possible. No less than 41 refugees were present at the Augsburg meeting on Easter morning, as compared to 45 Augsburgers. Occasionally there were even more foreigners than Augsburgers at a meeting. The refugees also tried to convert others to their belief: refugees from Switzerland and Swabia brought Anabaptism to Strasbourg. Fearing that Anabaptism would be spread in this way to their area, the authorities made desperate efforts to keep the refugees out. When, for example, Augsburg expelled Anabaptists in October 1527 and April 1528, the Nuremberg officials asked for a list of their names and then questioned newly arriving people carefully. The inns were watched and some of the "loose rabble" arrested. Express warnings against the Anabaptists were issued to the dyers and fustian weavers. By these methods the Nuremberg officials succeeded in identifying several refugees from Augsburg.

One aspect of the persecution is rarely recorded in the documents: the hardship suffered by the innocent relatives of the Anabaptists. Though the families of expelled Anabaptists were generally allowed to stay, the breadwinner was gone. Sometimes those left behind had to be supported by the Poor Law, which implied great humiliation. At Nuremberg the wives of expelled Anabaptists were warned that they would also be driven out if they sent their husbands sectarian books. They had to notify the town council whenever they received or sent letters. Often the wives were badly shaken by the strain of these harrowing events. When an Anabaptist came to tell a woman

at Augsburg that he had seen her husband at Strasbourg, he
noticed how terribly frightened she was and left at once.
The Anabaptists were too concerned with saving their souls to
waste much time worrying about their families.[98]

The Reaction of Non-Anabaptists

How did the general public react to the persecution of the
Anabaptists? The answer depends largely on what sort of material one consults. The officials and theologians complained that
the people thwarted effective measures against the sectarians; yet
the Anabaptists thought of themselves as lambs among wolves.

Many people were immensely impressed by the brethren, especially by their willingness to leave their property for the sake
of their faith. There was talk that the rulers and pastors had
banded together against the Anabaptists, though the brethren
were morally superior to them.[99] Violating the law, some people
flatly refused to support the fight against the Anabaptists. In
1530, 52 men of the villages of Rothenfluh and Andwil near
Basel even made a compact to leave the Anabaptists undisturbed.
All 52 were thrown into prison by the town council. In the village of Urbach in Württemberg the pastor was met with such
hostility whenever he preached against Anabaptist doctrines that
the *schultheiss*, the government representative in the village,
finally advised him not to mention the sect again. People who
went to see the pastor in the parsonage were suspected of being
traitors who had denounced the Anabaptists. In the end day
laborers even hesitated to work for the pastor. One man was
beaten up because he intended to report the participants in an
Anabaptist meeting. In particular, poor people who had received
employment, food, or money from the Anabaptists refused to
help round them up. The officials were called bloodhounds and
accused of jailing people without cause.[100] The governments
were aware of the mood of the people and sometimes ordered
that Anabaptists be taken to prison as quietly as possible.

Actually, some peasants thought that too much fuss was made

about these sectarians. What difference did it really make if an Anabaptist stayed in their village for a few weeks? They were more interested in good food and other worldly matters than in the church, the incensed pastors reported. Peasants who generally had a strong feeling for justice called the practice of confiscating the property of absent Anabaptists an iniquity. Those who were expelled should be allowed to take their property with them, "as was also done in Switzerland." [101] Some people simply did not share the confessional narrow-mindedness of their age. The church of the Anabaptists was also a church of God, a burgher of Strasbourg said. God had His church at Frankfurt, Geneva, Lausanne, or Strasbourg, at Saint Claus or Saint Andreas. Neither the Anabaptist nor the Lutheran doctrine was wrong: everyone who believed in God would be saved.[102]

The punishment of the Anabaptists sometimes caused the governments much embarrassment. If they put an Anabaptist on trial, the jury might refuse to sentence him to death. If, however, the government simply executed him on the basis of the imperial law, the condemned man might protest this injustice before the people. If an Anabaptist was given a regular trial, sentenced, and put to death, people might say that he must have been right, for he suffered and died for his belief. If, however, an Anabaptist was set free, they would say his belief evidently was not wrong.

At the place of execution the harangues delivered by the Anabaptists annoyed the officials terribly. To prevent the Anabaptists from speaking, the officials sometimes tied their tongues. Impressed by the piety and courage of the brethren, people would see miraculous signs at the place of execution the following night. The judge at Sonnenburg in the Tirol, known as a ferocious persecutor of Anabaptists, received threatening letters, and his stable was set on fire. The Tirolese government even feared armed resistance by the people; hence special guards were posted during the sentencing and execution of eighteen Anabaptists at Rattenberg on May 13, 1528, and the heretics were executed at a remote spot rather than the usual place. When justice was done without incident, the officials expressed relief. Their worries were not unreasonable: in 1529 at Schwäbisch Gmünd the people displayed such a menacing attitude that the town council sent an urgent demand to the Swabian League for help. Only after the league's troops had occupied the city did the town council dare to execute the Anabaptist ringleaders.[103] In order to prevent the Anabaptists from acquiring further publicity, the Innsbruck government occasionally ordered secret trials and executions. At Graz and Vienna executions sometimes took place at night or early in the morning.[104]

In Protestant Württemberg, Hesse, and the Palatinate, and in Catholic Solothurn, even the officials felt uneasy about government measures against the Anabaptists. The schultheiss, who was frequently a peasant, was responsible for driving Anabaptists out of the village. But would he carry out the government's orders if his own wife and children were Anabaptists? This was a serious problem in Württemberg, where the Anabaptists had found adherents in no less than 96 families of schultheissen, judges, and *heimbürgen* (administrators of village property) in 59 villages! In one village ten of the twelve judges had relatives in the Hutterite communities. At Urbach 29 close relatives of twelve judges, three heimbürgen, and one schultheiss belonged to the sect in the second half of the sixteenth century. It was largely because of these conditions that Anabaptism found an unusually wide following in this village.

There were also village judges who did not think that the Anabaptists had forfeited all their rights. Much to the chagrin of the government, the judges at Hohenstaufen restored the property of an old Anabaptist couple to them. Here and there, officials tacitly permitted Anabaptists to stay on in villages, even though they had been formally expelled. Others closed their eyes when expelled or fugitive Anabaptists visited relatives or attended a burial, or when Hutterite messengers brought letters and stayed for the night. One judge himself let a Hutterite stay overnight in his house. Whereas the pastor in some places repeatedly reported having seen an expelled Anabaptist in the village, the schultheiss and judges pretended they had not noticed anyone: nobody told them anything, they lamented. But when the pastor specifically told them that an Anabaptist had come, they excused themselves by saying they did not have orders from the government. Anabaptists whose arrest was planned were sometimes warned beforehand by a judge or his wife. There were officials who did not lift a finger when meetings were held in nearby forests. Some even had the effrontery to go to meetings themselves out of curiosity. Disregarding the mandates, some village officials allowed the Hutterites to sell their property and used the opportunity to acquire fields, meadows, and vineyards at greatly reduced prices. The governments had no illusions about what was going on in the villages. Officials who refused to comply with the law were threatened with severe punishment, and a few were even removed from their positions.

In the Hapsburg territories the law courts repeatedly obstructed the attempts of Ferdinand I to eliminate Anabaptism. In 1527 and 1528 the town of Freistadt flatly refused to put Anabaptists on trial, on the ground that it did not have jurisdictional powers. Sometimes the courts would not pass sentence according to the special mandates. At a trial at Steyr in March 1528, the majority of the jurors, 21 out of 34, simply disregarded the mandates by sentencing stubborn Anabaptists only to imprisonment and expulsion. Ferdinand I angrily voided the sentence and insisted that the Anabaptists be beheaded "without further solemnity of the law." When he also demanded the names of the jurors who had not complied with his mandates, he was met by strong protests from the jurors. In the same year jurors at Kitzbühel questioned whether the mandates of Ferdinand had ever been adopted by the Estates, or in other words, whether they were at all legal. Ferdinand now declared that mandates issued by the ruler for the elimination of Anabaptism had the force of law, even if they were not incorporated into the law of the country.

Even the top officials occasionally doubted whether the Anabaptists were really so dangerous. The *obermarschall* at Ansbach had the impression that Spittelmaier was an overwrought student, not a revolutionary.[105] Ferdinand I himself is said to have been horrified by the endless executions in the Tirol.[106] In 1539 and 1543 the government at Innsbruck proposed a temporary halt to all executions. Instead the Anabaptists would be ordered to sell their property and leave within a certain time. But Ferdinand rejected this proposal as a show of mildness that would only increase the number of heretics.[107]

At times the nobility shielded the Anabaptists. More than 38 noblemen in south Germany either employed fugitive and expelled Anabaptists on their estates as managers and craftsmen, or allowed them to live in their villages. What were their motives? The noblemen themselves generally had no Anabaptist leanings, but some, especially in Swabia, had been influenced by Schwenckfeld's broad-minded religious views. Warmhearted ladies with Schwenckfeldian leanings felt compassion for the brethren. The persecution of the Anabaptists also became an issue in the desperate struggle of the imperial knights to maintain their political independence. Some knights declared that they would employ Anabaptists whether the princes liked it or not, and they even forbade the territorial officials to proceed against Anabaptists in their part of a village. Philip of Hesse insinuated that these noblemen hoped to seize the church property in the event of a religious change.[108] Of course, the noblemen also knew that the Anabaptists were conscientious and hardworking. Furthermore, since the brethren were dependent on the nobleman who protected them, he could be certain that in the perennial feuds with his peasants over dues and services, the Anabaptist day laborers would not side with the peasants. This is probably also the reason why some peasants resented the employment of Anabaptists as managers or workers. Finally, there were noblemen who were simply impressed by the piety of their Anabaptist servants. One nobleman was prepared to bury his deceased Anabaptist servant in the chancel if the pastor refused to bury him in the cemetery.

Whatever their motives, many noblemen obstructed government campaigns against the Anabaptists. Ultimately, however, the princes could indeed force the noblemen to get rid of the Anabaptists, for the princes not only granted the noblemen some of their fiefs but also employed them as administrators, officers, and courtiers. Usually the Anabaptists stayed on the estate of a nobleman only a few years. Above all, it must be remembered that the majority of noblemen did not tolerate Anabaptists, just as the vast majority of jurors and officials obeyed the orders of the government and punished the Anabaptists according to the law.

It would also be a distortion to say that only the pastors bore malice against the brethren, whereas the population at large helped and admired them. As long as there were only a handful of Anabaptists in an area, people did not mind, but it was another matter when large numbers flocked to the same place. Tension developed at Markirch, a mining town in Alsace, where Egenolph von Rappoltstein tolerated not only Calvinists, Zwinglians and Schwenckfeldians but also various Anabaptists such as Gabrielites (disciples of Gabriel Ascherham), sundry followers of Marbeck and Sattler, and others. On May 29, 1561, the "common society, miners, and burghers" of Markirch formally asked Rappoltstein to get rid of these "cruel" sectarians. They were forced to make this request, they said, because first of all the Anabaptists were buying up houses and farms, so that a poor miner was unable to buy even a small house or a cottage; second, the Anabaptists did not pay the taxes that maintained government, pastor, church, and school, though they enjoyed the protection of the community; third, in times of war, the Anabaptists would simply ride away, leaving the poor miners to defend the country; and finally, the Anabaptists had created great religious confusion by insinuating themselves into houses and turning people's heads with their sophistries, so that no one clearly knew any longer what to believe. Determined to end this chaos, the people of Markirch voted democratically to adopt the Augsburg Confession as their faith. They would not tolerate Anabaptists in the mines, they said. The Anabaptists must either accept the Augsburg Confession or leave; otherwise, the miners would themselves leave.[109]

In Hesse, Alsace, and Württemberg, angry peasants also demanded that the Anabaptists either meet the obligations of an ordinary citizen and go to church like everyone else, or get out. The peasants were irritated by the Anabaptists' secret meetings, which they felt might lead to new conspiracies and bloodshed. People also grew weary of being called epicureans or drunkards. Sometimes Anabaptists were shunned by the peasants, evicted by their landlords, ridiculed and insulted in the streets. Some villagers even pursued the fleeing emigrants and took everything they had.[110] Such people obviously had no objection to the suppression of the sect.

How are we to explain this hostility? The persistent warnings of the authorities to avoid the Anabaptists, in the long run had their effect on public opinion. Many were genuinely shocked, too, by the excesses of the Anabaptist Kingdom of Münster. Even in later years, people were suspicious of sectarians who gathered at night in desolate places to conduct their rites.

If some people admired the Anabaptists and others disliked them, the mass of the population did not care one way or the other. A pious Catholic or Protestant simply regarded the Anabaptist doctrines as errors that did not interest him. Average Catholics and Protestants who went to church on Sunday but shied away from excessive piety were even less attracted by the religious intensity and moral rigor of the Anabaptists. Just as there were few who took monastic vows, so there were few who were willing to meet the exacting demands of this new sect. In any case, most people hardly ever encountered the Anabaptists, or if they did, forgot them in daily worries over food, work, health, or family. It was not only persecution but the limited appeal of the movement itself that prevented Anabaptism from ever attracting a large proportion of the population to its ranks.

Conclusion

During the sixteenth and the early seventeenth century thousands of perfectly harmless people suffered under harsh persecution because they were Anabaptists. Some got off relatively lightly by fleeing to Moravia, to be sure, but others had to pay with their lives. The persecution of Anabaptists may be viewed as one of the dark episodes of the sixteenth century, when people seem to have been driven by an irrational urge to suppress forcibly any religious view that conflicted with their own. Even so, it would be unfair to condemn the sixteenth century governments for trying to suppress Anabaptism. As we have seen, their attempt to maintain the monopoly of the established churches by law was based on time-honored principles of political philosophy. Certainly one cannot expect sixteenth-century governments to have displayed the same religious toleration characteristic of the liberal governments of the nineteenth century. The sixteenth-century governments have to be judged by sixteenth-century standards.

Nevertheless, one can only wonder whether—at least after the first turbulent years, or during the second half of the sixteenth century—the officials did not realize that the Anabaptists were only pious sectarians who did not harm anyone. As we have seen, some governments did begin to doubt the need for violent suppression and accordingly relented to a certain degree. But the imperial and territorial laws did not permit a basic change of policy, and it is unlikely that most governments and bureaucrats even considered such a change: that Anabaptists were not to be tolerated had become a widely accepted tradition. Furthermore, the general religious conditions were not conducive to a policy of toleration. As the sixteenth century wore on the animosity among Catholics, Lutherans, and Calvinists intensified until it exploded in the Thirty Years' War. In this atmosphere of religious hatred, the Anabaptists had even less chance to go their way in peace.

Whereas all Catholic and Protestant governments concurred in the policy of suppressing Anabaptism, their methods varied. First, in many Catholic territories, especially Bavaria and the Tirol, the death penalty remained the standard punishment for steadfast Anabaptists up to the Thirty Years' War. In the Protestant territories and cities, ordinary Anabaptists who refused to recant were usually expelled, and leaders imprisoned. Lutheran Saxony and the Zwinglian cities of Switzerland, which executed Anabaptists, were exceptions. Second, the legal charges used against Anabaptists by different governments were not quite the same. Catholic governments charged Anabaptists with heresy and rebellion; Luther's Saxony similarly charged them with blasphemy and rebellion. The Swiss cities, however, sentenced them to death for violating the civil laws.

Third, the legal proceedings were different. Courts of summary jurisdiction were used only by Catholic authorities, such as those in Austria, Salzburg, Bavaria, and the Swabian League in 1527 and 1528. Mass executions of a dozen or more Anabaptists were perpetrated only by Catholic governments. And only Catholic governments ever executed Anabaptists who had recanted. By contrast, the Protestant governments typically used all the persuasive powers at their command to win the sectarians back to the established church. At no time did any Protestant government pass the sentence of death on an Anabaptist who had abandoned his views. Finally, the difference between Protestant and Catholic policy toward the Anabaptists is borne out by the numerical evidence: 84 percent of all executions were perpetrated in Catholic territories, and only 16 percent in territories and cities that were Protestant or had Protestant leanings.

The severe methods used by the Catholic governments undoubtedly produced more successful results than the milder measures of the Protestant governments. In Catholic Austria, Salzburg, and Bavaria, Anabaptism was practically eliminated in 1527 and 1528. In the Tirol the mass executions achieved their aim by the middle of the sixteenth century. In Protestant Württemberg, Hesse, and the Palatinate, by contrast, Anabaptism flourished up to the Thirty Years' War.

In the long run, however, the refusal of most Protestant governments to put Anabaptists to death was much more significant than the success of the Catholic governments' harsher policy, for the German Protestants had unknowingly taken a decisive step toward religious toleration. It is unrealistic to expect the bloody intolerance of the late Middle Ages to have given way overnight to the universal religious toleration of nineteenth-century Germany: indeed, the evolution of religious toleration took centuries. But the step from executing heretics to letting them live was an essential one, even if the death sentence was replaced by expulsion. After all, the great dividing line is that between life and death: it was during the sixteenth century that most Protestant governments in the Empire chose life for the heretic. By focusing only on the views of the Reformers and disregarding the actual policy of the governments and the statistical evidence, most twentieth-century historians who have dealt with the subject, such as Ernst Troeltsch, Joseph Lecler, and Henry Kamen, have failed to grasp the role of the Reformation in the development of religious toleration.

It seems slightly paradoxical that the Catholic policy of killing stubborn Anabaptists was backward but effective, whereas the Protestant policy of expulsion instead of death was progressive but ineffective. Actually, the most progressive approach of all—toleration—might well have been the best method of eliminating the destructive tendencies of Anabaptism. The history of Dutch Anabaptism shows that the sect changed its nature once it was tolerated. When the brethren were given no occasion to suffer, their intellectual and emotional orientation changed drastically. Industrious and frugal, they soon became wealthy, and at least some of them subsequently developed into sects of prosperous bourgeois who finally abandoned their former condemnation of government, wealth, and worldly culture. Of course, this evolution took years. But it is possible that in the Empire, too, over the course of a century, toleration would have eroded some of the harsh features of Anabaptism into a less threatening form.

12

Conclusions

Over the course of a century almost any religious movement could be expected to show some signs of change. Even if its central doctrines were strictly upheld, the manifold events and forces in the surrounding society would inevitably have their effect. In spite of all loyalty to their faith, the new generations of believers would view some problems differently than their parents. It is not surprising, then, that the Anabaptist movement changed considerably between 1525 and 1618. First of all, the momentum of the movement fell off drastically. Whereas the early movement, owing to its vigorous leaders, had spread to hundreds of towns and villages throughout Switzerland, Austria, and Germany, by 1600 Anabaptism had been reduced to a small sect limited largely to the area of Zurich, to certain districts in Württemberg, the Palatinate, and Hesse, and to Moravia. Similarly, its membership base narrowed. Early Anabaptism had attracted at least some well-to-do burghers and intellectuals, but by 1600 those who accepted rebaptism were largely uneducated village folk who were far removed from the intellectual life of their time.

Although there had been numerous divergent tendencies in early Anabaptism, the brethren of the 1520s had regarded each other as fellow believers; the differences between the groups were still undefined and fluid. By the end of the sixteenth century, the Swiss Brethren and the Hutterites, the two major groups, were deeply divided by sharply distinct doctrines and customs, and by bitter hostility. Whereas the early Anabaptists had aimed at a sweeping spiritual reform, the later Anabaptists rarely saw beyond sectarian and parochial interests. At the same time, the Anabaptists were no longer divided by the feverish tendencies of certain groups—the eschatological expectations, ecstatic experiences, revolutionary schemes, and radical political views that had appeared sporadically during the 1520s and 1530s. Practices that had challenged the existing class structure of the sixteenth century, such as community of goods or the abolition of titles, by 1600 were viewed as harmless peculiarities of pious sectarians.

Even the spirit of Hutterite Anabaptism seems to have changed. Though the communities kept their religious characters, at least in some the former spiritual fervor and discipline slackened, perhaps owing to the absence of persecution in Moravia. This change is reflected in the Hutterite Chronicle. Whereas the early parts of the Chronicle are devoted to the heroic suffering of the Anabaptist martyrs, the sections dealing with the late sixteenth and the early seventeenth century frequently discuss only quarrels with the government and nobility or economic losses sustained during the Hapsburg wars.

In Germany and Switzerland, nevertheless, Anabaptism changed little over the years. Ironically enough, the fact that the German and Swiss brethren remained outlawed and were persecuted as heretics until the Thirty Years' War may well have kept alive their religious fervor. While the government of the Palatinate might have been lax at times in enforcing its laws, the governments of Hesse, Württemberg, and Zurich made great efforts to stamp out the Anabaptist congregations. In Zurich, and especially in Catholic territories such as Bavaria and the Tirol, loyal Anabaptists still faced the death penalty. Up until the Thirty Years' War the German and Swiss brethren had to meet secretly at night in forests and shacks to worship, baptize, and celebrate the Lord's Supper. Thus even in the early seventeenth century it required strong convictions and great courage for a German or a Swiss to accept a second baptism. The piety of those who did was as genuine and deep as that of the first congregation at Zollikon. From its beginnings in January 1525 until 1618, indeed, Anabaptism was primarily a religious movement rather than a political one. Thousands of documents reveal that throughout the century the overwhelming mass of brethren were deeply concerned with their salvation. If we do not recognize the spiritual force of Anabaptism, we fail to understand the movement altogether.

But if Anabaptism was based on religious impulses, the Anabaptists also introduced ideas that changed or were intended to change the most basic institutions and practices of sixteenth-century society. Like Müntzer, the Anabaptists were convinced that the existing society made it impossible to lead a truly Christian life. But whereas Müntzer chose the path of violent revolution, the Anabaptists only condemned the existing political institutions as unchristian and withdrew from the world as much as possible. Even so, their position had dangerous implications. By condemning law courts, oaths, the legal use of force, and indeed, government itself as unchristian, the peaceful brethren became a potential threat to civilization. Thus, ironically, these meek people, who endeavored in the name of Christ to establish the kingdom of love, in reality seemed to be bent on destroying civilization. Of course, the political doctrines of the Anabaptists never gained widespread acceptance. It appears that the Anabaptist leaders themselves did not expect the mass of mankind to accept their unusual doctrines, but aimed only at assembling small groups of pious believers, while government and law would continue to exist among unregenerate mankind.

The Anabaptists also challenged the basic tenets of sixteenth-century society by disregarding the traditional right of the spiritual authorities to decide doctrinal questions. Of course, Luther, too, had rebelled against pope and emperor. But in Saxony the learned theologians remained the final authority in deciding the true doctrine, and the decision was then enforced by the elector. In spite of the collapse of the Catholic Church, the sixteenth-century territorial state maintained a strict order.

Each social class had its functions: the theologian would not tell the craftsman how to do his job, nor would the craftsman decide questions of theology. It was this time-honored tradition the Anabaptists sought to discard. Grebel and his friends refused to recognize the theologians' authority and cared even less for orders issued by the government on matters of belief.

In other words, the Anabaptists rejected not only the prevailing religion, as Luther had done, but the principle of authority on which sixteenth-century society was based. Of course, this rejection of authority backfired on the Anabaptist leaders themselves, for their authority might in turn be questioned by any inspired believer. A new chapter in the history of Christianity had begun: from that time onward, numerous laymen were to reject the theologians' authority and start their own movements. Thus the small Anabaptist movement in our area eventually proliferated into at least twenty different groups, each with its own special doctrines and practices, and each rejecting the validity of the others.

The boldness of the Anabaptists in defying authority suggests a distinct democratic tendency in sixteenth-century Germany. The time was past when common people meekly submitted to orders from the church or government. Even when they faced powerful government officials, these courageous craftsmen and peasants demanded scriptural proof that they had erred, and often flatly refused to abandon their convictions. A similar democratic tendency can be seen in the congregational type of church, which the Anabaptists were the first to organize in Germany, Austria, and Switzerland: the individual congregation had no superior; it was independent and democratically organized. The Anabaptist church structure was thus totally different from the authoritarian and bureaucratic structure of the Catholic and Lutheran churches. At the same time Anabaptism foreshadowed the Pietist movement by offering a personal, intimate type of religious life in small circles. That there was no provision for pious conventicles within the established church was one of the signal failures of sixteenth-century Protestantism.

Some Anabaptists did distinguish themselves by their revolutionary tendencies, as we have seen, but whereas the few who dreamed of bloody revolution achieved nothing apart from incurring violent persecution by the authorities, the Hutterites, who eschewed the use of force and withdrew to Moravia, succeeded in building a new type of communistic and egalitarian society. While the sensational and bloody Kingdom of Münster gripped the attention of Europe, these simple Hutterite craftsmen and peasants achieved the most successful social revolution of the sixteenth century.

The Anabaptists, then, did go new ways. But did their ideas and actions have much influence on the rest of society? According to the evidence, the Anabaptists failed to attract large masses of the population in any area, although the Tirol might be an exception. We have seen that the Anabaptists had a relatively large following only during the first five years, from 1525 to 1529. From then onward, the number of believers steadily declined in Germany, Switzerland, and Austria for three reasons: suppression by the authorities, emigration to Moravia, and above all, the growing indifference of the population. We have estimated that an average of three thousand people joined the movement every ten years. But how significant are three thousand converts in a population of several million over the entire area of south and central Germany, Switzerland, and Austria? If in a town of a thousand inhabitants, two or three pious old women or journeymen refused to go to church and instead met in a barn to pray and read the Bible, we can hardly say that they represented a reformation movement. They were typical separatists or sectarians, earnest Christians who withdrew from the heathen world.

The Anabaptists had only token influence on the customs and organization of the Protestant churches in the sixteenth century. It was partly because of the Anabaptists that the confirmation service was introduced in many churches. As we have seen, the adoption of baptismal registers was also prompted by the appearance of this sect. But these innovations came about as part of the defense against Anabaptism rather than in any admiring imitation of Anabaptist customs.

The Anabaptists had no discernible impact on the political, economic, or social institutions of their age. It was a fantasy to hope that love could take the place of law and government. The Anabaptist doctrine that government must not interfere in religious affairs was not adopted by any government of the period. It is also questionable whether the Anabaptists really influenced the modern notion of separation of church and state, which developed in the Anglo-Saxon countries during the seventeenth and eighteenth centuries. The rejection of interest on loans by all Anabaptist groups, and commerce by some, could not stave off the growing commercialization of the sixteenth-century economy; of course, the more radical communism of the Hutterites had even less effect. Similarly, the Anabaptists had little, if any, influence on sixteenth-century culture. To be sure, some of their treatises and hymns reveal religious insight and powers of expression, but there is no evidence that these works circulated outside of Anabaptist circles. While the humanistic ideal of learning and elegance prevailed in both Catholic and Protestant Germany, higher education and aesthetic culture were angrily condemned by the brethren. Indeed, the Anabaptists in south and central Germany, Switzerland, and Austria already exhibited in the sixteenth century a cultural primitivism that has characterized some Anabaptist groups down to our own day.

We cannot deny that the Anabaptists displayed intense, genuine piety and outstanding moral vigor. The Hutterites also showed extraordinary organizational talent in creating an entirely new type of society. Yet these phenomena must be kept in proper perspective. However fascinating the Anabaptist movement was, it cannot be called more than a minor episode in the history of sixteenth-century German society.

Appendix A

The Density and Persistence of Anabaptism in Towns and Villages

The density of Anabaptism in towns and villages from 1525 to 1618 can be summarized as shown in the following table:

No. of Anabaptists	No. of towns and villages			
	1525–1529	1530–1549	1550–1618	1525–1618
1–4	352	607	602	1,220
5–9	48	74	69	169
10–30	34	39	44	106
31–100	18	12	12	36
Over 100	2	0	1	5
Uncertain	53	101	148	285
Total	507	833	876	1,821

Making allowances for the clandestine character of the sect, we assume that there was a certain continuity if Anabaptists were discovered in a town or village at least once every ten years, for example, in 1525, 1534, and 1543. If no new Anabaptist was reported within ten years after the appearance of the last Anabaptist, we assume that the continuity was broken. Of course, in some communities Anabaptism reappeared after twenty, thirty, or forty years. But it seems unlikely that Anabaptists could have lived in a town or village for dozens of years without being noticed by the authorities. Presumably outside leaders had again brought Anabaptism to such a town or village after the first Anabaptists had recanted, emigrated, or died.

In 78 towns or villages Anabaptists appeared for a period of ten years; in fourteen towns or villages, for twenty years; in five towns or villages, for thirty years; in two towns or villages, for forty years; and in two towns or villages, for fifty years.

Appendix B

Anabaptist Groups

Anabaptist groups that appeared in south and central Germany, Switzerland, Austria, and Moravia between 1525 and 1618 are listed below in alphabetical order, followed by their specific area and period of activity. In cases where the name of the group is unknown, the name of its leader is given.

Both: Sorga, 1527–33
Cornelians: Moravia, 1538–1622
Denck: Strasbourg, 1526; Bergzabern, Landau, and Worms, 1527; Regensburg, 1539
Gabrielites: Moravia, 1528–68; Markirch, 1561–62
Hofmann: Strasbourg, 1530–39
Hubmaier, Sword Bearers: Waldshut, 1525; Zurich(?), 1526; Moravia, 1526–35
Hut: Franconia, 1526–28; Salzburg and Passau, 1527; Bavaria, lower and upper Austria, and Swabia, 1527–28; Hesse, 1578 (Huttische Brüder)
Hutterites: The Tirol, 1528–1618; Swabia, Hesse, the Rhine valley, and Switzerland, 1530s–1618; Franconia, 1530s, 1570s; Moravia, 1531–1622
Kautz: Worms, 1527; Strasbourg, 1528
Marbeck: Strasbourg, 1530–1540s; Kinzig and Leber valleys, 1530s–1540s, 1560s–1590s; Moravia, 1538–1622; Graubünden and Augsburg, 1540s–1560s, Esslingen(?), 1544
Mennonites(?) or Hofmannites(?): Esslingen, 1535; Württemberg, 1540s
Philippites: Kraichgau and Bruhrain, 1528–29; Moravia, 1528–38; area of Heilbronn, 1529–39; areas of Worms and Strasbourg, 1535–39; Land ob der Enns, 1537–41

Römer: Thuringia, 1527–28
Sabbatarians: Moravia, ca. 1530–68
Scharf: Mühlhausen, 1534–37
Schnabel: Hesse, 1533–38
Spahl group: Spahl, 1532
Staff Bearers, Austerlitzers: Moravia, 1527–59
Swiss Brethren: Switzerland, 1525–1618; the Tirol, 1526–29; the
     Rhine valley and Swabia, 1526–1618; Moravia, late 1520s–1622;
     Hesse, 1553–87
Thuringian Anabaptism (leaders: Alexander, Kraut, Storger):
     Thuringia, 1530–37

Listed below are several Anabaptist leaders who may have founded
their own groups, though it is not known whether they did. Also
listed are several special groups that may or may not have been
Anabaptist.

Brandhuber: Linz, 1528–29
Bünderlin: Strasbourg, 1528
Entfelder: Eibenschitz (Moravia), 1526–28; Strasbourg, ca. 1530
Enthusiasts: Moravia, 1568
Fatalists: St. Gallen, 1525
Hessenbrüder: Eastern Hesse, 1555
Libertines: St. Gallen, 1525; Moravia, 1568
Rinck: Eastern Hesse, 1528–31
Spiritualists: St. Gallen, 1525

Appendix C

Statistics on the Occupations of Anabaptists

The occupations of known Anabaptist intellectuals between 1525 and 1618 are listed below, followed by the number of intellectuals in each occupation.

bishop, 1	German clerk
prior, 3	(*Teutsch schreiber*), 1
monk, 12	town clerk
priest or minister, 68	(*stadtschreiber*), 3
humanist scholar, 2	district clerk
magister, 1	(*landgerichts-*
schoolmaster, 34	*schreiber*), 1
student, 6	clerk of law court
book printer, 1	(*gerichtsschreiber*), 1
proofreader, 1	clerk of works
"corrector," 1	(*werkschreiber*), 1
book trader, 2	mining official, 3
physician, 16	notary, 1
apothecary, 1	artist, 6
judge, 1	architect, 1
clerk (*schreiber*), 4	uncertain, 4

The occupations of known Anabaptist craftsmen between 1525 and 1618 are listed below, followed by the number of Anabaptist craftsmen in each occupation, and in parentheses, the number of Anabaptist craftsmen and Anabaptist wives of craftsmen.

Textiles

bleacher, 2 (2)	clothmaker, 13 (17)
clothier, 1 (1)	cloth shearer, 13 (15)

crape maker, 2 (2)
dyer, 4 (6)
dyer in blue, 1 (2)
furrier, 28 (34)
hatter, 7 (8)
lace maker, 2 (3)
mangler, 3 (5)
netter, 1 (1)

old-clothes man, 1 (2)
rope spinner, 9 (10)
seamstress, 14 (14)
tailor, 133 (166)
weaver, 160 (203)
weaver of fine cloth, 3 (4)
weaver of grey cloth, 1 (1)
wool carder, 4 (6)

Metals

armorer, 2 (2)
blacksmith, 42 (48)
boilermaker, 6 (7)
borer, 3 (3)
coppersmith, 1 (1)
cutler, 20 (28)
goldbeater, 1 (2)
goldsmith, 13 (24)
gunpowder maker, 1 (2)
gunsmith, 3 (3)
haft maker, 1 (1)
harness maker, 2 (2)
harness polisher, 1 (1)
iron-lantern maker, 1 (1)
ironmaster, 1 (1)
locksmith, 12 (17)
miner, 32 (37)

needle maker, 7 (10)
pewterer, 1 (1)
pitcher maker, 5 (6)
ring maker, 5 (5)
saw filer, 1 (2)
scythesmith, 3 (3)
sicklesmith, 1 (1)
maker of points for shoes, 2 (2)
silver refiner, 1 (1)
spur maker, 5 (5)
sword cutler, 1 (1)
tinker, 1 (1)
tinsmith, 1 (1)
trap maker, 1 (1)
watchmaker, 5 (5)
windlass maker, 2 (2)

Foods

baker, 32 (48)
beer brewer, 2 (2)
butcher, 12 (18)
cellar man, 4 (4)
cook, 3 (3)
fisher, 4 (6)
gardener, 4 (4)
gatherer of herbs, 2 (3)
gingerbread baker, 2 (4)

innkeeper, 18 (24)
miller, 69 (90)
salt carrier, 1 (1)
salter, 1 (1)
sugar maker, 1 (2)
weigher of bread, 1 (1)
winegrower, 3 (4)
wine maker, 2 (3)

Wood

basket weaver, 3 (3)   maker of window frames, 1 (1)
bow maker, 2 (2)   papermaker, 0 (1)
cabinetmaker, 37 (44)   resin scraper, 1 (1)
cartwright, 7 (7)   sawmiller, 3 (5)
charcoal burner, 3 (4)   turner, 9 (9)
cooper, 19 (23)   wheelwright, 1 (1)
fence maker, 1 (1)   worker in wood, 2 (2)
maker of shoe trees, 2 (2)

Construction

bricklayer, 16 (19)   gauger, 1 (2)
bricklayer's man, 2 (2)   roofer, 1 (1)
carpenter, 28 (37)   well digger, 1 (1)
construction worker, 1 (3)   worker in water tower, 1 (1)
engineer, 1 (2)

Stone

brick burner, 2 (2)   potter, 11 (13)
cup maker, 1 (1)   slate cutter, 2 (4)
glassmaker, 19 (32)   stonemason, 10 (13)
master paver, 2 (2)   tile maker, 1 (1)

Leather

belt maker, 4 (5)   saddler, 8 (11)
cobbler, 103 (118)   strap maker, 1 (1)
purse maker, 11 (14)   tanner, 12 (19)

Other Crafts

barber, 1 (1)   bookbinder, 4 (4)
bathhouse keeper, 13 (15)   book printer, 2 (3)
midwife, 5 (5)   card maker, 2 (2)
wet nurse, 1 (1)   quill maker, 1 (1)

candlemaker, 1 (2)   boatman, 5 (5)
soap-boiler, 1 (1)   carter, 2 (2)

executioner, 1 (1)   fruit vendor, 0 (1)
gravedigger, 0 (1)   huckster, 11 (13)
knacker, 1 (1)   shopkeeper, 4 (5)

There were 25 (27) craftsmen whose exact occupation is not known. In addition, the occupation of several craftsmen could not be identified:

beschauer, (1)	*wescher*, 2 (3)
fewrer, 1 (1)	*zettelstube*, 3 (3)
korenruerer, 1 (1)	*zunft zum spiegel*, 1 (1)

The estimated number of Anabaptist craftsmen and farmers is given below. The percentages represent the proportion of craftsmen and farmers to the total number of Anabaptists during that period.

Group	1525–1529 No. (%)	1530–1549 No. (%)	1550–1618 No. (%)	1525–1618 No. (%)
Craftsmen				
Minimum *	1,492 (41.2)	1,124 (30.5)	545 (14.1)	3,161 (28.3)
Maximum †	2,200 (60.8)	1,526 (41.4)	826 (21.3)	4,552 (40.7)
Farmers				
Minimum ‡	1,214 (33.6)	2,058 (55.8)	2,984 (77.1)	6,256 (56.0)
Maximum §	1,922 (53.1)	2,460 (66.7)	3,265 (84.3)	7,647 (68.4)

* (1) Anabaptists in small towns and villages who were definitely craftsmen, plus (2) Anabaptists in imperial cities, capitals, or large territorial towns who were not nobles or intellectuals, or engaged in miscellaneous occupations, and therefore may be assumed to be craftsmen.

† (1)Anabaptists in villages who were definitely craftsmen, plus (2) Anabaptists in all towns who were not nobles or intellectuals, or engaged in miscellaneous occupations.

‡ Rural Anabaptists who were not nobles, intellectuals, or craftsmen, or engaged in miscellaneous occupations, and therefore may be assumed to be farmers.

§ Rural Anabaptists and Anabaptists in small towns who were not nobles, intellectuals, or craftsmen, or engaged in miscellaneous occupations.

The occupational structure of the Anabaptist movement is summarized in the table below:

Area and period	Total	Nobles	Intellectuals	Miscellaneous	Craftsmen	Rest (approx.)	Farmers (approx.)
Cities *							
1525–1529	1,347	1	48	72	1,226 †	0	0
1530–1549	958	1	19	43	895 †	0	0
1550–1618	262	2	5	4	251 †	0	0
Total	2,567	4	72	119	2,372 †	0	0
Small towns							
1525–1529	900	2	33	5	152	708	0
1530–1549	483	0	8	2	71	402	0
1550–1618	355	0	8	6	60	281	0
Total	1,738	2	49	13	283	1,391	0
Villages and farms							
1525–1529	1,079	3	15	10	102	0	949
1530–1549	1,736	10	3	13	122	0	1,588
1550–1618	2,838	1	10	12	202	0	2,613
Total	5,653	14	28	35	426	0	5,150
Residence unknown							
1525–1529	291	0	14	0	12	0	265
1530–1549	510	0	4	0	36	0	470
1550–1618	416	4	9	0	32	0	371
Total	1,217	4	27	0	80	0	1,106

* Imperial cities, Swiss cities, capitals, and large towns.
† Approximate number of craftsmen.

Appendix D

Statistics on the
Execution of Anabaptists

The number of Anabaptists known to have been executed between 1525 and 1618 is given below.

Period	Switzer- land	Rhine valley	Swabia	Hapsburg terri- tories	South- east	Fran- conia	Thurin- gia and Fulda	Total
1525–29	13	14	39	223+x	80	29	12	410+x
1530–39	48	24+x	47	167	20+x	3	61	370+x
1540–49	3	0	0	9	4	0	0	16
1550–59	0	x	0	2	3	3	0	8+x
1560–69	1	0	0	4	2	0	0	7
1570–79	1	1	1	1	0	0	1	5
1580–89	2	0	0	2	9	0	0	13
1590–99	1	0	0	3	2	0	0	6
1600–09	0	0	0	0	2	0	0	2
1610–18	1	0	0	2	0	0	0	3
Uncertain	3	0	0	0	0	0	0	3
Total	73	39+x	87	413+x	122+x	35	74	843+x

Note: In addition two persons were executed in unknown places, one in 1528 and the other in 1529. Thus the actual total known to have been executed is 845.

x signifies an additional unknown number of executed persons.

437

Notes

Full authors' names, titles, and publication data for works cited in the Notes will be found in the Bibliography. Sources from archives are identified in the Notes and Bibliography by bracketed numbers for convenience in citation.

Chapter 1

1. Bender, *Grebel*, 101.
2. *Liber Confutationis* and a little treatise on baptism (Fast, *Bullinger*, 126; Bender, *Grebel*, 186–88).
3. Muralt and Schmid, 23–28.
4. *Ibid.*, 13–21.
5. Fast, *Bullinger*, 77–106; Bender, "Zwickau Prophets."
6. Walther Köhler, "Wiedertäufer," in Herman Gunkel and Leopold Zscharnak, eds., *Religion in Geschichte und Gegenwart*, V (Tübingen, 1917); see also Muralt, 6–7.
7. Hillerbrand, "Anabaptism."
8. Hillerbrand, "Origin."
9. Clemen, II, 305.
10. "Liebhaber Gottes"; "die waren Liebhaber Gottes"; "die geliebten Gottes"; "die lieben Gottes" (*ibid.*; Jakobs, 521, 522; Zieglschmid, *Älteste Chronik*, 78).
11. Bender, "Discipline," 61.
12. Muralt and Schmid, 69.
13. "Von der Taufe, von der Wiedertaufe und von der Kindertaufe." In the Zurich documents the term Wiedertäufer, "Rebap-

tizer," appears for the first time in a report of Hans Brenwald, pastor of Hinwil, to the Zurich town council on November 13, 1525 (Muralt and Schmid, 129). Two days later it appears in a decree of the Zurich town council. *Ibid.*, 131.

14. The term Widertäufer appeared in 1526 at Strasbourg (Krebs and Rott, *Elsass*, I, 57), in 1527 at Constance, Überlingen, Landau, Frankfurt, the Palatinate, Ulm, Nuremberg, and Bavaria (Franz, *Urkundliche Quellen*, 1; Krebs, 116, 429, 451, 473; Schornbaum, Bayern, I, 28; Munich [28]); in 1528 at Esslingen, the bishopric of Speyer, Mainz, Heilbronn, Hesse, Württemberg, and Bamberg, and in the imperial laws and in resolutions of the Swabian League (Bossert 1*, 4; Karlsruhe [19], Esslingen, Jan. 10, 1528; Franz, *Urkundliche Quellen*, 16; Krebs, 477; Wappler, *Stellung Kursachsens*, 237, 238). At Bamberg, Nuremberg, Henneberg, and the area of Königsberg, the term Täufer first referred only to the leader who baptized (for Bamberg in 1527, Wappler, *Täuferbewegung*, 235, 239; Nuremberg [38], Ratsverlässe, Sept. 11, 1528; for Henneberg, 1527, Wappler, *Täuferbewegung*, 249; for the area of Königsberg, 1527, *ibid.*, 256). In the course of 1527 the authorities at Bamberg and Nuremberg began to refer to the sectarians in general as Täufer or Widertäufer (Wappler, *Stellung Kursachsens*, 238, and *Täuferbewegung*, 280; for Henneberg in 1531, *ibid.*, 325).

When the sectarians first appeared in Austria and Thuringia, the governments were not quite sure what to call them. In August 1527 the Austrian officials spoke of Hut and his followers (Mecenseffy, 1, 3, 13), but from October 1527 on the term Widertäufer became more and more common. In Thuringia and also at Nuremberg, the early sectarians were sometimes referred to as Schwermer (for Erfurt in 1527, Wappler, *Stellung Kursachsens*, 131; for the duchy of Saxony in 1527, Wappler, *Täuferbewegung*, 252, 253, and in 1530, *ibid.*, 320; Nuremberg [38], Ratsverlässe, Feb. 14 and 19, 1527) or Tauf Schwermer (for the duchy of Saxony, Wappler, *Täuferbewegung*, 275). Erfurt also spoke ironically of newly baptized Christian brethren (*ibid.*, 250–51), or the Christian Taufbrüder (*ibid.*, 251). On December 31, 1527, Duke Georg of Saxony used the term Widertäufer or Getewfte for the first time. In both the duchy of Saxony and Electoral Saxony, "Widertäufer" soon became the ordinary expression (*ibid.*, 327, 355; Wappler, *Stellung Kursachsens*, 134).

The term Täufer was used at Bamberg in 1527, for example, and sometimes at Strasbourg (Krebs and Rott, *Elsass*, II, 23).

15. For "Frytouffer," see Dürr and Roth, III, 353, 379, 380; for "Touffbrüder" in 1529, *ibid.*, IV, 337, and at Erfurt in 1527, Wappler, *Täuferbewegung*, 251; for "Contrateuffer" in 1528, Krebs, 477; for "Gartenbrüder" and "Gartenschwestern," Roth, "Geschichte der Wiedertäufer III," 14.

16. In German works it sometimes appeared in marginal remarks written in Latin (Krebs and Rott, *Elsass*, I, 66, 137) or as a note (*ibid.*, 528). For Latin works see *ibid.*, 72.

17. Zwingli, *In catabaptistarum strophus elenchus* (1527).

18. Bossert, 137, 393, 657, 808, 812, 833; Franz, *Urkundliche Quellen*, 400; Krebs, 324; Kluckhohn, I, 410; Wappler, *Täuferbewegung*, 346.

19. Franz, *Urkundliche Quellen*, 350.

20. Goshen, Ind. [13], Aug. 3, 1555; Wappler, *Täuferbewegung*, 440.

Chapter 2

1. As early as 1524 Clemens Ziegler, a spiritualist at Strasbourg, had rejected infant baptism and advocated the baptism of adult believers, but we have no evidence that Ziegler himself ever baptized anyone. In August 1525, however, a pastor at Basel referred to Anabaptists at Strasbourg (Krebs and Rott, *Elsass*, I, 586), and in January 1528 a woman at Landau claimed to have been baptized three years earlier at Rodt near Weissenburg (Krebs, 429). It is possible that Ziegler started this movement; it is also possible that refugees from Switzerland or Waldshut had come to Strasbourg and Weissenburg in 1525. In 1523 and 1524 the Zwickau prophets and Thomas Müntzer had also rejected infant baptism and demanded the baptism of believers, but there is no evidence that they baptized adults. In 1535, however, a woman claimed that more than ten years earlier she had been baptized by the leader Bernhardus at Lauterholz in the Harz

Mountains (Jakobs, 529). In 1529 a man at Königsberg in Franconia said that the brotherhood had started soon after the peasant uprising (Wappler, *Täuferbewegung*, 313). We do not know whether he meant 1525 or, as is more likely, 1526, when Hut indeed preached and baptized at Königsberg. A woman at Hünfeld in Hersfeld said in 1575 that she had been baptized during the Peasant War (Franz, *Urkundliche Quellen*, 380). Was she really referring to 1525?

2. Wappler, *Stellung Kursachsens*, 131.

3. Some of the Anabaptist groups formed as follows: in 1525 at Zurich, Basel, Schaffhausen, St. Gallen, and Waldshut; in 1526 at Strasbourg, Landau, Augsburg, Rottenburg, Freistadt, and Steyr; in 1527 at Bern, Lindau, Worms, Esslingen, Heilbronn, Ulm, Memmingen, Nuremberg, Windsheim, Passau, Regensburg, Munich, Burghausen, Salzburg, Linz, Wels, Enns, Melk, Vienna, Kitzbühel, Hall, Rattenberg, and Schwaz; and in 1528 at Bergzabern, Kaufbeuren, Schwäbisch Gmünd, Stuttgart, Vöcklabruck, Bruck an der Mur, Leoben, Kufstein, Sterzing, and Bozen.

4. In Switzerland, 46 communities; in the Empire, 43 communities, of which 28 were in Franconia.

5. The following major Anabaptist congregations were destroyed between 1527 and 1529:

Königsberg, Feb. 1527	Augsburg, April 1528
Horb and Rottenburg, Feb. and	Kaufbeuren, May 1528
July 1527	Landau, May 1528
Burghausen, Nov. 1527	Nuremberg, summer 1528–Jan.
Salzburg, Nov. 1527	1529
Munich, Jan. 1528	Worms, 1528
Passau, Jan. 1528	Heilbronn, 1529
Esslingen, Jan.–Feb. 1528	Schwäbisch Gmünd, Nov. 1529

6. In 1466 the Estates of the Tirol maintained that their country was inhabited by 600,000 people, which is probably an exaggeration. In 1532 only 375,000 persons are said to have received communion (Stolze, 262–63; Widmoser, "Unterland," 142).

7. Augsburg had 6,097 taxpayers in 1526. Assuming that a family consisted of four persons, Augsburg would have had a population of 24,388 persons in 1526. From 1526 through 1528, 298 persons

who permanently lived at Augsburg became Anabaptists, not including 56 Anabaptist refugees who appeared at Augsburg in 1527 and 1528. During the period 1526 to 1535, 359 persons, or about 1.5 percent of Augsburg's population, accepted baptism. Sixty-six Anabaptists are known to us at Esslingen and nearby villages from 1527 to 1530. Esslingen had approximately eight thousand inhabitants. In 1528 some Anabaptists claimed that there were two-hundred brethren at Esslingen, which would amount to 2.5 percent of the population.

8. Williams, 846, 857.

Chapter 3

1. Franck, 457; see also Fast, *Bullinger*, 128.

2. Hedio's list: Müntzerani, Orantes, Silentes, Somniantes, Pueris similes, Synceri, Impeccabiles a baptismo, Liberi, Binderliani, Sabbatarii, Maderani, Hofmannici, and nuper Circumcisi. Mentioned in the outline of Hedio's planned history of the Anabaptists (Fast, *Bullinger*, 172). For Gast, see *ibid.*, 128. Arzt's list: Anabaptistae Monasterienses, Anabaptistae Huterani, Anabaptistae Staeblarii, Anabaptistae Schwerterii, Anabaptistae Osterlicii, Anabaptistae Helvetii, Anabaptistae demonisalvi (Krebs, 511).

3. Bullinger, 1–66.

4. Fast, *Bullinger*, 129.

5. The lists of Eder and Erhard can be divided into three types of groups. First, there are eleven Anabaptist groups that are known to us on the basis of documentary evidence: Müntzerites, Sabbatarians, Mennonites, Huttites, Münsterite Brethren, Gabrielite Brethren, Austerlitzers, Swiss Brethren, Pilgram Brothers, Hutterites, and Staff Bearers. Second, there are seventeen groups, some of them probably taken over from Bullinger's book, that are not really known to us; if they existed at all, they were more likely to be restricted circles within the larger groups than separate groups: Secretive Anabaptists, also called Garden Brothers; Open Witnesses; Devilers; Weeping Brothers; Purists; Silent Ones; Apostolics; Barefooted Brothers; Spiritualists or Separatists; Praying Brothers; Vi-

sionaries or Enthusiasts; Adamers; Hypocritical Ones; Augustinians; Ambrosians; Scripturists or Paulinists; and a group including those who interpret the resurrection too spiritually, those who interpret the resurrection too bodily, and the universalists, who believe all will eventually be saved, even the devil. Third, there are groups that, if they ever existed, were hardly Anabaptists: Adamites, Free Livers, Cohabiters, Grubenheimers, David Georgians, Kesselgeist, Priest Murderers, Bloodthirsty Ones, Libertines, Anti-Christians, Judaizers, Devil Worshipers, Epicureans.

6. Hut's theology had probably formed by May 1526, the time of his baptism by Hans Denck at Augsburg. There is no evidence, however, that Denck and Hut were the founders of an indigenous Anabaptist movement in Germany, as Kiwiet maintains. There were no independent Anabaptist congregations in south Germany before Hubmaier and Reublin came from Zurich to Augsburg and Strasbourg. For Kiwiet's thesis on Denck and Hut see Kiwiet, 40–46.

7. Berbig, "Wiedertäufer" (1903), 316.

8. A man at Frankenhausen said in 1530 that the Son was under the Father and the Spirit above the Son (Wappler, *Täuferbewegung*, 320). Heinz Kraut and others maintained that the Father was almightiness; the Son, justice; and the Holy Ghost, mercy (*Corpus Reformatorum*, II, 998).

9. These brethren believed that like Christ they would rise not in the body but in the spirit (Wappler, *Stellung Kursachsens*, 203, 206).

10. Zieglschmid, *Älteste Chronik*, 105–19.

11. Krebs and Rott, *Elsass*, II, 318.

12. Klassen, 94–95.

13. Zieglschmid, *Älteste Chronik*, 242–43, 357–58; see also Bossert, 414.

14. Bossert, 412; Franz, *Urkundliche Quellen*, 393–94; Zieglschmid, *Älteste Chronik*, 360, 417, 422.

15. Bossert, 363–67.

16. Zieglschmid, *Älteste Chronik*, 363.

17. Beck, 96.

18. Erhard, 10b. The Hessian Anabaptists and the Philippites also condemned the Münsterites (Franz, *Urkundliche Quellen*, 255, 394;

Karlsruhe [19], Grafschaft Hohenlohe, Aug. 20, Sept. 16 and 18, 1535).

19. Krebs and Rott, *Elsass*, I, 289, and II, 298.

20. Schornbaum, *Bayern*, II, 63.

21. There is no factual basis to Kiwiet's claim (p. 66) that from 1554 on the Anabaptist community presented itself as one unit with Strasbourg as the center. A large meeting was indeed held near Strasbourg on March 17, 1554, but we do not know what happened there. Kiwiet's view that Marbeck paid a second visit to Moravia in 1550 is based on a misunderstanding of the word "Pilgram" in Beck (p. 188) which obviously refers to the Hutterites, not to Pilgram Marbeck.

22. If Marbeck's followers were not present, we can at least assume that they adopted the meeting's decisions. While Marbeck and Scharnschlager had formerly emphasized the human aspect of Christ and maintained that He could not have sinned, Scharnschlager in the last part of the *Verantwortung*, written between 1556 and 1558, bowed to the decisions made at Strasbourg. But there is no basis for Kiwiet's claim that this was a general assembly of all Anabaptist groups. We have no evidence that the Hutterites were present (Kiwiet, 66–67; Hulshof, 222).

23. The length of the mile varied from area to area; 150 miles would have amounted to between 1,113 and 1,333 kilometers, or 691 to 827 statute miles. But the figure is surely exaggerated, for even half the distance would have included faraway areas such as Moravia.

24. Zieglschmid, *Älteste Chronik*, 422–23.

25. The Concept of Cologne was signed by the Servants and Elders of the congregations in Alsace, Breisgau, Strasbourg, Weissenburg in Alsace, Landau, Neustadt, Lambsheim, Worms, and Kreuznach, and also by representatives of the congregation at Cologne, of all congregations in the "Landt van Millen and van der Mase, the congregation at Oderkerchke, Gladbeck and all congregations in Bergland and the one at Rees" (Rembert, 618).

26. Zieglschmid, *Älteste Chronik*, 359.

27. Such as Farwendel (*ibid.*, 417–19).

Chapter 4

1. Dürr and Roth, II, 485. In 1527 Hans Schlaffer met the leaders Oswald Glait, Wolfgang Brandhuber, and others at Regensburg. We do not know whether this was just an accidental encounter or whether a conference was held (Lydia Müller, *Glaubenszeugnisse*, 118).

2. Schlaffer also mentioned one Sigmund Hoffer; conceivably he may have meant Sigmund Salminger (*ibid.*).

3. Clemen, II, 305. Meihuizen argues that the "false brethren" rejected by the Schleitheim Articles were Denck, Hut, and Hubmaier. But the articles explicitly identify the false brethren as those who rendered themselves to "lasciviousness and liberty of the flesh."

4. Krebs, 113–14.

5. Wappler, *Täuferbewegung*, 271.

6. Schornbaum, *Bayern*, I, 170.

7. Text in Zieglschmid, *Älteste Chronik*, 83–85; see also Friedmann, "Oldest Church Discipline" (1958).

8. Scharnschlager, 354–56.

9. Bender, "Discipline," 57–66. In 1630 at "Hoffingen" in Switzerland, the Swiss Brethren agreed on four additional points.

10. Hege, 151.

11. Meyer, 248; Mecenseffy, 63–64. The congregation at Steyr may also have played a role in these appointments, for Schiemer said that he had been sent out by the believers at Steyr (Lydia Müller, *Glaubenszeugnisse*, 80–81).

12. Bossert, 207. Elections by vote seem to have been held among the Mennonites in north Germany, though it is not certain whether a majority or unanimity was required (Krahn, 122).

13. Wappler, *Täuferbewegung*, 496, 501.

14. Hege, 151; Wappler, *Inquisition*, 189.

15. Roth, "Geschichte der Wiedertäufer, III," 63.

16. A Thuringian leader told the officials in 1564 that he had been elected and confirmed (Wappler, *Täuferbewegung*, 496). See also Bender, "Discipline," 61.

17. Bender, "Discipline," 63.

18. Clemen, II, 310.

19. Bossert, 841–42.

20. Schornbaum, *Bayern*, I, 36.

21. Wappler, *Täuferbewegung*, 259.

22. Roth, "Geschichte der Wiedertäufer, II," 25–26.

23. Roth, "Geschichte der Wiedertäufer, III," 76; Brändly, 68; Karlsruhe [19], Esslingen, Jan. 20 and 21, 1528; Franz, *Urkundliche Quellen*, 57; Muralt and Schmid, 367; Meyer, 224; Schornbaum, *Bayern*, I, 57.

24. Lydia Müller, *Glaubenszeugnisse*, 160. The conference of the Mennonite leaders at Wismar in 1554 also decided that nobody was to engage in itinerant preaching unless he had been authorized to (Simons, 1042).

25. Clemen, II, 310.

26. Franz, *Urkundliche Quellen*, 267.

27. Zieglschmid, *Älteste Chronik*, 195–97; Franz, *Urkundliche Quellen*, 266–67.

28. Goshen, Ind. [13], July 4, 1576. In 1545 one Bastian, a helper, was dismissed also by the congregation at Strasbourg, but we do not know why (Hulshof, 210).

29. In 1530 a man at Strasbourg said he had heard that there were two thousand Anabaptists in the city (Krebs and Rott, *Elsass*, I, 277). The man was not an Anabaptist himself, and his figure was based on hearsay. Although we do not have precise figures, the available evidence indicates that there were not more than one hundred brethren in Strasbourg at that time.

30. Roth, "Geschichte der Wiedertäufer, III," 80–81, 89.

31. Kläui, 188.

32. A message sent to Jacob Kürschner at Wasselnheim near Strasbourg (Hulshof, 162).

33. Goshen, Ind. [13], July 4, 1576.

34. Hulshof, 209, 211.

35. Delbert Gratz, *Bernese Anabaptists and Their American Descendants* (Scottdale, Pa., 1953), p. 25.

36. The ster was an ancient Tirolese dry measure. Although there were many regional differences, in general one ster was equivalent to approximately 30 liters or 53 pints.

37. Krebs and Rott, *Elsass*, I, 63.

38. Bossert, 690.

39. Franz, *Urkundliche Quellen*, 400–401.

40. *Ibid.*, 397; 489–91; see also Bossert, 208, 420.

41. Wappler, *Täuferbewegung*, 350; Schacher, 115.

42. Krebs, 150.

43. Joachim Fleiner in Karlsruhe [19], Esslingen, April 20, 1529; see also Franz, *Urkundliche Quellen*, 57, 180–87, 276; Mecenseffy, 126; Mossmann, 5; and Schornbaum, *Bayern*, I, 168–70, 244–45.

44. Mecenseffy, 126.

Chapter 5

1. Roth, "Geschichte der Wiedertäufer, III," 65; Bossert, 384; Franz, *Urkundliche Quellen*, 65; Krebs, 321, 323, 410; Muralt and Schmid, 16, 126, 175, 218, 268, 280, 281, 287, 300, 321, 323, 397; Mecenseffy, 337, 339; Krebs and Rott, *Elsass*, I, 272, 275, 290, and II, 318; Wappler, *Täuferbewegung*, 354.

2. Bossert, 373.

3. Muralt and Schmid, 44–45, 123, 297.

4. The third demand was raised at the disputation at Zofingen, and not at Bern. At Bern the Anabaptists declared that the pastor should be maintained from justly acquired property (*Christenlich Gespräch*, "Von der Narung der dieneren des worts Gottes"; *Handlung oder Acta Gehaltner Disputation*, 125–28). Occasionally some pastors lived in such poverty that even the Anabaptists offered them help (Krebs and Rott, *Elsass*, II, 467).

5. *Mennonitisches Lexikon*, II, 454.

6. Bossert, 655; Karlsruhe [19], Heilbronn, trial of Wertz, statement of Hans Bersig; Hulshof, 213; Lydia Müller, *Glaubenszeugnisse*, 14, 89; Krebs and Rott, *Elsass*, I, 53.

7. Stuttgart [45]. There were fifteen changes in office in the district of Schorndorf and the small district of Lorch: one pastor was dismissed; three died; five were transferred to other parishes either by their request or because there had been difficulties; and one retired. What happened to the other five is not clear.

8. Bossert, 480; Franz, *Urkundliche Quellen*, 504; Krebs, 285, 380; Mecenseffy, 277. However, by the middle of the sixteenth century, the Swiss Brethren in the area of Kreuznach did make payments to the church (Zieglschmid, *Älteste Chronik*, 357).

9. Roth, "Geschichte der Wiedertäufer, III," 40, 43; Franz, *Urkundliche Quellen*, 63; Krebs, 495; Mecenseffy, 43, 159; Nicoladoni, 163; Schornbaum, *Bayern*, I, 354; Wappler, *Stellung Kursachsens*, 171, 175, 186.

10. The two pamphlets are "The Hearing of False Prophets or Antichristians" and "Concerning Evil Overseers," in Wenger, 277–78, 280–81. For instances where leaders allowed church attendance, see Muralt and Schmid, 180, and Wappler, *Täuferbewegung*, 309; where Anabaptists actually attended church, Schornbaum, *Bayern*, I, 183, 184.

11. Riedemann, 93–95.

12. Erhard, 6b–7; Fischer, *Ursachen*, 79; Karlsruhe [19], Heilbronn, May 12, 1530; Hubmaier, 320; Krebs, 278; Schornbaum, *Bayern*, I, 130; Sinzinger, 80; Wappler, *Täuferbewegung*, 252, 477; Zieglschmid, *Älteste Chronik*, 365.

13. Schornbaum, *Bayern*, II, 123.

14. Burckhardt, 101; Kläui, 185–93.

15. Goshen, Ind. [13], Oct. 13, 1567.

16. Muralt and Schmid, 306.

17. *Ibid.*, 75–76. In the sixteenth century waffle vendors were notorious for their insolence.

18. Römer in 1527 (Wappler, *Täuferbewegung*, 260).

19. Karlsruhe [19], Heilbronn, trial of Wertz; Schornbaum, *Bayern*, I, 130. This gesture was also used by Anabaptists who quarreled with each other (Zieglschmid, *Älteste Chronik*, 95).

20. Bossert, 550, 895; Dürr and Roth, IV, 382; Franz, *Urkundliche Quellen*, 149, 332; Krebs, 235; Muralt and Schmid, 33, 80, 388; Krebs and Rott, *Elsass*, I, 55–56, 70–71; Schornbaum, *Bayern*, I, 267; Schacher, 135; Esslingen [11], 79.

21. Muralt and Schmid, 38–39, 109–10; Mossmann, 5; Krebs and Rott, *Elsass*, II, 233; Widmoser, "Unterland," 210.

22. Dürr and Roth, II, 357; Krebs, 423; Kuppelwieser, 160–61; Schacher, 4; Sinzinger, 93, 186.

Chapter 6

1. Bossert, 207; Krebs, 235; Scharnschlager, 354; Augsburg [7], Urgichten, April 26, 1550; Wappler, *Täuferbewegung*, 499, 508.

2. Schornbaum, *Bayern*, I, 96; Karlsruhe [19], Esslingen, March 27, 1528.

3. Bossert, 207, 475; Franz, *Urkundliche Quellen*, 55, 305; Muralt and Schmid, 229; Schacher, 115.

4. Bossert, 732; Hulshof, 210; Goshen, Ind. [13], July 4, 1576.

5. Hulshof, 211.

6. Goshen, Ind. [13], July 4, 1576.

7. Franz, *Urkundliche Quellen*, 400–401. For other meetings see *ibid.*, 390, and Hulshof, 159–60, 212–16.

8. Franz, *Urkundliche Quellen*, 380.

9. Appenzeller, 121; Bossert, 1050; Karlsruhe [19], Esslingen, 1530s; Franz, *Urkundliche Quellen*, 291; Muralt and Schmid, 33, 124, 280; Schornbaum, *Bayern*, I, 218; Esslingen [11], A135, 74, Feb. 12, 1598; Karlsruhe [19], Ulm, July 13, 1528; Wappler, *Täuferbewegung*, 312, 386.

10. Bossert, 1050.

11. Franz, *Urkundliche Quellen*, 148, 281; Jakobs, 531; Wappler, *Stellung Kursachsens*, 197.

12. Schornbaum, *Bayern*, I, 203.

13. Franz, *Urkundliche Quellen*, 433; Krebs, 73.

14. Schornbaum, *Bayern*, I, 135, and II, 22.

15. Bossert, 654; Friedmann, "Felbinger's Confession," 152; Karlsruhe [19], Ulm, July 13, 1528; Wappler, *Stellung Kursachsens*, 168–69.

16. "Concerning Evil Overseers," in Wenger, 280–81; Wappler, *Stellung Kursachsens*, 138; see also Schornbaum, *Bayern*, I, 180–81; and for Ascherham, Zieglschmid, *Älteste Chronik*, 250.

17. Muralt and Schmid, 23–28; Riedemann, 77–78.

18. The analysis of Hut's and Hubmaier's thought is based on Armour's excellent study.

19. Mecenseffy, 18–21; Schornbaum, *Bayern*, I, 83, 85, 88–93; Wappler, *Täuferbewegung*, 242.

20. Schornbaum, *Bayern*, I, 79, 80, 87; Wappler, *Täuferbewegung*, 249.

21. For Franconia see Schornbaum, *Bayern*, I, 16–17, 70, 81, 183, and II, 170–72; and Wappler, *Täuferbewegung*, 237, 242, 244. For Thuringia see *ibid.*, 500.

22. Krebs, 209; Schornbaum, *Bayern*, I, 200, and II, 181–82.

23. Wappler, *Stellung Kursachsens*, 213, and *Täuferbewegung*, 500, 508.

24. Zieglschmid, *Älteste Chronik*, 238.

25. Wappler, *Inquisition*, 35.

26. Augsburg [7], Urgichten, May 5, 1550.

27. Some 35 were baptized by Jakob Gross, and 40 by Jörg Schad (Muralt and Schmid, 63, 105, 262).

28. Hubmaier, 349–50.

29. Berbig, "Wiedertäufer" (1903), 309, 310; Mecenseffy, 158–59; Nicoladoni, 208–9; Roth, "Geschichte der Wiedertäufer, II," 29; Schornbaum, *Bayern*, I, 79, 93; Wappler, *Täuferbewegung*, 239, 249.

30. In Thuringia three sets of questions have been preserved. The reference to a believer who was German might indicate that these formulas originated in an area with a mixed population, such as Bohemia. The threefold baptism on forehead, breast and heart mentioned in one of the formulas is also strange. Maybe these formulas were not of Anabaptist origin at all but were used by pre-Reformation sects (Wappler, *Täuferbewegung*, 305).

31. For instances where crosses were made on believers' foreheads, see Schornbaum, *Bayern*, I, 26, 67, 115–16. For those where water was sprinkled, *ibid.*, 57; Muralt and Schmid, 40. For those where water was poured, *ibid.*, 38, 177; Roth, "Geschichte der Wiedertäufer, II," 26, 28; Schornbaum, *Bayern*, I, 58; Wappler, *Stellung Kursachsens*, 138, and *Täuferbewegung*, 345; where water was poured three times, Franz, *Urkundliche Quellen*, 25.

32. Performed by Jörg Zeller in Franconia in 1527 (Schornbaum, *Bayern*, I, 125) and Claus Scharf in the area of Mühlhausen in 1537. Scharf was reprimanded by the brethren for this action (Wappler, *Täuferbewegung*, 439).

33. Kessler, 144.

34. In 1564 Andreas Ehrenpreis, the Hutterite bishop, still rejected the Polish Antitrinitarians' practice of baptizing by immersion. The Bible, Ehrenpreis argued, speaks only of baptism by water, not of baptism by immersion (Gross, 155).

35. Hulshof, 215–16; Krebs, 79, 272.

36. Judith, the wife of Hans Kimmich, claimed in 1535 at Passau that her name had been given her by the leader Wolf from Grötzingen at her baptism at Heilbronn in 1532 (Karlsruhe [19], Grafschaft Hohenlohe, Sept. 16, 1535). One Anna Krum at Göppingen is said to have received the name Sara when she was baptized around 1545 (Bossert, 1010).

37. Hubmaier, 367–68.

38. Clemen, II, 307; Franz, *Urkundliche Quellen*, 439–40; Hege, 151; Bender, "Discipline," 63; Scharnschlager, 356; Zieglschmid, *Älteste Chronik*, 84.

39. Roth, "Geschichte der Wiedertäufer, III," 64–65; Bossert, 634, 705; Burckhardt, 112; Karlsruhe [19], Esslingen, June 13, 1528; Hulshof, 211, 213; Krebs, 71; Scharnschlager, 356; Goshen, Ind. [13], July 4, 1576, and Aug. 7, 1583; Zieglschmid, *Älteste Chronik*, 211, 213, 229, 246, 250, 341, 409, 480.

40. Hulshof, 213–14.

41. *Ibid.*, 228. At the Frankenthal disputation in 1571 the Swiss Brethren also refused to defend the Mennonite position on marital avoidance.

42. Burckhardt, 112; Steck and Tobler, 675.

43. Goshen, Ind. [17], "Volgt mee eine Gesannt an die so man Schweizer Bruder nennt, 1543."

44. *Handlung oder Acta gehaltner Disputation*, 1532, 57b.

45. Steck and Tobler, 675.

46. Hulshof, 211.

47. Franz, *Urkundliche Quellen*, 213; Wappler, *Täuferbewegung*, 330. This is the term used in Acts 2:42 and 46, Acts 20:11, and Acts 27:35.

48. Roth, "Geschichte der Wiedertäufer, III," 54; Bossert, 410; Karlsruhe [19], Esslingen, July 4, 1539, Walter Liechtenstein; Franz, *Urkundliche Quellen*, 87–88; Krebs, 479, 530; Mecenseffy, 35;

Schornbaum, *Bayern*, I, 52, 68, 349; Sinzinger, 80, 187; Wappler, *Stellung Kursachsens*, 203, 207, and *Täuferbewegung*, 386; Zieglschmid, *Älteste Chronik*, 203.

49. Wappler, *Täuferbewegung*, 230, 358, 462, 500.

50. Bossert, 228. In 1602, *ibid.*, 1126.

51. Jakobs, 502; Wappler, *Täuferbewegung*, 320–21, 356.

52. Franz, *Urkundliche Quellen*, 88; Krebs, 46; Wappler, *Täuferbewegung*, 500.

53. Goshen, Ind. [16], "Das sechste Buch: Vom Brodbrechen der Heiligen"; Schornbaum, *Bayern*, I, 136–37, 148, 233; Wappler, *Täuferbewegung*, 425, 475.

54. Schornbaum, *Bayern*, I, 354; see also Wappler, *Täuferbewegung*, 358.

55. Riedemann, 82–85.

56. Bossert, 448, 541, 555; Franz, *Urkundliche Quellen*, 57, 264.

57. Wappler, *Täuferbewegung*, 330–31.

58. See John 6:32–58.

59. Bossert, 47, 433, 897; Krebs, 479; Schornbaum, *Bayern*, I, 52–53, 84, 175, 176–77, 178, 336, and II, 171; Wappler, *Stellung Kursachsens*, 138, and *Täuferbewegung*, 426.

60. Bossert, 241, 1085–86; Schornbaum, *Bayern*, I, 141, and II, 139–40.

61. Schornbaum, *Bayern*, I, 73, 82, 84, 95–96, 139, 152, 334, 335, 349; Goshen, Ind. [13], Oct. 13, 1567; Wappler, *Stellung Kursachsens*, 197, 203.

62. Schornbaum, *Bayern*, I, 52–53, 84, 127.

63. Jakobs, 508, 531.

64. Friedmann, "Felbinger's Confession," 153; Riedemann, 85–87.

65. Muralt and Schmid, 16.

66. Grebel seems to have celebrated the Supper already between January 15 and 22, 1525 (*ibid.*, 42). He cut bread into pieces and distributed them.

67. *Ibid.*, 38, 41, 43.

68. *Ibid.*, 304.

69. Bossert, 179, 242, 383; Wappler, *Täuferbewegung*, 475.

70. Bossert, 847; Dürr and Roth, II, 484; Krebs, 71; Krebs and Rott, *Elsass*, II, 489.

71. Bossert, 730.

72. *Ibid.*, 229, 557, 582, 1125; Krebs, 74.

73. Hubmaier, 355–56.

74. Franz, *Urkundliche Quellen*, 26; Jakobs, 503, 523, 528–29; Wappler, *Inquisition*, 112.

75. Krebs, 253; see also Bossert, 793, and Franz, *Urkundliche Quellen*, 390.

76. Bossert, 207, 209.

77. Bender, "Discipline," 61.

78. Bergsten, 312–13; Lydia Müller, *Glaubenszeugnisse*, 76; Widmoser, "Unterland," 69.

79. *Aussbund*, Nr. 13 and 119; *Lieder der Hutterischen Brüder*, 140.

80. Friedmann, *Schriften der Huterischen Täufergemeinschaften*, 159.

81. Hege, 151.

82. Grebel's own views are not clear. In December 1524 he spoke of the imminent sword, but at the disputation of November 6, 1525, he declared that the Messiah was already present (Muralt and Schmid, 30, 122).

83. Isaiah 3:24. Revelation 12:3. Jonah 3:4. Zwingli, IV, 43.

84. Roth, "Geschichte der Wiedertäufer, III," 36, 96, 102; Brändly, 70–72; J. C. Füsslin, "Bernard Weissen Kurze Beschreibung der Glaubenssonderung," in *Beyträge*, IV Theil (1749), p. 95; Karlsruhe [19], Heilbronn, trial of Wertz, statements of Hans Zehe; Krebs, 495; Karlsruhe [19], Reutlingen, about Feb. 2, 1528; Krebs and Rott, *Elsass*, I, 91.

85. Williams (pp. 858–62) exaggerates the role of eschatological expectations in Anabaptism.

86. For Thuringia see Franz, *Urkundliche Quellen*, 55, 57 (area of Mühlhausen in 1533); and Wappler, *Täuferbewegung*, 396 (area of Orlamünde in 1535). For Hesse see Franz, *Urkundliche Quellen*, 93 (Allendorf in 1535); and *ibid.*, 160, 166, 192, 193 (group around Tesch and Schnabel in 1538). For Franconia see Schornbaum, *Bayern*, I, 349 (Rosstal after 1533), and II, 205. (Rothenburg in 1536). See also Riedemann, "Ein annder Epistel," in Goshen, Ind. [15], fol. 407.

87. Wappler, *Inquisition*, 115.

88. Goshen, Ind. [17], "An die Aeltesten, samt der Gemeinde in Austerlitz . . . ," July 17, 1548.

89. For eschatological predictions made in 1572, see Bossert, 347, 350; in 1587, Franz, *Urkundliche Quellen*, 496–97; and in the 1580s by Hutterite emigrants from Knonau near Zurich, *Mennonitisches Lexikon*, IV, 630. Erhard wrote in 1588 that the Hutterites were constantly babbling about the Last Day (Erhard, 55); also Wolkan, 207, 251–53).

90. Muralt and Schmid, 223, 225. Grebel and Blaurock denied ever having mentioned revelations or visions (*ibid.*, 125, 217).

91. *Ibid.*, 161, 163.

92. Kessler, 154. Margret Hottinger was one of the first people in Zollikon to listen to the Bible readings of Manz and Grebel. She was baptized by Blaurock in January or February, 1525, and arrested before November 18, 1525. On March 1, 1526, she refused to abandon her belief and consequently was sentenced to stay in prison living on bread and water until she recanted or died. On May 1, 1526, she recanted and was probably set free. There is no indication in the Zurich documents that she held the views attributed to her by Kessler (Muralt and Schmid, 177, 178).

93. Steck and Tobler, 674–75.

94. Augustin from Bohemia was another. According to Bullinger, this Augustin, the founder of the Augustinian Brethren, believed in visions and dreams. We know that several years before 1532, the Swiss leader Martin Lincki banned one Augustin. Was this the same man as Augustin Bader of Augsburg, who in 1528 had visited Bohemia and Teufen in Appenzell, where he formally separated from the Anabaptists? (Bullinger, 44; *Handlung oder Acta gehaltner Disputation*, 57a.)

95. I Corinthians 15:31.

96. Acts 16:16–18. Kessler, 158; also Watt [Vadian], II, 405.

97. Clark, 116.

98. Miles, 308; Kessler, 162–64; Watt [Vadian], II, 405.

99. Kessler, 154–57; Sicher, 191. According to the records of the town council, Barbara Mürglin was expelled on April 9, 1526, and Magdalena Müllerin and Wybrat Vonwilerin on November 9, 1526:

Barbara Mürglin was expelled because she "had gone to the Anabaptists and died, and engaged in other unchristian matters"; Magdalena Müllerin because she had "mixed bodily with men," and together with her girl friends engaged in disorderly and offensive
conduct at Buch and elsewhere, such as calling herself the Son of
God and so on; Wybrat Vonwilerin because she had fornicated,
participated in the affair at Buch, and called herself Martha (Fast,
"Sonderstellung," 234).

100. Watt [Vadian], II, 407–8; Fridli Bluntschli, "Chronik," in
Fast, *Bullinger*, 170–71; Kessler, 159–62; Sicher, 191–92. According
to Sicher, Thomas Schugger thought that the sword would not
touch his brother unless God willed it (Schibli, 41–44).

101. Clemen, II, 320–21.

102. Krebs and Rott, *Elsass*, II, 257–59.

103. In 1530 Hofmann published *Prophetisches Gesicht* by Ursula
Jost, and in October 1532 a second edition of the prophecies of Lienhart Jost (Krebs and Rott, *Elsass*, I, 259, and see also II, 184, 185,
186, 388, 393).

104. For Reutlingen see Karlsruhe [19], Reutlingen, about Feb. 2,
1528; for Lauingen, Zieglschmid, *Älteste Chronik*, 195–96; for Esslingen, Karlsruhe [19], Esslingen, Dec. 1529, and Krebs and Rott,
Elsass, II, 17, 228, 290.

105. Meyer, 232.

106. The evidence on the Dreamers, consisting of 25 long and detailed transcripts of interrogations of individual members of the sect,
seems quite reliable. See Schornbaum, *Bayern*, I, 220–330. In my article "Medieval Heresies," I suggested that the heresy of the Free
Spirit might have influenced the Dreamers. Although nothing definite can be said, I am now inclined to think that Hut's influence was
decisive.

107. *Corpus Reformatorum*, II, 1002; Franz, *Urkundliche Quellen*,
265; Jakobs, 513, 530; Wappler, *Stellung Kursachsens*, 203, *Täuferbewegung*, 314, 360, 429, and *Inquisition*, 103.

108. On this group see Wappler, *Täuferbewegung*, 336–44; see
also Franz, *Urkundliche Quellen*, 299–300.

109. The documentary evidence on the Bloodfriends consists of
detailed transcripts of interrogations of four members of the sect

and two public letters by former followers of Ludwig (Franz, *Urkundliche Quellen*, 324–27; Hochhuth, 182–86; Wappler, *Täuferbewegung*, 480–94; Marburg, Staatsarchiv, 22a1, 12). I see no reason to question the veracity of the evidence.

110. See Cohn on how the book of Daniel and other Jewish and Christian prophecies influenced revolutionary medieval heresies.

111. Augsburg [7], March 6, 1541.

112. Roth, "Geschichte der Wiedertäufer, III," 128; Franz, *Urkundliche Quellen*, 40, 70; Fischer, *Ursachen*, 86; Muralt and Schmid, 215; Mecenseffy, 202; Nicoladoni, 163; Krebs and Rott, *Elsass*, I, 155; Schornbaum, *Bayern*, I, 130.

113. Kessler, 153; Karlsruhe [19], Heilbronn, trial of Wertz, statement of Hans Weik; *ibid.*, Grafschaft Hohenlohe, March 17, 1534.

114. Goshen, Ind. [14], "Verzeichniss viel notwendiger Puncten . . . (1612)."

115. Roth, "Geschichte der Wiedertäufer, III," 117.

116. Muralt and Schmid, 394–95.

117. Krebs, 171.

118. Franz, *Urkundliche Quellen*, 25.

119. Mark 10:15 and Luke 18:17.

120. Kessler, 152.

121. Bossert, 460, 687, 727; Krebs, 68, 73.

122. Bossert, 650–51, 808; Zieglschmid, *Älteste Chronik*, 158, 437, 481, 541. A man who had been forbidden by the courts to bear arms was taken for an Anabaptist (Clauss, "Wiedertäufer," 147).

123. Bossert, 217, 598, 616, 807.

124. Zieglschmid, *Älteste Chronik*, 437–38.

125. Krebs and Rott, *Elsass*, I, 338–39.

126. Mecenseffy, 159; Muralt and Schmid, 159.

127. Lydia Müller, *Kommunismus*, 30; Röhrich, 95; Wappler, *Täuferbewegung*, 496, 498, 507, and *Inquisition*, 189.

128. Bossert, 996; Burckhardt, 75, 105; Jakobs, 505; Kessler, 152–53; Lydia Müller, *Glaubenszeugnisse*, 100, 139; Riedemann, 135–36; Schornbaum, *Bayern*, I, 346; Zieglschmid, *Älteste Chronik*, 140, 433.

129. Augsburg [1], July 10, 1529.

130. Meyer, 228; *Mennonite Encyclopedia*, IV, 365.

131. Augsburg [8], Aug. 10, 1562, statement of Jacob Schneider;

Wappler, *Stellung Kursachsens*, 141, 168, and *Täuferbewegung*, 282.

132. Bossert, 371; *Corpus Reformatorum*, II, 1002; Jakobs, 521, 525; Sinzinger, 334; Augsburg [7], March 5, 1533; Wappler, *Täuferbewegung*, 396, 399, and *Inquisition*, 105.

133. Jedelhauser, 13; Fischer, *Ursachen*, 95.

134. See Roth, "Geschichte der Wiedertäufer, III," 61; Mecenseffy, 115; Krebs and Rott, *Elsass*, I, 232; Roth, "Geschichte der Wiedertäufer, II," 21, 23; Schornbaum, *Bayern*, I, 27, and II, 39; Wappler, *Täuferbewegung*, 263, 382.

135. Jakobs, 505; Wappler, *Täuferbewegung*, 382.

136. Wappler, *Täuferbewegung*, 382.

137. Fischer, *Taubenkobel*, 45; Krebs, 281, 530; Schornbaum, *Bayern*, I, 71; Zieglschmid, *Älteste Chronik*, 76.

138. Hubmaier, 273–74, 318–19, 583; Franz, *Urkundliche Quellen*, 438; Jakobs, 505; Schornbaum, *Bayern*, II, 22, 23, 29.

139. Bossert, 380; Karlsruhe [19], Esslingen, July 4, 1539; Krebs, 447; Augsburg [8], July 29, July 31, and Aug. 17, 1562; Karlsruhe [19], Ulm, Aug. 13, 1537.

140. Dürr and Roth, III, 254. See also the case of the Anabaptist midwife at Miedelsbach in Württemberg (Bossert, 391, 408, 505, 516).

141. Karlsruhe [19], Esslingen, April 1, 1529; Muralt and Schmid, 295, 383; Goshen, Ind. [13], July 2, 1572.

142. Krebs, 478–80.

143. Charles du Fresne du Cange, *Glossarium ad scriptores mediae et infimae Latinitatis . . .* (Niort, 1883), II, 648.

144. Appenzeller, 120.

145. Bossert, 706. For a case where it was forbidden to bury an Anabaptist in a cemetery, see *ibid.*, 614.

Chapter 7

1. Bergsten, 277–301.

2. The Anabaptists known to have taken part in the peasant uprising are as follows.

Thuringia: in the area of Erfurt, Hans Römer (Franz, *Urkund-*

liche Quellen, 55; Wappler, *Stellung Kursachsens,* 132), Georg
Fuchs (Wappler, *Täuferbewegung,* 270), Meister Andreas (*ibid.,*
270), Dionysius Mansfeld (*ibid.,* 257), Volkmar Fischer (*ibid.,* 258);
in the area of Mühlhausen, Heinz Kraut (*ibid.,* 410), Claus Scharf
(*ibid.,* 376), Heinrich Hutter (Merx et al., II, 758, 803, 925), Erhard
Stuess (Wappler, *Täuferbewegung,* 462–64), possibly Claus Stein-
metz and Christof Rudolph (Merx et al., II, 595–96, 649–50, 828).

The area of Hesse and Hersfeld: Melchior Rinck (Franz, *Urkundliche Quellen,* 49–50; Wappler, *Stellung Kursachsens,* 145),
Hans Plat, Heinrich Hutter, Zisenhans, Heinrich Lutz, Herman
Stolpf, Endres Lober, Schmidt Hen, Gilg Schneider (Franz, *Urkundliche Quellen,* 66–69; Merx et al., I, 370).

Franconia: Hans Hut (Meyer, 239, 241–42), Heinz Schar (Fries,
230–33), Friedrich Pretscher (Zumkeller, I, 376), Claus Fry (Baumann, *Quellen Rothenburg,* 85, 144, 149, 155, 315, 541, 545, 558,
616), Hans Hartmann (Schornbaum, *Bayern,* II, 223), Michel Maier,
Peter Wagner (Clauss, "Kleine Beiträge," 168–69).

Swabia: Michel Jungmann (Krebs, 358), Michel Sporer (Bossert,
1003–4), Hans Feigenbutz (Karlsruhe [19], Esslingen, 1529), Lienhart Wenig (*ibid.,* Jan. 17, 1528).

The Tirol: Friedrich Brandenberger (Sinzinger, 179), Christian
Lex am Kofel.

Switzerland: Hans Girenbader (Strickler, 134), Hans Füeger
(*Mennonitisches Lexikon,* III, 563).

3. Muralt and Schmid, 85–86, 98.

4. In 1467, Hinwil had 2,200 inhabitants (*Mennonitisches Lexikon,*
II, 193). Apart from Hinwil the district of Grüningen had eleven
villages and one town.

5. On this affair see Muralt and Schmid, 91–92, 110, 114, 131–33.

6. The claim of the amtleute that some pastors who had incited
the peasants during the uprising by preaching against tithes later
lured people into the Anabaptist sect is not quite correct. Impressed
by Grebel's arguments, Ulrich Zingg, pastor at Dürnten, preached
that salvation did not depend on the form of baptism; yet in spite
of momentary doubts he never became an Anabaptist. Sebastian
Ramsberger at Gossau made himself suspect by avoiding the baptism of children, but there is no evidence that he ever preached

Anabaptist doctrines. It is also revealing that two other pastors who had spoken out against tithes during the uprising, Hans Brenwald at Hinwil and Lorenz Keller at Egg, were strongly opposed to Anabaptism (*ibid.*, 183–88).

7. Although Römer was not an Anabaptist in the line of the early Swiss Brethren, his view of baptism as a promise to desist from evil, to love God and one's neighbor, and to lead a pure life, and his connections to the congregations at Sorga and Nikolsburg indicate that he belonged to the Anabaptist movement in a broader sense (Franz, *Urkundliche Quellen*, 55; Wappler, *Täuferbewegung*, 257, 259, 260, 262, 264, 271, 282).

8. The conspirators were Hans Römer, Christof Peisker, Volkmar Fischer, Herman Kommerstetten, Meister Andreas, Caspar von Fladungen, Niklaus Hofmann at Erfurt, the minister at Alpersdorf, and a tailor at Ilversgehofen who was identical with either George Fuchs or Meister Andreas.

9. Wappler, *Stellung Kursachsens*, 131, and *Täuferbewegung*, 253, 258–59.

10. Niklaus Hofmann said the uprising would take place on New Year's Day, but Georg Fuchs spoke of February 1528 (Wappler, *Täuferbewegung*, 265, 272).

11. During his first interrogation on September 3, 1534, Römer said they would have started fires at seven places at Erfurt, but on September 23, 1534, he mentioned only four houses of priests. Niklaus Hofmann said they had planned to set fires in four parts of the city, beginning with his own house.

12. *Ibid.*, 264, 269–73, 363, 364–67, 367–69, 371–74.

13. Lorenz Fries, the sixteenth-century historian of the uprising in Franconia, reports that shortly before May 30, 1525, a Thuringian furrier, a disciple of Müntzer, came to the Bildhausen peasant army advocating the extermination of the political authorities. When the preachers of the peasants objected to his extremely inflammatory sermons, and the peasants began to divide into factions, the leaders of the peasants asked the town of Neustadt on May 30, 1525, to send their two pastors to settle this dispute. It is possible that this revolutionary preacher was Hut, though he was not a furrier, or it may have been Römer. In the latter case, both Hut and Römer would have been with the Bildhausen peasants at the same time.

14. Neuser, 1–25.

15. Berbig, "Wiedertäufer" (1903), 312.

16. Spiritualists predicted at Zwickau in 1521 that the Turks would conquer Germany and that the world would be transformed within five to seven years. The Lutheran pastors and godless people would be slain. Then there would be one baptism and one belief (Wappler, *Müntzer*, 45).

17. Meyer, 228, 230–31, 239, 241–42.

18. Hut said that he had collected several articles to form a book known to the brethren as the "Book with the seven seals." It described the punishment of the sinners on the Last Day (*ibid.*, 240, 243). When Hut was arrested in September 1527, a so-called *Ratsbüchlein* was found in his possession, in which various doctrines are indicated by key words. Some of them do indeed deal with the end of the world, the future and the judgment, resurrection, the kingdom of God, eternal judgment, and hell (Roth, "Geschichte der Wiedertäufer, II," 39). Hut had also written a treatise, "Vom geheimnus des tauffs," which was found in the possession of Eitelhans Langenmantel, an Augsburg Anabaptist. Only five quotations used in this work have survived. They were taken from Revelation 7 and 9, from Ezekiel 14 and 9, and from Exodus. The first two refer to the signs or seals the servants of God received on their foreheads. The last three indicate that those who did not receive these signs would be slain together with their wives (*ibid.*, 40). Hut's treatise "Vom gehaimnus der tauf, baide des zeichens und des wesens, ein anfang eines rechten warhaftigen lebens" (in Lydia Müller, *Glaubenszeugnisse*, 12–28) does not mention eschatological questions. According to Langenmantel and his servant Anwald, the signs on the heads referred to baptism.

19. Hut admitted that Hubmaier might have taken the 52 articles from his *Book on Three Articles of the Faith*, though Hut said it had been distorted in 20 places, and from a concordance of 100 biblical passages. During his interrogation at Augsburg, Hut mentioned eleven of these 52 articles; three of the eleven (articles 1, 4, and 5) resemble five of the Nikolsburg Articles, which the Anabaptists were accused in 1527 and 1528 of having taught (Meyer, 235–37; Schornbaum, *Bayern*, I, 65). Friedmann maintains that neither Hut nor any other Anabaptist ever taught the Nikolsburg

Articles, but that they originated in malicious rumors that circulated before the Nikolsburg disputation (Friedmann, "Nikolsburg Articles"). Friedmann goes too far, however, for we do not know what Hut really taught in his *Book on Three Articles of the Faith*. There may well have been some among the early Anabaptists who held views similar to the Nikolsburg Articles. Early Anabaptism was a very diverse movement, with many tendencies. Still it is true that the Nikolsburg Articles do not reflect Anabaptist thought in general.

20. Roth, "Geschichte der Wiedertäufer, III," 65.

21. Lydia Müller, *Glaubenszeugnisse*, 12. According to Marx Maier, Hut had said at the meeting that the end would come in three and one-half years after the peasant uprising, that God would exterminate the authorities and punish sinners, and that he, Hut, would be one of those who were to eliminate the godless. Since Meir was not present at this meeting and made his report only three years after the event, we cannot accept it as definite proof of Hut's views (Schornbaum, *Bayern*, I, 198–99).

22. Schornbaum, *Bayern*, I, 37, 50, 54, 55.

23. Berbig, "Wiedertäuferei" (1912), 393.

24. Berbig, "Wiedertäufer" (1903), 309–16, 335–36; Wappler, *Täuferbewegung*, 228–43, and *Stellung Kursachsens*, 238.

25. Schornbaum, *Bayern*, I, 57, 61, 83, 84, 112, 148, 150, 168.

26. Mecenseffy, 44; see also Wappler, *Inquisition*, 39.

27. Lydia Müller, *Glaubenszeugnisse*, 54–55, 119. According to Schiemer the persecution of the brethren in Solothurn, Switzerland, had set in at the time predicted by Daniel.

28. Merx et al., I, 370.

29. Franz, *Urkundliche Quellen*, 65–70.

30. *Ibid.*, 22, 23, 25–26.

31. However, some Anabaptists in the area of Romrod are supposed to have said in 1530 that the Turks would introduce and confirm their belief (*ibid.*, 30).

32. For a single incident suggesting that one of them expected great social changes see *ibid.*, 29.

33. Hut's influence is indicated by the woman's views that the elect had signs on their foreheads, that the godless who had not

accepted these signs would be exterminated, and that Christ would appear at Easter 1528. She did not mention the Turks at all, however. Either Freisleben or refugees from Augsburg might have brought Hut's ideas or even his writings to Esslingen.

34. Karlsruhe [19], Reutlingen, about Feb. 2, 1528.

35. Karlsruhe [19], Esslingen, Jan. 15, 1528.

36. *Ibid.*, Sept. 13 and 17, 1527, and March 24 and 28, 1528; Bossert, 914.

37. Cataneus was one of the leading predictors of the sixteenth century (Dietrich Kurze, *Johannes Lichtenberger: Eine Studie zur Geschichte der Prophetie und Astrologie* [Lübeck, 1960], p. 67).

38. Krebs, 137–38, 484.

39. Franz, *Urkundliche Quellen*, 152; Krebs, 357, 406; Schornbaum, *Bayern*, I, 341.

40. Bossert, 279, 299; similarly, Wappler, *Täuferbewegung*, 501.

41. Muralt and Schmid, 51.

42. On the political theory of the Anabaptists, see Hillerbrand, *Politische Ethik*. Hillerbrand failed to notice the revolutionary trend in Anabaptism, the social criticism of the brethren, and the effect of their doctrines on sixteenth-century society.

43. A leader at Colmar said in 1535, however, that the authorities who persecuted his flock had been sanctioned by the devil, not by God (Mossmann, 6).

44. Riedemann, 110; Franz, *Urkundliche Quellen*, 65–69 (for 1533) and 281 (for 1543); Bergmann, 64 (for 1585); Bossert, 412.

45. Bossert, 170, 298; Steck and Tobler, 549; Wappler, *Stellung Kursachsens*, 198.

46. Bossert, 47, 355, 356, 730; Franz, *Urkundliche Quellen*, 191; Wappler, *Stellung Kursachsens*, 175.

47. *Corpus Reformatorum*, II, 999, 1000–1001; Wappler, *Täuferbewegung*, 417, 477.

48. Wappler, *Stellung Kursachsens*, 174; Krebs, 530.

49. Wappler, *Täuferbewegung*, 509.

50. Fast, "Krüsis Büchlein," 461.

51. *Ein Christenlich Gespräch*, "Von der Oberkeyt."

52. Krebs, 530; Wappler, *Täuferbewegung*, 503, and *Inquisition*, 103.

53. Muralt and Schmid, 200; Wappler, *Inquisition*, 31.

54. Sinzinger, 131; Wappler, *Inquisition*, 111; Zieglschmid, *Älteste Chronik*, 255.

55. Bossert, 359, 464; Krebs and Rott, *Elsass*, I, 274.

56. Bergsten, 50–53; Lydia Müller, *Glaubenszeugnisse*, 140; Zieglschmid, *Älteste Chronik*, 225.

57. Clasen, *Württemberg*, 97.

58. Bossert, 47, 198, 530, 727; Karlsruhe [19], Esslingen, July 3, 1544.

59. Franz, *Urkundliche Quellen*, 74–76.

60. Goshen, Ind. [13], April 10 and July 28, 1564, and Nov. 23, 1557.

61. Bossert, 1088; Zieglschmid, *Älteste Chronik*, 159.

62. Bossert, 1089. See also Schornbaum, *Bayern*, I, 105; and Wappler, *Stellung Kursachsens*, 177, and *Inquisition*, 108.

63. Dürr and Roth, V, 328–29, 367; Appenzeller, 132; Clasen, *Württemberg*, 109; Franz, *Urkundliche Quellen*, 309; Goshen, Ind. [13], 1564.

64. Bossert, 156–57.

65. Translation by Claudius Catiuncula (Basel, 1524). *Utopia* was translated into English for the first time in 1551; into French in 1550; into Italian in 1548; into Dutch in 1553 and 1562.

66. Wappler, *Müntzer*, 82.

67. See Jakob Holzwart, "Rustica Seditio Totius Fere Germaniae," in Baumann, *Quellen Oberschwaben*, 646–49.

68. On these letters see Schubert, 18–20.

69. In August 1524, Hergott's journeymen at Nuremberg secretly printed Müntzer's *Aussgetrückte Emplössung*. Called to account by the town council, Hergott disclaimed responsibility but preferred to leave the city. His wife continued to run the printing business. What Hergott did between October 1524 and January 1527 is unknown.

70. The pamphlet appeared anonymously. It was printed by Michael Blum at Leipzig. A note on the copy in the Leipzig archives says, "The rebellious book of Hans Hergott of Nuremberg, for which he was executed here with the sword. Monday after Cantate 1527."

71. Muralt and Schmid, 216, 217; see also Anthoni Roggenacher's denial in *ibid.*, 166.

72. Wappler, *Inquisition*, 36.

73. Schornbaum, *Bayern*, I, 66.

74. Franz, *Urkundliche Quellen*, 64–69.

75. For Bern see Steck and Tobler, 1041–42; for Augsburg, Roth, "Geschichte der Wiedertäufer, III," 65; for Esslingen, Clasen, *Württemberg*, 97–99; for Regensburg, Schornbaum, *Bayern*, II, 34, 39; for Passau, Nicoladoni, 208, 210; for Bruchsal, Schornbaum, *Bayern*, I, 238, 240; for Franconia, *ibid.*, 125–26, 234; for Saxony, *Corpus Reformatorum*, II, 998–99, and Wappler, *Täuferbewegung*, 349, 498, 500, 502, and *Inquisition*, 202; for Hesse, Franz, *Urkundliche Quellen*, 174, 197, and *Protocoll . . . Frankenthal*, 533–34.

76. For an instance in 1531 see Schornbaum, *Bayern* I, 231; in 1557, Krebs, 264; in 1604, *ibid.*, 322.

77. Krebs and Rott, *Elsass*, I, 274.

78. Konrad Huber was in charge of the money for five weeks in 1527, but he soon got rid of the dangerous duty. His successors Hans Kissling and Gall Vischer were expelled on October 14, 1527. During the following months Augustin Bader, Lucas Kreler, Hans Lauterwein, Simprecht Widemann, and Spitzendraht were elected but did not accept the office. In 1531 Narcis Stiermair was purse bearer. When he was arrested, two brethren went to his house and took possession of the fund, which amounted to six florins.

79. At Esslingen a hat was put upside down on a table during meetings to prevent people from seeing how much each believer contributed. The fund never exceeded one florin. At Strasbourg the believers decided in October 1528 either to administer the money themselves or to hand it over to Lucas Hackfurt, director of the Poor Administration of the city (Krebs and Rott, *Elsass*, I, 185). In the 1530s the brethren sent around the deacon, Hans Frisch, to collect the money in a box (*ibid.*, 289; Krebs and Rott, *Elsass*, II, 299). The fund at Passau never amounted to more than two pounds. Funds are also mentioned at Grossenbach in Fulda in 1528 and 1529 and at Alzey in the Palatinate in 1608 (Franz, *Urkundliche Quellen*, 22–23; Krebs, 243).

80. Scharnschlager, 355.

81. Kläui, 186.

82. Krebs and Rott, *Elsass*, I, 280.

83. Roth, "Geschichte der Wiedertäufer, III," 41.

84. Schornbaum, *Bayern*, II, 34; Nicoladoni, 210.

85. Augsburg [7], April 11, 1535.

86. Steck and Tobler, 675.

87. Mecenseffy, 42.

88. Lydia Müller, *Glaubenszeugnisse*, 137–38.

89. Sinzinger, 165, 218.

90. Kuppelwieser, 152.

91. Wappler, *Stellung Kursachsens*, 170, 174.

92. The Anabaptists in such places as Strasbourg, Kaufbeuren, Schwäbisch Gmünd, and Franconia were also said to preach communism. It is more likely that these Anabaptists thought of mutual help rather than a full community of goods (Krebs and Rott, *Elsass*, II, 63; Schornbaum, *Bayern*, II, 139; Wappler, *Täuferbewegung*, 280, 283).

93. My analysis of Hutterite views on property is largely based on Walpot's *Grosse Artikelbuch*, edited by Friedmann, in *Glaubenszeugnisse*, 175–238. Some of the other leaders who wrote on community of goods were Leonhard Dax, Claus Felbinger, Joseph Hauser, Peter Riedemann, Hans Schmid, and Ulrich Stadler. Their writings are listed in Loserth, 234.

94. Friedmann, "Oldest Known Hutterite Codex," 96.

95. Friedmann, *Schriften der Huterischen Täufergemeinschaften*, 151.

96. Lydia Müller, *Glaubenszeugnisse*, 139.

97. "It is almost impossible for a merchant and trader to keep himself from sin. And as a nail sticketh fast between door and hinge, so doth sin stick close between buying and selling." (Sirach 26, 29; 27, 2.)

98. Franz, *Urkundliche Quellen*, 436.

99. *Ibid.*, 383; Zeman, "Topography of Moravian Anabaptism," 46.

100. Hege, 152; Hulshof, 227; Bender, "Discipline," 62.

101. Muralt and Schmid, 30, 387.

102. Steck and Tobler, 1041; Burckhardt, 93. In 1525 Hans Krüsi did say, however, while preaching in the area of St. Gallen, that according to the living Word of God nobody was obliged to pay tithes (Brändly, 68).

103. The Anabaptists referred to Ezekiel 18, Psalm 15, and Luke 6.

104. *Ein Christenlich Gespräch*, "Von Zinsen"; see also *Handlung oder Acta gehaltner Disputation*, 128–31. A census, as Noonan defines it, was an obligation to pay an annual return from a fruitful property. The buyer of a census was in a lender's role: he furnished the cash. The seller was a debtor: he bound himself to the annual payment. Originally the return was paid in real fruits; when the money economy developed, in annual installments of cash. Such a transaction was considered different from a loan because a genuine sale was supposed to be involved. The census was one of the most popular investment contracts in Germany. On the other hand, it led to an alarming degree of indebtedness among the peasants. See John T. Noonan, Jr., *The Scholastic Analysis of Usury* (Cambridge, Mass., 1957), pp. 155–70; see also Ernst Ramp, *Das Zinsproblem: Eine historische Untersuchung* (Zurich, 1949).

105. Hubmaier, 341; Wappler, *Täuferbewegung*, 259; Krebs and Rott, *Elsass*, I, 53.

106. Krebs and Rott, *Elsass*, I, 218–23.

107. Karlsruhe [19], Esslingen, July 3, 1544; Franz, *Urkundliche Quellen*, 223–24, 437; reference to the example of Zachaeus (Luke 19:1–10) in Hulshof, 210; Krebs, 437.

108. Appenzeller, 117; Sohm, 192; see also Krebs, 312.

109. Bender, "Discipline," 62.

110. Bossert, 301, and see also 193.

111. Mecenseffy, 202; Wappler, *Täuferbewegung*, 323.

112. Spiritual marriage or promiscuity was reported at Basel before 1528 (Burckhardt, 111); at Augsburg in 1527 and 1528 (Sender, 186); at Heilbronn during 1528–1530 (Karlsruhe [19], Heilbronn, May 12, 1530); at Schwäbisch Gmünd in 1529 (Thoman, 158); at Neustadt an der Aisch in 1528 (Wappler, *Täuferbewegung*,

283); in Thuringia in 1532 (*ibid.*, 345); at Ellrich in the Harz Mountains in 1535 (*ibid.*, 381); and at Herda in Hesse (Franz, *Urkundliche Quellen*, 291).

113. Wappler, *Inquisition*, 37, 171, 176. Sturm had been baptized by Jakob Partzner, a disciple of Hut.

114. Wappler, *Stellung Kursachsens*, 214; Jakobs, 503.

115. Wappler, *Täuferbewegung*, 432, 433–34, and *Stellung Kursachsens*, 213; Franz, *Urkundliche Quellen*, 429.

116. Wappler, *Stellung Kursachsens*, 204, 206.

117. Jakobs, 514.

118. Goshen, Ind. [17], "Gemeine Vermanung und Erinnerung."

119. Muralt and Schmid, 287.

120. Bossert, 528; Franz, *Urkundliche Quellen*, 205; Hulshof, 162; Röhrich, 115; Roth, "Geschichte der Wiedertäufer, II," 112; Goshen, Ind. [13], Oct. 13 and Nov. 26, 1567, March 30 and April 23, 1568, and July 1573.

121. Augsburg [7], April 28, 1550.

122. Goshen, Ind. [13], Nov. 26, 1567.

123. Augsburg [7], April 28, 1550.

124. *Corpus Reformatorum*, II, 1002; Jakobs, 514; Wappler, *Täuferbewegung*, 445.

125. Bossert, 255, 520, 1010; Jakobs, 508, 522; Goshen, Ind. [13], April 10, 1564; probably also Bossert, 475, 476.

126. Bender, "Discipline," 61; Hege, 151.

127. Goshen, Ind. [17], "Gemeine Vermanung und Erinnerung." For examples of intermarriage see Krebs, 226, 230, 233.

128. Muralt and Schmid, 307, 320, 352–53, 357–58, 398, 399; see also Steck and Tobler, 458.

129. *Corpus Reformatorum*, II, 1001–2, 1004; Wappler, *Täuferbewegung*, 429, 441. Jakob Storger had been baptized in 1529 at Wels in Austria by Wolfgang Brandhuber. Brandhuber had also baptized in 1529 at Passau, where in 1528 some believers had begun to doubt whether they should stay with their unbelieving wives. Did Storger bring these radical views from Austria to Thuringia?

130. See, for example, *Corpus Reformatorum*, II, 1002; Jakobs, 515; Wappler, *Täuferbewegung*, 408, 409, 416, 421, 432, 442, 459, and *Inquisition*, 200.

131. Franz, *Urkundliche Quellen,* 385–86; Schornbaum, *Bayern,* I, 139; Wappler, *Stellung Kursachsens,* 172, and *Täuferbewegung,* 426, 427, 428, 432, 440, 442, 443, 444, 459.

132. Wappler, *Täuferbewegung,* 381, 429.

133. Franz, *Urkundliche Quellen,* 175–76, 430; Bossert, 199; Augsburg [1], March 6, 1531; Karlsruhe [19], Esslingen, July 3, 1544; Wappler, *Täuferbewegung,* 498, 502, 503.

134. "Das Grosse Artikelbuch," in Friedmann, *Glaubenszeugnisse,* 299–317; see also Riedemann, 97–103.

135. Erhard, 11b–12; Fischer, *Ursachen,* 33; Sinzinger, 417.

136. For instances where men left their wives, see Bossert, 594, 860, 868. For instances where women left their husbands, *ibid.,* 500, 514, 778; Sinzinger, 249; and Kuppelwieser, 189.

137. Bossert, 434, 499–500, 646, 670, 673, 676, 690, 804; Schacher, 135.

138. Muralt and Schmid, 313.

139. Roth, Geschichte der Wiedertäufer, III," 71.

140. Goshen, Ind. [13], July 28, 1564.

141. Augsburg [7], April 28, 1550.

Chapter 8

1. It has been suggested that Hubmaier fled to Moravia in the summer of 1526 to get away from the Hapsburg rule. He would have been unable to foresee, of course, that on August 29, 1526, a few weeks after his arrival at Nikolsburg, King Louis II would be killed in the battle of Mohacs and Moravia would pass under Hapsburg domination. (Zeman, *Anabaptists,* 132.) This theory might be correct, but it does not explain why Hubmaier did not flee to Strasbourg like so many Anabaptist leaders, or why he did not stay at Augsburg, where he baptized Denck in the spring of 1526.

2. In a long letter of January 26, 1531, Reublin reported to Marbeck his quarrel with Widemann at Auspitz and asked that his letter be circulated, especially at Zurich, to counter the lies of the Austerlitzers (Cornelius, II, 253.)

3. Bossert, 652.

4. Zieglschmid, *Älteste Chronik*, 181, 199, 210.

5. Erhard, 44a.

6. Mencik, 366.

7. The position of Hutterite missionaries who went abroad during the period 1530–1618 was as follows:

Area	Servant of the Word	Servant of temporal needs	Ordinary brother	Name unknown
Switzerland	2	0	15	12
Rhine valley	6	1	11	10
Swabia	8	0	30	7
Tirol	14	4	56	8
Austria	0	0	4	3
Southeast	2	0	30	1
Franconia	1	0	1	1
Thuringia	0	0	1	1

(Whenever missionaries visited several areas, they are listed in the area where they appeared first.)

8. Sinzinger, 504.

9. Wolkan, 206–9.

10. Kuppelwieser, 327–36.

11. Zieglschmid, *Älteste Chronik*, 370.

12. Loserth, 311, 312, 313–14.

13. See, for example, Franz, *Urkundliche Quellen*, 510–11, or Riedemann's letters in Goshen, Ind. [15].

14. Zieglschmid, *Älteste Chronik*, 163, 173, 344, 369, 378–79, 459–60, 481, 539–40, 541; Bossert, 172, 369, 653.

15. Franz, *Urkundliche Quellen*, 501–3; similarly, Sinzinger, 466, 508.

16. "How one should talk to the unbelieving people and nations in order to turn them from their errors and refute their false hopes, so that they might be brought to true penance." Preserved in Codex 1578 (Friedmann, *Schriften der Huterischen Täufergemeinschaften*, 163–64).

17. Erhard, 45–46.

18. Karlsruhe [19], Grafschaft Hohenlohe, March 17, 1534. For other reports of emigrants who traveled in small groups, see Bossert, 855; Beck, 141; Franz, *Urkundliche Quellen*, 314; Kuppelwieser, 280; Schornbaum, *Bayern*, II, 147; and Sinzinger, 198.

19. Sinzinger, 177, 198; Widmoser, "Unterland," 99.

20. Kuppelwieser, 196, 198, 217–18.

21. Karlsruhe [19], Heilbronn, trial of Wertz, statement of Wendel Meyer.

22. Kolb, 53–55; Sinzinger, 418.

23. Widmoser, "Unterland," 164; Sinzinger, 214.

24. Loserth, 313.

25. Schornbaum, *Bayern*, II, 141, 145, 149, 150, 153.

26. Routes taken by emigrants from the Tirol were as follows: (a) via Sillian and through Carinthia; (b) via Rodeneck to Sterzing, over the Brenner Pass to Matrei and Ellbögen, and then Hall; (c) through the district of Taufers, across the Krimler Tauern, through the Ziller valley to the lower Inn; (d) through the district of Rasen, the Antholz valley and across the Defereggen; (e) from Rodeneck via Pfitscher Joch to Rattenberg (Sinzinger, 364, 418; 423; Kuppelwieser, 344). From Bruhrain, the Kraichgau, the area of Heilbronn, and Hohenlohe, emigrants went via Schwäbish Hall or Dinkelsbühl to Donauwörth. From Württemberg, via Esslingen to Ulm or via Schorndorf to Nördlingen and Donauwörth (Clasen, *Württemberg*, 57). From the Palatinate, through Walldorf and Unterschefflenz near Mosbach (Krebs, 236); and from Hesse, sometimes via Fulda and Koburg (Franz, *Urkundliche Quellen*, 314).

27. Franz, *Urkundliche Quellen*, 497.

28. Tirolese emigrants boarded ships on the Inn River at Langkampfen, Jenbach, Hall, Kufstein, Kranzach, Rotholz, and the Volderer Bridge (Widmoser, "Unterland," 114, 164, 187, 191; Sinzinger, 418; Kolb, 53–55; Schornbaum, *Bayern*, II, 146).

29. Beck, 250.

30. Schornbaum, *Bayern*, II, 147; Karlsruhe [19], Ulm, May 27, 1587; Bossert, 855.

31. Some were arrested on land at Alzey, Artenburg, Carinthia, Hohenwart, Kropfsberg, Lienz, Nuremberg, and Schwäbisch Hall. Others were arrested on waterways at Burghausen, Grafenwörth,

Hall, Ingolstadt, Kösching, Kufstein, Linz, Neuburg, Neu-Ötting, Schärding, Stein near Krems, and Wasserburg.

32. Mencik, 366.

33. Emigrants from Hesse were living in Altenmarkt, Birnbaum, Damborschitz, Göding, Kobelitz, Landshut, Moskowitz, Neumühl, Pausram, Pribitz, Schakwitz, Schadowitz, Skalitz, Stiegnitz, Strassnitz, Teikowitz, Tracht, and Wischenau. For emigrants from Württemberg see Clasen, *Württemberg*, 58.

34. Widmoser, "Unterland," 201.

35. Franz, *Urkundliche Quellen*, 500, and similarly, 510.

36. Krebs, 272.

37. Schornbaum, *Bayern*, I, 212.

38. Bossert, 411, 795–96; 1111–12; Franz, *Urkundliche Quellen*, 496–97, 498, 501, 506, 509, 511.

39. Bossert, 796.

40. *Ibid.*, 411; see also Franz, *Urkundliche Quellen*, 515.

41. Munich [31].

42. Bossert, 397, 417, 476, 673, 699, 882, 907, 1104.

43. Wopfner, 202–32.

44. Kuppelwieser, 330.

45. Bossert, 689, 731; Heiz, 164; Mencik, 366; Schacher, 121, 125–26.

46. Bossert, 851, 855; Krebs, 207; Schornbaum, *Bayern*, I, 342.

47. Schornbaum, *Bayern*, II, 153. It must be added that at least in Württemberg, serfdom was not a cause of emigration (Clasen, *Württemberg*, 182). Whether it encouraged emigration in other areas is not clear.

48. Loserth, 175; Clasen, *Württemberg*, 182–83.

49. Loserth, 314; Zieglschmid, *Älteste Chronik*, 548–49; Beck, 295.

50. Bossert, 476.

51. Bossert, 691; Franz, *Urkundliche Quellen*, 521, 523; Heiz, 163; Krebs, 99; Kolb, 30–31; Kuppelwieser, 283; Schacher, 180–81.

52. Kolb, 87.

53. Zieglschmid, *Älteste Chronik*, 625.

54. Loserth, 229; Mencik, 366; Schornbaum, *Bayern*, II, 62.

55. Kuppelwieser, 293.

56. Erhard, 48; see also Erhard's preface to Jedelhauser's *Ursachen*, p. 2.

57. In 1533 some six hundred Tirolese believers were reported in the community at Auspitz. In 1544 four to five hundred believers and eight leaders were living at Schakwitz (Sinzinger, 214, 429).

58. Hruby (1933), 196–203.

59. Most emigrants were adults. Of course, many took their children with them, but there are reports that mortality in the schools was high. Also it seems quite possible that some of these children did not stay in the communities when they grew up; there were always defectors. The Hutterites also suffered losses during the persecutions of 1535 to 1536 and 1546 to 1550, and during the Hapsburg Wars of 1596 to 1608.

60. We have not included the communities in Slovakia because the evidence is incomplete.

61. Beck, 364; Zieglschmid, *Klein-Geschichtsbuch*, 128. Hruby (1933) assumes (p. 205) that these contracts were characteristic of the legal practices of German burghers. In reality the peasants and lords in Germany also drew up precise contracts when new villages were founded. See Franz, *Quellen*, 68.

62. Mais, 70–85.

63. Zieglschmid, *Älteste Chronik*, 198, 211, 433, 531, 554.

64. The Chronicle only occasionally reports the death of a servant of temporal needs. It is possible that not all servants of temporal needs were listed in the Hutterite Chronicle. Several "haushalters" mentioned in local sources at Nuslau cannot be identified in the Hutterite Chronicle (Zeman, "Topography of Moravian Anabaptism," 121).

65. Zieglschmid, *Älteste Chronik*, 158, 171, 522; Krebs and Rott, *Elsass*, II, 402.

66. Zieglschmid, *Älteste Chronik*, 92–93.

67. Fischer, *Ursachen*, 65–67.

68. Mencik, 366. It is not clear what "without books" meant.

69. During the same period (1539–1618) eight servants of the Word were confirmed about one year after their election; 55, about two years; 38, about three years; two, about four years; three, about

474

five years; one, about six years; one, about eight years; and one, about ten years.

70. The number of times servants were elected together during the period 1537–1618 was as follows:

No. of servants elected together	No. of times: servants of the Word	No. of times: servants of temporal needs
1	6	1
2	5	3
3–5	32	12
6–10	1	4
11–20	0	4
21–30	0	2

On eleven different occasions during the period 1539–1618 only one servant of the Word was confirmed at a time; on ten occasions, two servants were confirmed; on 21 occasions, three to five; and on one occasion, six.

71. Elections or confirmations were held four times at Pribitz, three times at Kostel, twice at Freischitz, and once at Steinabrunn, Gurdau, Holitsch, and Kuty. When several groups of servants were elected or confirmed the same day, the occasion is counted as only one election or confirmation. The name of the community is not reported in the case of 26 elections or confirmations.

72. The number of servants elected in various months was as follows:

Month	Servants of the Word	Servants of temporal needs
January	18	8
February	31	24
March	37	44
April	9	0
May	0	5
September	4	0
October	5	6

The number of servants elected on various days
was as follows:

Day	Servants of the Word	Servants of temporal needs
Sunday	89	70
Monday	3	5 (Pentecost)
Tuesday	o	o
Wednesday	9	3
Thursday	3	o
Friday	4	5
Saturday	o	1

We do not know the days on which the remaining servants were elected. It is strange that elections should not have been held on Tuesdays.

73. Four servants of temporal needs were promoted to servants
of the Word within two or three years; five within four or five
years; seven within six to ten years; four within eleven to fifteen
years; and one within sixteen to thirty years.

74. Reublin to Marbeck, Jan. 26, 1531, in Cornelius, II, 257.

75. Erhard, 17b–18, 37b–38; Fischer, *Ursachen*, 96–97; Jedelhauser, 10–11; Kot, 46; Sinzinger, 429; de Wind, 46.

76. Eight *mass* of wine. The Bavarian mass was the equivalent of
1.88 pints.

77. Zieglschmid, *Älteste Chronik*, 589.

78. Bishop Amon died at Schakwitz in 1542 (Beck, 150), and
bishops Lanzenstil and Riedemann were probably elected here.

79. Three bishops, Kräl, Braidl, and Dietrich, were elected at
Neumühl, and two, Kräl and Braidl, died there. Braidl lived in
Neumühl in the 1580s. Frequently servants of the Word and of
temporal needs were elected at Neumühl, and several large meetings
were held there. Neumühl was also one of the places where the
Hutterites celebrated the Lord's Supper. Hauptrecht Zapf, one of
the authors of the Hutterite Chronicle, lived at Neumühl. The bishops may not always have lived there, however, and some of the
larger meetings were also held at Schakwitz.

80. Those that "many years earlier had been written by our dear

forefathers" for servants of the Word and of temporal needs and for missionaries. The ordinances for missionaries must have been written before the exodus to Hungary, for the Hutterites did not proselytize in Germany after 1622. Nine ordinances were issued in the 1630s and 1640s; the others are undated. Several categories of craftsmen, such as shoemakers, bladesmiths, barber-surgeons, and carters, received two or more instructions. The individual instructions are counted here.

81. Mais, 67, 70–73. At Schakwitz in 1544, the bedrooms, common kitchen, school, and infirmary were located in one big building (Sinzinger, 429).

82. Franz, *Urkundliche Quellen*, 510, 513, 514.

83. Erhard, 18.

84. Goshen, Ind. [14], "Verzeichniss viel notwendiger Puncten . . ." (1612).

85. Riedemann, 97–102.

86. Bossert, 1107; Hruby (1933), 207.

87. There is evidence that the Hutterites felt responsible for their wives, however. Often letters from missionaries contained greetings to their wives. Riedemann even addressed several letters to his wife in Moravia.

88. Krebs, 272; see also Bossert, 186.

89. Sinzinger, 427–28; see also Bossert, 186.

90. Bossert, 412.

91. Goshen, Ind. [14], "Verzeichniss viel notwendiger Puncten . . ." (1612).

92. Bossert, 186.

93. Franz, *Urkundliche Quellen*, 315.

94. Sinzinger, 428–29.

95. Franz, *Urkundliche Quellen*, 510.

96. Erhard, 14.

97. Goshen, Ind. [14], "Mit den Haushaltern zu reden."

98. Zieglschmid, *Klein-Geschichtsbuch*, 534.

99. Sinzinger, 428.

100. Mais, 71, 83.

101. Friedmann, *Schriften der Huterischen Täufergemeinschaften*, 160.

102. Krebs, 271.

103. Zieglschmid, *Klein-Geschichtsbuch*, 529.

104. Goshen, Ind. [14], "Verzeichniss viel notwendiger Puncten
. . ." (1612).

105. Friedmann, *Schriften der Huterischen Täufergemeinschaften,*
156–57. Only a more detailed study would show whether any of
these sermons originated in the sixteenth century.

106. The man was baptized at Austerlitz, maybe in a non-Hutterite community (Schornbaum, *Bayern,* II, 62–63), and the others
at Nuslau (Bossert, 674).

107. At Nikolsburg 72 were baptized in 1527 or 1528; at Sobotiste, 70 in 1554 and a large number in 1556 (Schornbaum, *Bayern,* I,
132; Beck, 203, 250).

108. Friedmann, *Schriften der Huterischen Täufergemeinschaften,*
162–63.

109. Beck, 648. One former Hutterite said in 1597 he had been
obliged to promise to stay in their league, to declare that the Hutterites had the true belief, to promise never to get drunk, to agree
not to take a wife without their permission, and to submit to expulsion if he engaged in blasphemy, fornication, or drinking (Bossert,
701).

110. Goshen, Ind. [14], "Verzeichniss viel notwendiger Puncten
. . ." (1612).

111. Mencik, 367–70; Franz, *Urkundliche Quellen,* 315.

112. Friedmann, *Schriften der Huterischen Täufergemeinschaften,*
159.

113. Goshen, Ind. [14], "Verzeichniss viel notwendiger Puncten
. . ." (1612).

114. Mais, 70–85. The equivalent of twelve *joch* and one-half
achtel of vineyards and fourteen *gewandte* of fields. An Austrian or
Viennese joch was the equivalent of 7,883.45 square yards. One joch
was the equivalent of two *viertels* or four achtels.

115. Sinzinger, 504; Widmoser, "Unterland," 196.

116. Loserth, 170.

117. Goshen, Ind. [14], "Mit den Haushaltern zu reden."

118. Erhard, 61; Fischer, *Ursachen,* 70–71.

119. Hruby (1933), 179–83.

120. After the destruction of many of their communities in the
first years of the war, the Hutterites had been forced to use cash

for their maintenance. These sums would have to be added to the thirty thousand florins confiscated in 1621. The Hutterites also managed to withhold some of their cash during the confiscation of 1621 (Hruby [1935], 73–74).

121. *Ibid.*, 79.

122. Lydia Müller, *Glaubenszeugnisse*, 227–28.

123. Bossert, 696, 796, and similarly, 1112; Franz, *Urkundliche Quellen*, 500, 506, 507, 509.

124. Bossert, 186, 727, 808.

125. *Ibid.*, 511; Franz, *Urkundliche Quellen*, 276; Krebs, 272.

Chapter 9

1. Clasen, "Anabaptists in Bavaria," 20.

2. Krebs and Rott, *Elsass*, II, 432; Mecenseffy, 134–35; Kluckhohn, I, 628.

3. The prevailing religious conditions in major territories and cities where Anabaptism made a relatively strong appearance between 1525 and 1529 were as follows. (1) Catholic areas lightly affected by Protestantism: upper and lower Austria, Styria and Carinthia, Bavaria, Württemberg, Hohenberg, the bishoprics of Salzburg, Bamberg, Würzburg, and Speyer. (2) Areas that had not abolished the mass but had a strong Protestant movement: Zurich, Bern, Aargau, Basel, Schaffhausen, St. Gallen, Graubünden, Salzburg, Ulm, Memmingen, Kaufbeuren, Schwäbisch Gmünd, Esslingen, Worms, Regensburg, Ansbach. (3) Areas where the Reformation had been adopted or was in the process of being introduced: Electoral Saxony, Nuremberg, Augsburg, Heilbronn, Strasbourg, Landau. (4) Areas that were strictly Catholic: Schwyz, the Tirol (except Rattenberg, Schwaz, Hall), Passau, the bishopric of Augsburg, Grafschaft Mindelheim, Lahr, Rothenburg, Henneberg, the duchy of Saxony, the bishopric of Magdeburg, and Stift Quedlinburg.

4. Zwingli had preached them at Zurich since 1522; Haller at Bern since 1522; Oecolampadius at Basel since 1523; Hofmeister at Schaffhausen since 1522; Vadian and Kessler at St. Gallen since 1524.

5. The dates when Anabaptism definitely appeared and when the

Reformation was officially introduced (by the abolishing of the mass) in some major Swiss cities were as follows:

City or area	Appearance of Anabaptism	Reformation introduced
Zurich	Jan. 1525	April 1525
City of St. Gallen	early 1525	July 17, 1528
Schaffhausen	Feb.–March 1525	Sept. 1529
Graubünden	May 1525	May 1526
Basel	Aug. 1525	April 1, 1529
Bern	1525 or 1527	Feb. 7, 1528
Territory of St. Gallen	1525	1529

6. During 1530–49 Anabaptists appeared in the Catholic areas of Freie Ämter Aargau, the Tirol, Austria, the bishopric of Augsburg, Fürststift Kempten, Neuburg, the bishopric of Speyer, Grafschaft Solms, Mühlhausen, Grafschaft Schwarzburg-Blankenburg, and Grafschaft Mansfeld.

During 1550–1618 they appeared in the Catholic areas of Grafschaft Baden, Lucerne, Solothurn, Landvogtei of the Ten Free Imperial Cities in Alsace, Baden-Baden, the bishopric of Strasbourg, the bishopric of Speyer, Bavaria, the Tirol, and Grafschaft Solms.

7. During 1530–49 Anabaptists appeared in the Protestant areas of Zurich, Bern, Basel, Schaffhausen, Augsburg, Nördlingen, Ulm, Esslingen, Heilbronn, Strasbourg, Württemberg, Ansbach, Windsheim, Hesse, Hersfeld, and Electoral Saxony, and in Regensburg, a Catholic city with a strong Protestant movement.

During 1550–1618 they appeared in the Protestant areas of Zurich, Aargau, Baden-Durlach, Strasbourg, Electoral Palatinate, Pfalz-Zweibrücken, Leiningen, Hesse, Württemberg, Ulm, Schwäbisch Hall, and Augsburg.

8. See the example of the village of Urbach, cited in Clasen, *Württemberg*, 159–62.

9. Schornbaum, *Bayern*, I, 130.

10. Nine joined during the 1540s; five during the 1550s; two during the 1560s; and three during the 1570s.

11. Allen, VII, 338, 366; VIII, 113, 138, 473; X, 282; XI, 39.

12. Bossert, 1088.

13. *Ibid.*, 433.

14. Andreä, 83–86; Bossert, 655, 658; Lydia Müller, *Glaubenszeug-nisse*, 14; Loserth, 58.

15. Singling out the largest craft, weaving, we find that during the period 1526 to 1573, 36 weavers had no property whatsoever. Another eight were journeymen. Thus two-thirds of the Anabaptist weavers were really poor. But not all weavers were paupers. Fifteen had some property—worth up to fifty florins in seven cases; up to one hundred and fifty florins in one case, and three hundred in another; and up to five hundred in six cases. Another four were wealthy: three had property worth 501 to one thousand florins, and one had property worth up to three thousand. Even one of the heads of the guild of weavers joined the sect.

16. For example, in a small conventicle held by Jakob Gross in July 1527, we find a weaver, his wife, and a candlemaker, all with less than fifty florins' worth of property. But there also were some who were well-to-do: a goldsmith, a guildmaster, and a merchant. Finally, there was Salminger, a former monk, and his wife (Roth, "Geschichte der Wiedertäufer, III," 110–11).

17. *Ibid.*, 86.

18. *Ibid.*, 120.

19. *Ibid.*, 97, 101.

20. Mecenseffy, 101, 302; Krebs and Rott, *Elsass*, II, 311.

21. There are small differences between the figures presented here and those in my study of Anabaptism in Württemberg (*Württemberg*, p. 142). Whereas formerly I classified Anabaptists characterized as being poor but for whom no figures were available in the category of people with property worth 21 to 50 florins, I now regard them as being at the very bottom of society. I also included some Anabaptists who were called rich in the category of people with more than 500 florins' worth of property, but now I am putting them into the group of the well-to-do middle class (301–500 florins). In spite of these small variations, the basic results are the same.

22. Schacher, 14.

23. The real number of women executed was undoubtedly higher. Sometimes the officials reported only the number of executed Anabaptists without specifying whether they were men or women.

24. Schornbaum, *Bayern*, I, 155–57.

25. Kuppelwieser, 330.

26. Bossert, 662.

27. Muralt and Schmid, 41, 43. See also Bossert, 431, 842, 863; Karlsruhe [19], Grafschaft Hohenlohe, Aug. 25, 1535, statements of Katharina Haffner, Georg Lang, and Hans from Riblingen; Krebs, 255; Schornbaum, *Bayern*, I, 219–20; Sinzinger, 204.

28. Jakobs, 502, 508, 530; Muralt and Schmid, 287; Sinzinger, 184; Augsburg [1], March 13, 1531, and [8], 1562, statements of Veit Ulmann, Veit Dietrich, Barbara N.

29. Schornbaum, *Bayern*, I, 186–87; Wappler, *Stellung Kursachsens*, 169–75. See also Karlsruhe [19], Esslingen, Jan. 20, 1528; Franz, *Urkundliche Quellen*, 43; Krebs and Rott, *Elsass*, I, 309.

30. For example, in 1533 a man in Thuringia said that he had joined the Anabaptists because the government was after the people's livelihood and property like wolves (Franz, *Urkundliche Quellen*, 56).

31. Krebs and Rott, *Elsass*, I, 235–36; see also Goshen, Ind. [13], Dec. 16, 1560.

32. Franz, *Urkundliche Quellen*, 24–25.

33. Kuppelwieser, 297; Sinzinger, 90; Wappler, *Täuferbewegung*, 441–42.

34. Roth, "Geschichte der Wiedertäufer, III," 81. See also Bossert, 606; Dürr and Roth, II, 485–86; Krebs, 147–48; Roth, "Geschichte der Wiedertäufer, II," 15; Schornbaum, *Bayern*, I, 86; Goshen, Ind. [13], Nov. 23, 1557, and July 28, 1564.

35. Krebs, 329; see also Franz, *Urkundliche Quellen*, 344.

36. Schornbaum, *Bayern*, II, 77.

37. Bossert, 215.

Chapter 10

1. Muralt and Schmid, 14–15; Hubmaier, 274; Riedemann, 123. Much of this section on hymns draws on Duerksen's dissertation.

2. For instances when they sang psalms, see Karlsruhe [19], Heilbronn, trial of Wertz; and Wappler, *Täuferbewegung*, 350, 357, 435. Joachim Fleiner at Esslingen sang the Latin hymn "Clamavi ad te

Deum." For the singing of German hymns, see Franz, *Urkundliche Quellen*, 32, and Wappler, *Täuferbewegung*, 339, 345, 357.

3. Jakobs, 512; Wappler, *Täuferbewegung*, 396.

4. *Etliche schöne Geseng, wie sie in der Gefenknus zu Passaw im Schloss von den Schweizer Brüdern durch Gottes Gnad geticht und gesungen worden* (1564).

5. *Aussbund Etlicher schöner Christlicher Geseng, wie die in der Gefengnus zu Passaw im Schloss von den Schweitzern, und auch von anderen rechtgläubigen Christen hin und her gedicht worden: Allen und jeden Christen, welcher Religion sie auch seyen, unparteilich und fast nützlich zu brauchen* (1583).

6. Bossert, 738; Krebs, 284.

7. Bossert, 708, 725. To the dismay of the Lutheran pastors, some Anabaptist hymns found their way into Lutheran hymnbooks (Rathgeber, 337).

8. Ackermann, Adler, Ascherham, Boll, Bünderlin, Dachser, Entfelder, Christof Freisleben, Glait, Grebel, Hans Haffner, Hartmann, Has, Haug, Hintz, Hubmaier, Hut, Lienhart and Ursula Jost, Krüsi, Langenmantel, Manz, Marbeck, Rinck, Salminger, Sattler, Scharnschlager, Schiemer, Schlaffer, Schnabel, Schnell, Jörg Schoferl, Schrödin, Tesch, Trechsler, Vogel, Wetel, Ziegler.

9. The confessions of faith were written by Brem and friends, Freyberg, Gut, Hamann, Hechtlein, Kautz, Kenntlein, Hans Pauli, Lincki, Probst, Marbeck, Nadler, Pfersfelder, Sattler, Scharnschlager, Schiemer, Schlaffer, Schnabel, Spittelmaier, Tesch, Wagner and anonymous authors.

10. Apart from Hubmaier's formulas for baptism and the Lord's Supper, and three formulas of baptismal questions in Thuringia (Wappler, *Täuferbewegung*, 305).

11. Friedmann, *Schriften der Huterischen Täufergemeinschaften*, 152–55.

12. Braidl, Braitmichel, Dax, Hauser, Kräl, Preubler, Riedemann, Rumer, Schmid, Stadler, Walpot, Zapf, Zaunring.

13. Arbeiter, Felbinger, Geyerspühler, Gherlandi, Glock, Käls, Klampferer, Kropf, Mändl, Saga, Schwager. Dax, who has already been mentioned as an author of treatises, also wrote confessions of faith.

14. The figure of 58 brethren includes thirteen of the 24 authors mentioned in notes 12 and 13 above.

15. *Ibid.*, 150–66.

16. Gross, 150–52.

17. Friedmann, "Oldest Known Hutterite Codex," 96–107.

18. Friedmann, "Briefe der österreichischen Täufer," 44–49: Codex I (1571); Codex Ab (1572); Codex Wien (1577); Codex N (1581); Codex Artloff (1585); Codex VI (1615); Codex VIII (1618).

19. Two editions of Riedemann's *Account,* a treatise by Andreas Preubler, and Claus Braidl's book of 1604.

20. The Hutterites had theological treatises by Dachser, Denck, Freisleben, Glait, Haffner, Haug, Hubmaier, Hut, Langenmantel, Menno Simons, Rinck, and Schlaffer. They had letters and confessions of faith by Brandhuber, Sattler, Thomas von Imbroich, Jörg Wagner, and Thoman Waldhauser (Friedmann, *Schriften der Huterischen Täufergemeinschaften,* 132–38).

21. Dead were: Manz, Sattler, Schiemer, Hut, Langenmantel, and Hubmaier. In prison were Dachser and Rinck. Freisleben and Schoferl had recanted.

22. Treatises by Hans Schnell and Jakob Hartmann (Bender, "New Discoveries," 73); see also the anonymous commentary on the disputation of Frankenthal, written in 1590 (*Eine kurtze, einfaltige erkanntnus*).

23. Sorg printed at least twelve books by Hubmaier, one treatise of Oswald Glait ("Entschuldigung" [1527]), and another by Jörg Haug. Hubmaier's "Summa eines christlichen Lebens" (1525), was printed by Melchior Ramminger at Augsburg, though Ramminger did not put his name on the book. Philip Vollandt printed the second edition of Riedemann's *Account of our Religion* in 1565.

24. The tracts were written by Dachser, Langenmantel, Hut, and Jörg Haug (Schottenloher, 54–57, 59–90).

25. In February 1527 the city of Nuremberg was informed by officials at Koburg that the Anabaptists ran their own printing press in the back room of a master borer in the district of St. Clara (Clasen, "Nuernberg," 27; also Schornbaum, *Bayern*, I, 130). Freisleben wrote in 1528 that his book on baptism had been printed in

the hiding place Moab (Karlsruhe [19], Esslingen, Jan. 1528), perhaps referring to Worms or Strasbourg. At Worms, Peter Schöffer
is said to have printed Anabaptist writings (*Mennonitisches Lexikon*,
IV, 85). Balthasar Beck at Strasbourg printed three books of Melchior Hofmann. In 1539 two Anabaptists from Moravia had books
bound at Regensburg (Schornbaum, *Bayern*, II, 76).

    26. Augsburg [7], May 5, 1550.

    27. Schornbaum, *Bayern*, I, 244.

    28. Roth, "Geschichte der Wiedertäufer, III," 96 (Augsburg in
1528); Nicoladoni, 201 (Schorndorf or Passau in 1528); Schornbaum, *Bayern*, I, 79, 84 (Uttenreuth in 1527); Wappler, *Täuferbewegung*, 253 (Erfurt in 1527).

    29. Burckhardt, 114; Nicoladoni, 202.

    30. *Mennonitisches Lexikon*, II, 14–15; Kiwiet, 75, 78–79; Franz,
Urkundliche Quellen, 380; Goshen, Ind. [13], July 4, 1576; Friedmann, *Schriften der Huterischen Täufergemeinschaften*, 98.

    31. Kiwiet, 75. Marbeck also used the *Kleine Deutsche Testament-
lein* by Wolf Rofel.

    32. Dürr and Roth, V, 39.

    33. Roth, "Geschichte der Wiedertäufer, III," 96; Bossert, 854.

    34. Roth, "Geschichte der Wiedertäufer, II," 20, 24, 29, 30–31.
One of Hut's books was also found in the possession of Andreas
Menser, a pastor at Hildburghausen in Saxony-Koburg who had
Anabaptist leanings (Berbig, "Wiedertäuferei" [1912], 384).

    35. Karlsruhe [19], Esslingen, March 27, 1528; Franz, *Urkundliche
Quellen*, 19; Wappler, *Stellung Kursachsens*, 145. Other books that
circulated among the brethren were the writings of Tesch, found in
Hesse in 1538; Menno Simons' *Fundament*, in Württemberg during
the second half of the sixteenth century; and Claus Felbinger's
Schriftliche Verantwortung, in the area of Zurich around 1590
(Franz, *Urkundliche Quellen*, 169; Clasen, *Württemberg*, 67; Berg-
mann, 65).

    36. Sinzinger, 82–83; Widmoser, "Unterland," 62–63.

    37. The writings are listed in Bergdolt, 108.

    38. Augsburg [7], April 23, 1550; Bergmann, 65; Wappler, *Täu-
ferbewegung*, 257, 347, and *Inquisition*, 121. Herxheimer was a follower of Schwenckfeld. About 1554 he published *Fassnachtsküchlein
oder Warnungsbüchlein durch Bernhard Herxheimer*.

Chapter 11

1. The theological foundations of religious intolerance have been discussed in great detail by Lecler. Schraepler's study is limited to the mandates passed against the Anabaptists. I am interested not only in the legal basis but above all in the practical aspects of the persecution.

2. Clasen, "Anabaptists in Bavaria," 246; Bossert, 3; Mecenseffy, 91.

3. Karlsruhe [19], Reutlingen, April 14, 1528. Spies were also used in Styria (Mecenseffy, 182).

4. Goshen, Ind. [13], May 19, 1561. Spies were proposed also in Ansbach (Schornbaum, *Bayern*, I, 337).

5. For Ansbach in 1533 see Schornbaum, *Bayern*, I, 337.

6. There were exceptions. The 25 Anabaptists imprisoned at Zurich in early February 1525 were questioned by a commission consisting of Zwingli, Judd, Kaspar Megander, and several town councilors. The next month, however, a second group of sectarians was first interrogated by a commission of town councilors only.

7. Hans Spittelmaier and Hans Nadler may have been permitted to write their answers (Schornbaum, *Bayern*, I, 47–56, 131–41).

8. Zurich, Augsburg, Pfalz-Zweibrücken, Baden-Durlach (Franz, *Urkundliche Quellen*, 104–5; Krebs, 27, 62–63). In the Palatinate the Anabaptists were warned in 1596 that if they did not attend church within a month, they would be forbidden to use water and pasture or the common land (*ibid.*, 204).

9. Bossert, 644, 645, 845.

10. Goshen, Ind. [15], "Die epistel Peter Ridemanns den Gefangenen . . . zue Güglingen."

11. Clasen, "Nuernberg," 35: "Gründtlich unterrichtung, eins erbarn Rats der Statt Nürnberg, Welcher gestalt, Jre Pfarrher und Prediger in den stetten und auf dem land, das volck, wider etlich verfurische Lere der Widerteufer, in jren predigen auz heyliger götlicher schrift, zum getreulichsten ermanen und unterrichten sollen." Jakob Andreä's *Drei und dreissig Predigen von den fürnemsten Spaltungen in der Christlichen Religion*, delivered at Esslingen in 1567, were published in 1568, 1573, 1576, and 1589. Eight of them

dealt with Anabaptism. In 1600 the superintendents in the Palatinate were ordered to instruct the village pastors on how to proceed with the Anabaptists (Krebs, 227).

12. Wappler, *Stellung Kursachsens*, 82. For the examples of Lutz at Reutlingen and Pfudler at Strasbourg, see Clasen, *Württemberg*, 11.

13. The punishments varied from territory to territory. See, for example, Roth, "Geschichte der Wiedertäufer, III," 2, 3; Schornbaum, *Bayern*, II, 179, 191; Mecenseffy, 71–72; Krebs, 425, 482–83, 492, 493; Clauss, "Kleine Beiträge," 172, 175; Franz, *Urkundliche Quellen*, 37, 142; Schacher, 6, 8.

14. Schornbaum, *Bayern*, I, 179, 197, and similarly at Windsheim (*ibid.*, 128).

15. In 1531 at the latest, the Anabaptists began to keep lists of the number of executions. The earliest known list was found in the possession of the leader Julius Lober, who on his way from Bruchsal to Moravia was arrested in the duchy of Ansbach on April 10, 1531. The list indicates the number of executions in various towns and the type of execution (Schornbaum, *Bayern*, II, 278–79). The Hutterites also kept lists of executions. The chronicle edited by Zieglschmid contains a long list under the year 1542. The chronicler added that more executions had taken place than the brethren could remember (Zieglschmid, *Älteste Chronik*, 232–35). Beck included in his excerpts of chronicles a similar list for the year 1581 (Beck, 277–80).

16. More precisely, eleven governments executed eleven to twenty Anabaptists; nine executed six to ten; sixteen executed two to five; and twenty-one executed only one each.

17. Muralt and Schmid, 224–26, 332–33, 363–74. In the cases of Jakob Falk and Heini Reimann no mention is made of their having broken their oaths. Hans Landis was sentenced to death in 1614 on the ground that his refusal either to stop preaching and baptizing or to leave the country undermined both church and state.

18. De Quervain, 124–44; Burckhardt, 40–43; Bächtold, 101–4.

19. Roth, "Geschichte der Wiedertäufer, III," 58; Krebs, 425; Berbig, "Wiedertäufer" (1903), 322–23; Schornbaum, *Bayern*, I, 19–20, 109–11; Wappler, *Täuferbewegung*, 370.

20. The Codex Justinianus, the Codex Theodosianus, and the Con-

stitutions contain laws passed by the emperors Gratian, Valentianus, Theodosius, and others against Manicheans and Donatists (Stiasny, 111; Köhler, 16).

21. Meissner's theory, repeated by Schraepler, was based on insufficient evidence.

22. Bossert, 32–33, 996; Franz, *Urkundliche Quellen*, 71–73.

23. Mandates of February 24, 1528, and April 1, 1528, for the Tirol (Widmoser, "Unterland," 62, 258–61). For Austria see Mecenseffy, 88–89, 120, 136–37, 189.

24. For the Austrian mandate of 1530 see Mecenseffy, 216–18; for the policy in Austria, *ibid.*, 139, 174, 243; for the Tirolese mandates of 1529, of December 10, 1544, and of July 12, 1567, see Kuppelwieser, 361–62, 386, 393. In a few exceptional cases even leaders were pardoned: for example, Hans Perger at Kitzbühel in 1549 (Kolb, 72).

25. For orders to destroy houses see Mecenseffy, 7, 85, 198, 239; and Sinzinger, 118, 119. For the actual destruction of houses, Mecenseffy, 203, 227; Widmoser, "Unterland," 67, 126; and Sinzinger, 433.

26. However, several burghers at Munich were sentenced to death not by the duke but by the town council "in secret quiet procedure, behind closed doors" (Pernöder, 27).

27. *Ibid.*, 24.

28. *Ibid.*, 26.

29. Zieglschmid, *Älteste Chronik*, 542, 627.

30. *Ibid.*, 540, 542, 551, 563, 627.

31. See Oyer's study and the older study by Meissner.

32. Franz, *Urkundliche Quellen*, 109, 119.

33. Bossert, 161–68.

34. Krebs and Rott, *Elsass*, I, 80–87; see also Krebs, 130–35.

35. Schornbaum, *Bayern*, I, 224–27.

36. *Ibid.*, 210–11, 215–16, 259–62, and II, 288–89.

37. *Ibid.*, I, 105–7.

38. *Ibid.*, 174.

39. *Ibid.*, 35–36.

40. Fabian, 30.

41. Schornbaum, *Bayern*, II, 200.

42. Zieglschmid, *Älteste Chronik*, 248–49.

43. Bossert, 464, 581, 1087, 1096. Similarly, see the example of Kress (Bossert, 645).

44. Goshen, Ind. [15], "Ein epistel vom petter Ridemann."

45. Protestant governments banishing Anabaptists: Ansbach-Bayreuth, Augsburg, Baden-Durlach, Basel, Bern, Esslingen, Heilbronn, Hesse, Kaufbeuren, Leiningen, Nördlingen, Nuremberg, Palatinate, Pfalz-Neuburg, Pfalz-Zweibrücken, Regensburg, Schaffhausen, Strasbourg, Ulm, Württemberg, Zurich (1525). Some territories began to expell Anabaptists right after Protestantism had been adopted: Hesse in 1528, Württemberg in 1536, and Ansbach in 1529 (Franz, *Urkundliche Quellen*, 2, 17–19; Clasen, *Württemberg*, 35; Schornbaum, *Bayern*, I, 147, 162). In the Palatinate executions had already been stopped under Elector Frederick II (1544–56), before the adoption of Protestantism. In Leiningen mandates ordering expulsion were issued in 1566, 1587, and 1609 (Krebs, 301–2, 326). In 1557 Pfalz-Zweibrücken ordered the expulsion or execution of obstinate Anabaptists (*ibid.*, 269), but none were executed. The government of Baden-Durlach recommended in 1570 and 1578 that leaders be expelled under all circumstances. Obstinate adherents were also to be expelled (*ibid.*, 48, 62–63).

46. Ulm granted a period of grace in 1536 (Franz, *Urkundliche Quellen*, 121). Hesse granted a final month from 1537 on (*ibid.* 143–44). The Count von Fürstenberg granted half a year in 1582 (Krebs, 369).

47. Constance granted six days in 1527 (*ibid.*, 451); Strasbourg, one or two weeks in 1534 and two weeks in 1536 (Krebs and Rott, *Elsass*, II, 317, 354; Franz, *Urkundliche Quellen*, 124); Landau, three to eight days in 1528 (Krebs, 429, 430, 432), two weeks in 1562 (*ibid.*, 439), and a month in 1557 (*ibid.*, 436); Ansbach, one month in 1529 (Schornbaum, *Bayern*, I, 162); the bishopric of Speyer and the Palatinate, two weeks in later years (Krebs, 482, 165–66); Leiningen, 45 days in 1609 (*ibid.*, 326); Hesse, two weeks in 1528 and a month in 1536 (Franz, *Urkundliche Quellen*, 18, 137).

48. Goshen, Ind. [13], Aug. 27, 1566.

49. Roth, "Geschichte der Wiedertäufer, III," 17, 30, 44, 66, 75, 91, 116.

50. In Ansbach, however, some Anabaptists were apparently whipped before their expulsion just because they were obstinate (Schornbaum, *Bayern*, I, 348).

51. Bossert, 50, 191, 1031; Franz, *Urkundliche Quellen*, 38, 142; and Krebs, 62, 166. In 1572 a law in Württemberg stipulated that Anabaptists be put on trial only after their second return. (Bossert, 315).

52. Zieglschmid, *Älteste Chronik*, 205–6; Sinzinger, 426; *Mennonitisches Lexikon*, IV, 632.

53. Emperor Frederik II's law of 1238 against heretics had ordered that the property of heretics be confiscated.

54. For an instance of confiscation in Grafschaft Fürstenberg, see Krebs, 369. The city of Constance administered the property of absent Anabaptists in 1579 (*ibid.*, 471). In 1571 Hans Georg von Seebach in Oberhamersbach valley allowed two Anabaptists to sell their belongings and leave within four weeks (*ibid.*, 381); this was an exceptional case. The bishopric of Speyer first confiscated property, then allowed the Anabaptists to take their belongings with them, and then switched to a policy of administering the property (*ibid.*, 508, 524–25, 513–14).

55. Karlsruhe [19], Heilbronn, April 8, 1557; Krebs, 44, 63, 166.

56. Only the government at Bern, as far as we know, seems to have confiscated the property of Anabaptists permanently (Schraepler, 61).

57. Franz, *Urkundliche Quellen*, 18.

58. For the decrees of 1571, 1584, and 1612, see Schraepler, 74–75.

59. Krebs, 48, 166.

60. The places and dates of disputations are as follows:

Zurich, Jan. 17, 1525	Teufen, Oct. 10, 1529
St. Gallen, June 1525	Basel, Dec. 29, 1529
Basel, Aug. 1525	Laufen, 1530
Zurich, Nov. 6–8, 1525	Bremgarten, 1531
Waldshut, 1525	Bern, April 18–20, 1531
Strasbourg, Dec. 22–23, 1526	Strasbourg, Dec. 11–12, 1531; Jan.
Basel, June 10, 1527	19, 1532
Bern, Jan. 12, 1528	Zofingen, June 30–July 9, 1532

Strasbourg, June 11, 1533   Pfeddersheim, Aug. 25–26, 1557
Bern, March 11–17, 1538   Frankenthal, May 28–June 18, 1571
Marburg, Oct. 30–Nov. 3, 1538 Wädenswil, Jan. 26, 1613
Schaffhausen, Jan. 11–15, 1543 Grüningen, March 3, 1613

61. Fast and Yoder, 83–95.

62. Krebs, 200.

63. Yoder, 51.

64. Fast, *Bullinger*, 115; Yoder, 75.

65. Karlsruhe [19], Grafschaft Hohenlohe, Sept. 18, 1525.

66. Augsburg [4], Sept. 9, 1529.

67. Appenzeller, 121; see also Schornbaum, *Bayern*, II, 171.

68. Wappler, *Täuferbewegung*, 397.

69. Krebs, 323–24.

70. Bossert, 144, 384, 513, 543, 799, 863, 890; *Corpus Reformatorum*, II, 1004; Franz, *Urkundliche Quellen*, 187–88; Jakobs, 535; Krebs, 228–29, 272–73; Wappler, *Stellung Kursachsens*, 176.

71. Krebs, 233–34.

72. Wappler, *Inquisition*, 174–75.

73. Bossert, 1057; Krebs and Rott, *Elsass*, I, 64–65, and II, 403. For the Anabaptists' anger at being compelled to go to church, see Bossert, 426, 490.

74. Augsburg [7], May 12, 1533.

75. Wappler, *Stellung Kursachsens*, 12; Augsburg [7], May 7, 1533.

76. For examples see Bossert, 63, 219, 220, 225, 343–44, 492; Dürr and Roth, V, 93–94; and Sinzinger, 509.

77. Dürr and Roth, V, 373, and VI, 447.

78. Nicoladoni, 198; Sinzinger, 187; Augsburg [1], March 13, 1531, Christoff Starck; Wappler, *Stellung Kursachsens*, 135, 137, 140, 171; Widmoser, "Unterland," 147.

79. Roth, "Geschichte der Wiedertäufer, III," 10; see also Muralt and Schmid, 252–53.

80. Krebs, 484; Franz, *Urkundliche Quellen*, 201; Kolb, 28; Mecenseffy, 344; Schornbaum, *Bayern*, I, 54; Augsburg [7], Sept. 12, 1573; Wappler, *Täuferbewegung*, 449; Zieglschmid, *Älteste Chronik*, 241.

81. Erhard, 39; Schornbaum, *Bayern*, II, 49.

82. Wappler, *Täuferbewegung*, 446, 455–56; see also Zieglschmid, *Älteste Chronik*, 406.

83. For examples see Muralt and Schmid, 253; Schornbaum, *Bayern*, II, 137; Wolkan, 21–22; and Zieglschmid, *Älteste Chronik*, 72–73.

84. Zieglschmid, *Älteste Chronik*, 389, 548.

85. *Ibid.*, 534–35.

86. Krebs and Rott, *Elsass*, I, 284–87.

87. Karlsruhe [19], Heilbronn, June 10, 1540.

88. For instances where orders to leave were rejected, see Bossert, 375, 582; Dürr and Roth, III, 268; Franz, *Urkundliche Quellen*, 179, 505; Krebs, 383; Muralt and Schmid, 77, 127; Krebs and Rott, *Elsass*, I, 238; Steck and Tobler, 1042, 1046, 1053; and Wappler, *Stellung Kursachsens*, 174.

89. Karlsruhe [19], Heilbronn, June 1, 1540; Dürr and Roth, III, 289.

90. Bossert, 441, 442, 702.

91. *Ibid.*, 426, 454, 472, 473; Franz, *Urkundliche Quellen*, 41–42, 391–92; Krebs, 444, 447.

92. For instances where expelled Anabaptists returned to their villages, see Bossert, 385, 387, 406, 430, 506, 554, 644; Augsburg [7], April 12 and 15, 1535; and Goshen, Ind. [13], April 24, 1557, and July 29, 1577.

93. Goshen, Ind. [17], "Gemeine Vermanung und Erinnerung."

94. Krebs, 234, 238.

95. Refugees were discovered as follows:

Place	Date	No. of refugees
Strasbourg	1527–35	73
Augsburg	1527–28	56
Heilbronn	1529	30–45
Heilbronn	1530s and 1540s	possibly 18
Ulm	1528–31	18
Esslingen	1527–28	17
Nuremberg	1527–28	8
Nuremberg	1539	3
Regensburg	1527	5
Grafschaft Schwarzburg	1530	7
Grafschaft Schwarzburg	1533	1

96. Roth, "Geschichte der Wiedertäufer, III," 19, 20.

97. Krebs and Rott, *Elsass*, II, 385, 466.

98. Bossert, 662.

99. Krebs, 68–69; Muralt and Schmid, 356; Goshen, Ind. [13], Nov. 3, 1557.

100. Bossert, 853; Clasen, *Württemberg*, 159–62; Dreytwein, 234.

101. Bossert, 483.

102. *Ibid.*, 428; Clasen, *Württemberg*, 157; Goshen, Ind. [13], Dec. 29, 1557.

103. Clasen, *Württemberg*, 16–18; Sinzinger, 89; Wappler, *Täuferbewegung*, 393; Widmoser, "Unterland," 85.

104. Kuppelwieser, 157–58; Mecenseffy, 244; Sinzinger, 387; Zieglschmid, *Älteste Chronik*, 260, 267.

105. Schornbaum, *Bayern*, I, 104. Similarly, in 1534 the governor of Styria referred to imprisoned Anabaptists as "pious, simple-minded people" (Mecenseffy, 276).

106. Sinzinger, 122–23.

107. Kuppelwieser, 384.

108. Franz, *Urkundliche Quellen*, 157.

109. Goshen, Ind. [13], May 29, 1561.

110. Bossert, 294; Franz, *Urkundliche Quellen*, 30; Sohm, 191; Goshen, Ind. [13], June 3, 1577, and Nov. 25, 1578.

Bibliography

SOURCES IN ARCHIVES

Augsburg, Stadtarchiv

[1]Literalien. Aug.–Dec. 1527; Jan.–Feb. 1528; Jan.–March 1529; Jan.–March, April–Dec. 1531.

[2]Der Rat der Dreizehn. 1527–29.

[3]Ratsprotokolle. 1526–29, 1529–32, 1545, 1554.

[4]Selekt Schwenckfeldiana und Reformationsakten. Faszikel Wiedertäufer zu Schellenbach.

[5]Steuerlisten. 1526–73.

[6]Strafbücher. 1549–53, 1554–62, 1571–80.

[7]Urgichten. 1527, 1530–31, 1533, 1534, 1535, 1541–42, 1550, 1554, 1564, 1573.

[8]Wiedertäuferakten. 1562.

[9]Wiedertäufer- und Religionssachen. I, Wiedertäufer; II, ca. 1520–79.

Esslingen, Stadtarchiv

[10]Bürgerbuch. 1500–1556.

[11]Faszikel 135/208.

[12]Rathsbuch. Vol. CDI.

Goshen, Indiana, Mennonite Historical Library

[13]Collection of documentary material on sectarians in Alsace, 1557–1616.

[14]Ehrenpreis, A. Auszug etliche der Gemeindeordnungen, geordnet und geschrieben zu der Gemein Besserung und Auferbawung im Monat February 1640.

[15]Epistel Buech mit fleiss geschriben von vilen streitern und zeugen gottes allenn frummen zum Trosst. 1566.

[16]Handbichel wider den prozess, der zu Worms am Rhein wider die Brüder, so man die Hutterischen nennt, ausgangen ist im 1557. Jahr, dessen sich dann Philippus Melanchthon und Johannes Barentius selbst ander mehr aus ihren Mittel unterschrieben haben. Wehe aber denen, die das Böse gut und das Gut böse nennen, die Finsternus zu Licht und das Licht zu Finsternus machen. Esaie (ca. 1560).

[17]Kunstbuch. Erster Teil der Epistlen oder Sandbriefen auch anderen Schrifften etlicher deren so man nent die widertöuffer.

Heilbronn, Stadtarchiv

[18]Beetbücher. Vols. XIII–XX (1528–58).

Karlsruhe, Generallandesarchiv

[19]Collection Bossert. Documentary material on Anabaptism in Herrschaft Hohenberg, Grafschaft Hohenlohe, and the free imperial cities of Esslingen, Heilbronn, Reutlingen, Schwäbisch Gmünd, Schwäbisch Hall, Ulm, Weil der Stadt.

Landshut, Staatsarchiv

[20]Land- und Stadtgericht Landsberg. ABN 57/32, Rep. 18, Fasz. 363, Nr. 1527 and 1528.

[21]Passau. Blechkastenarchiv 38.

Lauingen, Stadtarchiv

[22]Ratsprotokolle.

[23]Steuerliste 1525.

Ludwigsburg, Staatsarchiv

[24]A 282 Kirchenrat, Nr. 3084–96: Akten zur Verwaltung des Täuferbesitzes. Nr. 3094c Spezialfaszikel II, Schorndorf 1598–1600, L 1–20: Akten über die grosse Visitation in Urbach 1598.

Munich, Bayerisches Hauptstaatsarchiv
[25]Freising. Hochstift Freising, Literalien, Nr. 669.
[26]Ingolstadt. Bestand Staatsverwaltung, 2842, 2843.
[27]Landshut. Staatsverwaltung, Kirche und Schule, Nr. 2791.
[28]Mandate. Bestand Staatsverwaltung, 3221.
[29]Pfalz-Neuburg. Bestand Staatsverwaltung 2780.
[30]Pfalz-Neuburg. Literalien, Nr. 1267, 1275, 1286, 1292.
[31]Urfehden, Urgichten und Urteile, Stift Kempten, Nr. 1605, Neuburger Abgabe.

Munich, Staatsarchiv für Oberbayern
[32]Landgerichte Friedberg, Mörmoosen, Kraiburg, Tittmoning. G.R. 1260.
[33]Landschreibeamt Burghausen. Rentmeisterlisten, Fasz. Nr. 216-267a.

Munich, Stadtarchiv
[34]Blutbannbuch. 1574–86.
[35]Stadt München. Chamerpuch 1527, 1528, 1529, 1530.
[36]Stadt München. Ratsprotokolle 1527, fols. 37 and 42.
[37]Steuerliste 1527.

Nuremberg, Staatsarchiv
[38]Documentary material on Anabaptism in the free imperial city of Nuremberg, Collection Dr. Braun.

Rifton, New York, Society of Brothers, Woodcrest
[39]EAH 164. Schulordnung von 1568, mit Zusatz von Claus Braidl von 1588.
[40]EAH 167. Ordnungen, von Andreas Ehrenpreis gesammelt, 1640–50.

Stuttgart, Hauptstaatsarchiv
[41]A 54 (Steuerwesen). Türkenschatzung 1544.
[42]B 169–74. Reichsstadt Esslingen, Büschel 36: Esslinger Täuferakten.

[43]B 177–85. Reichsstadt Schwäbisch Gmünd.
[44]Tomi Actorum. Vols. VII, VIII.

Stuttgart, Landeskirchliches Archiv
[45]Synodus Protokolle. 1581–90.

WORKS CONSULTED

Abel, Wilhelm. *Agrarkrisen und Konjunktur in Mitteleuropa vom 13. bis zum 19 Jahrhundert.* Berlin, 1935.
Allen, Percy Stafford, ed. *Opus Epistolarum Des. Erasmi Roterdami.* 12 vols. Oxford, 1906–58.
Andreä Jakob. *33 Predigen von den fürnemsten Spaltungen in der Christlichen Religion . . . Von newen widerumb übersehen und mit 6 Predigen gemehret.* Tübingen, 1568.
Appenzeller, Gotthold. "Solothurner Täufertum im 16. Jahrhundert." In *Festschrift Eugen Tatarinoff*, pp. 110–34. Solothurn, 1939.
Armour, Rollin Stely. *Anabaptist Baptism: A Representative Study.* Scottdale, Pa., 1966.
Aussbund Etlicher schöner Christlicher Geseng, wie die in der Gefengnus zu Passaw im Schloss von den Schweitzern, und auch von anderen rechtgläubigen Christen hin und her gedicht worden: Allen und jeden Christen, welcher Religion sie auch seyen, unparteilich und fast nützlich zu brauchen. N. p., 1583.
Bächtold, C. A. "Die Schaffhäuser Wiedertäufer in der Reformationszeit." *Beiträge zur Vaterländischen Geschichte* (Historischer Verein des Kantons Schaffhausen), VII (1900), 71–118.
Baumann, Franz Ludwig. *Quellen zur Geschichte des Bauernkrieges in Oberschwaben.* Bibliothek des Litterarischen Vereins in Stuttgart, Vol. CXXIX. Tübingen, 1876.
——. *Quellen zur Geschichte des Bauernkrieges in Rothenburg.* Bibliothek des Litterarischen Vereins in Stuttgart, Vol. CXXXIX. Tübingen, 1878.
Beck, Josef, ed. *Die Geschichts-Bücher der Wiedertäufer in Österreich-Ungarn, 1526–1785.* 2d ed. Nieuwkoop, 1967.
Bender, Harold S. *Conrad Grebel (c. 1498–1526): The Founder of the Swiss Brethren.* Goshen, Ind., 1950.

——. "The Discipline Adopted by the Strasburg Conference of 1568." *Mennonite Quarterly Review*, I (1927), 57–66.

——. "New Discoveries of Important Sixteenth-Century Codices." *Mennonite Quarterly Review*, XXX (1956), 72–77.

——. "The Zwickau Prophets, Thomas Müntzer and the Anabaptists." *Mennonite Quarterly Review*, XXVII (1953), 3–16.

Berbig, Georg. "Die Wiedertäuferei im Ortslande zu Franken, im Zusammenhang mit dem Bauernkriege: Eine Ergänzung zu Die Wiedertäufer im Amt Königsberg i.fr." *Zeitschrift für Kirchenrecht*, LIV (1912), 378–403.

——. "Die Wiedertäufer im Amt Königsberg i.Fr. i.J. 1527/28: Aktenmässig dargestellt." *Zeitschrift für Kirchenrecht*, XXXV (1903), 291–353.

Bergdolt, Johannes. *Die freie Reichsstadt Windsheim im Zeitalter der Reformation (1520–1580)*. Quellen und Forschungen zur Bayerischen Kirchengeschichte, Vol. V. Leipzig-Erlangen, 1921.

Bergmann, Cornelius. *Die Täuferbewegung im Kanton Zürich bis 1660*. Leipzig, 1916.

Bergsten, Torsten. *Balthasar Hubmaier: Seine Stellung zu Reformation und Täufertum, 1521–1528*. Kassel, 1961.

Blanke, Fritz. *Brothers in Christ*. Scottdale, Pa., 1961.

Bossert, Gustav, ed. *Herzogtum Württemberg*. Quellen zur Geschichte der Wiedertäufer, Vol. I. Leipzig, 1930.

Brändly, Willy. "Täuferprozesse in Luzern im 16. Jahrhundert." *Zwingliana*, VIII (1944–48), 65–78.

Bullinger, Johann Heinrich. *Der Wiedertöuffern ursprung, fürgang, Secten, wäsen, fürnemen und gemeine Irer leer Artickel, ouch ire gründ, unnd warumb sy sich absünderind und ein eigne kirchen anrichtind, mit widerlegung und antwort uff alle jre gründ und artickel sampt Christenlichen bericht und vermanen, dass sy jres irrtumbs und absünderens abstandind und sich mit der kirchen Christi vereinigind, abgeteilt in VI bücher*. Zurich, 1560.

Burckhardt, Paul. *Die Basler Täufer: Ein Beitrag zur Schweizerischen Reformationsgeschichte*. Basel, 1898.

Ein Christenlich Gespräch gehalten zu Bern zwüschen den Predicanten und Hansen Pfister Meyer von Arouw den Widertouff, Eyd, Oberkeyt, und andere Widertöufferische Artickel Betreffende. Zurich, 1531.

Clark, Elmer Talmage. *The Small Sects in America.* Nashville, Tenn., 1937.

Clasen, Claus-Peter. "The Anabaptists in Bavaria." *Mennonite Quarterly Review,* XXXIX (1965), 243–61.

——. "Medieval Heresies in the Reformation." *Church History,* XXXII (1963), 392–414.

——. "Nuernberg in the History of Anabaptism." *Mennonite Quarterly Review,* XXXIX (1965), 25–29.

——. *Die Wiedertäufer im Herzogtum Württemberg und in benachbarten Herrschaften: Ausbreitung, Geisteswelt und Soziologie.* Stuttgart, 1966.

Clauss, Hermann. "Kleine Beiträge zur Geschichte der Wiedertäufer in Franken." *Zeitschrift für bayerische Kirchengeschichte,* XV (1941), 105.

——. "Wiedertäufer in der ehemaligen Reichsstadt Nördlingen." *Jahrbuch des historischen Vereins für Nördlingen und Umgebung,* XVII (1934), 145–48.

Clemen, Otto Constantin, ed. *Flugschriften aus den ersten Jahren der Reformation.* 4 vols. Nieuwkoop, 1967.

Cohn, Norman. *The Pursuit of the Millennium: Revolutionary Messianism in Medieval and Reformation Europe and Its Bearing on Modern Totalitarian Movements.* New York, 1961.

Cornelius, Carl Adolf. *Geschichte des Münsterischen Aufruhrs.* 2 vols. N.p., 1855–60.

Corpus Reformatorum: Philippi Melanchthonii opera, quae supersunt omnia. Edited by Carolus Gottlieb Bretschneider. Vol. II. Halle, 1835.

de Quervain, Theodor. *Kirchliche und soziale Zustände in Bern unmittelbar nach Einführung der Reformation (1528 bis 1536).* Bern, 1906.

de Wind, Henry A. "A Sixteenth-Century Description of Religious Sects in Austerlitz, Moravia." *Mennonite Quarterly Review,* XXIX (1955), 44–53.

Dreytwein, Dionysius. *Esslingische Chronik, 1548–1564.* Bibliothek des Litterarischen Vereins in Stuttgart, Vol. CCXXI. Stuttgart, 1901.

Duerksen, Rosella Reimer. "Anabaptist Hymnody of the Sixteenth

Century: A Study of Its Marked Individuality with Dependence on Contemporary Secular and Sacred Musical Style and Form." Ph.D. dissertation, Union Theological Seminary, 1956.

Dürr, Emil, and Paul Roth. *Aktensammlung zur Geschichte der Basler Reformation in den Jahren 1519 bis zu Anfang 1534.* 6 vols. Basel, 1921–50.

Eine kurtze einfaltige erkanntnuss uff die dry zehen artikell so verlouffens 1572. Jars zu Franckenthal In dr pfaltz disputiert worden. . . . zuschreben angefangen Sambstag den 6. tag Jenners des Newen Kalenders Im 1590. Jar.

Erhard, Christoph. *Gründliche kurtz verfaste Historia Von Münsterischen Widertauffern: Und wie die Hutterischen Brüder so auch billich Widertauffer genent werden, im Löblichen Marggraffthumb Märhern, deren über die sibentzehen tausent sein sollen, gedachten Münsterischen in vilen ähnlich, gleichformig und mit zustimmet sein.* Munich, 1588.

Fabian, Ekkehart. *Die Schmalkaldischen Bundesabschiede, 1530-1532.* Schriften zur Kirchen- und Rechtsgeschichte, Vol. VII. Tübingen, 1958.

Fast, Heinold. "The Dependence of the First Anabaptists on Luther, Erasmus and Zwingli." *Mennonite Quarterly Review,* XXX (1956), 104–19.

——. "Hans Krüsis Büchlein über Glauben und Taufe: Ein Täuferdruck von 1525." *Zwingliana,* XI (1962), 456–75.

——. *Heinrich Bullinger und die Täufer.* Schriften des Mennonitischen Geschichtsvereins, Vol. VII. Weierhof, 1959.

——. "Die Sonderstellung der Täufer in St. Gallen und Appenzell." *Zwingliana,* XI (1960), 223–56.

——, and John Howard Yoder. "How to Deal with Anabaptists: An Unpublished Letter of Heinrich Bullinger." *Mennonite Quarterly Review,* XXXIII (1959), 83–95.

Fischer, Christoph Andreas. *Der Hutterischen Widertauffer Taubenkobel, in welchem all ir Wüst, Mist, Kot und Unflat . . . zu finden, Auch des grossen Taubers, dess Jacob Hutters Leben . . . angehenckt.* Ingolstadt, 1607.

——. *Vier und funfftzig Erhebliche Ursachen Warumb die Widertauffer nicht sein im Land zu leyden.* Ingolstadt, 1607.

Franck, Sebastian. *Chronica, Zeytbuch und geschychtbibel von an-begyn bisz inn disz gegenwertig M.D. xxxj jar.* Strasbourg, 1531.

Franz, Günther. *Quellen zur Geschichte des Deutschen Bauern-standes in der Neuzeit.* Munich, 1963.

——. *Urkundliche Quellen zur Hessischen Reformationsgeschichte.* Vol. IV: *Wiedertäuferakten, 1527–1626.* Marburg, 1951.

Friedmann, Robert. "Die Briefe der Österreichischen Täufer: Ein Bericht." *Archiv für Reformationsgeschichte,* XXVI (1929), 30–80, 161–87.

——. "Claus Felbinger's Confession of 1560." *Mennonite Quarterly Review,* XXIX (1955), 141–61; XXX (1956), 78.

——. "The Doctrine of Original Sin as Held by the Anabaptists of the Sixteenth Century." *Mennonite Quarterly Review,* XXXIII (1959), 206–14.

——. "The Nikolsburg Articles: A Problem of Early Anabaptist History." *Church History,* XXXVI (1967), 391–409.

——. "The Oldest Church Discipline of the Anabaptists." *Mennonite Quarterly Review,* XXIX (1955), 162–66; XXXII (1958) 236–37.

——. "The Oldest Known Hutterite Codex of 1566: A Chapter in Anabaptist Intellectual History." *Mennonite Quarterly Review,* XXXIII (1959), 96–107.

——. *Die Schriften der Huterischen Täufergemeinschaften: Gesamt-katalog ihrer Manuskriptbücher, ihrer Schreiber und ihrer Li-teratur, 1529–1667.* Graz, 1965.

——, ed. *Glaubenszeugnisse Oberdeutscher Taufgesinnter,* Part II. Quellen zur Geschichte der Täufer, Vol. XII. Gütersloh, 1967.

Fries, Lorenz. *Die Geschichte des Bauernkrieges in Ostfranken.* Edited by August Schäffler and Theodor Henner. 2 vols. Würz-burg, 1876–83.

Gross, Leonard. "Newly Discovered Codices of the Hutterites." *Mennonite Quarterly Review,* XLII (1968), 149–55.

Handlung oder Acta gehaltner Disputation und Gespräch zu Zof-fingen inn Bernner Biet mit den Widertöuffern: Geschehen 1532. Zurich, 1532.

Hartung, J. "Die Augsburgische Vermögenssteuer und die Entwick-lung der Besitzverhältnisse im 16. Jahrhundert." *Jahrbuch für*

Gesetzgebung, Verwaltung und Volkswirtschaft im Deutschen Reich, XIX (1895), 867–83.

Heberle, Urban. "Die Anfänge des Anabaptismus in der Schweiz." *Jahrbuch für Deutsche Theologie*, III (1858), 225–80.

Hege, Christian. *Die Täufer in der Kurpfalz: Ein Beitrag zur Badisch-Pfälzischen Reformationsgeschichte*. Frankfurt, 1908.

Heiz, J. "Täufer im Aargau." *Taschenbuch der historischen Gesellschaft des Kantons Aargau* (1902), pp. 107–205.

Hergott, Johann. "Von der newen wandlung eyenes Christlichen lebens: Hütt dich Teuffel, die Hell wirdt zurbrechen." In *Neudrucke deutscher Literaturwerke des 16. und 17. Jahrhunderts: Flugschriften aus der Reformationszeit*, Vol. XX, edited by A. Götze and L. E. Schmitt. Tübingen, 1953.

Hillerbrand, Hans Joachim. "Anabaptism and the Reformation." *Church History*, XXIX (1960), 404–24.

——. "The Origin of Sixteenth-Century Anabaptism: Another Look." *Archiv für Reformationsgeschichte*, LIII (1962), 152–80.

——. *Die politische Ethik des Oberdeutschen Täufertums: Eine Untersuchung zur Religions- und Geistesgeschichte des Reformationszeitalters*. Leiden, 1962.

Hochhuth, Karl Wilhelm Herman. "Landgraf Philip und die Wiedertäufer." *Zeitschrift für die historische Theologie*, XXVIII (1858), 538–644; XXIX (1859), 167–209.

Hruby, Frantisek. "Die Wiedertäufer in Mähren." *Archiv für Reformationsgeschichte*, XXX (1933), 1–36, 170–211; XXXII (1935), 1–40.

Hubmaier, Balthasar. *Schriften*. Edited by Gunnar Westin and Torsten Bergsten. Quellen zur Geschichte der Täufer, Vol. IX. Gütersloh, 1962.

Hulshof, Abraham. *Geschiedenis van de Doopsgezinden te Straatsburg van 1525 tot 1557*. Amsterdam, 1905.

Jakobs, Ed. "Die Wiedertäufer am Harz." *Zeitschrift des Harz-Vereins für Geschichte und Altertumskunde*, XXXII (1899), 423–536.

Jedelhauser, Hans. *Zwelf wichtige und starke Ursachen Hansen Jedelhauser . . . warumb er mit seinem Weib . . . von den Wi-*

*dertauffern, so man Hutterische Brüder nennt, sey abgetretten
. . . sich aber zu der Catholischen Kirche bekehrt habe.* Edited
by Christoph Erhard. Ingolstadt, 1587.

Keller, Ludwig. *Die Reformation und die älteren Reformparteien in
ihrem Zusammenhange dargestellt.* Leipzig, 1885.

Kessler, Johannes. *Sabbata mit kleineren Schriften und Briefen.*
Edited by Emil Egli and R. Schoch. St. Gallen, 1902.

Kiwiet, Jan J. *Pilgram Marbeck: Ein Führer der Täuferbewegung
im Süddeutschen Raum.* Kassel, 1957.

Klassen, William. *Covenant and Community: The Life and Writings
and Hermeneutics of Pilgram Marpeck.* Grand Rapids, Mich.,
1968.

Kläui, Paul. *Geschichte der Gemeinde Horgen.* Horgen, 1952.

Kluckhohn, August, ed. *Briefe Friedrichs des Frommen von der
Pfalz.* 2 vols. Brunswick, 1868, 1872.

Köhler, Walther. *Reformation und Ketzerprozess.* Tübingen, 1901.

Kolb, Franz. *Die Wiedertäufer im Wipptal.* Vol. LXXIV of
Schlern Schriften. Innsbruck, 1951.

Kot, Stanislaus. "Polish Brethren and the Problem of Communism
in the Sixteenth Century." *Transactions of the Unitarian Historical Society,* XI (1956), 38–54.

Krahn, Cornelius. "The Office of Elder in Anabaptist-Mennonite
History." *Mennonite Quarterly Review,* XXX (1956), 120–27.

Krebs, Manfred, ed. *Baden und Pfalz.* Quellen zur Geschichte der
Täufer, Vol. IV. Gütersloh, 1951.

Krebs, Manfred, and Hans Georg Rott, eds. *Elsass,* Part I: *Stadt
Strassburg, 1522–1532.* Quellen zur Geschichte der Täufer, Vol.
VII. Gütersloh, 1959.

——. *Elsass,* Part II: *Stadt Strassburg, 1533–1535.* Quellen zur Geschichte der Täufer, Vol. VIII. Gütersloh, 1960.

Kreider, Robert S. "Anabaptism and Humanism: An Inquiry into
the Relationship of Humanism and Evangelical Anabaptism."
Mennonite Quarterly Review, XXVI (1952), 123–41.

Kuppelwieser, Karl. "Die Wiedertäufer im Eisacktal." Dissertation,
Leopold-Franzens-Universität, Innsbruck, 1949.

Lecler, Joseph. *Histoire de la tolérance au siècle de la réforme.* 2
vols. Paris, 1955.

Lenckner, Georg. "Täufer im Gebiet der Reichsstadt Schwäbisch Hall." *Württembergisch-Franken*, XXXVIII (1964), 16–28.

Lieder der Hutterischen Brüder: Gesangbuch hg. von den Hutterischen Brüdern in Amerika. Scottdale, Pa., 1914.

Littell, Franklin H. *The Anabaptist View of the Church.* Studies in Church History, Vol. VIII. New York, 1952.

Loserth, Johann. "Der Communismus der Mährischen Wiedertäufer im 16. und 17. Jahrhundert: Beiträge zu ihrer Geschichte, Lehre und Verfassung." *Archiv für österreichische Geschichte*, LXXXI (1894), 135–322.

Mais, Adolf. "Das Grundbuch von Neumühl: Das älteste Grundbuch der Hutterischen Brüder." *Jahrbuch für die Geschichte des Protestantismus in Österreich*, LXXX (1964), 66–88.

Mecenseffy, Grete, ed. *Österreich*, Part I. Quellen zur Geschichte der Täufer, Vol. XI. Gütersloh, 1964.

Meihuizen, H. W. "Who Were the 'False Brethren' Mentioned in the Schleitheim Articles?" *Mennonite Quarterly Review*, XIL (1967), 200–222.

Meissner, Erich. "Die Rechtsprechung über die Wiedertäufer und die anti-täuferische Publizistik." Dissertation, Georg-August-Universität, Göttingen, 1921.

Mencik, Ferd. "Ein Schreiben über die Wiedertäufer ex 1607." *Zeitschrift des deutschen Vereins für die Geschichte von Mähren und Schlesien*, XV (1911).

The Mennonite Encyclopedia: A Comprehensive Reference Work of the Anabaptist-Mennonite Movement. Vols. I–IV. Hillsboro, Kans., 1955–59.

Mennonitisches Lexikon. Vols. I–IV. Frankfurt, 1913–67.

Merx, Otto, Günther Franz, and Walther Peter Fuchs, eds. *Akten zur Geschichte des Bauernkrieges in Mitteldeutschland.* 2d ed. 2 vols. Aalen, 1964.

Meyer, Christian. "Zur Geschichte der Wiedertäufer in Oberschwaben, I: Die Anfänge des Wiedertäufertums in Augsburg." *Zeitschrift des Historischen Vereins für Schwaben und Neuburg*, I (1874), 207–53.

Miles, Hermann. "Die Chronik des Hermann Miles." Edited by

Ernst Götzinger. In *Mitteilungen zur vaterländischen Geschichte*, Vol. XXVIII, pp. 275–385. St. Gallen, 1902.

Mossmann, X. *Les Anabaptists à Colmar, 1534–1535.* 1869.

Müller, Ernst. *Geschichte der Bernischen Täufer: Nach Urkunden dargestellt.* Frauenfeld, 1895.

Müller, Lydia. *Der Kommunismus der Mährischen Wiedertäufer in der Reformationszeit.* Leipzig, 1927.

———, ed. *Glaubenszeugnisse Oberdeutscher Taufgesinnter*, Part I. Quellen zur Geschichte der Wiedertäufer, Vol. III. Leipzig, 1938.

Muralt, Leonhard von. *Glaube und Lehre der Schweizerischen Wiedertäufer in der Reformationszeit.* Zurich, 1938.

———, and W. Schmid, eds. *Zürich.* Quellen zur Geschichte der Täufer in der Schweiz, Vol. I. Zurich, 1952.

Neusser, Wilhelm. *Hans Hut: Leben und Wirken bis zum Nikolsburger Religionsgespräch.* Berlin, 1913.

Nicoladoni, Alexander. *Johannes Bünderlin von Linz und die Oberösterreichischen Täufergemeinden in den Jahren 1525 bis 1531.* Berlin, 1893.

Oyer, John Stanley. *Lutheran Reformers against Anabaptists: Luther, Melanchthon and Menius, and the Anabaptists of Central Germany.* The Hague, 1964.

Peachey, Paul. *Die soziale Herkunft der Schweizer Täufer in der Reformationszeit: Eine religionssoziologische Untersuchung.* Schriftenreihe des Mennonitischen Geschichtsvereins, Vol. IV. Karlsruhe, 1954.

Pernöder, Andreas. "Chronik, 1506–1528." Bayerische Staatsbibliothek Munich, Cgm 1594.

Protocoll. Das ist Alle Handlung des Gesprechs zu Frankenthal inn der Churfürstlichen Pfaltz, mit denen, so man Widertäuffer nennet. Heidelberg, 1571.

Rathgeber, Julius. *Strassburg im sechzehnten Jahrhundert, 1500–1598: Reformationsgeschichte der Stadt Strassburg dem evangelischen Volk erzählt.* Stuttgart, 1871.

Rembert, Karl. *Die "Wiedertäufer" im Herzogtum Jülich: Studien zur Geschichte der Reformation, besonders am Niederrhein.* Berlin, 1899.

Riedemann, Peter. *Account of Our Religion, Doctrine and Faith,*

Given by Peter Rideman of the Brothers Whom Men Call Hutterians. Translated by Kathleen E. Hasenberg. Suffolk, England, 1950.

Ritschl, Albrecht. "Prolegomena zu einer Geschichte des Pietismus." *Zeitschrift für Kirchengeschichte,* II (1878), 1–55.

Röhrich, Timotheus Wilhelm. "Zur Geschichte der Strassburgischen Wiedertäufer in den Jahren 1527 bis 1543: Aus den Vergichtbüchern und anderen archivalischen Quellen mitgeteilt." *Zeitschrift für die historische Theologie,* XXX (1860), 3–121.

Roth, Friedrich. "Zur Geschichte der Wiedertäufer in Oberschwaben, II: Zur Lebensgeschichte Eitelhans Langenmantels von Augsburg." *Zeitschrift des Historischen Vereins für Schwaben und Neuburg,* XXVII (1900), 1–45.

——. "Zur Geschichte der Wiedertäufer in Oberschwaben, III: Der Höhepunkt der Bewegung in Augsburg und der Niedergang im Jahre 1528." *Zeitschrift des Historischen Vereins für Schwaben und Neuburg,* XXVIII (1901), 1–154.

Schacher, Josef. "Luzerner Akten zur Geschichte der Täufer." *Zeitschrift für Schweizerische Kirchengeschichte,* LI (1957), 113–35, 173–98.

Scharnschlager, Leupold. "A Church Order for Members of Christ's Body." *Mennonite Quarterly Review,* XXXVIII (1964), 354–56, 386.

Schibli, Hans Rudolf. "Die Wiedertäufer in St. Gallen im 16. Jahrhundert." Thesis, Universität Zurich, 1950.

Schornbaum, Karl, ed. *Bayern,* Part I: *Markgraftum Brandenburg.* Quellen zur Geschichte der Wiedertäufer, Vol. II. Leipzig, 1934.

——. *Bayern,* Part II: *Reichsstädte Regensburg, Kaufbeuren, Rothenburg, Nördlingen, Schweinfurt, Weissenburg.* Quellen zur Geschichte der Täufer, Vol. V. Gütersloh, 1951.

Schottenloher, Karl. *Philipp Uhlhart, Ein Augsburger Winkeldrucker und Helfershelfer der "Schwärmer" und "Wiedertäufer."* Munich-Freising, 1921.

Schraepler, Horst W. *Die rechtliche Behandlung der Täufer in der deutschen Schweiz, Süddeutschland und Hessen, 1525–1618.* Schriften zur Kirchen- und Rechtsgeschichte, Vol. IV. Tübingen, 1957.

Schubert, Hans von. *Der Kommunismus der Wiedertäufer in Münster und seine Quellen.* Sitzungsberichte der Heidelberger Akademie der Wissenschaften: Philos.-histor. Klasse, Vol. XI. Heidelberg, 1919.

Sender, Clemens. "Die Chronik des Clemens Sender von den ältesten Zeiten der Stadt Augsburg bis zum Jahr 1535." In *Die Chroniken der Deutschen Städte*, Vol. XXIII, edited by Friedrich Roth. Leipzig, 1894.

Sicher, Fridolin. *Fridolin Sichers Chronik.* Edited by Ernst Götzinger. Mitteilungen zur vaterländischen Geschichte, Vol. XX. St. Gallen, 1885.

Simons, Menno. *The Complete Writings of Menno Simons (c. 1496–1561).* Translated by L. Verduin and edited by John C. Wenger. Scottdale, Pa., 1966.

Sinzinger, Katharina. "Das Täufertum im Pustertal." Dissertation, Leopold-Franzens-Universität, Innsbruck, 1950.

Sohm, Walter. *Territorium und Reformation in der hessischen Geschichte, 1526–1555.* Marburg, 1915.

Steck, Rudolf, and G. Tobler, eds. *Aktensammlung zur Geschichte der Berner Reformation, 1521–1532.* Bern, 1923.

Stiasny, Hans. *Die strafrechtliche Verfolgung der Täufer in der freien Reichsstadt Köln, 1529 bis 1618.* Reformationsgeschichtliche Studien und Texte, Vol. LXXXVIII. Münster, 1962.

Stolze, Otto. *Geschichte des Landes Tirol.* Innsbruck, 1955.

Strickler, Gustav. *Geschichte der Herrschaft Grüningen: Das ist Geschichte des Zürcher Oberlandes und seiner Beziehungen zur Stadt Zürich und dem See.* Zurich, 1908.

Thoman, Nicolaus. "Weissenhorner Historia." Edited by Franz Ludwig Baumann. Bibliothek des Litterarischen Vereins in Stuttgart, Vol. CXXIX, pp. 1–240. Tübingen, 1876.

Wappler, Paul. *Inquisition und Ketzerprozess in Zwickau zur Reformationszeit: Dargestellt im Zusammenhang mit der Einwirkung der Ansichten Luthers und Melanchthons über Glaubens- und Gewissensfreiheit.* Leipzig, 1908.

——. *Die Stellung Kursachsens und des Landgrafen Philipp von Hessen zur Täuferbewegung.* Reformationsgeschichtliche Studien und Texte, Vols. XIII–XIV. Münster, 1910.

———. *Die Täuferbewegung in Thüringen von 1526–1584.* Beiträge zur neueren Geschichte Thüringens. Vol. II. Jena, 1913.

———. *Thomas Müntzer in Zwickau und die "Zwickauer Propheten."* 2d ed. Gütersloh, 1966.

Watt, Joachim von [Vadian]. *Deutsche Historische Schriften.* Edited by Ernst Götzinger. Vol. II: Chronik der Aebte des Klosters St. Gallen. St. Gallen, 1877.

Wenger, John C. "Three Swiss Brethren Tracts." *Mennonite Quarterly Review*, XXI (1947), 275–84.

Widmoser, Eduard. "Das Täufertum im Tiroler Unterland." Dissertation, Leopold-Franzens-Universität, Innsbruck, 1948.

———. "Das Tiroler Täufertum." *Tiroler Heimat*, XV (1951), 45–89, 103–28.

Wiedemann, Hans. "Die Wiedertäufergemeinde in Passau, 1527–1535." *Ostbairische Grenzmarken: Passauer Jahrbuch für Geschichte, Kunst und Volkskunde*, VI (1962/63), 262–76.

Williams, George Hunston. *The Radical Reformation.* Philadelphia, 1962.

Wolkan, Rudolf. *Die Lieder der Wiedertäufer: Ein Beitrag zur Deutschen und Niederländischen Litteratur- und Kirchengeschichte.* Berlin, 1903.

Wopfner, Hermann. "Güterteilung und Überbevölkerung Tirolischer Landesbezirke im 16., 17. und 18. Jahrhundert." *Südostdeutsche Forschungen*, III (1938), 202–32.

Yoder, John Howard. *Täufertum und Reformation in der Schweiz: I. Die Gespräche zwischen Täufern und Reformatoren, 1523–1538.* Karlsruhe, 1962.

Zeman, Jarold Knox. *The Anabaptists and the Czech Brethren in Moravia, 1526–1628: A Study of Origins and Contacts.* The Hague, 1969.

———. "Topography of Moravian Anabaptism." *Mennonite Quarterly Review*, XL (1966) 266–78; XLI (1967), 40–78, 116–60.

Zieglschmid, A. J. F. *Die älteste Chronik der Hutterischen Brüder.* Ithaca, N.Y., 1943.

———. *Das Klein-Geschichtsbuch der Hutterischen Brüder.* Philadelphia, 1947.

Zumkeller, Adolar, ed. *Urkunden und Regesten zur Geschichte der*

Augustinerklöster Würzburg und Münnerstadt: Von den Anfängen bis zur Mitte des 17. Jahrhunderts. 2 vols. Würzburg, 1966, 1967.

Zur Linden, Friedrich Otto. *Melchior Hofmann, Ein Prophet der Wiedertäufer.* Haarlem, 1885.

Zwingli, Huldreich. *Huldreich Zwinglis sämtliche Werke.* Edited by Emil Egli and Georg Finsler. Vols. LXXXVIII–C of *Corpus Reformatorum.* Leipzig, 1905–44.

Index

Library of Congress Cataloging in Publication Data
(For library cataloging purposes only)

Clasen, Claus Peter.
  Anabaptism; a social history, 1525–1618.

  Bibliography: p.
  1. Anabaptists—History. I. Title.
BX4931.2.C57   284' .3   78-37751
ISBN 0-8014-0696-X